MENTORING SCIENCE TEACHERS IN THE SECONDARY SCHOOL

This practical guide helps mentors of new science teachers in both developing their own mentoring skills and providing the essential guidance their trainees need as they navigate the rollercoaster of the first years in the classroom. Offering tried-and-tested strategies based on the best research, it covers the knowledge, skills and understanding every mentor needs and offers practical tools such as lesson plans and feedback guides, observation sheets and examples of dialogue with trainees.

Together with analytical tools for self-evaluation, this book is a vital source of support and inspiration for all those involved in developing the next generation of outstanding science teachers. Key topics explained include:

- Roles and responsibilities of mentors
- Developing a mentor–mentee relationship
- Guiding beginning science teachers through the lesson planning, teaching and self-evaluation processes
- Observations and pre- and post-lesson discussions and regular mentoring meetings
- Supporting beginning teachers to enhance scientific knowledge and effective pedagogical practices
- Building confidence among beginning teachers to cope with pupils' contingent questions and assess scientific knowledge and skills
- Supporting beginning teachers' planning and teaching to enhance scientific literacy and inquiry among pupils
- Developing autonomous science teachers with an attitude to promote the learning of science for all the learners

Filled with tried-and-tested strategies based on the latest research, *Mentoring Science Teachers in the Secondary School* is a vital guide for mentors of science teachers, both trainee and newly qualified, with ready-to-use strategies that support and inspire both mentors and beginning teachers alike.

Saima Salehjee is a Lecturer in Chemistry Education at the University of Strathclyde. She is responsible for teaching and research work with particular emphasis on STEM education.

MENTORING TRAINEE AND NEWLY QUALIFIED TEACHERS

Series edited by: Susan Capel, Trevor Wright, Julia Lawrence and Sarah Younie

The **Mentoring Trainee and Newly Qualified Teachers** Series offers subject-specific, practical books designed to reinforce and develop mentors' understanding of the different aspects of their role, as well as exploring issues that mentees encounter in the course of learning to teach. The books have two main foci: First, challenging mentors to reflect critically on theory, research and evidence, on their own knowledge, their approaches to mentoring and how they work with beginning teachers in order to move their practice forward. Second, supporting mentors to effectively facilitate the development of beginning teachers. Although the basic structure of all the subject books is similar, each book is different to reflect the needs of mentors in relation to the unique nature of each subject. Elements of appropriate theory introduce each topic or issue with emphasis placed on the practical application of material. The chapter authors in the subject books have been engaged with mentoring over a long period of time and share research, evidence and their experience. We, as series editors, are pleased to extend the work in initial teacher education to the work of mentors of beginning teachers.

We hope that this series of books supports you in developing into an effective, reflective mentor as you support the development of the next generation of subject teachers.

For more information about this series, please visit: https://www.routledge.com/Mentoring-Trainee-and-Newly-Qualified-Teachers/book-series/MTNQT

Titles in the series

Mentoring Physical Education Teachers in the Secondary School
Edited by Susan Capel and Julia Lawrence

Mentoring Design and Technology Teachers in the Secondary School
Edited by Suzanne Lawson and Susan Wood-Griffith

Mentoring English Teachers in the Secondary School
Edited by Debbie Hickman

Mentoring Science Teachers in the Secondary School
Edited by Saima Salehjee

MENTORING SCIENCE TEACHERS IN THE SECONDARY SCHOOL

A Practical Guide

Edited by Saima Salehjee

First published 2021
by Routledge
2 Park Square, Milton Park, Abingdon, Oxon OX14 4RN

and by Routledge
52 Vanderbilt Avenue, New York, NY 10017

Routledge is an imprint of the Taylor & Francis Group, an informa business

© 2021 selection and editorial matter, Saima Salehjee; individual chapters,
the contributors

The right of Saima Salehjee to be identified as the author of the editorial material,
and of the authors for their individual chapters, has been asserted in accordance with
sections 77 and 78 of the Copyright, Designs and Patents Act 1988.

All rights reserved. No part of this book may be reprinted or reproduced or utilised
in any form or by any electronic, mechanical, or other means, now known or
hereafter invented, including photocopying and recording, or in any information
storage or retrieval system, without permission in writing from the publishers.

Trademark notice: Product or corporate names may be trademarks or registered trademarks,
and are used only for identification and explanation without intent to infringe.

British Library Cataloguing-in-Publication Data
A catalogue record for this book is available from the British Library

Library of Congress Cataloging-in-Publication Data

Names: Salehjee, Saima, editor.
Title: Mentoring science teachers in the secondary school : a practical
guide / edited by Saima Salehjee.
Description: Abingdon, Oxon ; New York : Routledge, 2021. | Series:
Mentoring trainee and newly qualified teachers | Includes
bibliographical references and index.
Identifiers: LCCN 2020028603 (print) | LCCN 2020028604 (ebook) | ISBN
9780367023119 (hardback) | ISBN 9780367023126 (paperback) | ISBN
9780429400308 (ebook)
Subjects: LCSH: Science--Study and teaching (Secondary) | Science
teachers--In-service training. | Mentoring in education.
Classification: LCC Q181 .M436 2021 (print) | LCC Q181 (ebook) | DDC
507.1/2--dc23
LC record available at https://lccn.loc.gov/2020028603
LC ebook record available at https://lccn.loc.gov/2020028604

ISBN: 978-0-367-02311-9 (hbk)
ISBN: 978-0-367-02312-6 (pbk)
ISBN: 978-0-429-40030-8 (ebk)

Typeset in Interstate
by SPi Global, India

Visit the eResources: www.routledge.com/9780367023126

This book is dedicated to an inspirational science educator, Professor Mike Watts, whose mentoring support has (trans)formed a large cohort of science graduates to become effective teachers and researchers in the UK and beyond.

CONTENTS

List of illustrations	x
Tasks	xiii
Case studies	xvii
Appendices	xviii
List of contributors	xix
Acknowledgements	xxiv
An introduction to the series: Mentoring trainee and newly qualified teachers	xxv

Introduction: A practical guide to mentoring science education   1

SECTION 1 FOUNDATIONS OF MENTORING   9

1 Models of mentoring   11
Gill Golder, Alison Keyworth and Clare Shaw

2 About you as a mentor   22
Nicklas Lindstrom

3 Beginning science teachers' expectations of their mentors   32
Stephen P. Day

4 Accountabilities of a reflective mentor   47
Jodi Roffey-Barentsen and Richard Malthouse

5 Developing a mentor-mentee relationship   59
Michelle Wormald

viii *Contents*

SECTION 2 BASIC MENTORING PRACTICES 71

6 Supporting beginning teachers with lesson planning 73
Gareth Bates, Ralph Littler, Morag Findlay and Saima Salehjee

7 Supporting beginning science teachers to teach and evaluate their lessons 93
Morag Findlay, Saima Salehjee and Stavros A. Nikou

8 Pre-lesson discussions, lesson observation and post-lesson discussions in mentoring beginning science teachers 116
Morag Findlay

9 Holding weekly mentoring meetings 137
Stephen P. Day

SECTION 3 EXTENDING BASIC MENTORING PRACTICES 153

10 Supporting beginning teachers to develop pedagogical content knowledge 155
Michael Allen and Simon Parry

11 Supporting beginning teachers to cope with contingencies 171
Mike Watts

12 Supporting beginning teachers to develop their ability to assess pupils 183
Helen Gourlay

13 Supporting beginning teachers to link learning, memory and inquiry 201
Jonathan Firth

14 Supporting a beginning teacher to apply features of the nature of science 214
Nqobile Nkala

15 Supporting beginning teachers in embedding scientific literacy 228
Saima Salehjee and Mike Watts

16 Mentoring beginning teachers in implementing process-oriented guided inquiry learning: An example of an inquiry-based pedagogical approach of teaching science 244
Sheila S. Qureshi, Adam H. Larson and Venkat Rao Vishnumolakala

Contents ix

SECTION 4 MOVING BEYOND 263

17 Supporting a beginning teacher to become autonomous 265
Gareth Bates and Ralph Littler

18 Supporting a beginning teacher to implement extension and enrichment 278
Jane Essex

19 Supporting beginning teachers to work with pupils with special educational needs and disability 291
Darren Moore and Alison Black

20 To conclude 305
Saima Salehjee

References 309
Author index 325
Subject index 328

ILLUSTRATIONS

Figures

1.1	Helping to learn styles	19
2.1	Motivation-readiness matrix for mentoring	23
2.2	The traditional model of mentoring	28
4.1	Situated reflective practice	57
7.1	Stages of teacher development related to a beginning teacher's increasing responsibility and autonomy	95
7.2	A schematic representation showing that as beginning teachers become more confident, they tend to talk less and the pupils tend to talk more	99
8.1	Three dimensions for providing lesson observation and feedback	122
10.1	A learning progression approach to develop PCK	158
15.1	Connecting scientific literacy dimensions and scientific literacy elements to form learning outcomes	235
16.1	The POGIL learning cycle	251

Tables

1.1	Key external drivers influencing mentoring work	14
3.1	Some characteristics of an effective and ineffective mentor	34
3.2	Some key actions of an effective and ineffective mentor	35
3.3	An induction programme checklist for a beginning teacher	39
3.4	A beginning teacher's progression profile	43
3.5	Some aspects of expected support by a mentor associated with some unreasonable expectations	44
4.1	A template for time offering challenges to achieve targets	51
4.2	Weekly reflections by applying the four elements of RP	54
4.3	Using Kolb's learning cycle to evaluate sample reflective accounts	55
5.1	First meeting checklist	63
5.2	Tracking emotional changes	65

6.1	Learning outcomes and pupils learning	79
6.2	Possible key questions (KQ) for the learning outcomes (LO) presented in Table 6.1	80
6.3	A lesson plan	82
6.4	Planning tasks according to pupil's different competence levels	86
6.5	Using a range of questions to target the particular needs	88
6.6	Planning differentiated tasks	89
7.1	Some examples of basic teaching skills (based on Bassett, Bowler and Newton, 2019, pp. 172–174; and Kyriacou, 2018) aligned with some characteristic behaviours of an effective teacher	101
7.2	Links between the characteristic behaviours of effective teachers, associated basic teaching skills and a beginning teacher's next steps in developing these skills	102
8.1	The MERID model	118
8.2	Lesson observation template	126
8.3	WRAP feedback chart for post-lesson discussion	130
8.4	Mentoring checklist before, during and after a lesson observation	131
9.1	Weekly mentoring meetings verses the lesson debriefs	139
9.2	Some example purposes of weekly mentoring meetings and lesson debriefs	140
9.3	A professional development plan adopting teacher standards	142
9.4	A sample professional development plan to achieve teacher standards	142
9.5	The GROW model	146
12.1	The three dimensions of assessment	184
12.2	A checklist for inducting beginning teachers into your school's assessment policies and practices	188
13.1	A beginning teacher's views on retrieval practice	209
14.1	Articulating a beginning teacher's views about NoS	216
14.2	Sources of guidance for practical activities	222
14.3	A lesson plan pro forma to include the elements of the NoS in the planning and teaching of practical work (including health and safety)	224
15.1	Mentor's reflection in relation to scientific literacy	233
15.2	Verbs for writing learning outcomes to incorporate scientific literacy in lesson planning	235
15.3	Supporting a beginning teacher to plan for group work	237
15.4	Enhancing scientific literacy by maximising a pupil's participation	238
15.5	Lesson evaluation template focused on planning and teaching scientific literacy dimensions	240
16.1	A beginning teacher's self-reflections on philosophical orientation towards teaching and learning science	246
16.2	Analysing and/or planning different lesson activities according to the four levels of inquiry	248
16.3	A POGIL plan	251

xii *illustrations*

16.4 A POGIL lesson plan for a series of lessons 257
17.1 A weekly log to record my involvement with the wider school community to enhance teacher's autonomy 273
19.1 A template to promote scientific literacy 297

TASKS

1.1	Mentor's reflection: Reflecting on your understanding of mentoring	12
1.2	Mentor's reflection: Understanding the term mentoring	13
1.3	The context in which you carry out your mentoring duties	16
1.4	Three different mentoring models	17
1.5	Responsibilities of the mentor and beginning teacher at each stage of Katz's stages of development model (1995)	19
1.6	Helping a beginning teacher to learn using Clutterbuck's (2004) model	19
1.7	Attributes of an effective mentor	20
1.8	Mentor's reflection: Reflecting on your mentoring practice	21
2.1	The motivation-readiness matrix	23
2.2	What is good mentoring?	24
2.3	Identifying yourself	25
2.4	Reflections on Case study 2.1: Harry	26
2.5	Reflections on Case study 2.2: Razina	27
2.6	Which is your preferred style of mentoring?	29
2.7	Your beliefs: Teaching and mentoring	30
3.1	Reflecting on your perspectives on the main characteristics of mentoring a beginning teacher	33
3.2	Mentoring actions of an effective mentor	35
3.3	Mapping Hudson's factors for effective mentoring	36
3.4	Supporting a beginning teacher to recognise their personal teaching and learning developmental needs and communicate their expectations with you as a mentor using a PRoP form	37
3.5	Unreasonable expectations of a mentor	44
4.1	The mentor you wish to become	49
4.2	Apply the four elements of RP to view the impact on mentoring difficult situations	52
4.3	Mentor refection: Selecting a model of RP	58
5.1	Sharing personal experiences of teaching with a beginning teacher	61
5.2	Mentor's reflection: Am I judgemental or not?	62
5.3	Knowing me, knowing you	62
5.4	Managing expectations and commitments	64

xiv *Tasks*

5.5	Developing a beginning teacher's confidence	67
5.6	Emotional intelligence to recognise negative emotions	68
6.1	Mentoring to support lesson planning by using the experiential learning cycle	74
6.2	Mentor's self-reflection on supporting a beginning teacher to plan a single and/or series of lessons	75
6.3	Mentoring to support effective planning through arranging lesson observations of experienced teachers for a beginning teacher	77
6.4	Supporting a beginning teacher to identify pupils learning	79
6.5	Writing key questions to accomplish a smooth progression of a lesson	80
6.6	Embedding key questions as part of a beginning teacher's planning to strengthen pupils' learning	81
6.7	Mentoring to support planning for differentiated questions	87
6.8	Long-term planning	90
7.1	Characteristic behaviours of effective teachers	96
7.2	Supporting a beginning teacher to identify strengths and areas of challenge in becoming an effective teacher	99
7.3	Characteristic behaviours of an effective teacher and basic teaching skills	100
7.4	Assisting a beginning teacher to develop their basic teaching skills at the early stages of development	101
7.5	Survival stage: Micro-teaching and mentoring support	103
7.6	Recognising difficulties stage and mentoring support	105
7.7	Hitting a plateau – mentoring support	109
7.8	Self-evaluation and mentor–mentee discussions	111
7.9	Supporting a beginning teacher to self-evaluate their practice based on pupils' feedback	112
8.1	What sort of mentor are you?	117
8.2	Mentoring approaches for Jane	118
8.3	Pre-lesson discussions and teacher standards	121
8.4	Focused feedback	122
8.5	Undertaking lesson observation	123
8.6	To intervene, or not to intervene, in a lesson	124
8.7	Reflecting on John's lesson and Brian's observation	127
8.8	Reflecting on mentoring approaches	129
9.1	Running the weekly mentoring meetings – reflective questions	138
9.2	Weekly mentoring meetings verses the lesson debriefs	139
9.3	Teacher standards: Professional developmental targets and strategies	141
9.4	What are the common internal drivers to consider when establishing the weekly meetings?	143
9.5	Mentor's reflection	148
10.1	What mentoring support is needed to develop PCK?	157
10.2	Subject knowledge audit for a beginning science teacher	159
10.3	Mentoring a beginning teacher, with an emphasis on using PCK to enhance pupils' learning	162
10.4	Content Representation (CoRe) tool	163

Tasks xv

10.5	An action plan to help a beginning science teacher by developing subject knowledge and PCK and linking them effectively	164
11.1	A contingent moment for a beginning science teacher	172
11.2	A contingent moment in the middle of a planned lesson experienced by a beginning teacher	173
11.3	Supporting a beginning teacher to build a scientific explanation for pupils	174
11.4	Beginning teacher's judgment, explanation and contingent question	177
11.5	Mentor's reflection: Building confidence of a beginning teacher	179
12.1	Identifying what a beginning teacher knows about assessment	185
12.2	A checklist for inducting beginning teachers into your school's or department's assessment practices	187
12.3	Construction and analysis of summative tests	189
12.4	Assessing pupils' scientific inquiry skills using summative styled rubrics	189
12.5	Reflection on pupils' summative tests	190
12.6	Developing effective questioning practices among beginning teachers	193
12.7	Developing comment-only marking	194
12.8	A formative analysis of summative tests	196
12.9	The KMOFAP approach	197
13.1	Mentor's reflection on effective learning	203
13.2	A beginning teacher's beliefs and understanding about memory and learning	204
13.3	Supporting beginning teachers to use the spacing effect in the school context	206
13.4	Supporting beginning teachers to use interleaving	207
13.5	Supporting beginning teachers to use retrieval practice	208
13.6	Mentor's reflection on strategies to support a beginning teacher in developing learning, memory and inquiry	211
14.1	Aspects of science teaching and mentoring	215
14.2	Articulating a beginning teacher's views about NoS	216
14.3	Supporting a beginning teacher to exemplify the elements of NoS	217
14.4	An audit on the presence of NoS in the science curriculum	218
14.5	Reflecting on what aspects of the NoS can be taught through a given practical activity	219
14.6	'A matter of terms'	220
14.7	Sources of guidance	221
14.8	Induction to the laboratory on dealing with serious contingency issues	222
14.9	PDW to unravel NoS elements and health and safety procedures in practical science lessons	225
14.10	Lesson planning to incorporate practical activities, along with the elements of the NoS and instruction on health and safety	226
15.1	An introduction to pedagogical practices associated with scientific literacy	230
15.2	A beginning teacher outlining scientific literacy-mediated events and experiences	231
15.3	Mentor's reflection on prior mentoring in relation to scientific literacy	232
15.4	Supporting a beginning teacher to plan for group work	236
15.5	Mentor-mentee evaluations	239
16.1	Self-reflection of inquiry-based and experiential science education	245

xvi *Tasks*

16.2 Classifying pupil activities using Fitzgerald, Danaia and McKinnon's (2019) four levels of inquiry — 247

16.3 Challenges to implementing inquiry-based pedagogical approaches — 249

16.4 The POGIL learning cycle: Developing a POGIL plan — 250

16.5 The POGIL learning cycle: Analysing a POGIL activity — 252

16.6 Considering group roles — 253

16.7 Incorporating POGIL process skills in science lessons — 256

17.1 Mentor's reflection: Mentoring strategies related to supporting the development of an autonomous teacher — 267

17.2 Supporting Andrew in increasing autonomy — 268

17.3 Supporting Liam in increasing autonomy — 269

17.4 Sharing practices that makes an autonomous teacher — 270

17.5 My peer's autonomous development as a teacher — 271

17.6 Mentoring support to strengthen participatory appropriation plane — 276

18.1 Mentor's reflection: Looking at the context of differentiation — 279

18.2 Mentoring strategies for Zarah — 280

18.3 Supporting a beginning teacher to start thinking about planning enrichment activities — 282

18.4 Mentor's strategies for Chen — 283

18.5 Signposting the beginning teacher to sources of support — 287

18.6 Reflection and review of the five-steps of the framework — 288

19.1 A beginning teacher's reflection on SEND information and provision — 293

19.2 A beginning teacher's preconceptions and knowledge on managing pupils with SEND — 294

19.3 A template to promote scientific literacy among pupils with SEND — 298

19.4 Incorporating inquiry-based learning practices for pupils with SEND — 300

19.5 A case study task — 301

19.6 In-depth discussion — 302

CASE STUDIES

2.1	Harry	26
2.2	Razina	27
3.1	Amy's reflections on her experience of school-based mentoring	36
5.1	Michael and Claire	66
5.2	Sarah and Alison	66
7.1	Hanniyah and Henry	103
8.1	Jane: Mentoring meeting targeting lesson observations	118
8.2	Brian and John (pre-lesson discussion)	120
8.3	Brian's approach one	128
8.4	Brian's approach two	128
13.1	Paul's mentoring meeting	202
13.2	Dorothy and Viktoria	209
15.1	Sarah: Mentor-mentee discussion points	232
17.1	Andrew (a beginning science teacher)	267
17.2	Liam	268
18.1	Zarah: Reach for the stars	280
18.2	Chen: Field trip	283

APPENDICES

3.1	Personal Record of Progress (PRoP) form	46
6.1	Handout for pupils investigating the relationship between the voltage across a resistor and the current through it	92
7.1	Self-evaluation and mentor–mentee discussion template	114
8.1	Lesson observation template for John	134
9.1	An example template of a weekly meeting record document	150
10.1	Subject knowledge audit for beginning teachers	166
10.2	A CoRe matrix to develop PCK	169
10.3	An example of a completed CoRe matrix, for teaching enzymes to 14–16-year-old pupils	169
10.4	A three-step process to help a beginning teacher to develop their subject knowledge and PCK	170
12.1	Action plan template	200
13.1	Task 13.2 suggested answers	213
15.1	A lesson plan template: Scientific literacy dimensions	242
16.1	Rates of reaction	260

CONTRIBUTORS

Michael Allen is currently Associate Professor in the School of Education at Kingston University, London. His research interests include preschool science, particularly conceptual development in the early years, science misconceptions at all levels of education and quantitative methodologies. As a school teacher himself, Michael taught science at secondary and middle schools in Berkshire for 12 years and has mentored numerous trainee secondary science teachers. As part of his current role, Michael teaches science to trainee primary school teachers, supervises students undertaking school experience and lectures on masters and doctoral programmes.

Gareth Bates is a Lecturer of Teacher Education – science specialism at the University of Bedfordshire, where as part his role he coordinates the Post Graduate Certificate in Education (PGCE) secondary science course. He works closely with mentors and provides regular CPD throughout the year, including a mentor conference. Previously in his teaching career he has been a head of science and was an advocate of professional development. Additionally, during his teaching career Gareth supported a number of trainee teachers and newly qualified teachers as both a mentor and delivering bespoke professional development sessions.

Alison Black graduated as a teacher with a specialism in primary science in 2001. She has taught in primary and secondary schools, and is now a Lecturer in Inclusive and Special Education at the University of Exeter. She is programme lead for the Masters in Special Educational Needs (SEN) and is also the coordinator for SEN across the teacher training programmes the university offers. She has been a mentor for teacher trainees and newly qualified teachers in the schools she worked in and holds a range of mentoring roles at the university.

Stephen P. Day is Head of Division (Education) at the University of the West of Scotland and is a lead science tutor. His research interests focus on the handling of socio-scientific discussion; constructivist approaches to learning for sustainability; the learning and teaching of ideas that challenge pupils in the sciences; and models of coaching and mentoring for beginning science teachers and initial teacher education (ITE) Tutors. He is an experienced science mentor having supported many beginning science teachers into the profession. He also mentors new ITE tutors as they transition into their new role from primary and secondary education.

xx *Contributors*

Jane Essex has taught science in state secondary schools in England for 16 years and mentored student teachers for two different universities. While in school, she undertook a doctorate looking at whether mentoring could raise pupil attainment in chemistry. She subsequently moved to an initial teacher education (ITE) post as a Chemistry PGCE tutor at Keele University and was then appointed to ITE posts at Brunel University London. While at Keele, she also directed a pilot phase pre-ITE chemistry subject knowledge enhancement course. Most recently, she was appointed as a Chemistry Education lecturer at Strathclyde University. In all of these posts she has been extensively involved in supporting and developing school-based mentors to work with student teachers.

Morag Findlay has worked as a physics and mathematics teacher from the Highlands of Ethiopia to the Northwest Highlands of Scotland and has experience of both the English and Scottish education systems. As a science teacher educator at the University of Strathclyde, she completed her EdD in physics teacher education. She has extensive experience of working with student teachers on a range of science and education modules on campus as well as mentoring student teachers before, during and after observed lessons in schools. She is currently the programme External Examiner for another Scottish Professional Graduate Diploma in Education (PGDE) course.

Jonathan Firth is a psychology teacher, author, and researcher. Alongside his teaching and teacher-education roles he is currently doing a PhD at the University of Strathclyde, focusing on the practical applications of memory research to education. He has written several school psychology textbooks, and his latest book, *Psychology in the Classroom* (Routledge, co-authored with Marc Smith), focuses on the application of psychological theories and concepts to teaching. He is a board member of the British Psychological Society's Psychology of Education Section.

Gill Golder is a director of teacher education, department head for education and programme leader for secondary education at the university of St Mark and St John, Plymouth. For details please, visit www.marjon.ac.uk/about-marjon/staff-list-and-profiles/golder-gillian.htmlDirector

Helen Gourlay is a Development Lead for Teach First, where she works with trainee teachers and newly qualified teachers. Before working in ITE, Helen was a successful and innovative science teacher. She taught science across the secondary age range for 17 years in comprehensive schools in London and Hertfordshire. This experience included working as a Team Leader for Science in two schools. Prior to working for Teach First, Helen was a lecturer in science education at King's College London, the University of East Anglia and Brunel University, where her responsibilities included leading a secondary ITE programme, leading on science teacher education (with a specialism in physics), School Direct, and Teach First. Her research interests include science teacher development and children and young people's learning in science.

Alison Keyworth is a director of the Institute of Education at the university of St Mark and St John, Plymouth. For details please, visit www.marjon.ac.uk/about-marjon/staff-list-and-profiles/keyworth-alison.html

Adam H. Larson is Lecturer of English at Weill Cornell Medicine-Qatar where he teaches the First-Year Writing Seminar, an intensive writing course introducing academic writing through disciplines in the social sciences and humanities. He has mentored science instructors at several institutions in Saudi Arabia, and developed curricula in technical communications for programmes in engineering, health science and information technology. Larson received his Doctorate in Education from King's College London, where his research involved the philosophy and sociology of education. His current research interests include the philosophy and sociology of education, youth transitions from school to work, professional learning, and teacher/faculty development.

Nicklas Lindstrom has been teaching secondary school science for 20 years as head of chemistry, head of science and latterly lead practitioner. Throughout this time he has mentored numerous trainees acting as subject mentor working with the University of Warwick, Birmingham, Wolverhampton and Northampton. In 2018 Nicklas took up the post of Lecturer of Science Education at King's College London and continued to mentor both trainee teachers and also support school based science mentors. He will this year begin his PhD studies at Birmingham University in secondary school chemistry education, investigating 'how student can use interconnected units of chemical knowledge to develop solutions to chemical problems'.

Ralph Littler is an enthusiastic teacher with over 25 years' experience across the private, mainstream and custodial sectors. He researched mentoring from a communities of practice perspective as part of his master's degree. Formally a founding member and subject leader of an education custodial facility, mentoring and training new staff, more recently he has worked in mainstream education teaching science to middle school pupils. With a track record for turning 'at risk' trainees in to quality teachers, he is now a freelance advisor focusing on science, delivering teacher/mentor training sessions, and supporting early career teachers who find their role a challenge.

Richard Malthouse is Senior Lecturer on the BA (Hons) Education Studies programme at the University of East London. He currently lectures in Education with Psychology and engages in seminars with Early Years students. Prior to this, he lectured at the University of West London and as a Teaching Fellow at Brunel University, lecturing on the BA in Contemporary Education. He is currently researching elements of metacognition and the transition from Levels 3 to 4 and has developed a new model of reflective practice aimed to assist Year 1 students.

Darren Moore teaches in the Graduate School of Education at the University of Exeter. He has worked on the Secondary Science PGCE programme there since 2009, leading the course since 2017. He also leads master's modules on Special Educational Needs (SEN). He has experience working with learners with SEN from primary age to Further and Higher Education and been involved in a range of research involving learners with SEN, often focused on social and emotional mental health. Through PGCE work at Exeter and as an External Examiner for Manchester Metropolitan University, Darren sees mentoring relationships from both beginning teachers and experienced mentors' perspectives.

Stavros A. Nikou is a Lecturer in Digital Education at the University of Strathclyde, UK. He holds a PhD in Information Systems, an MSc in Computer Science and a BSc in Physics. He has many years of experience in STEM and ICT education and mentoring teachers in

ICT and technology-enhanced learning. His research expertise is in the fields of learning technologies, context-aware mobile learning and assessment, smart learning environments, teacher education and computational thinking. He has published in scientific peer-reviewed journals and international conferences as well as book chapters.

Nqobile Nkala holds a Master's in Education and an EdD in science education from The Open University, Milton Keynes, UK. He is a senior lecturer in education at Canterbury Christ Church University, Kent, UK, working on the Teach First programme. His academic interests are in science education, teacher education, critical pedagogy and sociocultural theory. He has over 20 years of science teaching experience, during which he led a science department and mentored trainee teachers on various initial teacher education routes. He has worked with and trained a number of effective mentors across the East of England.

Simon Parry has been a secondary science teacher for almost 30 years, and for almost all of that time he has been a mentor to beginner teachers, both PGCE students and NQTs. He has taught Biology, Chemistry and Physics to GCSE, and biology to A-level, including being an A-level examiner. He has been a head of science, and was an Advanced Skills Teacher from 2006–2013, much of which involved supporting teachers in local secondary and primary schools. From 2013 to 2016 he has been a facilitator for the OLEVI Outstanding Teacher Programme.

Sheila S. Qureshi is an Associate Professor of Chemistry at Weill Cornell Medicine in Qatar (WCM-Q), obtained her BSc degree in Chemistry and Biology from University of London, Goldsmiths College. Dr Qureshi received her PhD in Synthetic Organic Chemistry from Cardiff University (UWIST). After working in the pharmaceutical industry, she received her PGCE from the University of Nottingham. Dr Qureshi's teaching strives to develop students as independent learners. She uses innovative teaching strategies, such as Process Orientated Guided Inquiry Learning (POGIL) and has trained and mentored chemistry teachers in schools in implementing POGIL in Qatar. Her research has demonstrated clear benefits from blending lecture with POGIL workshops.

Jodi Roffey-Barentsen is Senior Lecturer at the School of Education at the University of Brighton. She is Programme Leader of the BA (Hons) Early Childhood Education and Care and contributes to postgraduate programmes such as the MA and EdD, and supervises PhD students. Prior to this she was involved in Education Studies and Teacher Training programmes. Her research interests include Reflective Practice and Learning Support. Jodi is a Senior Fellow of the Higher Education Academy.

Saima Salehjee is a Lecturer in Chemistry Education at the University of Strathclyde. She is responsible for teaching and research work with particular emphasis on STEM education. Saima's research focuses on science literacy, public understanding of science, science identity and identity transformations over a lifespan of individuals from a different ethnic, religious and sexual backgrounds. She mentors national and international (student) teachers and collaborates with scholars and researchers at an international level.

Clare Shaw is a Senior Lecturer in primary initial teacher education at the university of St Mark and St John, Plymouth. For details please, visit www.marjon.ac.uk/about-marjon/staff-list-and-profiles/shaw-clare.html.

Venkat Rao Vishnumolakala has served as an academic in STEM Education at Curtin University, Australia before joining Abu Dhabi University as a visiting faculty in Education since fall, 2017. He specialises in students' understanding of science concepts in small group active learning pedagogies in trans-national settings. He mentors graduate students, new professionals and collaborates with scholars and researchers. He has taught at secondary and tertiary levels in Australia, New Zealand and India since 1992. He earned his doctorate from Science and Mathematics Education Centre of Curtin University, Australia.

Mike Watts is a Professor of Education at Brunel University London. Mike supervises a strong group of doctoral students and teaches on a wide range of courses across Education. He is HEA National Teaching Fellow (2003) and was elected Fellow of the Institute of Physics in 2004. He has just completed a decade-long project to explore approaches to teaching and learning in university science. Most recently, he has been consultant to the Teaching Council of Ireland and external examiner for the National University of Ireland. Mike leads the STEM Education Research Group at Brunel, and has published widely in science education over many decades.

Michelle Wormald is currently a Lecturer in Education at the University of Hull. Trained as a primary teacher specialising in science, Michelle has taught in both primary and secondary settings. She has worked as a mentor for 20 years as part of her roles as pastoral leader, head of science and director of learning.

ACKNOWLEDGEMENTS

I am most grateful to Susan Capel for the opportunity to edit this book. Completion of this book could not have been possible without your continued support, guidance and encouragement. Thank you, Susan.

I am thankful to all the contributors for their willingness in sharing their expertise, thoughts and ideas – without them, there would simply be no book. I am grateful to the Strathclyde University's School of Education Heads – Mrs Linda Brownlow and Professor Ian Rivers – for their support in the completion of this book.

A special thanks to my family. Words cannot express how grateful I am to my mother and sister for their continued motivation and encouragement.

My warm thanks also go to many people from Routledge who have supported and guided me in the production of this book.

AN INTRODUCTION TO THE SERIES: MENTORING TRAINEE AND NEWLY QUALIFIED TEACHERS

Mentoring is a very important and exciting role. What could be better than supporting the development of the next generation of subject teachers? A mentor is almost certainly an effective teacher, but this doesn't automatically guarantee that he or she will be a good mentor, despite similarities in the two roles. This series of practical workbooks covers most subjects in the secondary curriculum. They are designed specifically to reinforce mentors' understanding of different aspects of their role, for mentors to learn about and reflect on their role, to provide support for mentors in aspects of their development and enable them to analyse their success in supporting the development of beginning subject teachers (defined as trainee, newly qualified and early career teachers). This book has two main foci: first, the focus is on challenging mentors to reflect critically on theory, research and evidence, on their own knowledge, how they work with beginning teachers, how they work with more experienced teachers and on their approaches to mentoring in order to move their practice forward. Second, the focus is on supporting mentors to effectively facilitate the development of beginning teachers. Thus, some of the practical activities in the books are designed to encourage reflection, while others ask mentors to undertake activities with beginning teachers. This book can be used alongside generic and subject books designed for student and newly qualified teachers. These books include Capel, Leask and Younie's *Learning to Teach in the Secondary School: A Companion to School Experience*, 8th edition (2019b), which deals with aspects of teaching and learning applicable to all subjects. This generic book also has a companion Reader: *Readings for Learning to Teach in the Secondary School* by Capel, Leask and Turner (2010) containing articles and research papers in education suitable for master's-level study. Further, the generic book is complemented by two subject series: *Learning to Teach [subject] in the Secondary School: A Companion to School Experience*; and *A Practical Guide to Teaching [subject] in the Secondary School*. These books are designed for student teachers on different types of initial teacher education programmes (and indeed a beginning teacher you are working with may have used/ currently be using them). However, these books are proving equally useful to tutors and mentors in their work with student teachers, both in relation to the knowledge, skills and understanding the student teacher is developing

xxvi *An introduction to the series*

and some tasks that mentors might find it useful to support a beginning teacher to do. It is also supported by a book designed for newly qualified teachers, Capel, Lawrence, Leask and Younie's *Surviving and Thriving in the Secondary School: The NQT's Essential Companion* (2019a), as well as Capel, Heilbronn, Leask and Turner's *Starting to Teach in the Secondary School: A Companion for the Newly Qualified Teacher* (2004). These titles cover material not generally needed by student teachers on an initial teacher education course, but which is needed by newly qualified teachers in their school work and early career.

The information in this book should link with the information in the generic text and relevant subject book in the two series in a number of ways. For example, mentors might want to refer a beginning teacher to read about specific knowledge, understanding and skills they are focusing on developing, or to undertake tasks in the book, either alone or with their support, then discus the tasks. It is recommended that you have copies of these books available so that you can cross-reference when needed.

In turn, the books complement a range of resources on which mentors can draw (including other mentors of beginning teachers in the same or other subjects, other teachers and a range of other resources including books, research articles and websites).

The positive feedback on *Learning to Teach* and the related books above, particularly the way they have supported the learning of student teachers in their development into effective, reflective teachers, encouraged us to retain the main features of that book in this series. Like teaching, mentoring should be research- and evidence-informed. Thus, this series of books introduces theory, research and professional evidence-based advice and guidance to support mentors as they develop their mentoring to support beginning teachers' development. The main focus is the practical application of material. Elements of appropriate theory introduce each topic or issue, and recent research into mentoring and/or teaching and learning is integral to the presentation. Tasks are provided to help mentors identify key features of the topic or issue and reflect on and/or apply them to their own practice of mentoring beginning teachers. Although the basic structure of all the subject books is similar, each book is different to reflect the needs of mentors in relation to the unique nature of each subject.

The chapter authors in the subject books have been engaged with mentoring over a long period of time and are aiming to share research/evidence and their experience. We, as series editors, are pleased to extend the work in initial teacher education to the work of mentors of beginning teachers. We hope that this series of books supports you in developing into an effective, reflective mentor as you support the development of the next generation of subject teachers.

Susan Capel, Julia Lawrence, Trevor Wright and Sarah Younie
December 2020

Introduction
A practical guide to mentoring science education

By the time a beginning teacher is given a full teaching timetable, significant effort has been expended by many people, including the beginning teachers themselves, university staff members and school mentors. Science teachers work hard to educate pupils by extending their scientific knowledge/expertise and adopting effective strategies to promote scientific learning by all pupils they teach. Schools and governments also play a vital role in supporting the development of beginning teachers; their effort is to provide support for their recruitment, training and retention in schools as effective science teachers.

This investment does not end once a beginning teacher attains qualified teacher's status (QTS); rather, they will be taken to the next level of support and guidance. So, why is it worthwhile investing in science teacher education programmes? It is valuable, because it develops effective teachers who can, locally and regionally, meet the challenge of inspiring young people to carry on with the study of science after it ceases being compulsory in school. At a minimum, it produces scientifically literate citizens who can achieve a better lifestyle and can help others to live a better life (Salehjee and Watts, 2020). Further, it is a way of generating skilful future scientists to meet the demands of the global market (see, for example, Confederation of British Industry (CBI), 2012 and House of Lords, 2012; US President's Council of Advisors on Science and Technology (PCAST), 2014). Further, investment in supporting teacher education (both initial and continuing) has more value if a beginning teacher receives support from university staff and school mentors.

So, how much are you, as a mentor of a beginning teacher, responsible for training and retaining beginning science teachers? Recently, in some countries, there has been a move away from traditional university-based postgraduate courses to more school-led teacher education for beginning teachers. With these changes there are now more classroom-teachers, like you, who are acting as mentors in school-led teacher education programmes – arguably, without the same level of support from university staff (both in preparation for being a mentor and in working as a mentor of a trainee teacher), as was previously the case with university-based courses. Teachers in schools are involved not just in working with beginning teachers; they also mentor newly qualified and early career teachers. Consequently, a lot of responsibility lies with you to train and retain these beginning teachers in the teaching profession. More responsibility requires more preparation; however, Clarke, Triggs, and Nielsen (2014) are of the opinion that generally classroom-teachers with mentoring responsibility lack preparation and can exhibit a lack of ability in providing high-quality individualised support to their mentees. This lack of

2 *Introduction*

high-quality support is evident because many classroom-teachers, mentoring beginning science teachers, are left to learn the complexity of the mentoring processes on their own, without explicit support and proper training.

The purpose of this book

In a similar way to teaching, the mentoring role requires proper training, planning and practice. Simply having a number of years in science teaching does not ultimately enable classroom-teachers to mentor beginning teachers effectively (Gareis and Grant, 2014; Stanulis and Brondyk, 2013). With that in mind, this book is designed to fill the gap in both the training of and support for school-based mentors to enable you to support beginning science teachers effectively. Indeed, it is anticipated that, as more teacher education is school-led, there will be a greater need for practical books such as this to support school staff working with beginning teachers.

In expanding your role from being a science classroom-teacher to a science mentor, you could intentionally or unintentionally pass your initial teacher education (ITE) experiences onto a beginning teacher. However, in actuality, your initial teacher education cannot be the same as that of the beginning teacher, you mentor. The journey of becoming a science teacher depends on the individual beginning teacher, their relationships with mentors and other school staff members, diverse cohorts of pupils, differences in coping with internal and external pressures and various teaching and learning contexts. Therefore, this book will take you through the journey of supporting a beginning teacher's development into becoming an effective science teacher.

This practical workbook is designed to help you develop further as a science mentor, in turn supporting beginning teachers to become effective science teachers who can offer a range of science learning opportunities to secondary school pupils. In preparing this book, I have attempted to draw on a broad range of science specialist expertise. The authors of the chapters have been chosen based on their expertise as science teachers, science mentors, university tutors of beginning science teachers and/or their academic work in the field of teacher education. These authors have drawn on research to provide evidence-based practice in mentoring beginning science teachers. This research is supported by practical examples of existing good practice, alongside a range of teaching and learning strategies for mentors and beginning teachers to use in their work.

This book covers a wide range of practical guidance for mentoring; however, it cannot cover everything that a mentor will experience while working with an individual beginning teacher. Nevertheless, this book can help a mentor to understand the complexities of mentoring beginning teachers. This book aims to support a mentor to:

- Develop their knowledge, understanding and skills about effective mentoring
- Use basic mentoring strategies to meet the needs of supporting a beginning teacher to survive and progress in teaching science to secondary aged pupils
- Support a beginning teacher's development over time using professional judgements and expertise
- Reflect critically on their practices, responsibilities, perceptions, disposition and beliefs as a mentor of a beginning science teacher.

Introduction 3

In reading this book, you will be able to recall, refine, adjust or change your mentoring style to complement an individual beginning teacher's stage of development. You will also be able to evaluate aspects of mentoring through the eyes of the authors of chapters in this book and begin to strengthen, change or even transform your own values, outlook, dispositions and beliefs about mentoring beginning science teachers.

About this book

This book contains 20 chapters in four sub-sections, which cover the following topics:

Section 1 Foundations of mentoring. This section includes five chapters, which cover theories and models of mentoring, understanding of your motivations and readiness to be a mentor, beginning science teachers' expectations of their mentor, embedding reflective practices in your mentoring and strengthening the mentor–mentee relationship to support a beginning teacher's professional development.

Section 2 Basic mentoring practices. This section includes four chapters focusing on supporting a beginning teacher to plan, teach and evaluate lessons, mentoring steps to employ a lesson observation cycle effectively (pre-lesson discussions, lesson observations and post-lesson discussions), and holding weekly mentoring meetings to support a beginning teacher's development in a constructive manner.

Section 3 Extending basic mentoring practices. This section comprises of six chapters to build beginning science teachers' knowledge for teaching the science curriculum, not only developing pupil's knowledge but also to develop pupils as effective science learners. In so doing, the chapters focus on supporting beginning teachers to develop their pedagogical content knowledge, to cope with pupils' contingent questions, to assess pupils' scientific learning effectively, to link learning, memory and inquiry, to enhance pupils' scientific learning, incorporate learning about the nature of science in their lessons, to embed scientific literacy, and to adopt inquiry-based learning approaches to teaching science.

Section 4 Moving beyond. This section comprises of four chapters. Following from the previous section, it focuses on knowledge, skills and understanding about communities of practice to support beginning science teachers to become autonomous teachers, extending and enriching their planning further and teaching special educational needs and disability (SEND) pupils in a full class context. Finally, the last chapter concludes the book, highlighting some key aspects that this book has offered – to develop and continue with effective mentoring practices.

Although this book is divided into sub-sections and chapters, some similar content is covered in several chapters. In such cases, the content is expressed in a different context or can be viewed as extended material and activities. Where similar content is covered, there is cross-referencing to the relevant chapter.

Each chapter is laid out as follows:

- **Introduction**, presents the background, rationale and organisation of the chapter.
- **Objectives,** highlight the points for a mentor to take from reading the chapter and completing the tasks.

4 Introduction

- **The main content** of the chapter is underpinned by research and evidence with a focus on practical support and guidance. Throughout the chapter, links between theory and practice are emphasised by including examples, checklists, case studies and tasks. In particular, tasks are designed to reinforce the practical impact of the book. Some tasks specifically ask you to reflect on your perceptions, knowledge, understanding, skills and practices, while others require you to undertake activities with a beginning teacher.
- **Summary and key points**, highlight the take-home message offered by the chapter.
- **Further resources**, include some selected resources to find out more about the content of each chapter.

eResources

The main text is supported by online eResources (www.routledge.com/9780367023126). This contains all the appendices, checklists, tables and tasks that require you to insert information. They can be downloaded and completed or printed off. It also includes some further electronic resources associated with particular chapters.

Other resources

Various secondary resources are identified both in additional resources provided at the end of each chapter and in the references. These resources include books, articles, reports, websites and blogs relevant to the content of the chapter.

In addition, the book can be used alongside science subject-specific books and generic books for beginning science teachers, such as:

- Capel, S., Leask, M. and Younie, S. (eds). (2019) *Learning to teach in the secondary school: A companion to school experience*, 8th edition. Abingdon, Oxon and New York: Routledge.
- Capel, S., Lawrence, J., Leask, M. and Younie, S. (eds). (2020) *Surviving and thriving in the secondary school: The NQTs essential companion*. Abingdon, Oxon and New York: Routledge.
- Newton, D. P. (2008) *A practical guide to teaching science in the secondary school*. Abingdon, Oxon and New York: Routledge.
- Taber, K. S. (2019) *The nature of the chemical concept: Re-constructing chemical knowledge in teaching and learning*, Vol. 3. UK: Royal Society of Chemistry.
- Taber, K.S. and Kind, V. (2005) *Science: Teaching school subjects 11-19*. London and New York: Routledge.
- Toplis, R. and Frost, J. (2010) *Learning to teach science in the secondary school: A companion to school experience*. London and New York: Routledge.
- White, E. and Jarvis, J. (2013) *School-based teacher training: A handbook for tutors and mentors*. London: Sage.

Some of these books are written for mentors and beginning teachers, while others are written specifically for beginning teachers. In either case, you can use these books to support beginning teachers in their development as science teachers, either in terms of their readings or in terms of activities to support their development.

About you

This book is addressed to you as a mentor of a beginning science teacher. It acknowledges that we cannot generalise about all mentors for a variety of reasons; for example, you are individuals with unique personalities, you have a varying number of years of experience as a science teacher and mentor, and you work in different secondary school contexts. With these differences in mind, this book recognises the fact that professional development is an ongoing process and requires consistent reflection and opportunities for lifelong learning. Therefore, if you have considerable experience in one or different secondary school settings, you are encouraged to reflect on how you can develop and enhance your practice further.

In addition, a beginning teacher you are mentoring will differ in the range of their experience of teaching. For some, it is their first time teaching in school, while others will have some prior teaching experience. Some beginning teachers are associated with university-based initial teacher education courses, while others are learning as part of a school-based programme or have just gained QTS. As a mentor, you might be well supported (or not) by a university, other teacher education provider or local authorities in mentoring a beginning science teacher. Within all these different contexts and support, you will notice that different beginning teachers begin from a different starting point, so you cannot use the same mentoring strategies for all beginning teachers. Moreover, an individual beginning teacher's mentoring support and accompanied challenges also vary from one school to another, from one class to another and even between lessons, which requires you to change mentoring support according to the developmental needs of the beginning teacher.

There is no one best way to use this book. You can consider reading this book chapter by chapter, or you can read selected chapters depending on your need at any point. There are activities in every chapter (except Chapter 20), which are called tasks, adding to the practical nature of the book. You can undertake all of these or pick and choose, as appropriate. Some tasks are designed to support you in developing your knowledge, skills and qualities to be an effective mentor of beginning science teachers. Other tasks support you with reflection on your role, responsibilities and practice as a mentor. The content of yours and/or the beginning teacher's actions and reflection forms the basis of these tasks. We encourage you to extend your discussion about the tasks and linked texts with the beginning teacher, school colleagues, laboratory assistants and other staff members to further enhance the process of reflection within the community of practice. In this way, you can reflect on your own responses and elicit other potential responses and views.

Further, it is important that you and a beginning teacher record and keep answers, thoughts, descriptions, explanations and notes after reading a chapter and completing the associated tasks. These recordings will help you to contemplate further in undertaking activities in the other chapters. In addition, you can revisit, adapt or change your reflective accounts, outcomes and planned activities as a result of future mentoring practices. This will enable you and a beginning teacher to evidence learning and teaching developments.

6 *Introduction*

Terminology used in the book

Different terminology is used in various secondary school settings. These differences range from local, to regional and global understanding of the terms used. Some of the terminology used in this book might not be used in the school context in which you are working as a science mentor and teacher.

One example of the terminology used in the book is 'subject knowledge' which is sometimes called content knowledge. In this book the term subject knowledge is used to mean any scientific knowledge that is brought into the classroom by teachers and pupils, not only from the science curriculum's recommended units of work (blocks/sections of the curriculum) but also from a variety of other sources, which links with the science taught and learned in the classroom. These other sources include science fiction books and other reference books, science magazines, newspapers, internet resources, life experiences, social interaction et cetera.

In this book the word science covers mainly the biology, chemistry and physics parts of secondary school science. Some examples, scenarios and tasks explicitly reference topics linked to either biology, chemistry or physics, which can be adapted/adopted for other topics in the secondary science curriculum. Where this book refers to some recommended units of work, it is referring to the science curriculum in England. The two most recent Government documents used in this book are:

- Department for Education (DfE). (2013) *Science programmes of study: Key stage 3 National Curriculum in England* (for age group 11–14)
- DfE. (2014) *Science programmes of study: Key stage 4 National Curriculum in England* (for age group 14–16).

The General Certificate of Secondary Education (GCSE) aligns its assessment requirements with these DfE documents. These DfE curriculum documents might not correspond exactly to curriculum documents and recommended units of work that you are using in your country/school. In each case, use/refer to the relevant documents in your school and mentoring situation.

This book is gender neutral, where possible, rather than using he/she. Secondary school children are referred to as pupils to avoid confusion with the term student. For instance, the term student-centred is read as pupil-centred in this book.

The focus of this book on beginning science teachers (trainee, newly qualified teacher (NQT), and early career teacher with QTS), whatever country they reside in. Generally, mentoring suggestions and tasks given are designed for one beginning teacher with an understanding that you are (or about to) mentor at least one beginning teacher. However, the same mentoring suggestions and tasks can be adopted/adapted for use with more than one beginning teacher.

Also, this book has addressed you as mentors on whatever type of route to teaching you are mentoring (Post Graduate Certificate in Education (PGCE), Post Graduate Diploma in Education (PGDE), undergraduate teaching led courses leading to QTS, School Direct, School-Centred Initial Teacher Training (SCITT)), or indeed, if you are mentoring full-time teachers with no university-based professional teaching qualification status, newly qualified

Introduction 7

or early career teachers. Hence, to maintain consistency, this book uses the term beginning teacher or beginning science teacher to cover the trainee/newly qualified and early career science teachers you are mentoring.

The focus of the book is generally UK specific, but it is written generically to have broader appeal beyond the UK. Hence, some specific teaching standards from the UK, USA and Australia are introduced in Chapter 1 and subsequently country-specific content is either signposted to Chapter 1 or is not focused entirely on one country. However, some authors have talked explicitly about specific teacher standards of a particular country, but at the same time, it is recognised that there are different arrangements in place in the other countries, as appropriate. For instance, reference is made to the English National Curriculum, the Northern Ireland Curriculum, the Scottish Curriculum for Excellence and the Welsh School Curriculum. In these kinds of instances, it is suggested that you ensure you recognise the requirements of mentoring in the context in which you are working.

This book provides numerous example ways of planning lessons, assessing pupil's knowledge and understanding and observing beginning teachers' knowledge and skills development. These are some examples of good practice. The intention here is not that you use all of it or use it precisely in the way it is presented in this book. Instead, you are advised to focus on an individual beginning teacher's requirement and your school and mentoring context and then adopt/adapt, reflect and keep a check on the pace of delivery accordingly, before you apply the suggested mentoring styles, models and practices.

So, let's start to recall, learn, act and reflect as a mentor with a vision of making active, reflective and autonomous beginning science teacher for the future.

Saima Salehjee
December 2020

SECTION 1
Foundations of mentoring

1 Models of mentoring

Gill Golder, Alison Keyworth and Clare Shaw

Introduction

Your job as a mentor is to develop a positive working relationship with a beginning teacher to enable them to grow and develop both professionally and personally. How you go about this will be influenced by a number of factors, such as your own experience of being mentored in the past and your common-sense opinions of the role. These are important starting points, but you are likely to grow as an effective mentor when you also base your approaches on evidence. This chapter (and this book) is designed to support you in considering the evidence to underpin your practice.

The chapter starts by looking at different definitions of mentoring. It then looks at the importance of the context in which you are working as a mentor, highlighting a number of documents from England and other countries, which impact on your mentoring practice. The chapter then considers three mentoring models that a mentor could adopt to inform their practice. These models underpin various roles you undertake and hence the other chapters in this book.

Objectives

At the end of this chapter, you should be able to:

- Have a greater understanding of what is meant by the term 'mentoring' for a beginning teacher
- Have an appreciation of the key context in which you work that may influence the manner in which you act as a mentor in school
- Have an awareness of the plethora of mentoring models that exist. Compare and contrast three developmental mentoring models and how these could be used to support your role as a mentor.

Before reading further, Task 1.1 asks you to reflect on your understanding of mentoring.

12 *Golder et al.*

Task 1.1 Mentor's reflection: Reflecting on your understanding of mentoring

Reflect on what you understand by mentoring by considering the following questions:

1. How would you define mentoring?
2. How does your definition inform your practice as a mentor?
3. How do the various policy and guidance documents relevant to your context influence your mentoring practice?
4. Do you base your mentoring practice on personal experience or on a model(s) of mentoring? If a model, which one(s)? Why?

1.1 Definitions of mentoring

Mentoring is widely used in many contexts for the purpose of helping people to learn and develop, both professionally and personally. There are numerous and frequently contradictory definitions of mentoring, with accompanying models of how mentoring is best approached (Haggard, Dougherty, Turban and Wilbanks, 2011). Whilst different models might utilise different terminology and vary in emphasis regarding the role of a mentor, what remains consistent is the view that mentoring is a supportive, learning relationship. The mentor, with his or her more extensive experience, is there to support a learner's development. The quality of the relationship between mentor and a beginning teacher is extremely important.

The terms mentoring and coaching are at times used interchangeably. Both aim to develop the professional or professional competencies of a client or colleague. Although mentoring and coaching have much in common, an important difference between the two is the focus of developmental activities. In mentoring, the focus is on development at significant career transitions, whereas in coaching the focus is on the development of a specific aspect of a professional learner's practice (Centre for the Use of Resource and Evidence in Education (CUREE), 2005).

Montgomery (2017) suggested that definitions of mentoring often involve the concept that advice and guidance to a novice, or a person with limited experience, is given by an experienced person. In this way, mentoring can be seen to be hierarchical, a top-down approach largely based on a one-way flow of information.

> Mentoring involves the use of the same models and skills of questioning, listening, clarifying and reframing associated with coaching. Traditionally, however, mentoring in the workplace has tended to describe a relationship in which a more experienced colleague uses his or her greater knowledge and understanding of the work or workplace to support the development of a more junior or inexperienced member of staff.
>
> (Chartered Institute of Personnel and Development (CIPD), 2012, p. 1)

In contrast, other definitions of mentoring follow a less hierarchal structure. These include peer mentoring (Driscoll, Parkes, Tilley-Lubbs, Brill and Pitts Bannister, 2009) and group mentoring (Kroll, 2016). In these approaches to mentoring, the flow of information is more bidirectional.

Models of mentoring 13

Montgomery (2017) suggested that they are more personalised as mentoring is adapted to an individual mentee's goals and needs more effectively. Higgins and Thomas (2001) suggested that top-down mentoring had a greater impact on short-term career outcomes and individually driven mentoring supported long-term career development more effectively. Whether the focus is on short- or long-term tailored development of a mentee, there are common aspects to all forms of mentoring. CIPD (2012, p. 1) identified four characteristics of mentoring:

- It is essentially a supportive form of development.
- It focuses on helping a person manage their career and improve skills.
- Personal issues can be discussed productively.
- Mentoring activities have both organisational and individual goals.

In education, school-based mentors play a vital role in the development of student teachers and the induction and development of newly qualified teachers (NQTs). They also support other staff at points of career development. As with mentoring in other contexts, there is a focus on learning, development and the provision of appropriate support and encouragement. The definition of a mentor outlined in the National Standards for School-based Initial Teacher Training (ITT) Mentors in England (Department for Education (DfE), 2016b, p. 11) is someone who 'is a suitably experienced teacher who has formal responsibility to work collaboratively within the ITT partnership to help ensure the trainee receives the highest quality training'. However, in initial teacher education (ITE) in many countries, including England, assessment of a student teacher is integral to the mentor's role. This is supported by Pollard (2004) who suggested that the role of the mentor in ITT has developed because of three aspects, the complexity of the capabilities teachers need to meet, the focus on high professional standards in school and the transfer of knowledge from one generation to another. Task 1.2 asks you to consider what you understand the term mentoring to mean.

Task 1.2   Mentor's reflection: Understanding the term mentoring

- Research the terms 'mentoring' and 'coaching'.
- List a variety of terms that you associate with mentoring and coaching.
- Make a list of common and unique characteristics for both.

1.2 The context in which you are working that underpins your mentoring practice

Mentoring is increasingly important in a range of fields, both in the UK and internationally, as a tool to support recruitment into a profession, retention in that profession, professional learning, networking and career development. In teaching, it is widely recognised that there is a strong relationship between professional learning, teaching knowledge and practices, educational leadership and pupil results (Cordingley, Higgins, Greany, Buckler, Coles-Jordan, Crisp, Saunders and Coe, 2015). As such, there has been an increase in the development of policy and guidance documents as well as frameworks, toolkits and factsheets produced over the past few years to support educators and others in fulfilling their roles as mentors.

14   *Golder et al.*

As a mentor, it is important to recognise and embed current policy and statutory guidance into your mentoring practice. There are a number of key documents that underpin the mentoring process in ITE and beyond in England and elsewhere. These constitute key external drivers in shaping mentoring practice in school. Being aware of these is important, but knowing how to use them to support your work with a beginning teacher can add purpose and validity to what you do (there are examples of how to do this in other chapters in this book). They also enable you to recognise the value of being a mentor in school, as 'effective professional development for teachers is a core part of securing effective teaching' (DfE 2016d, p. 3).

Table 1.1 highlights policy and guidance documents that influence the work you do in school with a beginning teacher in England and also signposts you to examples of international equivalence documents to enable you to make comparisons internationally.

Table 1.1 Key external drivers influencing mentoring work

	Policy/guidance document	*Author and date introduced*	*Key purpose*
Teacher standards documents	Teachers' Standards (England)	DfE (2011)	Used to assess all student teachers working towards qualified teacher status (QTS) as well as NQTs completing their statutory induction period. 'Providers of ITT should assess trainees against the standards in a way that is consistent with what could reasonably be expected of a trainee teacher prior to the award of QTS' (DfE, 2011, p. 6).
	The Australian Professional Standards for Teachers (Australia)	Australian Institute for Teaching and School Leadership (AITSL) (2011)	The standards are designed so that teachers know what they should be aiming to achieve at every stage of their career; to enable them to improve their practice inside and outside of the classroom. 'The Standards do this by providing a framework which makes clear the knowledge, practice and professional engagement required across teachers' careers' (AITSL 2011, p. 2).
Core content requirements for ITE	Framework of Core Content for Initial Teacher Training (England)	DfE (2016a)	The aim of this framework is to improve the consistency and quality of ITT courses by supporting those involved in training teachers and student teachers themselves to have a better understanding of the key elements of good ITT content.
	Differentiated Primary and Lower Secondary Teacher Education Programmes for Years 1-7 and Years 5-10 (Norway)	Ministry of Education and Research (2010)	These regulations apply to universities and university colleges that provide primary and lower secondary teacher education. They aim to ensure that teacher education institutions provide integrated, professionally oriented and research-based primary and lower secondary teacher education programmes of high academic quality.

Models of mentoring   15

	Policy/guidance document	Author and date introduced	Key purpose
National or regional standards for educators acting as mentors	National standards for school-based initial teacher training (ITT) mentors (England)	DfE (2016b)	The standards were developed to bring greater coherence and consistency to school-based mentoring arrangements for student teachers. They set out the minimum level of practice expected of mentors. They are used to foster consistency in the practice of mentors, raise the profile of mentoring and build a culture of mentoring in schools.
	The New York State Mentoring Standards Albany (USA)	The State Education Department/ The University of The State Of New York (2011)	A set of standards that guide the design and implementation of teacher mentoring programmes in New York State through teacher induction.
National or regional guidelines for general coaching and mentoring practice	National framework for mentoring and coaching (England)	CUREE (2005)	The framework was developed in order to help schools implement mentoring and coaching to assist with continuing professional development and other activities. It sets out ten principles based on evidence from research and consultation that are recommended to inform mentoring and coaching programmes in schools. The framework provides a tool for reflection on existing practice and further development and assists a mentor in self-regulation and monitoring of their own practice.
	NTC Continuum of Mentoring Practice (USA)	New Teacher Centre (NTC) (2011)	Designed to assist programme leaders as they seek to implement mentoring to support induction programmes that are capable of accelerating the development of beginning teacher effectiveness, improving teacher retention, strengthening teacher leadership and increasing pupil learning. 'It presents a holistic view of mentoring, based on six professional standards ... The continuum of mentoring practice describes three levels of development, labelled Exploring/ Emerging, Applying, Integrating/ Innovating' (NTC 2011, p. 2).

(continued)

16   *Golder et al.*

Table 1.1 (Cont.)

	Policy/guidance document	Author and date introduced	Key purpose
Professional development expectations for teachers	Standards for teachers' professional development (England)	DfE (2016d)	This is intended for 'all those working in and with, schools in order to raise expectations for professional development, to focus on achieving the best improvement in pupil outcomes and also to develop teachers as respected members of the profession' (DfE 2016d, p. 4). There is an emphasis on using the standards to support regular reflection on existing practice and discussion between all members of the teaching community. There are five parts to the standard which, when acted upon together, ensure effective professional development.
	Ohio Standards for Professional Development (USA)	Ohio Department for Education (2015)	These define the essential elements of a strong professional learning system, which is one way that school systems can support all educators and encourage improved teaching and learning.

Task 1.3 looks at the context in which you carry out your mentoring duties.

Task 1.3   The context in which you carry out your mentoring duties

Reflect on the context in which you carry out your mentoring duties. Ensure you are familiar with the relevant documents above (or, if you are working outside England, documents specific to your context). What aspects of these documents do you identify as being of most use to your work and why?

1.3 Effective mentoring models

As alluded to above, there are a number of models of mentoring that a mentor could adopt in order to support the growth and development of a beginning teacher. Attempts have been made to categorise different approaches to mentoring, for example Maynard and Furlong (1995) suggested that there are three categories of mentoring, the apprenticeship model, the competence model and the reflective model. The apprenticeship model argues that the skills of being a teacher are best learned by supervised practice, with guidance from and imitation of, experienced practitioners. The competence model suggests that learning to teach requires learning a predefined list of competences (the current Teachers' Standards

Models of mentoring 17

in England (DfE, 2011) could be described as a competence model). In this model, the mentor becomes a systematic trainer supporting a beginning teacher to meet the competences. In the reflective model, the promotion of reflective practice through mentoring is key. This requires a beginning teacher to have some mastery of the skills of teaching to be able to reflect upon their own practice and for the mentor to be a co-enquirer and facilitator rather than instructor. Task 1.4 asks you to look at three different mentoring models.

Task 1.4   Three different mentoring models

- What are the features of practice for each of these models: apprentice, competence and reflective?
- Which features of these models do you use/want to use in our mentoring?
- When do/would you use each model of mentoring?

Maynard and Furlong (1995, p. 18) acknowledged that these three models exist but suggested that they should be taken together, in order to contribute to 'a view of mentoring that responds to the changing needs of trainees'. It is this recognition that mentoring practices and approaches evolve as a beginning teacher develops and the need for an examination of different stages of development that lead us to exploring three models of mentoring in more detail. We explore three well-known models (Daloz, 2012; Katz, 1995; Clutterbuck, 2004), all of which focus on the need for the mentor to be flexible in their style and approach to best fit the needs of a mentee, at any given stage of their development, in ITE and/or their teaching career.

Daloz's (2012) developmental model identifies two key aspects that need to be present in order for optimal learning to take place: **challenge** and **support**. The challenge aspect refers to your ability as a mentor to question a beginning teacher to enable them to reflect critically on their own beliefs, behaviours and attitudes. The support aspect relies on you being able to offer an empathetic ear, actively listen and encourage a beginning teacher to find solutions in order to continue to develop and progress.

Daloz (2012) argues that a combination of high challenge and high support needs to be offered by you as the mentor for a beginning teacher to learn effectively and to **'grow'** (high challenge + high support = **growth)**. At the opposite end of this spectrum is what Daloz refers to as **'stasis'**. A beginning teacher's learning in this zone is very limited as a result of their mentor offering low levels of challenge and support (low challenge + low support = **stasis).** Where challenge is high but support is low, a beginning teacher is likely to **'retreat'** from development (high challenge + low support = **retreat).** However, where challenge is low but support is high, a beginning teacher is unlikely to move beyond their present situation despite their potential for growth being on the increase. Daloz refers to this as **'confirmation'** (low challenge + high support = **confirmation).** You therefore need to be aware of both the level of challenge you offer and the level of support needed by the beginning teacher.

18 *Golder et al.*

The second model is Katz's stages of development model (1995) which describes a model for professional growth in four stages:

1. Survival stage
2. Consolidation stage
3. Renewal stage
4. Maturity stage.

During the first stage, '**survival**', a beginning teacher is likely to show signs of being self-focussed and just 'getting by' or coping from day-to-day. They are likely to experience their practice from a position of doubt and be asking questions like 'can I get to the end of the week?' or 'can I really do this day after day?'. During this initial stage, a beginning teacher may show a reluctance to take responsibility for things and, instead, look to blame others, for example, the pupils, colleagues, the school. As a mentor, observing a beginning teacher during the survival stage, you are likely to see elements of confusion and a lack of any clear rules and routines in their lessons. The beginning teacher may also demonstrate little, if any, consistency in their approach to managing behaviour. Their teaching style is often very teacher-centric and they show a reluctance to deviate from their 'script' in any way.

By the second stage, '**consolidation**', it is likely that a beginning teacher will have begun to implement clearer rules and routines into their classrooms. There is evidence of them starting to question their own practice and being more open to alternative ways of doing things. Whilst observing a beginning teacher at this stage, you are likely to notice that their classes are generally well managed and that the needs of the average pupil are predominantly well catered for. In addition, the beginning teacher is likely to demonstrate a greater awareness of individual pupils and their learning needs. However, they are unlikely to have gained a true grasp of how to support and cater for the needs of pupils within specific subgroups, for example, special educational needs and disability (SEND), English as an additional language (EAL) and gifted and talented (G and T).

The '**renewal**' stage is the point at which a beginning teacher becomes much more self-aware and self-critical. They have generally mastered the basics and are now striving for ways in which they can improve their practice. They are looking for strategies and ideas of how to introduce more creative and innovative activities into their lessons. As a general rule of thumb, at the 'renewal' stage a beginning teacher is often at their most self-motivated and is eager to contribute to departmental discussions, offer suggestions, design additional resources and/or become involved in the running of lunch time and after-school clubs.

The final stage of Katz's model, '**maturity**', is where a beginning teacher is demonstrating signs of developing their own beliefs, teaching strategies and styles. They are regularly asking themselves a number of questions that support deeper levels of reflection, both in and on practice (Schön, 1983). They are still looking to improve their practice and are still interested in new ideas and resources. However, their focus has shifted from an inwards perspective to a much broader one. They are now very much interested in the impact of their teaching on their pupils' learning and progress. Task 1.5 focuses on the responsibilities of the mentor and beginning teacher at each stage of Katz's stages of development model (1995).

Models of mentoring 19

> **Task 1.5 Responsibilities of the mentor and beginning teacher at each stage of Katz's stages of development model (1995)**
>
> In each of Katz's stages, there are responsibilities for both the mentor and beginning teacher. Identify what you would do to support a beginning teacher at each stage.

Clutterbuck's (2004) model of developmental mentoring suggests that an effective mentor wants to draw on all four of the 'helping to learn' styles (guiding, coaching, counselling and networking) (see Figure 1.1). Figure 1.1 shows that in any given mentoring relationship, a mentor may need to adopt a different style and/or approach to challenge and support a beginning teacher at various stages of their development. In developmental mentoring the beginning teacher sets the agenda based on their own development needs and the mentor provides insight and guidance to support the beginning teacher to achieve the desired goals. A more expert mentor will be able to select the right 'helping to learn' style for a beginning teacher's needs.

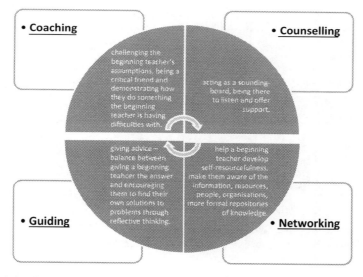

Figure 1.1 Helping to learn styles
(Source: Adapted from Clutterbuck's model of developmental mentoring (2004, p. 9))

Now complete Task 1.6, which looks at Clutterbuck's model.

> **Task 1.6 Helping a beginning teacher to learn using Clutterbuck's (2004) model**
>
> - Which of the four 'helping to learn' styles you consider the most comfortable and why.
> - Which do you use the least often and/or feel the least comfortable with and why?
> - What could they do to overcome this?

20   *Golder et al.*

Your ability to assess and identify the developmental stage in which a beginning teacher is operating at any given point is a significant aspect of your role in becoming an effective mentor and ensuring growth takes places. Of equal importance, however, is your skill in adapting your own approach to fit the developmental needs of a beginning teacher. It is worth remembering that none of the three models (Daloz, 2012; Katz, 1995; or Clutterbuck, 2004) are linear in structure, and, therefore, it is likely that a beginning teacher will move 'to and fro' between stages/zones, for example, if teaching different aspects of the curriculum in which they have greater or lesser knowledge and/or confidence or starting at a new school. With each of the models considered above, it is possible to see elements of all three approaches to mentoring described by Maynard and Furlong (1995). Regardless of the mentoring model on which you prefer to base your practice, the attributes of the mentor play a crucial role in making decisions about the approach to mentoring.

There have been a number of attempts to characterise attributes of mentors. For example, Child and Merrill (2005) sought to generate an understanding of the attributes of a mentor in ITE. Cho, Ramanan and Feldman (2011) described personal qualities that lie at the core of a mentor's identity and professional traits that relate to success in work-related activities. The DfE (2016b) described four separate, but related, areas in the *National Standards for School-based Initial Teacher Training (ITT) Mentors*, i.e. personal qualities, teaching, professionalism and self-development and working in partnership. Ragins (2016) described the attributes of a mentor as an antecedent to high-quality mentoring; as something that needs to be in place before a mentor–mentee relationship begins. Task 1.7 asks you to consider the attributes of an effective mentor.

Task 1.7   Attributes of an effective mentor

1. Considering the context and models of mentoring outlined in this chapter, reflect upon what you think the attributes of an effective mentor are. Attach a level of significance to each attribute, using three categories of significance: *essential*, *desirable* and *highly desirable*.
2. Having identified the attributes and the levels of significance, place five of the attributes in a prioritised list that best captures the ideal profile of a mentor of a beginning teacher.
3. Reflect on your own practice as a mentor; how might you develop the attributes that you have prioritised?

Finally, Task 1.8 asks you to reflect again on your mentoring practice after having read this chapter.

> ### Task 1.8   Mentor's reflection: Reflecting on your mentoring practice
>
> After having read this chapter, reflect how your understanding of definitions of mentoring, relevant policy and guidance documents and models of mentoring have/will impact on your practice.

Summary and key points

Effective mentoring is a complex and demanding task, but, as with any role that enables you to have a positive impact on the development of others, it is hugely rewarding. In this chapter, we have considered the importance of:

- Being aware of different definitions of mentoring
- Understanding the context in which you are carrying out your role and what moral, political or theoretical drivers might influence the education system that you work in and/or your work as a mentor
- Having a broad understanding of different models, or approaches to, mentoring in order to make decisions about how to carry out your role as a mentor.

Further resources

Cordingley, P., Higgins, S., Greany, T., Buckler, N., Coles-Jordan, D., Crisp, B., Saunders, L. and Coe, R. (2015) *Developing great teaching: Lessons from the international reviews into effective professional development*. London: Teacher Development Trust.
This book should help you to gain an understanding of how mentoring fits into current ideas of effective continued professional development and learning.

Maynard, T. and Furlong, J. (1995) 'Learning to teach and models of mentoring', in T. Kerry and A. Shelton-Mayes (eds) *Issues in mentoring*. London: Routledge, pp. 10-14.
This chapter should help to deepen your knowledge of the three categories of mentoring, the apprentice model, the competence model and the reflective models.

Newton, D.P. (2008) *A practical guide to teaching science in the secondary school*. Abingdon, Oxon and New York: Routledge.
This practical guide is designed to help beginning science teachers to learn how to teach science in secondary schools, with an emphasis on practical skills and subject knowledge.

Pedersen, J., Isozaki, T. and Hirano, T. (eds) (2017) *Model science teacher preparation programs: An international comparison of what works*. Charlotte, North Carolina: Information Age Publishing.
This book will help you to view, gain knowledge and adapt successful models, implemented in different countries, to incorporate effective science teacher preparation programmes.

2 About you as a mentor

Nicklas Lindstrom

Introduction

Taking time to reflect on who you are as a professional is not something at the forefront of a teacher's considerations in the day-to-day cut and thrust of a secondary school. These are, dynamic and emotional places to work. They can feel chaotic, busy and vibrant so often there is little time for self-reflection. However, knowing something about yourself and your motivations can lead to understanding why you react and behave as you do in your work. The beliefs and values you hold shape your conduct and the interactions and relationships you have, as a teacher and as a mentor.

You have probably been mentored, certainly at the beginning of your careers, and maybe you have engaged with mentoring during professional development throughout your career. The manner in which you were mentored influences what you think of as good mentoring and how effective or otherwise the process of professional mentoring is in the development of your own teaching (Chu, 2019) and in the development of beginning teachers. This chapter asks you to become more conscious of who you are as a teacher and a mentor. It asks you to make more explicit why you come to the decisions you do and to what extent you want to share these.

Objectives

At the end of this chapter, you should be able to:

- Analyse your motivations and readiness to mentor beginning teachers
- Identify what good mentoring means to you
- Have a sense of self and how it impacts on your mentoring role
- Understand mentoring styles and their relationship to your beliefs and values
- Reflect on what your beliefs and values say good mentoring and teaching is
- Understand teacher beliefs and values and their impact on you as a mentor.

2.1 Analysing your motivations and readiness to mentor

Developing your mentoring skills is a key component of continuing professional development for many teachers. It is important to understand your context and address the 'how' and 'why' you arrive at the stage where mentoring beginning teachers is where you want to be. Although the role of a mentor may well sound like a daunting prospect, you should be aware

About you as a mentor 23

there is support for you from your school or from an initial teacher education (ITE) provider with whom you are working. However, it is important to understand your motivation and readiness to be a mentor. Task 2.1 asks you to consider Figure 2.1, which presents a matrix to examine your motivation and readiness to be a mentor. This task is designed to help you to understand your motivation, fears and enthusiasm for the mentoring journey, as well as to understand where the emotions you are feeling come from.

Task 2.1 The motivation-readiness matrix

Consider where you are on the motivation-readiness matrix in Figure 2.1. You should not view this analysis as pertaining to a better or worse place to be, but as a starting point to reflect on your role as a mentor of a beginning teacher. There are four quadrants, namely;

Instructed - motivated:
You have not put yourself forward to mentor, but have been assigned it. However, you are engaged in and are enthusiastic about the role.

Self-nominated - motivated:
As with instructed - motivated, but you have put yourself forward to mentor.

Instructed - demotivated:
You have been instructed by someone to carry out the role, but you have very little or no interest in being a mentor.

Self-nominated - demotivated:
You have volunteered, perhaps out of a sense of duty or motivated by professional development to carry out such a role, but you are not personally invested in it.
When identifying where you are on the matrix:

1. Be honest with yourself and mark where you think you are
2. Ask yourself why you have placed yourself in that area
3. What impact do you think this could have on your role as a mentor?

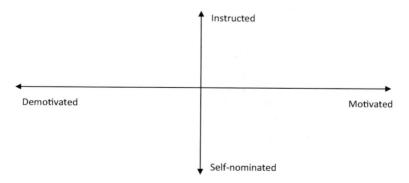

Figure 2.1 Motivation-readiness matrix for mentoring
(Source: Adapted from Henderson (1970))

24 *Lindstrom*

Understanding your starting point will give you some perspective on the challenges facing you and your motivation to overcome these as they arise. If you are completing Task 2.1 before you decide to take up the role, then it may well inform your decision to continue or decline offers or opportunities to begin your mentoring journey. Regardless of your starting point, it is important to become well informed about what mentoring is and how it works before becoming a mentor.

2.2 What does good mentoring mean to you?

Mentoring in schools has been defined as a procedural formal activity, controlled by an external organisation, such as a university or work place (Lofthouse, Leat and Towler, 2010). This definition implies you need to make accurate judgements to share with the beginning teacher. You act as a supportive and nurturing colleague, encouraging a beginning teacher to develop and flourish. However, you also need to make judgements about progress against teacher standards towards which a beginning teacher is working (in England, Department for Education (DfE), 2011), and you may feel varying degrees of conflict in these aspects of the role. Also, be aware that judgements can lead to reluctance or hesitance from a beginning teacher to share all of their experiences with you. So, the role of a mentor is a balancing act between the trusted mentor and an assessor (Yusko and Feiman-Nemser, 2008).

To achieve an appropriate balance, it is important to be able to identify what good mentoring is. Knowing what good mentoring means to you allows you to focus on the beliefs and values you have. You can then evaluate how your beliefs and values align with ideas about 'good mentoring' from other people you work with, such as the beginning teacher and other colleagues. Task 2.2 asks you to consider what good mentoring is.

Task 2.2   What is good mentoring?

- Write down what your immediate response is to the question. What is good mentoring?
- If you can, compare your response to those of another mentor/teacher.
- Do you feel your beliefs about what good mentoring is are aligned with those of other colleagues you work with? Can you foresee any sources of tension or support?
- What are the similarities or are there any differences between your views and other institutions such as an ITE provider?
- This could well inform who you choose to work alongside you and the beginning teacher you mentor.

2.3 Your sense of self and how it impacts on your mentoring role

Your beliefs and values determine who you are as a teacher and, by extension, as a mentor (Chu, 2019). The process of working closely with a beginning teacher can affect how you perceive yourself and can change how you see good teaching and good mentoring (Beauchamp and Thomas, 2009). Before reading any further, Task 2.3 asks you to consider your own personality.

Task 2.3   Identifying yourself

Undertake an internet search for personality questionnaires and complete one. For example, 16 Personalities (see further resources), provides detailed feedback and allows exploration of your impact on those around you. You need to answer the questions as honestly as you can.

Next consider the following questions:

1.   How accurately does it reflect your beliefs and values?
2.   How do you reflect on your own motivations for taking the decisions you do?
3.   Do you recognise the way you deal with others as an accurate description of you as a mentor and a teacher?

Your responses to the questionnaire are a starting point. Your responses will change over time as your identity is re-shaped by your interaction with others (Gee, 2000). Overtime, the relationship you have with a beginning teacher will undoubtedly contribute to and re-shape your own sense of self as a teacher–mentor and as an individual (Hobson, Ashby, Malderez and Tomlinson, 2009).

It is argued that mentoring and being mentored can have a positive impact on your own professional development. These influences come from a number of contexts, such as participating in mentoring training sessions offered by an ITE provider, other developmental courses and, importantly, your ability to self-reflect on your own mentoring practice. This is because reflection is a vital component of your development. Mentor training provides you with opportunities to share experiences and best practice with fellow mentors and the opportunity to learn from researchers in the field. However, there are always a number of different contexts (these are explored further in the section below on Teacher beliefs and values and its impact on you as a mentor), that govern decisions you make and this is also true of a beginning teacher in your charge. This is because beginning teachers' own perspectives are likely to change rapidly as they progress from being a student teacher to becoming a professional. Sachs goes someway to explain what teacher identity is. He suggested it is that sense of 'how to be' and 'how to act' (Sachs, 2005). This is also true for mentor identity.

2.4 Mentoring beliefs and values and their impact on the styles of mentoring

Your style of mentoring will be governed by the many motivations and sense of self already alluded to in the previous two sections. It should be said that the reason why such an emphasis has been placed upon your own understanding of who you are is because your role is pivotal in the development of a beginning teacher. Essentially, the beliefs and values you hold as a teacher and as a mentor determine very much the actions you take (Korthagen, 2004). This is illustrated through your reflections on the two Case studies below. Now read these two Case studies (2.1 and 2.2) and answer the questions in Task 2.4 and 2.5.

Case study 2.1: Harry

Harry is a beginning teacher in his ITE year. He is placed in a school with a good reputation and he likes the department, the school and the people in his department. However, he is growing increasingly concerned about the feedback he is receiving from his mentor. Feedback is framed most often as 'I wouldn't do it like that' and also 'I would do it like this, because I know it works'. Harry feels as if he is being asked to conform to a particular style of teaching that his mentor values, but one that he is less convinced by. Harry would prefer teaching to be more pupil focussed and less teacher directed. Harry shares this with his university tutor who asks Harry if he would like her to intervene on his behalf. Harry does not want the tutor to do this as he feels this may cause friction, which he is keen to avoid. It is this which has stopped him from raising his concerns directly with his mentor so far. After considerable reflection and conversations with his university tutor, Harry chooses to comply with the instructions coming from his mentor as he does not want to alienate his mentor or other staff in the department.

Task 2.4   Reflections on Case study 2.1: Harry

Answer the following questions:

1. How do you perceive this situation?
2. What would you advise the mentor and Harry to do?
3. How would you respond if you were in this position as a mentor?
4. Are your values and beliefs so important that you would want to pass these onto a beginning teacher you mentor?

About you as a mentor 27

> ## Case study 2.2: Razina
>
> Razina was placed in a science department of over 12 full-time staff and a further four part-time staff in a large secondary school. It was a lively department full of teachers with differing experience. Her mentor was not one of the most experienced staff but had taught for a few years. Razina liked the messages she was getting from her university course, which championed an approach to assessment for learning based around a dialogue between the teacher and the pupils. There appeared to be no specific policy in the department about the way written feedback was given, only that there was an expectation that it occurred every two weeks. Razina initially thought this was a straightforward instruction for her. Razina was diligently responding to her pupils work in the manner she had interpreted; the 'two weeks' making her feedback relevant to the activities. Her mentor kept asking Razina to stick to written comments in a particular format, one on spelling, one on presentation and one for progress. Her mentor was insistent that this was how it was supposed to be done. Razina was becoming anxious as she was unsure about the 'best' way to provide written feedback, given the number of different perspectives she had been given and the structure reiterated by her mentor.

Task 2.5   Reflections on Case study 2.2: Razina

Answer the following questions:

1.   What do you think is happening in this Case?
2.   What extent do you think the mentor's actions are justified?
3.   What advice would you give Razina and how would you see this issue being resolved?

In your mentoring, the aim is to avoid what Bullough (2008, p. 70) described as 'becoming little more than a weak exercise in vocational socialisation', or supporting beginning teachers in becoming part of a group of others doing the same thing. What is commonly happening is that mentors in situations such as that experienced by Razina are re-enacting the status quo of the department as it already exists and asking beginning teachers to follow these norms (Jian Wang, Odell and Schwille, 2008). It would be useful to reflect on the extent to which you may do this when mentoring and what, if any, impact this may have on your relationship with a beginning teacher.

2.5 Mentoring styles and your beliefs and values

The previous sections should have given you some insight into the type of mentor you wish to be. This section explores some different models of mentoring. As you read through these, think about which you recognise in yourself and which you aspire to be like.

Trevethan (2017) described a number of mentoring models, namely:

- The traditional model
- The reflective practitioner model
- The learning partnership model.

The traditional model (Bullough and Draper, 2004) is categorised as a supervisory one. It can be viewed as a triad between a beginning teacher, the school mentor and a third party, often a university tutor, but can be from school-based training provider, in, for example, School-Centred Initial Teacher Training (SCITT) or Teach First. This is shown in Figure 2.2.

In this traditional model the beginning teacher acts in a subordinate role accepting instruction from the school mentor, whereby the school mentor models teaching. The ITE provider exists to moderate the interactions taking place and is slightly removed from the process.

The reflective practitioner model (Ethel and McMeniman, 2000) is one that you may be more familiar with and recognise as typical mentoring. In this model, a mentor is meant to be a reflective practitioner in order to effectively support and nurture the beginning teacher to develop and become resilient and reflective themselves. This allows the beginning teacher to prepare for uncertainties, adopt and acquire attributes and abilities needed to deal with the complexity of teaching. However, French and Raven (1960) noted that the mentor in this model still acts as an expert and has a powerful influence over the beginning teacher as they do in the traditional model.

The learning partnership model is a more realised version of the reflective practitioner model in that it espouses the mentor's own development by developing a learning community (Le Cornu, 2010; McIntyre, Hagger and Hagger, 1993). Here, the mentor acts as a trusted colleague to the beginning teacher and the classroom is viewed as a place of inquiry. This allows both participants in the relationship to learn how to develop their teaching practices (Langdon, 2014). McDonald and Flint (2011) aptly noted that the mentor in this model would use a constructivist approach (Piaget, 1952), thus establishing prior knowledge and using explorative questioning to support both their own and the beginning teacher's development. These styles therefore describe not only the process of mentoring but also the outcome of

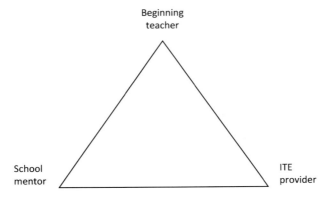

Figure 2.2 The traditional model of mentoring

such styles used by a mentor. Task 2.6 is designed to help you identify your preferred style of mentoring. By now you should have a sense of how your beliefs and values and thus your style of mentorship impact and inform you behaviour.

Task 2.6 Which is your preferred style of mentoring?

Reflect on the three styles of mentoring (traditional, reflective and the learning partnership model) by answering the following questions:

1. What are the pros and cons of each style? Perhaps use a table to organise your thoughts.
2. How do your beliefs and values fit with the description of the models?
3. Do you see yourself as fitting into one of these styles or do you think they are useful at different stages of mentoring?

2.6 Teacher beliefs and values and its impact on you as a mentor

Your beliefs and values give voice to the person you are, but specifically those aspects of your character that guide your decisions as a teacher and as a mentor. Your mentoring role is bound up in who you are as a teacher. The next two sections explore some significant influences on these.

2.6.1 Cultural beliefs

There are influences that are so pervasive that they colour not only your decisions as a teacher but also as a person. For example, religious beliefs and aspects of culture rooted in your socio-economic background. It is said that teachers' beliefs are the most important psychological construct in teachers' education and it is these beliefs that are the best indicator for pedagogic decisions. Therefore, beliefs influence a teacher's perception and consequently their behaviour in the classroom (Pajares, 1992). You will need to make a conscious choice about the degree to which you feel these beliefs are part of your own philosophy of teaching and awareness of these will help you to reflect on the decisions you make as a mentor. Self-awareness of your beliefs and values allows choices to be made about what impact these beliefs have on your mentoring role. For example, beliefs about the efficacy of practical work or the use of games in learning science could shape advice you give to a beginning teacher.

2.6.2 Other external forces

Mediating factors exist that generate barriers to any personal belief system. They prevent an individual enacting their beliefs. Structural and relational aspects of a school, such as work overload, working conditions, pupil behaviour and lack of resources may all mitigate against

30 *Lindstrom*

this enactment. You need to negotiate these, considering which impact the way you want to carry out your mentoring role. You may, for example, need to speak to colleagues to support you to obtain a suitable space for mentoring discussions, time for reflection and space to make contacts with the beginning teacher effective. Some of these may be out of your control and it is useful to acknowledge this.

However, there are influences over which you do have autonomy. Most science teachers are concerned about what kind of science teacher they should be (Wolf-Watz, 2000). For example, the amount of practical work and the degree to which they try to link scientific knowledge to the everyday experiences of their pupils. Another factor highlighted in the work of Wolf-Watz (2000) was the prevailing conception on the nature of boys' and girls' learning, and whether boys prefer technology more than girls. Knowing how you respond to these and other considerations will allow you to reflect on the degree to which you shape and mediate between your own beliefs on teaching and those which you relay to a beginning teacher as best practice. Decisions need to be made about the extent to which your own beliefs and values are communicated both consciously and subconsciously in the advice shared with a beginning teacher and the decision you make in your mentoring role.

Task 2.7   Your beliefs: Teaching and mentoring

1. What do you consider to be the keystones to your philosophy of teaching and teaching science? For example, the value you place on practical work, group work and discussion. You may wish to consider teaching and teaching science separately or think about them holistically. Write a list of these.
2. Once you have listed these, ask yourself how much of this you would want to impart into your mentoring and if this would be a conscious effort to direct the teaching style of a beginning teacher or if you would explain your motivations for holding these beliefs and allow the beginning teacher to explore these alongside their own beliefs.
3. What are the structural barriers you may encounter in your role as a mentor?
4. How will you deal with those times of the year when your capacity to act as the mentor and teacher you want to be, are challenges by tiredness and stress?

Summary and key points

This chapter has highlighted that knowing a little more about yourself allows you to:

*   Analyse your motivations and readiness to mentor beginning teachers
*   Identify what good mentoring means to you
*   Have a sense of self and how it impacts on your mentoring role
*   Understand mentoring styles and their relationship to your beliefs and values
*   Reflect on what your beliefs and values say good mentoring and teaching is
*   Understand teacher beliefs and values and their impact on you as a mentor.

About you as a mentor 31

This will enable you to choose how much of your own teaching values and beliefs you impart to a beginning teacher and also how these can influence ongoing decisions you make.

Becoming more self-aware means you can reflect on and more consciously formulate the kind of mentor you want to become and how this can best benefit a beginning teacher under your care and guidance. Ultimately, though, the mentoring journey will also enable you to better build upon your own ideas about teaching and what good teaching and mentoring is.

Further resources

DfE (Department for Education) (2016b) *National Standards for School-based Initial Teacher Training (ITT) Mentors*, London: DfE, viewed 20 January 2020 from: https://assets.publishing. service.gov.uk/government/uploads/system/uploads/attachment_data/file/536891/Mentor_ standards_report_Final.pdf
These are the DfE standards for mentors of beginning teachers in England. They make for interesting reading and you may well want to reflect to what extent they support your own values and beliefs about mentoring.

NERIS Analytics Limited (2020) *16 Personalities: Personality Test*, viewed 2 January 2020 from: www.16personalities.com
Not only will this resource give you guidance about your own personality traits, but it will also allow you to explore those of others, enabling you to better understand the kind of person you are mentoring and those with whom you need to form relationships, such as your line manager and your subject lead.

3 Beginning science teachers' expectations of their mentors

Stephen P. Day

Introduction

In initial teacher education (ITE) programmes in the UK and many other countries, the mentor is expected to perform a dual role: a supporter, as a beginning teacher develops their classroom practices, and an assessor against the relevant teacher standards (for example, in England the Teachers Standards (Department for Education (DfE), 2011), Professional Competencies (General Teaching Council for Northern Ireland (GTCNI) 2018a), the General Teaching Council for Scotland's Standards for Registration (GTCS, 2012), and the Professional Standards for Teaching and Leadership (Welsh Government, 2018)). Therefore, to act as an effective supporter and assessor, as a mentor you need to consider a beginning teacher's expectations, of you in supporting their development as an effective teacher.

This chapter aims to allow you to reflect upon your mentoring practices. It asks you to consider what a beginning teacher might reasonably expect from you as a mentor, the characteristics and some actions of effective/ineffective mentors. Next, the chapter introduces Hudson's constructivist approaches to effective mentoring. That is followed by some effective mentoring actions to support beginning teacher expectations of you, such as: enabling a beginning teacher to self-reflect and discuss their expectations of themselves and expectations of you, conducting an induction programme, suggesting ways to balance working (teaching) life with other commitments and supporting the beginning teacher to meet teacher standards. Finally, attention is drawn to the fact that you might not always be able to fulfil a beginning teacher's expectations of you.

Objectives

At the end of this chapter, you should be able to:

- Reflect on key characteristics of mentoring from a beginning teacher's perspective
- Consider some effective and ineffective actions of a mentor

Beginning science teachers' expectations   33

- Understand constructivist approaches to establish effective mentoring
- Support a beginning teacher's expectations by getting to know their expectations of you and undertake mentoring actions to aid their expectations, such as supporting them in adjusting to the school environment, planning, teaching and observing others or being observed, suggestions on balancing home and working life, and supporting them to meet the teacher standards
- Discuss some unreasonable expectations by a beginning teacher of a mentor.

3.1 Self-reflection on the characteristics of effective mentoring from a beginning teacher's perspective

Before you start reading about some of the expectations a beginning science teacher may have and how you can support their expectations, Task 3.1 encourages you to reflect on your perspectives on what the main characteristics of an effective mentor of a beginning teacher are.

Task 3.1   Reflecting on your perspectives on the main characteristics of mentoring a beginning teacher

Reflect on the following questions:

1. Write a list of what to you are the main characteristics of a good mentor of a beginning teacher.
2. Do you possess some, most, all of these characteristics?
3. Recall some positive and negative feedback (if any) on your mentoring by beginning teachers, from your previous mentoring experiences. What lessons did you learn from them?
4. Based on the answers to questions 1–3, list some key characteristics that you think a beginning teacher should be expecting of a mentor.
5. Next, compare your effective mentoring list with the information contained in Table 3.1, by answering the following questions:
    -   What list of characteristics of an effective mentor did you come up with that resemble the characteristics of an effective mentor identified in Table 3.1? How will you strengthen some of your perceived mentoring characteristics in future?
    -   Which characteristics from Table 3.1 did you not have on your effective mentoring list? Do you wish to develop these characteristics in your mentoring? If yes then how, and if not then why not?
    -   Are there any barriers in developing some of the characteristics of an effective mentor? What can you do to overcome such barriers?

---

34 S. P. Day

Table 3.1 Some characteristics of an effective and ineffective mentor

Characteristics of an effective mentor	Characteristics of an ineffective mentor
Availability	Distant and unfriendly
Consistency	Unapproachable
Honesty	Unreliable
Professionalism	Intimidating
Assertiveness	Unpredictable
Effective communicator	Overprotective
Resourcefulness	Incapable
Reliable	Unreliable

(Source: Adapted from the work of Anderson (2011))

3.2 Mentoring actions from a beginning teacher's perspective

Mentoring a beginning science teacher necessarily requires the mentor to adopt a twin tracked approach to the way they co-construct a beginning teacher's professional identity, since they are to be a teacher first and a science specialist second. More generally, a beginning teacher's concerns about planning include the science curriculum, especially their engagement with areas of general science with which they may not be familiar, given their own academic subject preparation and field experiences (Ingersoll, 2003; Chapter 10), as well as having to cope with how best to teach practical techniques along with health and safety issues required in science teaching (Chapter 14, pp. 220-224), et cetera. Therefore, a beginning teacher will expect a mentor to guide them to understand and overcome planning and teaching challenges, which places an onus on the mentor to help the beginning teacher navigate these challenges. In order to effectively plan and enact science pedagogy, a beginning teacher will also expect their mentor to support them in making a variety of decisions with regards to what content to teach, how best to teach it (see Chapter 7), as well as what and how to assess the learning (see Chapter 12) that emerges from that teaching. In supporting them to plan and teach science autonomously, you will want to act as a facilitator rather than a dictator.

The expectations a beginning teacher has of their mentor to support them with planning and teaching challenges might vary in terms of the balance between direction, challenge and support, in part because of the beginning teacher's prior science-based learning and scientific experiences with previous and current mentors, confidence in using their subject knowledge in developing their pedagogical content knowledge (PCK), and life circumstances, et cetera. Therefore, the first few weekly mentoring meetings should be designed to help a beginning teacher to agree on what level, type and manner of support they require from their mentor (see Task 3.4 below, Section C for an example of how this might be operationalised).

A beginning teacher's expectations of effective mentorship may also be linked to their values, attitudes and beliefs towards the mentoring process itself, in much the same way that your own values, attitudes and beliefs influence the way you mentor. It is fair to say that one of the most difficult aspects of mentoring a beginning teacher effectively lies in the fact that there is often a difference between your expectations and the beginning teacher's expectations. For example, a beginning teacher might have no prior observing and/or teaching experiences, or

Beginning science teachers' expectations 35

have previously volunteered as a support worker in your (or another) school for some time and/or have been a full- or part-time staff member in a school (such as a laboratory technician or teacher assistant or as administration staff). Whether or not a beginning teacher has prior experience of teaching and/or working in a school, it is important that each beginning teacher receives individual support and guidance by a mentor as part of their professional development. Therefore, you need to establish with a beginning teacher how they feel about their teaching role, what their perceptions are of a science teacher, what they expect from you, and how they wish to engage with you as one of their main professional supporters.

Research from across several professional settings suggests some converging themes as to what some key actions of an effective mentor are. Table 3.2 lists some key actions of an effective and ineffective mentor. In addition, Task 3.2 asks you to map your mentoring actions against Table 3.2 and revisit Task 3.1 to establish further grounds on becoming an effective mentor, based on a beginning teacher's expectations.

Table 3.2 Some key actions of an effective and ineffective mentor

Some actions of an effective mentor	*Some actions of an ineffective mentor*
Displays an interest in a beginning teacher's learning	Displays a lack of interest in a beginning teacher's learning
Treats a beginning teacher as an individual	Generalises their beginning teacher's needs
Recognises a beginning teacher's stage of learning	Delegates unwanted duties to a beginning teacher
Establishes a learning environment	Noticeably dislikes their mentoring role
Understands a beginning teacher's learning needs and requirement of the ITE	Lacks knowledge of the ITE programme that the beginning teacher is following
Identifies learning goals with the beginning teacher	Discourages the beginning teacher from practising innovative teaching in the classrooms
Includes the beginning teacher as part of the department team	Does not allow the beginning teacher to take part in departmental discussions
Explains what is being done and why	Breaks promises
Demonstrates pedagogy and skills to be modelled	Throws the beginning teacher in at the deep end
Balances practice with educational theory and applies evidence-based practice	Does not see educational theory as important
Assists the beginning teacher to evaluate and reflect upon their learning experience	Lacks experience themselves as a teacher

(Source: Adapted from the work of Anderson (2011))

Task 3.2   Mentoring actions of an effective mentor

Follow the below steps:

Step 1. By using Table 3.2 as a checklist to consider your effectiveness as a mentor, reflect on your actions. Add other mentoring actions, if needed.
Step 2. Revisit Task 3.1 and accompanied Table 3.1 and map some effective mentoring actions with effective characteristics of a mentor.

3.3 Constructivist approaches to establish effective mentoring

It is fair to suggest that most ITE programmes subscribe to constructivist approaches to teacher education. It is therefore reasonable for a beginning teacher to expect their mentors to adopt an approach to mentoring that aligns to this perspective. The mentoring role within these factors frames the beginning teacher's teaching experience from a constructivist perspective where the mentor scaffolds, facilitates and supports the beginning teacher towards a level of proficiency in science teaching. Hudson's (2004) research in the Australian context confirmed that constructivist mentoring in teacher education can be characterised by a model defined by five factors, where constructivist theory complements effective mentoring within a school placement, as it can be used to build upon prior understandings towards developing a beginning science teacher's knowledge and skills for teaching. Hudson's (2005) effective mentoring factors include:

1. Personal attributes that the mentor needs to exhibit for constructive dialogue.
2. System requirements that focus on curriculum directives and policies.
3. Pedagogical knowledge for articulating effective teaching practices.
4. Modelling, i.e. demonstrating efficient and effective practices.
5. Feedback for the purposes of reflection for improving teaching practices.

Task 3.3 asks you to evaluate Case study 3.1 against Hudson's (five) effective mentoring factors.

Task 3.3   Mapping Hudson's factors for effective mentoring

Read Case study 3.1 and answer the following questions:

1. Which of Hudson's five factors did Amy find most effective? and why?
2. How do you incorporate Hudson's factors in your mentoring?
3. What will you do to strengthen the incorporation of these factors in your mentoring practices further?

Case study 3.1: Amy's reflections on her experience of school-based mentoring

The key characteristic which I have found most important in all of my mentors is approachability. Having loads of questions and feeling like a bit of a burden with teachers, who you understand have a big workload, can sometimes leave you feeling unwilling to ask questions which might seem 'silly'. Being reassured that you can approach your mentor at any time with any question, big or small, really made a difference during my time on [school] placement and during the beginning of my probation.

The mentors I had on placement were experienced and were familiar with work I was required to carry out for my [ITE] course, and were supportive in helping organise activities such as shadowing, observations, looking through lesson plans and

Beginning science teachers' expectations 37

> reflections and genuinely took an interest in giving me constructive feedback to further my practice. They were also familiar with the teacher standards and helped keep my teaching relevant to the key areas I would finally be assessed on. This expertise and understanding of my workload as a student teacher are also a key indicator of a good mentor, from my experience.

Reflecting on your self-perception of mentoring from a beginning teacher's perspective allows you to sketch a picture of an effective mentor to support the development of a beginning teacher you are working with. Tasks 3.1, 3.2 and 3.3 have possibly allowed you to picture an effective mentor. The next section of this chapter presents some suggestions for you to strengthen your efforts in becoming an effective mentor to support a beginning science teacher's development.

3.4 Supporting a beginning teacher's expectations

Any one beginning teacher differs from other teachers (beginning or experienced) in a number of ways, including their level of resourcefulness, creativity and confidence, as well as their expectations of you. Hence, as mentioned above, getting to know a beginning teacher's expectations is vital for you to undertake mentoring actions which align their expectations. You begin to know a beginning teacher by first gathering information about their prior teaching and learning experience, to design some questions for later conversations about their expectations of you (some example questions are provided in Section B of Task 3.4). But before asking these questions, allow the beginning teacher to reflect on their expectations of becoming an effective teacher because you might find that some beginning teachers will not be able to clearly communicate what they expect of you as their mentor. The cause of this lack of clarity in communication could be that the beginning teacher has not explicitly self-reflected on their personal teaching and learning developmental needs, and so their understanding of your expectations of them and their expectations of you might not be clear. Task 3.4 asks you to encourage a beginning teacher you are mentoring to reflect on their developmental strengths and needs, and communicate their expectations of you using a Personal Record of Performance (PRoP) form.

Task 3.4   Supporting a beginning teacher to recognise their personal teaching and learning developmental needs and communicate their expectations with you as a mentor using a PRoP form

Complete the three sections of the PRoP form (see Appendix 3.1) by following the steps below:

Section A: Before a mentoring meeting, ask the beginning teacher to complete Section A of the PRoP form independently. Encourage them to record their reflections of their practices and note down three or four areas of perceived 'strength' and three or four 'areas to be developed' over the next week or so. Moreover, based on their self-identified strengths and areas to be development, encourage them to signpost the kind of 'support' they are expecting from you to strengthen their identified strengths and work on the areas for development.

Section B: Next, along with the beginning teacher, complete Section B by discussing Section A of the PRoP form. In this section you and the beginning teacher record specific discussions that chart their prior teaching and learning experiences, and discuss how you can support them. Through this discussion you will elicit a lot of basic and specific support the beginning teacher requires from you. It may be useful to discuss how these experiences have influenced their development so far. You could ask the following questions:

- How have the beginning teacher's prior teaching and learning experiences influenced their development to become an effective teacher?
- What aspects of teaching science makes them feel anxious, more confident?
- What level of guidance do they value to become a confident teacher?
- What teaching and learning support would they expect to engage with?
- What do they expect from a mentor to strengthen their teaching practices in becoming an effective teacher?

Section C: This section on areas of concern is to be completed by you in agreement with the beginning teacher on the level, type and manner of support you can offer to them. For example, the beginning teacher needs to know if there are any aspects of their teaching and learning practices that require immediate action. In accomplishing such actions, you should discuss what support the beginning teacher can expect from you, and what aspects they need to work out on their own. It should be noted that this section may be left blank but that 'areas of concern' may be a natural part of a beginning teacher's development and may just be a persistent issue that is taking time to resolve. Finally, sign the form and date it.

Using the PRoP form in subsequent mentoring meetings, ideally every week, will be useful for the beginning teacher as it will establish a routine that they can follow. Continued use of the PRoP form could help them to manage their expectations of themselves and to clearly communicate their expectations of you. It can evidence mentor–mentee discussions in a systematic way. These discussions will help you assess their ability to reflect on their progress since the last meeting and to evaluate how they are progressing towards meeting agreed targets that have previously been set for upcoming meetings. Such discussions will also help them to focus on their growing subject knowledge, pedagogical abilities, teaching and learning skills and/or other skills and abilities. Four possible aspects

Beginning science teachers' expectations 39

of support, discussed below, that the beginning teacher will be expecting from a mentor, which you can offer to them, are:

- Support to understand the school environment
- Suggestions on balancing teaching life with other commitments
- Facilitate a beginning teacher's teaching of science
- Support to meet teacher standards.

3.4.1 Support to understand the school environment

Beginning teachers expect mentors to help them understand a number of aspects relating to the general school environment in a practical, quick and easy manner, so that they can adjust to the new environment and begin functioning as quickly as possible. Therefore, an induction programme is a vital part of a beginning teacher's orientation into the workings of the school, regardless of their prior experience. In addition, it can give you an opportunity to plan some focused mentoring actions for the beginning teacher you are mentoring, to support their expectations of you in relation to them settling into the school effectively. Your school can subtly vary from other schools in terms of culture, ethos and physical environment – thus the aim of an induction programme is to develop a beginning teacher's ability to function effectively within your school. In other words, it aims to help them 'fit in' to the school by making them aware of information, resources, policies and procedures used to govern the work of the school.

It is reasonable to suggest that any new member of the staff (beginning or experienced teacher) ought to receive some practical information to help them function within the new environment soon after their arrival at the school. Table 3.3 can be used as a checklist to induct a beginning teacher to the school. Many schools have a tailored induction programme

Table 3.3 An induction programme checklist for a beginning teacher

Checklist items	Mentor's actions	Date	Beginning teacher's queries and additional requirements	Mentor's additional support
School and senior leadership team	Welcome a beginning teacher to the school. Provide verbal introductions to the school's culture, ethos, key principles, and names and roles of the senior leadership team			
School handbook	Give a copy of the school's handbook, including details about the school, such as information about: • contact details • ethos • the school day • school staff • the curriculum • assessment • school policies.			

(continued)

40   S. P. Day

Table 3.3 (Cont.)

Checklist items	Mentor's actions	Date	Beginning teacher's queries and additional requirements	Mentor's additional support
A beginning teacher's activities within the whole school	Provide an overview of some of the whole school expectations/ requirements to be undertaken by a beginning teacher, such as:			
	The schools safeguarding protocol			
	Professional expectations			
	School Health and Safety procedures			
	Overview of the school's behaviour policies			
	Inclusion policies and procedures			
	Tracking and monitoring policies			
	Pupil support arrangements.			
A beginning teacher's activities within the science department	Provide an overview of the expected activities from a beginning teacher that are practised in the Science Department:			
	Observing experienced science teachers			
	Observing experienced teachers from other practical subjects like design and technology, home economics or physical education			
	Discussions with science technicians			
	Practice of experiments and other practical activities			
	An overview of departmental assessment practices (summative and formative)			
	Tracking and monitoring pupils progress			
	Shadowing pupils (see Chapter 19, Tasks 19.5 and 19.6).			

for beginning teachers, which should provide an elementary understanding of the mechanics of how the school works to support their professional development. Therefore you can adopt/adapt the first two columns of Table 3.2 according to your school's procedures on inducting a beginning teacher, and then use this table to record: date (column three) of when you have conducted (or will be conducting) the actions in the second column, the beginning teacher's queries and expected further support (column four), and your suggestions and agreed support in response to the beginning teacher's expectations (column five).

Once the beginning teacher has been introduced to key people within the school and department, they then need to become acquainted with the expectations of the school and department. Therefore, while completing the last two columns of Table 3.3 with the beginning teacher, it is important that your discussions involve framing of the school context within which they are expected to make progress in their teaching and learning practices.

You need to be mindful that many beginning teachers display some level of anxiety during the first few weekly mentoring meetings and so you might not be able to gather all the required information about their initial expectations in these meetings. Therefore, it is important that you establish a mentor–mentee relationship during the first few meetings, by putting the beginning teacher at their ease, by providing them with emotional support, along with professional guidance. Refer to Chapter 5, for guidance on establishing a mentor–mentee relationship based on emotional support during initial mentoring meetings (Table 5.1). During this initial stage, you should also indicate to the beginning teacher that they will be expected to take increasing responsibility for the learning of their pupils and thereafter become less dependent upon support from you and other members of staff as they gain more experience.

3.4.2 Suggestions on balancing teaching life with other commitments

In addition to differences in their prior experiences and expectations, a beginning teacher might be seeking your support in balancing their professional and personal lives. You need to be mindful that a beginning teacher you mentor might be doing a weekend job to meet financial needs, have childcare responsibilities, et cetera. Therefore, as a mentor it is useful to know early about a beginning teacher's other commitments and responsibilities that they would like to share with you, for example, you could ask:

- What aspects of their commitments other than teaching do they see as helping or hindering their professional development?
- How you can support them?
- Do they use any strategy to keep their professional and personal life in balance (such as creating and adhering to a work schedule, socialising with people outside the work environment, et cetera)?

You should be resourceful in giving a beginning teacher some guidance that can support them to manage their teaching commitments along with other responsibilities. This may include guidance on available funding for teachers and science graduates, student loans, childcare facilities, access to health and well-being organisations, et cetera. You can also share some of the day-to-day strategies that help you balance your teaching life with some other commitments (see above).

3.4.3 Facilitate a beginning teacher's teaching of science

It is noted that a beginning teacher expects you to support them with their lack of prior teaching experiences. This requires you to understand and acknowledge the beginning teacher's expectations of you in relation to, for example, co-planning, co-teaching, observing experienced teachers, being observed by experienced teachers and evaluating their teaching practices.

A variety of strategies to support a beginning teacher to gain science teaching experience through your guidance are presented in other chapters in this book, including: Chapter 6 associated with planning, Chapter 7 on teaching, Chapter 8 on observation, and the use of PRoP in this chapter on evaluating teaching practices. These chapters or sections of the chapters consider some mentoring strategies to cater for differentiated support on an ongoing basis.

At this point, you need to acknowledge a beginning teacher's previous teaching experiences as a student teacher. For example, they may have had a good first school placement but may struggle with the second school placement due to a change of school in terms of setting and organisation. It is therefore important for you to determine how the beginning teacher's learning expectations are influenced by their earlier learning gains/setbacks through planning and teaching experiences, observing other teachers and/or being observed by the experienced teachers.

3.4.4 Support to meet teacher standards

A major expectation of a beginning teacher is for you to support them to meet the requirements of the teacher standards towards which they are working. Table 3.4 presents a beginning teacher's progression profile, which can be adopted and adapted to support them to develop their progression profile by mapping against the professional teacher standards used in your context. This profile acts as a progression profile as it requires the beginning teacher to identify further actions that they will undertake to support areas for development they have identified in the profile. It is ideal if you can encourage a beginning teacher to start building this progression profile before attaining newly qualified teacher (NQT) status, and to continue after they have achieved it. You can guide them to reflect, review, and modify Table 3.4 by extending the third and fourth column and review it, ideally every six months, and at least for the first three years of their teaching career.

Moreover, in supporting a beginning teacher's expectation of attaining qualified teacher status (QTS), you need to be aware of the current guidelines on mentoring used in your country. These guidelines provide a structured approach to mentoring beginning teachers and mentoring models for you to adopt. Such frameworks have evolved and developed over time and have tended to focus on either the apprenticeship, competence or reflective models (see description of these models in Chapter 1). Currently, for example, the 'self-evaluation framework' for initial teacher education in Scotland (Education Scotland, 2018), tends to merge the three models of mentoring given that all ITE is university-based, validated by the GTCS and by definition is standards driven, with a heavy emphasis on the practicum component where mentoring is often shared between a university-based tutor and a school-based mentor.

Beginning science teachers' expectations 43

Table 3.4 A beginning teacher's progression profile

Professional teacher standards progression profile entry, for example:	Some indicators (adopted from General Teaching Council for Scotland GTCS, 2012)	Beginning teacher's evidence	Beginning teacher's expectations of their mentor in achieving teacher standards
Professional values and commitment	Mutual respect and rapport		
	Honesty and integrity		
	Collaboration		
	Rights of all learners		
	Wider school community		
Professional knowledge and understanding	Curriculum knowledge		
	Pedagogical theories into practice		
Professional skills and abilities	Teaching and learning		
	Classroom organisation and management		
	Assessment/ pupils learning.		

The mentoring model you are using in your country/school might not be shared with university-based tutors, hence a beginning teacher will rely more on you, and so you have a greater responsibility to support their expectations to migrate from apprenticeship, guided and participatory planes of development over time. Along these lines, this chapter and other chapters in the book are designed to support you to develop the best possible mentoring practices, even if you have minimal support from the other external bodies, to assist the gradual development of current and upcoming beginning teachers.

3.5 Unreasonable expectations by a beginning teacher of a mentor

The chapter has, so far, presented what a beginning teacher could be expecting from you and how you can support them during the time you are mentoring them. The PRoP form highlights the beginning teacher's expectations of a mentor. While completing the PRoP form, a beginning teacher should be aware that a mentor may not always be able to support what they expect from them, for example, if they expect written feedback on each and every lesson. Therefore, while completing the PRoP form, it is recommended that you discuss with the beginning teacher what you can or cannot do. In addition, Task 3.5 asks you and the beginning teacher to discuss some unreasonable expectations they might have of a mentor.

44 S. P. Day

Task 3.5   Unreasonable expectations of a mentor

- Complete the second column of Table 3.5, which asks you to list what a beginning teacher might expect of you, but which it is not possible for you to act upon it. Some examples are provided in the table.
- Ask the beginning teacher to complete the second column of Table 3.5 separately.
- Next, discuss each other's thoughts and complete the last two columns of the table together by highlighting the responsibilities of the beginning teacher and mentor to accomplish the aspects of expected support below:
  - To understand the school environment
  - To balance teaching life with other commitments
  - Facilitate a beginning teacher's teaching science
  - To meet teacher standards.

With the beginning teacher, add other aspects of support in the table, as appropriate. Moreover, during these discussions highlight that a beginning teacher's expectations and your support will evolve over time.

Consider Task 5.4 Managing expectations and commitments (p. 64) before conducting a discussion with the beginning teacher about some reasonable and unreasonable expectations of a mentor.

Table 3.5 Some aspects of expected support by a mentor associated with some unreasonable expectations

Some aspects of expected support	Some unreasonable expectations from a beginning teacher	A beginning teacher's responsibilities	A mentor's responsibilities
Understand the school environment	Expecting the mentor to go through the school's handbook with the beginning teacher	To read the handbook thoroughly. Could ask the mentor about specific points from the handbook for clarity	To provide school handbook, highlighting aspects of school's ethos, value and culture.
Balance teaching life with other commitments	Expecting the mentor to organise a timetable for them to use to balance teaching life with other commitments	To construct and modify a timetable themselves	Provide some model strategies to balance their teaching life with other commitments.
Facilitate a beginning teacher's teaching practices	Expecting written feedback on each and every lesson	Self-evaluate lessons	Provide some written and some oral feedback.
Meet teacher standards	Expecting mentor to revise and recap the subject knowledge	Revise and recap subject knowledge independently	Point a beginning teacher to some books and other resources, including online resources, to develop their subject knowledge.

Summary and key points

In order to effectively mentor a beginning science teacher, I suggest that it is the responsibility of a mentor to acknowledge the expectations that the beginning teacher may have of them as a mentor. Key points from the chapter are:

- Reflecting, understanding and considering characteristics of an effective mentor from the beginning teachers' perspectives.
- Adopting constructivist approaches to mentoring that acknowledge the beginning teacher's perspectives.
- Facilitating support to the beginning teacher to communicate their expectations of a mentor effectively.
- Plan and undertake mentoring steps to support the beginning teacher's expectations by providing an induction programme and opportunities to discuss, for example, balancing home and work life, offering guided support on planning, teaching, observing, evaluations, and providing support to meet the teacher standards.

Further resources

Luft, J.A. (2009) 'Beginning secondary science teachers in different induction programmes: The first year of teaching', *International Journal of Science Education*, *31* (17), pp. 2355-2384. This article provides a useful insight into how different types of induction programme facilitate the development of beginning secondary science teacher's development over the course of a session. This article shows that teachers who participated in science-specific induction programmes significantly changed their beliefs and used more investigations in their classroom lessons than did their peers in other induction programmes. This indicates that science specific mentoring has a significant positive effect on the beginning science teachers' professional identity and classroom practice.

National Academies of Sciences, Engineering, and Medicine. (2019). *The Science of Effective Mentorship in STEMM*, Washington, DC: The National Academies Press, viewed 20 January 2020, from: https://doi.org/10.17226/25568.
This report outlines findings from a North American consensus study report. The report provides a rich picture of why mentoring is needed, what mentoring is, why professional identities matter, what form mentoring takes, how effective mentorship can be achieved and why assessment and evaluation is required. While this focuses on STEMM in general rather than science education in particular, this report provides the reader with a simple, easy to read starter.

Watson, S.B. (2006) 'Novice science teachers: Expectations and experiences', *Journal of Science Teacher Education*, *17* (3), pp. 279-290.
This text explores a project that aimed to investigate how novice science teachers perceived a lack of preparation to deal with common problems in the classroom could be addressed. It outlines several trends that emerged such as recognising the importance of effective, organized instruction during the term of the study, along with the importance of effective classroom management and discipline skills. The study emphasises that a focus on supporting developing novice science teachers' ability to plan and prepare lessons, and develop adequate knowledge of subject matter is important. Importantly, all novice science teachers in this study felt that they were well prepared by their university classes in their primary content area, but less prepared in supporting areas of science. That said, this article is useful for mentors since it indicates where potential gap may be in novice science teachers developing teaching practice.

46 S. P. Day

Appendix 3.1 Personal Record of Progress (PRoP) form

Personal Record of Progress (PRoP) Please discuss this with your mentor.	**Week:**

Section A

Area(s) of perceived strength:

Expected support from the mentor:

Area(s) to be developed:

Expected support from the mentor:

Spoken and written communication: Satisfactory / Improving / Needs Attention

Section B

Specific discussion
Main area of strength this week (or strengths identified previously):

Main area for development next week (or areas for development before the next meeting):

Section C

Area(s) of concern at this stage   No ☐   Yes ☐

If yes:

• What steps a mentor would undertake to support the beginning teacher?

• What steps a beginning teacher would undertake to support their development?

Beginning science teacher's signature....................................... Date ....

Mentor's signature .... Date ....

4 Accountabilities of a reflective mentor

Jodi Roffey-Barentsen and Richard Malthouse

Introduction

Recent research suggests that both mentors and beginning teachers benefitted most when a reflective model of mentoring was adopted (Tonna, Bjerkholt and Holland, 2017). However, as discussed by Malthouse and Roffey-Barentsen (2014), not all scientists immediately embrace the notion of reflective practice (RP). This may result in a tension when they embark upon an initial teacher education (ITE) programme in which RP is an inherent part. One reason for this may be that science teachers occupy two concurrent and contradictory paradigms. On the one hand, their grounding in the sciences has embedded them firmly within a 'positivist' paradigm that relies upon hard facts and objectivity. However, being a teacher introduces them to what some might view as a conflicting 'interpretative' paradigm, where truth is constructed and is subjective. Therefore, a science teacher could find themselves trapped between the two paradigms and may struggle to come to terms with the need to embrace both (Malthouse and Roffey-Barentsen, 2014). Arguably, beginning teachers gain most from being mentored by subject specialists (McIntyre and Hobson, 2016), therefore both scientists, mentor and beginning teacher, may need to overcome their prejudices and assumptions and learn to engage with what one chemistry teacher referred to as 'waffle and frilly stuff' (Malthouse and Roffey-Barentsen, 2014, p. 163).

This chapter is designed to equip you with a deeper understanding of RP. It discusses some models of RP and offers techniques to enable you to be a reflective mentor and to support a beginning science teacher to reflect on the extent of their progress and to identify the direction of their development. It should also enable you to support a beginning teacher to use RP to realise: any limitations they may be experiencing; their learning needs; the effect they may have on others; and the effect others may have upon them. Thus, the models offered can be applied to meet your needs as a mentor and the needs of a beginning teacher you mentor.

48 *Roffey-Barentsen and Malthouse*

Objectives

At the end of the chapter, you should be able to:

- Identify aspects of reflective mentoring practice
- Consider four elements of reflective practice in your mentoring and also be able to encourage a beginning teacher to consider these elements
- Support change by sharing conversations and documenting reflective accounts
- Employ a number of models of reflective practice to support you in the mentoring process.

4.1 Some important aspects of reflective mentoring

Reflective mentoring requires a trusting, supportive and affirming relationship and the creation of a safe space for honest and critical reflection for both parties (Tonna, Bjerkholt and Holland, 2017). Highlighting the element of being non-judgmental and building trustworthiness in effective mentor-mentee relationships, Hobson (2016, p. 103) argued that 'the key is for mentors to gain mentees [beginning teachers]' trust as soon as possible to facilitate mentees' readiness to take full advantage of mentoring support and participate in a wide range of potentially powerful mentoring activities'. He designed the ONSIDE mentoring framework, which has the promotion of trust at its centre (ibid.). ONSIDE is the mnemonic for mentoring that is 'off-line' or non-hierarchical; 'non-evaluative and non-judgemental'; 'supportive' of mentees' psychosocial needs and well-being; 'individualised' and tailored to the specific and changing needs (emotional as well as developmental) of the mentee; 'developmental' and growth oriented; and 'empowering' (ibid., p. 101). When the aim of mentoring, for the beginning teacher, is critical reflection, then a mentor should be non-judgemental (Tonna, Bjerkholt and Holland, 2017). Hobson (2016) referred to 'judge-mentoring as an inappropriate enactment of mentoring....' (p. 93). Judgementoring can happen, especially where a mentor is involved in the line-management of the beginning teacher, when a mentor is reliant on the strategy of observing and providing mentor-led 'feedback' on the beginning teacher's lessons, which can focus on the negative aspects of the teaching (ibid.).

As mentioned above, every beginning teacher is unique and has different needs, aspirations, temperaments, goals and a multitude of other characteristics; therefore, you need to fashion your practice to accommodate the needs of a beginning teacher on an individual basis. RP enables a mentor and beginning teacher to understand and express themselves in a way that is exclusive to them and to their mentor-mentee relationship. The beginning teacher needs to adopt a reflective model that works for them and off they go in a spiral of reflection and action planning. During this process of a spiral of reflection and action planning, the beginning teacher may get stuck – where a mentor can intervene with their own mentoring approaches and support them to become reflective teachers. Later in the chapter we discuss elements of RP and a few models of RP (Roffey-Barentsen and Malthouse, 2013; Malthouse, Roffey-Barentsen and Watts, 2014, 2015) but before that, Task 4.1 asks you to identify your personal mentoring style. Your answers from Task 1. 6 on mentoring styles will help you to complete Task 4.1.

> **Task 4.1   The mentor you wish to become**
>
> Reflect on your mentoring style by responding to the following questions:
>
> 1.   What are your expectations of being a mentor?
> 2.   How will you deal with a very competent beginning teacher?
> 3.   What coping strategies do you have to support a less confident beginning teacher?
> 4.   Will you be mirroring a significant individual in your own life?
>
> Make notes to assist your thinking.

4.2 Elements of reflective practice (RP)

RP is a process of thinking, whereby a person can make sense of an event, situation, occurrence or phenomenon. It is different to everyday thinking as it involves thinking on a higher plane. RP is a form of metacognition, which brings about an understanding of a person's own thought processes, with an idea that individuals are an expert in relation to themselves. If individuals are honest about themselves and realistic about others within the 'communities of practice' (see also Chapter 17), they can then benefit from the process of engaging in thinking deeply about teaching and learning practices.

From our extensive reading and writing on RP, we acknowledge that there are four elements that can affect the way you and a beginning teacher you mentor, think, reflect upon their own thinking and act accordingly, i.e. ourselves, other people, the environment and time. These are considered below.

4.2.1 Ourselves

This relates to internal activities such as thinking, emoting and doing. Thinking involves cognitive activities associated with problem solving, working out an issue, identifying the component parts of a situation or following instructions. Emoting can include valuing others or embracing safe practices. However, certain emotions can be inappropriate in some circumstances, such as anger. The ability to do something, such as undertaking a new task, can be challenging for some and previous experiences may influence the ability to engage in a task. We recommend that a good starting place when it comes to reflecting, is to start with questioning ourselves from the position of the 'I'.

With a focus of being the mentor of a beginning teacher, you can ask yourself the following reflective questions:

*   What do I want?
*   Why do I want it?
*   How do I get it?
*   What do I not want?
*   How do I avoid it?

50 *Roffey-Barentsen and Malthouse*

In addition to your reflections, you can use similar questions with the beginning teacher, but with the focus of their reflection based on the aspects of teaching and learning practices which they are currently focusing on in becoming a reflective teacher. You can support the beginning teacher in answering these questions and encourage them to keep a track of their changing perceptions of teaching and learning. Keeping a track can help them to map their progression of becoming a reflective teacher.

4.2.2 *Other people*

Other people can have a very significant effect upon us. Working with others can be challenging and may evoke various emotions as we attempt to negotiate with them. It is in dealing with others that most challenges exist. Mentor and beginning teacher need to work together. In addition, the beginning teacher will also have to engage with other colleagues (teaching and non-teaching staff members) in the subject team and the wider school, as well as with pupils and maybe pupils' parents or caregivers. This can involve a number of things such as their interrelatedness or the possible impact they may have upon you as their mentor. RP works on a principle of connectedness. McIntosh (2010) argued that the 'ideas of connectedness suggest that we are always in relation with someone' (p. 37).

You can answer the following reflective questions focusing on the beginning teacher you are currently working with:

- Who are they to you?
- What are they to you?
- What do they want in general?
- What do they want from you specifically?
- What will be likely to occur in the event of this or that happening?

You can also encourage the beginning teacher to answer the above reflective questions focusing on their interactions with you, other colleagues and pupils. They can share some or all of their answers with you for suggestions, comments and discussion.

4.2.3 *The environment*

This includes the more concrete elements in which we function such as offices, teaching rooms, laboratories, meeting rooms, schools, universities or colleges, towns or cities. Sometimes they are fit for purpose and on other occasions they hinder intended actions. This positionality can relate to geographical features or can relate to a position within an organisation.

You could ask yourself questions like:

- Where am I now?
- Where do I want to be?
- Why do I want to be there?
- How will I get there?

Accountabilities of a reflective mentor 51

The answers to these questions will help you to recognise an environment in which you are comfortable (or not) in establishing a mentor-mentee relationship. You can ask the beginning teacher to answer the above questions as well and later offer some time during the weekly mentoring meetings to discuss each other's responses. This discussion can support and challenge you and/or the beginning teacher to work in partnership, sometimes even outside of each other's comfort zones.

4.2.4 Time offers new challenges

A mentor or the beginning teacher may be short of time or may have to wait a long time for something. Situations can change over time; issues can be resolved or environments can change. Some questions related to time can include:

- When do I want it?
- When do I want the change to begin?
- When do I want the situation to stop?
- When do I need the skill?
- What are the advantages/disadvantages to putting it off?
- What are the advantages/disadvantages to doing it now?

The questions above can be answered by you from the perceptive of mentoring a beginning teacher and by a beginning teacher from the perspectives of their teaching and learning approaches, targeting a challenging situation (such as dealing with behaviour management during science practical sessions). Table 4.1 can be used to record a description of a challenging situation in the first row of the table. Then record each other's (mentor and beginning teacher) perspectives in Table 4.1. Next, use the middle column of Table 4.1 to collaboratively come up with an agreed timeline. The use of this template not only helps the mentor and the beginning teacher to view what needs to be achieved (or not) in a given time interval but can also provide some room to understand each other's expectations, challenges and barriers to achieve certain targets.

Table 4.1 A template for time offering challenges to achieve targets

Description of the target:

A mentor's perception	Timeline (By when?)	A beginning teacher's perception
When do I want it?		When do I want it?
When do I want the change to begin?		When do I want the change to begin?
When do I want the situation to stop?		When do I want the situation to stop?
When do I need the skill?		When do I need the skill?
What are the advantages/disadvantages to putting it off?		What are the advantages/disadvantages to putting it off?
What are the advantages/disadvantages to doing it now?		What are the advantages/disadvantages to doing it now?

4.3 RP to support change among beginning teachers

The four RP elements interact with each other to a greater or lesser extent. Asking the questions in Table 4.1, guided by the mentor, ensures that RP is a useful tool for a beginning teacher who is unsure of what to reflect on or what self-reflective questions to consider. Arguably, within RP there may be an element of reluctance among beginning teachers involving the kind of reflection that can result in change.

RP is primarily concerned with bringing about change with a view to improve practice. However, before this change-oriented journey begins, it is often necessary for you to first stop, turn around and see where you have been and how will you support the beginning teacher's journey. This form of calibration is an important element when embarking upon the thinking process. If you have not identified what needs to be addressed first, you will not know where the beginning teacher stands on that learning journey. Then, having given some thought to your calibration, it may be that a different path from the one you are taking may be more appropriate. Therefore, Task 4.2 asks you to reflect on your mentoring practices by applying the four RP elements to a mentoring situation significant to you.

Task 4.2   Apply the four elements of RP to view the impact on mentoring difficult situations

Think of an occasion or situation that was significant to you in relation to difficult moments when you were mentoring a beginning teacher. Then relate those difficult moments to the four elements, i.e. ourselves, other people, the environment and time. Make notes if helpful and answer the following questions:

1.   What do you notice? Consider different perspectives.
2.   Is using the RP elements of use to the beginning teacher?
3.   How does this assist analysis of the difficult situation you are referring to?

Another key characteristic of RP is responsibility. It is the responsibility of a practitioner to engage in the process of RP. However, the reality is that, initially, a beginning teacher may not fully understand the purpose of RP. A beginning teacher you are mentoring may have preconceived ideas about RP and may feel a little bit unsure of what exactly is expected of them, or be unwilling to engage with the process. Many beginning teachers seem to just accept situations as they have occurred without properly using the RP approach as a way to direct their professional development. Some have not realised that they are capable of not only directing their own affairs but are able to take their own advice; arguably, an individual should be an expert on themselves. RP is not easy for some beginning teachers and requires a certain amount of effort by all. We now propose some mentoring strategies that can be used to involve a beginning teacher with RP to support their teaching journey.

4.3.1 RP and experience sharing conversations

Although reflection can be traced back as far as Socrates, its roots in education are in the early twentieth century. Dewey (1933), for instance, considered a number of ways in which an individual can think including imagination, belief and stream of consciousness. However, it was reflection that appeared to interest him the most. He observed reflection as being a meaning-making process, which led to a deeper understanding of a subject whereby an individual was able to identify and connect experiences and ideas, and the relationship between them (Dewey, 1933). Dewey was of the opinion that, in order to reflect, it is necessary to value the intellectual and personal development of oneself and others. Furthermore, he posited that an experience has no value until it has been shared in some form (Dewey, 1938). Therefore, you and a beginning teacher you are mentoring, share many experiences and ideas in the form of conversations for mutual (personal and professional) development. Some of these conversations could be at a superficial level of reflection that focusses on what works or what does not work. This superficial level of reflection is not enough, therefore you should encourage the beginning teacher to reflect upon the learning process in a critical way. You can do this by using an effective open-ended questioning strategy involving 'Why', 'Why not', 'But if' questions. It is advisable to give the beginning teacher enough time to answer these reflective oriented questions in order to avoid over-burdening them during their thought-processes. Asking them to self-evaluate their strengths and areas for improvement is often an effective way of starting them to reflect at critical levels (Chapter 7, pp. 110–112).

4.3.2 RP and documenting reflective accounts

In addition to sharing conversations verbally, the expectations of a beginning teacher on many ITE programmes is also to document their reflections in a reflective journal – ideally on a weekly basis. This, maintaining of a reflective journal, is important for a beginning teacher to recognise the positive and negative impact of their teaching on pupil's learning and areas for further development in their teaching and learning approaches.

Task 4.2 asked you to reflect on a critical situation as a mentor using the four RP elements. Table 4.2 provides a template using the same four elements of RP, which can be used by a beginning teacher you are mentoring to record their weekly reflections. The first row asks the beginning teacher to give a description of a selected situation and the reason for choosing it. The following four rows of the table ask them to reflect on the selected situation with the aid of the four RP elements (in this table, 'your' refers to the beginning teacher). Before giving this template to the beginning teacher, make sure to support them in recognising and understanding the four elements of RP. Ask the beginning teacher to discuss their reflections during weekly mentoring meetings, where you can support them with their teaching and learning practices by promoting the use of RP elements further.

Schön (1987) introduced RP elements through the concepts of reflection-in-action and reflection-on-action. Reflection-in-action relates to a person who finds themselves in a situation where they need to think on their feet, i.e. when and possibly what they are doing is not working particularly well. A reflection-in-action example for you as a mentor could be that you have planned a particular pedagogical exercise for a beginning teacher you are

Table 4.2 Weekly reflections by applying the four elements of RP

Write a description of a selected situation for reflection and the reason of this selection

Ourselves
What was your initial emotional response/action to it? Did it change later?

Others
How did the pupils respond/act to this situation and your response to it? Why do you think a pupil or a group of pupils responded/acted in this manner?

Environment
What was the impact of the environment? Did it support the response/action or hinder the intended actions?

Time
What have you learned from this situation and subsequent reflection? Would these experiences and reflections change over time? Why (or why not)? How would this experience change your approach to teaching and learning?

---

mentoring; however, as you endeavour to engage the beginning teacher with the planned pedagogical exercise, you become aware that your expectations are not going to plan. You decide to change your pedagogical exercise and mentoring style. You have no time; the mentoring meeting is in progress, and you have to come up with something. You decide on the changes necessary and implement these on the spot, i.e. thinking on your feet and planning as you go. Later that day, you begin to reflect on what happened. You ask yourself if, having decided to change the exercise, did you do the best thing in hindsight? You consider the effects of the changes you made and decide on the mentoring styles and strategies you will employ on the next occasion. This is reflection-on-action; which is after the event.

Schön did not have a model. His observations were temporal in nature; they took the form of considerations at the time and after. Griffiths (2000) explained the role of reflection on teachers' professional practices as immediate effects (of reflection) may be minimal, but the process of reflection-on-action stays in the mind and adds to the store of professional knowledge that can be drawn on later. The weekly reflective journal template (Table 4.2) will support a beginning teacher to accomplish a reflection-on-action approach. You can discuss these weekly reflections with the beginning teacher during weekly mentoring meetings. In addition, you can encourage the beginning teacher to aggregate and discuss their weekly reflections on a monthly basis with you, by communicating (written or oral) two most prominent achievements and a minimum of one wish which they would like to achieve in the following month(s).

Griffiths viewed the importance of reflection-on-action on (beginning) teacher's professional development. We believe reflection-on-action is equally important for mentor's

Accountabilities of a reflective mentor 55

professional development. In this way, reflection can be seen as part of, and contributing to, mentors' personal and professional capability. Therefore, like beginning teachers, we recommend that, as a mentor, you should also keep a reflective journal entering accounts including (i) the target of focused mentoring session(s); (ii) a description of the context and mentoring strategies; (iii) the response received from the beginning teacher; and (iv) your evaluations, learning and future actions.

4.4 Models of reflective practice (RP) for unreflective beginning teachers

We believe that these mentoring strategies will support you and a beginning teacher you mentor towards becoming reflective practitioners. These useful strategies can be further strengthened by introducing RP models, such as Kolb's (1984) cycle, Brookfield's (1995, 2017) lenses and situated RP (Malthouse, Roffey-Barentsen and Watts, 2014). These models will provide some structure to the beginning teacher by which they can evaluate their own and other teachers' lessons and grade the reflective accounts of self-and/or others.

4.4.1 Model 1: Kolb's learning cycle

Kolb's (1984) learning cycle has four-stages (Table 4.3). The first point of the cycle is an actual, or concrete experience (CE), where the beginning teacher does something. The next stage is reflective observation (RO), where the beginning teacher reflects upon what they have done. Abstract conceptualisation (AC) takes the form of the beginning teacher finding out more about what they have done. Frequently, this takes the form of reading some relevant literature to support or change their existing practices. Having done something, reflected upon it and found out more about it/read some relevant literature, the final stage is that of active experimentation (AE) where the beginning teacher plans for the next CE.

Table 4.3 Using Kolb's learning cycle to evaluate sample reflective accounts

Kolb's four-steps (Adapted from Kolb, 1984)	Grade the given sample self-reflective teacher's accounts on teaching from most reflective to least reflective		
	Reflective account 1	Reflective account 2	Reflective account 3
concrete experience (CE)			
reflective observation (RO)			
abstract conceptualisation (AC)			
active experimentation (AE)			

The model is cyclical and can be employed as often as it is necessary (Chapter 6, p. 74) uses Kolb's four-stages of learning cycle to reflect on lesson planning).

This model could be beneficial for a beginning teacher, especially for those who value RP but are unable to reflect on their practices appropriately. You can support a beginning teacher to use RP approaches in their teaching practices by first sharing some sample in-depth and some superficial teacher's reflective accounts with them. Next, ask the beginning teacher to grade the accounts from most reflective to least reflective, using Kolb's four steps as the four criteria for grading. This exercise could help the beginning teacher to understand what RP entails and assist them to begin the in-depth process of understanding reflection.

4.4.2 Model 2: Brookfield's lenses

Brookfield (1995, 2017) recognised the importance of scrutinising assumptions. In order to do this, he advocated observing a phenomenon from a number of perspectives. He called this 'his four complementary lenses of reflective practice' (2017, p. xi). These lenses comprise the following:

- The point of view of the teacher
- The point of view of the learner
- The point of view of colleagues
- The point of view of theories and literature (Roffey-Barentsen and Malthouse, 2013, p. 8).

However, not all of these perspectives align to the practice of mentoring and so we offer a second set of alternative lenses:

- The point of view of the beginning teacher
- The point of view of the mentor
- The point of view of colleagues and/or pupils
- The point of view of theories and literature.

We believe that this model could help a beginning teacher, especially those who lack the ability to view self and others' perspective and those who do not value the importance of RP in their teaching practices. It is best if you can convince a beginning teacher you are mentoring to value the perceptions of others and the important role RP plays in their personal development. You can do this by asking them to:

1. Observe some lessons taught by experienced science and/or non-science teachers, and evaluate those lessons. Encourage them to document why they think certain aspects of teaching went well or which they felt could be improved
2. Next, ask them to converse with the observed teacher to record their perspectives on their lesson
3. Finally, meet with the beginning teacher to discuss the perceptions of self (beginning teacher) and others (observed teachers). You can then ask the following questions to support this discussion:
   - Does literature exist in relation to their perceptions?
   - In what way does it relate to their teaching and learning practices?

- How do their ideas relate to Brookfield's (adapted by Roffey-Barentsen and Malthouse, 2013) model?
- In light of the above, what are their perceptions now?

4.4.3 Model 3: Malthouse and Roffey-Barentsen's situated reflective practice

This situated reflective practice model is anticipatory in nature, i.e. this model allows a person to reflect upon what they would do should a certain situation arise. Figure 4.1 represents an overview of this model (Malthouse, 2012; Malthouse, Roffey-Barentsen and Watts, 2015). You can use this model to support a beginning teacher who finds themselves in a situation in which they feel they have no control. You could introduce the five interlinked stages in Figure 4.1 to the beginning teacher you are mentoring to support them in reflecting their personal reflective account.

You could use the five-stages, presented in Figure 4.1, in the following ways:

1. Identify a situation – Ask the beginning teacher to describe a difficult situation (such as struggling to properly complete the lessons in a 40-minute period).
2. Relate – Having identified the situation, support the beginning teacher to relate the impact of such a situation to their professional development.
3. Reflect – Encourage the beginning teacher to think about the likelihood of the identified situation (see above) and next steps.
4. Plan – Allow the beginning teacher to formulate a contingency plan in the event of the changes actually occurring, which can be discussed with you if required.
5. Act – The beginning teacher plan is acted upon. Together, you can review the action and ask open-ended questions to further incorporate the reflective process.

This model (Figure 4.1) is quite flexible and the situation can be reviewed at any stage. Further, it is not necessary for the model to be employed in its entirety. For example, if it becomes apparent that something needs to be done at the 'relate' stage, then it may be necessary to act without the need to 'reflect' or 'plan'.

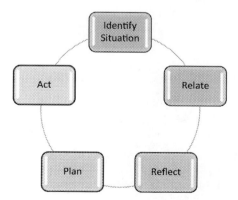

Figure 4.1 Situated reflective practice
(Source: Adapted from Malthouse (2012) and Malthouse, Roffey-Barentsen and Watts (2015))

58 *Roffey-Barentsen and Malthouse*

Finally, Task 4.3 is designed to enable you to reflect on RP models in your mentoring practices. It also asks you to identify which model is most suitable for the beginning teacher you are currently mentoring.

Task 4.3   Mentor refection: Selecting a model of RP

1. Ask yourself which RP model you prefer to use and why?
2. Which model is most suitable for the beginning teacher you are currently mentoring? Why?
3. Would you consider using different RP models for different beginning teachers? Why (not)?

Summary and key points

The key considerations that have been made in this chapter for you as a mentor concern what you are trying to achieve as a mentor and the different approaches you might adopt to develop reflective mentoring practices and to support a beginning teacher to develop RP, focusing on:

*   The elements of RP that have been identified as including ourselves, other people, the environment and time
*   An experience has no value unless it has been shared; reflection-in-action and reflection-on-action can be ways of sharing
*   Reflective mentoring involves a mentor–mentee relationship that is trusting, supporting and affirming
*   Kolb's learning cycle, Brookfield's lenses and situated reflective practice were offered to enable you to support a beginning teacher to become a reflective teacher.

Keeping your answers, notes, discussions and reflections from this chapter will be helpful for you to reflect progressively as you work with a beginning teacher and as you read other chapters in the book.

Further resources

Bolton, G. and Delderfield, R. (2018) *Reflective Practice: Writing and Professional Development*. London: Sage.
The newly updated fifth edition of this bestselling book explores reflective practice as a creative and dynamic process. This book encourages you to reflect thoughtfully on your role as a mentor to improve your own self-awareness, effectiveness and professional development.

Roffey-Barentsen, J. and Malthouse, R. (2013) *Reflective Practice in Education and Training*. 2nd edn. London: Sage.
This is a practical guide to RP for mentors and mentees in educational settings. RP is a key element of teaching and this comprehensive and accessible guide introduces and explains this area of practice for mentors and beginning teachers. It asks 'what is reflective practice?' and includes an explanation of the processes of reflection and tips on reflective writing.

5 Developing a mentor-mentee relationship

Michelle Wormald

Introduction

The role of a teacher is definitely rewarding but has many challenges. For a beginning teacher, it is easy to become overwhelmed, lost in a sea of endless marking and demands of paperwork. Therefore, it is vital that a beginning teacher is supported in the early stages of their career to overcome challenges and celebrate successes (New Teacher Centre, 2011). As mentioned in Chapter 1, it is one of your responsibilities to develop a positive and rewarding mentor-mentee relationship, which can be the lynchpin to a successful early career, enabling a beginning teacher to go beyond the survival stage of development and to realise both their own potential and that of their pupils (Hudson, 2016a). However, the role of the mentor will be perceived differently by different parties involved (Davis and Fantozzi, 2016), so to have a successful mentor-mentee relationship based on trust, a consistent understanding of expectations needs to be set out to ensure both you and the beginning teacher understand each other's roles in the relationship.

This chapter explores different factors that impact on the mentor-mentee relationship, and what you, as a mentor, can do to create a successful relationship, leading to mutual professional development. It also considers the views of the beginning teacher and their concerns about planning and teaching, allowing you to understand what they are experiencing and enabling you to support them more effectively. The tasks highlight specific approaches that can be used to build the relationship between a mentor and beginning teacher by improving communication with and emotional support for the beginning teacher. In this chapter, the term 'mentee' is used when referring to the 'mentor-mentee relationship'; otherwise, the term 'beginning teacher' is used.

Objectives

At the end of this chapter you should be able to:

- Understand the need for building an effective mentor-mentee relationship
- Recognise and practise mentoring approaches that support the emotional needs of a beginning teacher

60 *Wormald*

- Promote an effective mentor-mentee relationship by establishing mentoring strategies to build a beginning teacher's confidence in their planning and teaching practices
- Establish a strong mentor-mentee relationship by utilising emotional intelligence in your mentoring practice.

5.1 The need for building a mentor-mentee relationship

Teachers may become a mentor once they are successfully established in the classroom, want to take on another challenge in their career and want to share their skills with a beginning teacher. Some mentors volunteer for the role, some are chosen. Whatever your reasons are for becoming a science mentor, you should be totally committed to the role of supporting the development of beginning teachers. A beginning teacher you are mentoring must be given the support they need both in their initial teacher education (ITE) and in the transition into becoming an established practitioner, as a newly qualified and early career teacher. Beginning teachers need to understand the need for, and value, the support given to them by their mentors (see also Chapters 1 and 2). However, a mentor-mentee relationship is sometimes considered to be a one-way street, with the beginning teacher being too reliant on a mentor. At the start, this may be the case as a beginning teacher has less experience and knowledge than the mentor, resembling an apprentice level or plane of development (Chapters 1, 6 and 17). However, a mentor-mentee relationship evolves over time, going through different phases; the balance changes and becomes more symbiotic (Kochan and Trimble, 2000; Trubowitz, 2004; Chapter 17).

The effectiveness of the mentor-mentee relationship depends on a mentor's ability to build a collaborative relationship with a beginning teacher, using their communication skills to clearly explain strategies and analyse discussions to identify areas for development (Hanson, 2010) and being open towards offering support and challenge (see Chapters 1 and 17). Skills required for providing emotional support and to build collaborative relationship are transferable to supporting the professional development of the beginning teacher (Schwille, 2008). For example, good listening skills not only enable a mentor to identify what the beginning teacher is feeling at the time, but also help to develop a trusting relationship (Kochan and Trimble, 2000). Later in this chapter (see Section 5.4), a few tried and tested strategies in strengthening mentor-mentee relationships are presented.

Aligning with the development of an autonomous teacher, research by Davis and Fantozzi (2016) found that each mentor-mentee relationship is unique. Therefore, rather than using the same mentoring strategies for all beginning teachers, for a relationship to reap personal and professional rewards, any approaches to mentoring need to be tailored to an individual beginning teacher's needs. This requires you to develop a good knowledge of the beginning teacher's needs through cultivating a sound mentor-mentee relationship as this relationship is the key to success. Being dismissive of a beginning teacher's concerns could make them unwilling to be open and honest about their situation and perhaps reluctant to share their mistakes for fear of not being understood and supported. The impact of this would be to undermine the level of trust between the mentor and beginning teacher, which in turn will damage the relationship. Therefore, you need to give importance to a beginning teacher's

Developing a mentor-mentee relationship 61

concerns to establish a trusting relationship with them. Some areas of concern that beginning teachers report most frequently are:

- Providing a rich platform for learning by maintaining good behaviour in the classroom, looks at beginning teachers' perceptions on the issue of behaviour management while teaching pupils with special educational needs and disability (SEND).
- Health and safety in relation to conducting practical work as it could lead to explosions, breaking of glass, burning and injury (see some mentoring suggestions on health and safety while planning and teaching science practical lessons in Chapter 14, pp. 220–224).
- The majority of beginning teachers express their worries about subject knowledge when teaching non-specialist science topics (see some mentoring suggestions on supporting a beginning teacher with subject knowledge and pedagogical content knowledge (PCK) in Chapter 10). Beginning teachers are also concerned whether they will be able to teach, and how pupils will respond to, controversial topics such as Big Bang theory, In-Vitro Fertilization (IVF) and contraception, or teaching that involves learning outside the classroom (you can refer to Task 18.3 (p. 282) on planning a field trip as an enrichment activity).
- Beginning teachers often feel apprehensive about assessing pupils' scientific understanding and skills development (see some mentoring suggestions on assessment in Chapter 12).

These concerns of beginning teachers will evolve and most probably lessen with experience (Schwille, 2008). That said, a mentor must be able to recognise what an individual beginning teacher needs at a particular point in time to ensure the correct type of support is provided. This depends, in part, on the beginning teacher's levels of resilience, which will vary according to their previous and current experiences. Before reading any further, Task 5.1 asks you to share some of your personal experiences of teaching with a beginning teacher you are mentoring, to acknowledge their concerns, and support their understanding that these teaching associated concerns are part of their development.

Task 5.1 Sharing personal experiences of teaching with a beginning teacher

Recall and list some personal experiences of teaching that:

1. Could have put you off from science teaching. What did you do to overcome such concerns?
2. Have encouraged you to remain as a secondary science teacher.

Share some examples with a beginning teacher you are mentoring and encourage them to talk about some of their fears and anxieties towards becoming a science teacher and discuss ways to overcome their fears and anxieties.

5.2 Mentoring approaches that support the emotional needs of a beginning teacher

A mentor can be a source of conflict, especially from a beginning teacher's point of view. Starting with reflecting on your own practice, you need to reflect on the idea of a mentor being 'judgemental'. The feeling of being continuously judged can be seen by a beginning teacher as criticism and can lower their self-esteem. This could upset the balance in the mentor–mentee relationship, making it difficult for a beginning teacher to trust their mentor. This distrust in their mentor could undermine the experience for both mentor and beginning teacher. Trust is one of the most important areas in the mentor–mentee relationship to develop and nurture. Therefore, retaining, polishing and strengthening your support is vital to build a bond of trust between you and a beginning teacher you are mentoring (Hudson, 2016a; Izadinia, 2016).

There is an expected level of discretion in a mentor-mentee relationship that aids the development of a trusting relationship, including listening without judgement, as mentioned above, and ensuring that a beginning teacher knows that their feelings are valid (Trubowitz, 2004). Trust is developed over time, but it starts with the mentor doing what they say they will and following up on actions they said they will do. Before reading about such practices, Task 5.2 asks you to self-reflect on your experiences and relationships in mentoring a beginning teacher.

Task 5.2 Mentor's reflection: Am I judgemental or not?

In keeping with the attributes of an ONSIDE mentoring framework (see Chapter 4, p. 48) consider:

1. An occasion when a particular beginning teacher reported to you that they were being overtly judged and criticised (by you or other experienced teachers). How did you overcome this issue?
2. How did this affect the relationship between you and the beginning teacher? How would you approach such an issue if it arose again?

Task 5.3 asks you to recall the support you received from mentors you have worked with and whether (or not) you have (can) adopted and/or adapted those mentoring practices with the beginning teacher you are currently mentoring.

Task 5.3 Knowing me, knowing you

Recall some positive mentor-mentee relationships that you have experienced in your own teaching career either with a mentor or a supportive colleague. Then reflect on how your mentor and/or a supportive colleague helped you to: (i) be open about your fears and concerns, or (ii) cope when you made a mistake (such as during a practical lesson or using incorrect scientific vocabulary in the classroom). Now, using these reflections:

1. List what would help you as a mentor to know about the beginning teacher.
2. Consider what the beginning teacher might want to know about you.

Developing a mentor–mentee relationship   63

Mentors also need to recognise the emotional needs of their beginning teachers on an individual level. Therefore, to start and maintain a healthy mentor–mentee relationship, a mentor needs to identify and support a beginning teacher's emotional needs (along with cognitive and social support), which should ideally start from the first mentoring meeting.

To prepare for the first mentoring meeting, consider the information about the beginning teacher initial teacher training available to you. This can be obtained from their last end-of-school placement report, previous teacher development profile/portfolio listing their strengths and areas for development or from asking their university tutor (if any) about the beginning teacher, et cetera. Next, expand upon the available information about the beginning teacher through one-to-one discussions with them, ideally meeting face-to-face to introduce yourself and get to know a little more about them before the mentoring process starts. This meeting could be in a less formal space than where you normally meet the beginning teacher, as it will help them to talk freely in a relaxed atmosphere.

You may use the following checklist (Table 5.1) to ensure you and the beginning teacher you are mentoring get the most out of this initial mentoring meeting. The last point of the checklist (Table 5.1), refers to the importance of drawing a line for this mentor–mentee relationship. You need to decide how much of yourself you are willing to give to maintain this relationship. It is not necessary to share your entire teaching career with a beginning teacher, but a few insights based on your teaching ambitions help to develop trust between you and the beginning teacher. Likewise, it is not essential to know absolutely everything about the beginning teacher. However, understanding their social context, cultural background and teaching and learning philosophy could provide you with some indication of the 'hot spots' where the beginning teacher might have particular issues/challenges. This understanding will allow you to put appropriate support in place for them.

Table 5.1 First meeting checklist

Checklist	Yes	No	Mentor's pre-meeting notes	Mentor's post-meeting notes
Identify a neutral space, date and time where you can talk without interruptions				
Arrange refreshments to put the beginning teacher at ease				
Plan to allow the beginning teacher to ask questions				
Plan a series of some closed- and some open-ended questions to direct and stimulate conversations				
Decide where you want to draw the line between your professional and personal life				

64 *Wormald*

While a mentor and a beginning teacher match cannot always be carefully planned; it is important for you to be aware of a beginning teacher's perceptions and expectations of the mentor–mentee relationship (Chapter 3). Therefore, you need to discuss and agree on mentor–mentee relationship-based expectations with the beginning teacher. Also discuss some commitment-oriented ground rules, including an outline of what information is shared with other members of staff (such as the head of science), to ensure some level of confidentiality. During discussions with you, these ground rules allow the beginning teacher to feel sufficiently comfortable to be open and honest about their experiences with other staff members.

Chapter 3 suggests that you use a Personal Record of Performance (PRoP) form (see Task 3.4, p. 37) to allow the beginning teacher you are mentoring to identify 'their' expectations of you. Task 5.4 asks you to consider your expectations and commitments to build an effective mentor–mentee relationship.

Task 5.4 Managing expectations and commitments

1. Reflect on the conversations you have had with a beginning teacher during your first meeting. What did you learn about them that might influence how you manage a mentor–mentee relationship?
2. Think about your own working days. How much time will you make available to the beginning teacher? Think about where you want boundaries to be set in terms of your availability, especially beyond agreed meeting times, where the beginning teacher might seek advice or require support when they are struggling, and how and when you prefer to be contacted (for example, through emails and when you will respond to emails).
3. Construct a mind map or a list of your expectations and commitments to establish a mentor–mentee relationship. Ask the beginning teacher to do the same. Then share, discuss and clarify any differences in opinions. These thoughts could be captured in a shared document that can be referred to and modified throughout the mentoring process.

After completing Task 5.4 (and Task 3.4), design a mentoring programme in discussion with the beginning teacher, with frequent opportunities to review and update the programme, and which gives the beginning teacher ownership of the process, thereby encouraging a greater level of participation. This will allow changing emotions held by the beginning teacher to be reflected in the programme. For example, the beginning teacher may become more confident in planning simple practical tasks (such as displacement reactions of metals), but may still fear teaching a challenging practical task (say, fractional distillation).

The design of the mentoring programme must offer opportunities to track emotional changes from low to high confidence and stress and anxiety levels, to identify and address potential emotionally ascribed barriers to the beginning teacher's teaching and learning

Table 5.2 Tracking emotional changes

Some example teacher standards	Emotional changes - Week 1
Subject knowledge	Positive changes
	Negative changes
	Required support
	Next steps
Teaching	Positive changes
	Negative changes
	Required support
	Next steps
Classroom management	Positive changes
	Negative changes
	Required support
	Next steps
Pupil's assessments	Positive changes
	Negative changes
	Required support
	Next steps
Trust and respect	Positive changes
	Negative changes
	Required support
	Next steps
Professional commitments	Positive changes
	Negative changes
	Required support
	Next steps
Any other	Positive changes
	Negative changes
	Required support
	Next steps

practices. You could track the beginning teacher's emotional changes against some broad teacher standards using Table 5.2. Table 5.2 suggests you encourage the beginning teacher to document and discuss emotional changes during weekly mentoring meetings; however, this can be conducted more or less frequently, depending on the beginning teacher's needs. The first, left-hand, column, of Table 5.2 presents some indicators that can be altered in

66 *Wormald*

accordance with the emotional challenges experienced by the beginning teacher. The 'positive' and 'negative' emotional changes in the second column should be completed by the beginning teacher and the aspects on 'required support' and 'next steps' should be filled in by them in discussion with you. You can then encourage the beginning teacher to add columns on the right as week 2, week 3, and so on. This document will help a beginning teacher to pen-down their feelings and provide a platform for them to discuss their emotional changes openly with you. In turn, it allows you to follow up with these emotional changes on a regular basis.

5.3 A mentor-mentee relationship to support the development of confidence by a beginning teacher

Case studies 5.1 and 5.2 below show two examples of positive mentor-mentee relationships in supporting beginning teachers to plan and teach lessons with confidence.

Case study 5.1: Michael and Claire

Michael, a beginning science teacher, has not taught a lesson on the reactivity of alkali metals before and raised this concern in a weekly mentor meeting. Instead of just advising Michael to carry on with it, Claire, the mentor, co-planned a lesson on alkali metals with him, and arranged a solo-teaching session for Michael. She then observed the lesson, which was followed up with lesson feedback entailing a discussion to critique the lesson, evaluate the effectiveness of the strategies and the safety precautions used to teach the lesson. Michael appreciated that his concern was heard and not judged and appropriate support was administered according to the expectations and commitments promised by his mentor.

Case study 5.2: Sarah and Alison

Sarah, in her first year of teaching, had to teach a lesson that included a heart dissection. She was concerned about a challenging pupil in the class, especially about that pupil's potential behaviour. Alison, the mentor, took time to listen to Sarah's concerns without being judgmental, and used coaching techniques by asking Sarah open-ended questions on behaviour issues, discussing the reasons behind such an issue and revisiting the school's behaviour policies with Sarah. These mentoring actions helped Sarah to plan and implement effective classroom management strategies to address the pupil's behaviour, which eventually built her confidence to include the activity on heart dissection.

Developing a mentor–mentee relationship 67

Like Claire and Alison, you must be approachable and accessible to a beginning teacher's concerns and at the same time give them autonomy to work on the challenges (Laminack, 2017).

You should also be mindful that a beginning teacher can feel quite isolated while planning lessons themselves. Therefore, collaboration between you and a beginning teacher to plan aspects of a lesson could provide opportunity to share good practice, consider different approaches and stimulate more engaging teaching practices in future by giving the beginning teacher confidence to try new pedagogical practices. This collaboration should not only strengthen the mentor–mentee relationship but should also offer a balance between providing support and giving autonomy to a beginning teacher on their teaching and learning practices (see Chapter 7 on your support to increase a beginning teacher's teaching responsibilities and autonomy over time).

A mentor is viewed as a more knowledgeable other, as described by Vygotsky (Kumpulainen and Wray, 2002; Knight and Benson, 2014). You could reverse this view by asking a beginning teacher to suggest a new teaching strategy that you might not have tried before, and make the collaborative process beneficial for mutual development. This collaboration between the mentor and beginning teacher can remove anxiety by identifying key safety and organisational points in the planning process. Then, co-teaching, with the beginning teacher taking the lead, provides them with the confidence to lead, along with the comfort of knowing support is in the class. Once the beginning teacher experiences a successful outcome, for example with practical work, they are more likely to incorporate practical work into future lessons (see Chapter 6 for mentoring strategies to incorporate co-planning and Chapter 7 for co-teaching).

In addition to planning and teaching lessons, you are also observing a beginning teacher's classroom practices regularly (Chapter 8). You could ask the beginning teacher to observe some of your lessons and give feedback to you. The beginning teacher may find it difficult to give constructive feedback to you on your planning and teaching of lessons (Hudson, 2016a) at first, but going through this process, with your encouragement, will enable them to see that teaching is a continuous journey of development and that an experienced teacher is not a finished article. Before moving on, Task 5.5 asks you to reflect on opportunities you have had to work with a beginning teacher on planning and teaching lessons.

Task 5.5   Developing a beginning teacher's confidence

Think about the questions below:

1. What opportunities have you had to work with a beginning teacher on planning and teaching lessons?
2. How did you support the beginning teacher to overcome their concerns? How will you help a beginning teacher in future?
3. How did you/will you ensure that you are building their confidence with planning, teaching and understanding that there is always room for improvement?

5.4 Mentoring to strengthen the mentor–mentee relationship through emotional intelligence

It is possible that a beginning teacher will find difficulty in expressing and articulating their emotional needs appropriately so, for them, your emotional intelligence skills help to interpret and manage the beginning teacher's emotions, such as fear, panic or happiness. Interpretation of these positive and/or negative emotions starts with a mentor picking up a beginning teacher's verbal clues such as: 'I hope pupil X isn't here today' or 'I'm dreading teaching period 4 today', which could indicate a particular issue/challenge that they are experiencing and with which they may require your support. Sometimes non-verbal clues can also be given by the beginning teacher, such as tiredness; lacking enthusiasm or feeling ill; missing deadlines; coming late to school and showing disengagement with pupils while teaching. If, as a mentor, you overlook such indicative clues then there is a possibility that the situation will worsen and the beginning teacher might display further signs of an escalating issue. For example, a pattern of absence, especially when they are due to teach certain classes, aggressiveness, anxiety and stress, which could ultimately result in them withdrawing from the teaching profession.

Task 5.6 asks you to contemplate signs and clues of, for example, fear, panic and unwillingness to listen by a beginning teacher and ways to find out the underlining issue that is causing negative emotions.

Task 5.6   Emotional intelligence to recognise negative emotions

First, ask a beginning teacher you are mentoring to identify an issue with which they are finding difficulty coping. Then unpick the situation to get to the underlying issues by carefully observing their actions in lessons and during weekly mentoring meetings with you, as well as in other school-based situations. Next, list any observed verbal and non-verbal clues that could indicate an underlying issue. The following questions could help you to identify underlying issues, by tracking some of the negative emotional changes:

1. Has the beginning teacher reacted in an unexpected way to a situation or comment, perhaps in a way that could be perceived as over-reaction? Why do you think they reacted in such a way?
2. Has the beginning teacher displayed any avoidance strategies, such as a pattern of absence or used pupil behaviour as an excuse to avoid practical tasks or whole class experiments?
3. Is the beginning teacher ignoring your (or other staff members') emails, isolating themselves from you and/or others during non-teaching times and breaks?

If any answers to the above questions indicate that there could be an underling issue in relation to the beginning teacher's actions, then:

- Arrange an informal meeting with the beginning teacher at a place and time where you will not be disturbed and have sufficient time to talk.
- Gently explain the concerns you have and ask how you can support them.

Developing a mentor-mentee relationship 69

- Most beginning teachers are relieved when they are given the opportunity to discuss such issues, but some might be more hesitant to admit something is not right. In this instance, reassure the beginning teacher that you are there to listen when they are ready.
- For those who do share their worries, list two or three actions for the beginning teacher that will help resolve their concerns, and state what you will do to support them (this might be to revisit the conversation in the next planned meeting or a specific action such as making an action plan, et cetera). You could revisit Table 5.2 to support this discussion.

Task 5.6 can be further supported by using the suggestions below:

1. Be aware of your own emotions

   Ensure there is a calm environment in which the beginning teacher can express their feelings, fears and worries. Although you may yourself feel frustrated, impatient, disappointed and irritated, especially if the beginning teacher is not responding in the way you had hoped, it is important to be in control of how you react. This does not prevent you from challenging any inappropriate behaviour by the beginning teacher, but keeping your personal emotions out of the discussion will prevent you from becoming judgmental and support the beginning teacher in moving forward.

2. Practice

   Facing a challenging conversation can be daunting, so pre-plan how you want the conversation to play out, including planning some key questions to unpick underlying issues, identifying positive actions where possible and planning some specific mentoring strategies that will be supportive. It is also important to be aware of the language used during the discussion. This pre-planning helps to take emotions out of the discussion and keeps the focus on the actions rather than the people (pupils, other staff members, et cetera) involved. You could perhaps ask another experienced mentor to join the discussion.

3. Using appreciative comments

   Employ some appreciative and affirmative comments during your discussions, as positive reinforcement could encourage the beginning teacher to reflect on their teaching and learning strategies constructively by looking at both sides of the coin (positive and further actions required).

4. Identify the cause of negative feelings

   Identify with the beginning teacher, when and why they feel (i) unconfident, (ii) fearful, (iii) apprehensive or nervous, (iv) confident, (v) relieved, (vi) positive, et cetera. Ideally, you should be discussing these negative (and positive) feelings with the beginning teacher during your weekly mentoring meetings and, with careful questioning, you should be able to uncover underlying problems and possible solutions to overcome these feelings. However, in some situations, a more challenging conversation may be required. If this is the case, it is vital that, as a mentor, you are prepared for the discussion by clearly identifying the issues with the use of evidence.

70 *Wormald*

5. Resolving issues
    You must resolve an issue by a focused intervention. However, in some situations, the beginning teacher might become defensive and unwilling to accept and act upon targeted interventions. Here, it could be useful to share your own experiences to demonstrate that it is possible to recover the situation.

Summary and key points

A successful mentor–mentee relationship can only be built over time through the positive actions of both the mentor and beginning teacher. Through developing a successful mentor–mentee relationship, there is a much greater chance of a beginning teacher developing their teaching and hence enhancing pupils learning. Specifically, you need to:

- Take time to learn about a beginning teacher's emotional needs at the start of the relationship – this investment of your time will form the basis of the relationship
- Identify what you and a beginning teacher expect from each other, set boundaries and establish commitment outlines
- Be mindful of a beginning teacher's emotions, as they may indicate underlying issues, they have not raised in meetings
- Develop trust – act on your promises of support, listen without being judgemental and be approachable
- When a challenging conversation is required, prepare by planning the structure of the conversation, perhaps practise the key discussion points, and have any evidence to hand. Discuss and resolve the issue in a collaborative way.

Further resources

ACAS (The Advisory, Conciliation and Arbitration Service) (undated) *Challenging conversations and how to manage them*, ACAS, viewed 28 April 2020, from: https://archive.acas.org.uk/conversations
The ACAS website offers useful tips and guidance about having challenging and difficult conversations in a constructive way. Whilst not aimed specifically at education, the advice will help you prepare for difficult conversations, and allow you to control the situation more effectively. It should be helpful in maintaining a mentor–mentee relationship.

Goleman, D (2008) *Working with Emotional Intelligence*. London: Bloomsbury.
This book provides an exploration of emotional intelligence. It provides helpful suggestions to raise your own awareness of emotions and how they influence people to act in a specific way. It should help you to identify and understand some of the issues a beginning teacher faces and enable you to understand and influence the dynamics of a mentor–mentee relationship.

Teacher Tapp website (undated) *Ask. Answer. Learn*, Education Intelligence Ltd Venture, viewed 7 April 2020, from: http://teachertapp.co.uk/
The Teacher Tapp website is a useful, easy-to-use application. It asks routine, day-to-day questions and offers appropriate research and articles reflecting the work being done by a teacher at the time. This could provide an extra source of support in working with a beginning teacher, allowing them to develop their practice and build on their pedagogical knowledge.

SECTION 2

Basic mentoring practices

6 Supporting beginning teachers with lesson planning

Gareth Bates, Ralph Littler, Morag Findlay and Saima Salehjee

Introduction

The planning and teaching of lessons are integral to the role of a teacher. In our experience as teacher educators and school-based mentors, a series of lessons that are carefully planned and clearly articulated by the teacher are the ones that are most successful for pupils' learning. Our experience aligns with the quote allegedly by Benjamin Franklin, 'If you fail to plan, you are planning to fail.' However, as experienced teachers, we know that not all lessons go according to plan. As a mentor, you need to be resilient and accepting of the fact that a beginning teacher could 'fail' due to insufficient understanding of the long-term effect of planning on pupils' learning. As a consequence, you need to have well-developed strategies in place to support a beginning teacher to cultivate understanding of advanced practices of lesson planning.

This chapter addresses issues that a beginning teacher might have with lesson planning. It draws on strands from Chapter 4 on reflective practices by adapting Kolb's learning cycle (Kolb, 1984) to the planning process, exploring potential strategies that you can implement to support a beginning teacher. Using Daloz's mentoring model (Daloz, 2012) (see Chapter 1) and Rogoff's (1995) adapted model, this chapter explores when and how you can support and challenge a beginning teacher to become autonomous in planning for pupils' learning. Additionally, using perspectives from cognitive psychology on learning, the chapter frames how you can facilitate a beginning teacher to plan lessons that support a long-term curriculum plan.

Objectives

At the end of this chapter, you should be able to:

- Use the experiential learning cycle to reflect on supporting a beginning teacher to plan lessons
- Support a beginning teacher's transition from being able to plan sections of lessons (micro-planning), to single three-part lessons for a whole class, and, finally, to plan differentiated long-term curriculum plans - using Rogoff's apprenticeship, guided participation and participatory appropriation developmental planes.

74 *Bates et al.*

6.1 **Lesson planning as a reflective process**

Effective lesson planning is a reflective process. You could use Kolb's (1984) 'experiential learning' theory as a framework to explore how you can best support a beginning teacher to plan lessons for pupils' learning. Kolb (1984) described the idealised learning cycle (see also Chapter 4, p. 55, on using Kolb's learning cycle to support a beginning teacher to write self-reflective accounts) as a recursive process where the learner, in this case a beginning teacher, experiences (concrete experience (CE)), reflects (reflective observation (RO)), thinks (abstract conceptualisation (AC)) and then acts (active experimentation (AE)). As an example, a beginning science teacher's direct experience (CE) is teaching a lesson to a class. The next lesson for the same class is planned by them after reflecting (RO) on how the lesson went, which leads to some development or organisation of resources (AC), which are then deployed in the next lesson (AE). Task 6.1 asks you to use the experiential learning cycle to reflect on your mentoring approaches to support a beginning teacher in lesson planning

---

Task 6.1   **Mentoring to support lesson planning by using the experiential learning cycle**

Address the questions below:

1. At what point in the experiential learning cycle should you be asking for a lesson plan or lesson plans from a beginning teacher and why?
2. If you request lesson plan(s) from a beginning teacher in advance of teaching a lesson, how far in advance?
3. What feedback should you be giving to the beginning teacher before they teach the lesson?
4. How far in advance should you be giving feedback on a lesson plan and/or series of lesson plans to the beginning teacher?
5. Once you have observed a lesson, what feedback should you be giving to the beginning teacher that can support them to plan for the next lesson and/or series of lessons?
6. How will you incorporate the use of the experiential learning cycle in the beginning teacher's planning routine?

You will notice that your answers to Task 6.1 differ as a beginning teacher gains more experience in planning lessons over time. Hence, while using the experiential learning cycle, you need to acknowledge the prior experiences and developmental needs of the beginning teacher. Different feedback could be given about lesson plans to a beginning teacher at different stages of their development, for example:

Beginning teachers with lesson planning   75

- When a beginning teacher is co-planning with you and/or an experienced teacher, then your feedback on lesson plans prior to the lesson should be focused on procedural errors such as practical timing and choice of activities.
- During the initial stages of lesson planning, we believe that you should let a beginning teacher try out some of their self-planned approaches to teaching. But be mindful, if you see that they have planned a new strategy that could possibly fail in practice, then tell them why they need to modify/change it and offer suggestions.
- Once a beginning teacher has started to plan full lessons more independently then you should be constructive in your feedback on lesson planning; for example, you can talk about the relevance of pedagogical theories and assessments and curriculum for planning a lesson to enhance pupils' learning.
- Throughout the feedback process you should be encouraging a beginning teacher to reflect on their pre-lesson planning, teaching and post-lesson planning, consequently facilitating the experiential learning cycle.

In addition to the above points, your support to a beginning teacher during the course of their developmental journey should be aimed at the development of pupils' long-term learning. However, the constraints of a school's timetable, wider curricula, the demands of the standardised curricula (such as the National Curriculum for England) and examination constraints, limit a beginning teacher to planning learning for their pupils within a short number of lessons. Before reading further on supporting a beginning teacher to gradually develop their planning skills to plan for pupils long-term learning, Task 6.2 asks you to reflect on the process of planning that you have established (or intend to establish) to support a beginning teacher you are mentoring.

Task 6.2   Mentor's self-reflection on supporting a beginning teacher to plan a single and/or series of lessons

Reflect on the following questions:

1. How do you, as a mentor, support a beginning teacher to plan lessons?
2. Do you use any particular template and/or reflective model to assist a beginning teacher?
3. What resources do you provide a beginning teacher to use for planning (such as units of work, sample lesson plans, et cetera)?
4. What institutional and curriculum-based influences (positive and/or negative), do you think can impact the way in which a beginning teacher plans for long-term benefits to pupil's learning?
5. Do you recommend single lesson plans and/or long-term plans? and Why?
6. What mentoring methods could you employ to support a beginning teacher in planning lessons aiming for pupils' learning?

6.2 Supporting a beginning teacher's developmental journey of planning

This section of the chapter provides some mentoring strategies to support a beginning teacher to plan lessons at different stages of their development towards becoming an autonomous teacher. We use Rogoff's (1995) three planes of development that a beginning teacher generally goes through in their journey. A short description of these three planes, along with its resemblance to Katz's (1995) stages of development (a detailed description on Katz (1995) four-stages of development is given in Chapter 1) are:

1. Apprenticeship plane, this stage is typically at the start of a beginning teacher's placement in your school. It resembles Katz's (1995) survival stage and exhibits some signs of the consolidation stage. In this plane a beginning teacher is contributing to planning some sections of the lessons.
2. Guided participation, this plane of development covers a beginning teacher's development from Katz's consolidation stage to the renewal stage, where they are given responsibility to plan full lessons for different classes.
3. Participatory appropriation, at the end of this stage, a beginning science teacher should be autonomously planning series of lessons with an aim to plan for a sequence of learning rather than focusing on a short number of lessons of learning gains for all the pupils. This plane resembles Katz's maturation stage.

The next section presents the three planes and some possible mentoring suggestions that you can employ to support a beginning teacher's developmental journey of planning effective lessons. The sequence of mentoring suggestions covering a specific developmental plane are not fixed. These suggestions are simply some guidelines for you to adopt/adapt according to the needs of a beginning teacher you are mentoring.

6.2.1 Apprenticeship plane

At this early stage of development, a beginning teacher needs support in settling in. Using Daloz's (2012) model of mentoring, in order to achieve 'growth' in learning, you need to give a beginning teacher high support and high challenge. In order to give high support at this stage, we suggest that you allow the beginning teacher to observe experienced teachers planning, and micro-plan some of the lessons with the classes you intend them to co-teach.

This apprenticeship plane is a modelling phase, where you share some example lesson plans as models of your own practice and discuss ideas on how to plan effective lessons. During these discussions, you may want to emphasise the importance of planning and indicate to the beginning teacher that, at the start of their teaching career, they may observe experienced teachers who 'just know' how much to put into each part of a lesson and can effectively and quickly change/adapt their planning according to the need of pupils. This is probably because they have planned just about every conceivable situation, and have a better control on changing strategies as they go along, either in planning single or a series of lessons. In addition, your discussions could involve sharing your experiences of altering your lesson plans on a regular basis, with a focus on the idea that one planned lesson or a series of lessons – for a particular age group of pupils – is not a finished article. Rather, teachers are

Beginning teachers with lesson planning 77

required to continually refine and adapt their plans according to the teaching and learning circumstances, such as school/classroom context and pupils' learning needs.

After these initial discussions with a beginning teacher you could consider how your colleagues can have an input into supporting the development of the beginning teacher to plan effective lessons. To initiate this involvement, you could arrange for a beginning teacher to observe an experienced teacher's lesson(s) (ideally a science teacher, if there is more than one science teacher in your school). It is important to involve experienced science teachers at this early stage of development, because it is unlikely that a beginning teacher will only be teaching lessons solely to the classes you normally teach. Before arranging these observations, you need to ensure the best support for the beginning teacher. Therefore, think about the following:

- What are the strengths and expertise of the experienced science (or non-science) teacher that can support the beginning teacher?
- What could the beginning teacher learn from them?
- What information would you give to the teacher about the beginning teacher?
- What support would you like the teacher to provide them?

After considering the above points, select an experienced teacher who can support the beginning teacher in planning effective lessons. Task 6.3 asks you to arrange lesson observations of an experienced teacher for a beginning teacher that provide opportunities for the beginning teacher to learn about the importance of effective planning for their teaching practices.

Task 6.3 Mentoring to support effective planning through arranging lesson observations of experienced teachers for a beginning teacher

1. Prior to arranging an observation of an experienced teacher's lesson (ideally a science teacher), encourage the beginning teacher to list some questions that they would like to ask the experienced teacher about planning, such as what planning of the lesson or a series of lessons have they undertaken and why? What will they do if the planning does not go according to plan? et cetera.
2. During the lesson observation, ask the beginning teacher to make notes on the ways the experienced teacher uses planned activities to benefit pupils' learning. What was good about it? What teaching strategies did the experienced teacher use in the class and how did they detail these teaching strategies in their lesson plans?
3. Discuss these observational notes in your next weekly mentoring meeting with the beginning teacher.

[You might arrange more than one lesson observation for the beginning teacher. In this case, repeat the above steps for the selected experienced teacher or teachers.]

During this stage, in addition to observing and evaluating an experienced teacher, you can support a beginning teacher with micro-planning. Micro-planning involves a beginning teacher planning certain parts of a lesson, for instance, preparing for lesson starters, mini-plenaries, experiments, et cetera. Discussions on micro-planning can then support the beginning

78 *Bates et al.*

teacher to co-plan a complete lesson with you and/or with other experienced teachers. As they grow in confidence, the beginning teacher can start planning activities for a co-planned lesson and you can provide feedback on these planned activities. This co-planning of lessons can start from the apprenticeship plane and can be continued to the advanced participatory appropriation plane of development. The kind, manner and level of mentoring support in co-planning lessons will differ between the beginning (apprenticeship) and advanced (participatory appropriation) planes of development.

6.2.2 Guided participation plane: Understanding the science curriculum to plan learning outcomes and key questions

Using Daloz's (2012) model, at this plane of development, the high challenge for a beginning teacher is from the accountability and responsibility they have for planning full lessons for different classes. Therefore, initially, you can provide high support through co-planning of full lessons. Ideally a co-planned lesson should be a contemporaneous account of a face-to-face conversation about the lesson. Therefore, at this stage, co-planning should involve discussion about effective planning with a focus on pupils' learning progression, i.e. emphasising what pupils are expected to have learned at the end of the lesson, indicating one or more learning expectations recommended under the specific unit of work.

In this chapter, the term unit of work is used to indicate different units or blocks of work that originate from the government's approved science curriculum. In England, these units of work can be found in the relevant curriculum documents, for example, Department for Education (DfE) (2013) for Key Stage 3 (age group 11–14) and DfE (2014) for Key Stage 4 (age group 14–16). As mentioned in the introduction to this book, you might need to adopt/adapt these curriculum documents according to the curriculum requirements of the country/examination boards/ school in which you are working. A list of some units of work is also presented in Appendix 10.1 (p. 166) of Chapter 10, which can be shared with the beginning teacher for guidance.

This co-planning support is part of the early development of a beginning teacher, 'however, it is most beneficial when it is ongoing, as the demands and expectations of the lesson plan become increasingly pupil-centred' (Binney, Barrett, Green, Pocknell and Smart, 2019, p. 167). Depending on the developmental stage and needs of a beginning teacher, your support with guided co-planning can vary; therefore, the steps outlined in this section are not absolute and can be adopted/adapted respectively.

Some mentoring support you could provide to a beginning teacher to continue with the co-planning associated discussions on planning a whole lesson is considered next. Some different and more advanced approaches to support a beginning teacher to plan lessons are also covered in other chapters of the book, for example, Chapter 15. You can choose and select a mentoring approach according to the needs of a beginning teacher and focus of your support.

6.2.2.1 Learning outcomes and pupils learning

An understanding of a unit of work is an ongoing process for a beginning teacher, for which you can provide support to plan learning outcomes that support pupils' learning identified in the unit of work. Before supporting a beginning teacher to write learning outcomes, you need to share some example learning outcomes with them. You could then support the beginning teacher to write learning outcomes for lesson plans they intend to teach. This

Beginning teachers with lesson planning 79

provides a source of evidence that they can use to demonstrate 'what learning is intended?' before the lesson and 'what outcomes have been achieved (or not)?' after the lesson. While supporting the beginning teacher to write learning outcomes, it is noted that most beginning teachers often find it easy to identify the activities pupils will complete during a lesson, but they find difficulty identifying the learning which will take place. To this end, Task 6.4 asks you to support a beginning teacher by sharing some example learning outcomes.

Task 6.4 Supporting a beginning teacher to identify pupils learning

Undertake the following steps to support a beginning teacher to identify learning expected by pupils from each of the planned learning outcomes:

1. Ask the beginning teacher to look at Table 6.1, which indicates five-example learning outcomes (LO1–LO5) in the first column; for the 'electricity' unit of work, specifically on 'current, resistance and voltage relationships for different circuit elements; including their graphical representations' (DfE, 2014, p. 15). In the second column the beginning teacher is asked to write about the relevance of each of the six learning outcomes in achieving expected learning for the given aspect of the unit of work.
2. Next, encourage the beginning teacher to discuss Table 6.1 with you for further guidance.
3. These steps could be followed in the similar way for other aspects of the same unit of work (or other units of work) that you think are appropriate to share.

Table 6.1 Learning outcomes and pupils learning

Learning outcomes (LO) for 'Exploring current, resistance and voltage relationships for different circuit elements; including their graphical representations' (DfE, 2014, p. 15).	The relevance of the learning outcomes (LO) in achieving the expected pupils' learning for 'Exploring current, resistance and voltage relationships for different circuit elements; including their graphical representations' (DfE, 2014, p. 15).
LO1 Set up a series electrical circuit to measure the current through a resistor and the voltage across it as the current in the circuit is varied	
LO2 Record the results in a table and calculate the ratio of the voltage across the resistor to the current through the resistor	
LO3 State that the value of voltage divided by current is approximately constant	
LO4 State the formula for Ohm's law and explain the meaning of the symbols used	
LO5 Plot a graph of voltage against current	
LO6 State that the resultant straight-line graph shows that the voltage across a resistor is directly proportional to the current through it	

80   *Bates et al.*

6.2.2.2 Learning outcomes and key questions

After supporting a beginning teacher to discuss learning outcomes and associated pupils' learning expectations identified in the science curriculum's units of work, you can then support them to use key questions characterising the course of the lesson. Key questions can give the skeleton of the lesson or provide a series of waypoints that a beginning teacher has to reach to organise the lesson. How the lesson progresses between the waypoints depends on the interaction between the beginning teacher and the class. The key questions are often linked to learning outcomes. In addition to the scripted key questions, a beginning teacher and/or the pupils could ask many spontaneous questions as the lesson progresses (Chapter 11). Task 6.5 looks at a beginning teacher writing key questions for the learning outcomes presented in Table 6.1. Task 6.6 then focuses on mentoring steps to support the beginning teacher to embed key questions in their lesson planning.

Task 6.5   Writing key questions to accomplish a smooth progression of a lesson

Ask the beginning teacher to follow these steps:

1.   Look back at Task 6.4 (Table 6.1) and write some key questions for each learning outcome.

[You could use Table 6.1 to focus on learning outcomes and pupils learning from a different unit of work and ask the beginning teacher to write key questions accordingly.]

2.   What question(s) would they ask in an exit pass at the end of the lesson?
3.   Compare the beginning teacher's key questions with the (possible example) key questions presented in Table 6.2.

Table 6.2 Possible key questions (KQ) for the learning outcomes (LO) presented in Table 6.1

LO1: KQ1 How can pupils design an electrical circuit to measure the current through a resistor and the voltage across it?
LO2: KQ2 Looking at the results table, what can pupils tell about the value of the voltage across the resistor as the current through it increases?
LO3: KQ3 What happens to the voltage across the resistor when the current through it doubles?
LO4: KQ4 Can pupils describe the relationship between the current through the resistor and the voltage across it?
LO5: KQ5 What sort of line can pupils draw on the graph? (straight-line or curve of best fit)
LO6: KQ6 What is the relationship between the current and the voltage for a resistor?
LO4/6: KQ4/6 What is the relationship between the voltage across a resistor and the current through it?

Beginning teachers with lesson planning 81

Task 6.6   Embedding key questions as part of a beginning teacher's planning to strengthen pupils' learning

After completing Task 6.5 with a beginning teacher, follow the steps below:

1. Ask the beginning teacher to plan a series of lessons within a specific unit of work, focusing on the use key questions. Review the lesson plans and ask the beginning teacher to justify their questioning choices to evaluate pupils' progress.
2. Following the series of lessons, support the beginning teacher to evaluate the effectiveness of their key questioning technique using pupils' feedback as a means to assess pupils' progress formatively and how they can improve the effectiveness of this strategy further.
3. Encourage the beginning teacher to differentiate the above questions catering for all the pupils (some examples are provided in Table 6.5).

Once the beginning teacher masters the use of key questioning, you could refer them to Chapter 11, which introduces other ways of planning rich questioning to develop classroom dialogue and building confidence among pupils. See also Chapter 15 (pp. 234-235), which suggests ways to support a beginning teacher to construct learning outcomes by embedding scientific literacy approaches to learning using a range of verbs (Table 15.1), and Chapter 18 (282-283) to promote enrichment activities.

6.2.3 *Guided participation plane (continued): Three-part lesson plan*

At this stage of guided participation, some full lessons for a specific class of pupils could be planned over a period of time, a week or two, which could later build up into series of lessons comprising a complete (or some aspects) unit of work. At this stage of guidance, you could use a three-part lesson plan design (comprising a lesson starter, the main body of the lessons and the consolidation parts) to support a beginning teacher to plan a whole class lesson under your guidance (Fautley and Savage, 2013). The beginning teacher needs to understand that the boundaries between start (lesson starter), middle (main body) and end (consolidation) of the three-part lesson plan should be fluid, to allow ease of flow between the three parts, to present a whole lesson picture rather than three isolated parts of a lesson.

Table 6.3 presents a co-planned lesson plan for one of the lessons in a unit of work on electricity. The learning outcomes (Table 6.1) and key questions (Table 6.2) are revisited in this lesson plan.

Table 6.3 A lesson plan

Class: 3A

Year group: Year 9/Secondary 2

Date: XXXX

Lesson number: XX

Unit of work: Electricity

Topic: 'Current, resistance, voltage and Ohm's law', specifically on 'exploring current, resistance and voltage relationships for different circuit elements; including their graphical representations' (DfE, 2014, p. 15).

Learning outcomes (LO)

All pupils will be able to:

LO1 Set up a series electrical circuit to measure the current through a resistor and the voltage across it as the current in the circuit is varied

LO2 Record the results in a table and calculate the ratio of the voltage across the resistor to the current through the resistor

LO3 State that the value of voltage divided by current is approximately constant

LO4 State the formula for Ohm's law and explain the meaning of the symbols used

Some pupils will be able to:

LO5 Plot a graph of voltage against current

LO6 State that the resultant straight-line graph shows that the voltage across a resistor is directly proportional to the current through it.

Activity	Time	Teacher activities	Pupils' activities
Part one: Start			
Lesson starter	5 minutes	What would be different if there was a power cut right now? Why is electricity important?	Pupils write down two or three things that would be different in a power cut. Brief class discussion.
Part two: Main body			
Designing the investigation	10 minutes	**KQ1** How can you design an electrical circuit to measure the current through a resistor and the voltage across it? Eliciting ideas from the pupils and mark the investigation pro forma (Appendix 6.1) to assess their understanding and scientific skills Guiding pupils to include all relevant data in the table	Think-pair-share activities to develop the circuit. Designing a table for results. Draw a circuit diagram and add the table headings in the investigation handout in Appendix 6.1.

Beginning teachers with lesson planning 83

Activity	Time	Teacher activities	Pupils' activities
Carrying out the investigation	20 minutes	Giving instructions about collecting the equipment	Working in groups.
		Monitoring progress by patrolling the laboratory	Setting up the circuit.
		Interacting with groups of pupils and assessing their experimental skills	Recording results.
		KQ2 Looking at the results table, what can pupils tell about the value of the voltage across the resistor as the current through it increases?	Looking for the relationship between the variables in tabular or graphical form as appropriate (Appendix 6.1).
		Asking questions to assess and guide progress	Tidying up equipment.
		KQ3 What happens to the voltage across the resistor when the current through it doubles?	
		KQ4 Can pupils describe the relationship between the current through the resistor and the voltage across it?	
		Asking quick finishers to plot a graph of their results	
		KQ5 What sort of line can pupils draw on the graph? (Straight-line or curve of best fit.)	
		KQ6 What is the relationship between the current and the voltage for a resistor?	

Part three: Consolidation

Exit pass question: What is one thing you learned today and one thing you want to find out about?

Plenary	10 minutes	Discussing results	Working individually, in pairs, practical groups or as a class to reach conclusion.
		Eliciting relationship from pupils both as a verbal relationship and as a formula	
		KQ4/6 What is the relationship between the voltage across a resistor and the current through it? See also KQ2, KQ3 and KQ5	Recording conclusion and formula on exit passes.
		Giving instructions for exit pass using pencil and paper/electronic devices	
		Dismissing pupils	

Links to the following lesson(s)

- Homework will be set after the next lesson.
- Apply Ohm's law to solve problems.
- Investigate what happens when the temperature of a resistor/component changes.

84   *Bates et al.*

A brief description on the three-part lesson plan in Table 6.3 is as follows:

6.2.3.1 Part one: Start
The first part of the lesson plan could include a starter activity to engage and challenge pupils at the start of the lesson. You can support the beginning teacher to plan lesson starters by:

- Asking them to come up with three lesson starters from different sources such as textbooks and internet search. Encourage the beginning teacher to plan the first lesson starter linking to the everyday use of Ohm's law, second starter from the news, third starter, some questions that can evaluate what pupils' misconceptions were gained from the previous lesson(s)
- Ask the beginning teacher to plan the timings of the starters. This should not be longer than 10% of the lesson time. This will support them in setting the pace of starter activity
- Encourage the beginning teacher to plan for rewards for pupils who effectively complete the starter activity in a given time
- Finally, discuss the benefits and drawbacks of the three lesson starters, the suitability of them with the planned learning outcomes and, together with the beginning teacher, agree on one of the lesson starters that will be used for the upcoming lessons on electricity.

6.2.3.2 Part two: Main body
This section looks at pupil and teacher activities that can be outlined according to the planned key questions in Table 6.2. Through discussions, you can support the beginning teacher to plan some activities according to the possible key questions. Next, you can advise the beginning teacher to plan two to three specific mini-sections of part two (main body). Some ideas for mini-sections could be:

- *Problem-solving* activities, such as allowing pupils to solve problems in building electrical circuits
- *Skill development*, such as after a series of teacher demonstrations the class have the task of explaining the relationships between current, resistance and voltage, using existing resources and/or resources pupils make for themselves
- *Writing-based* activities such as pupils critiquing the laboratory report of peers prior to producing their own.

The example lesson plan on current, resistance, voltage and Ohm's law, under the unit of work electricity (Table 6.3) includes mini-sections, such as problem-solving (*think-pair-share activities* to develop electrical circuit), skill development (*setting up* the circuit), and writing-based activities (pupils *writing down two or three things* that would be different in a power cut) within the two broad divisions of designing the investigation for 10 minutes and carrying out the investigation for 20 minutes.

Some other suggestions you could make to the beginning teacher at this plane of development could be to plan:

- Individual, peer or group work resources and the physical environment
- Teacher's activities to support pupils' activities

Beginning teachers with lesson planning   85

- An introduction to differentiating teacher's activities to support the learning of all pupils (see also participatory appropriation plane section below)
- Time allocation accounting for classroom routines (such as the time it will take to set up an investigation, carrying out the investigation and clearing away)
- Formative styled assessment procedures.

Some examples to these suggestions can be seen in Table 6.3.

6.2.3.3 Part three: Consolidation

The plenary forms the third section of the three-part lesson plan. It completes the lesson, consolidates the lesson for pupils and the beginning teacher and provides planning avenues for the next lesson. You can support the beginning teacher to plan some plenary questions that consolidate the learning of pupils and enable them to signpost learning for the next lesson or a series of lessons. You can support the beginning teacher to plan plenaries, for example on electricity (focusing on current, resistance, voltage and Ohm's law), by:

- Asking the beginning teacher to come up with some plenary ideas from different sources, such as implementing what ideas they have observed experienced teachers using that they believe work well for pupils or using some online plenary ideas
- Asking the beginning teacher to plan the timings of the plenary as an essential part of their lesson planning to avoid cutting the plenary short to complete the lesson on time
- Sharing some plenary ideas with them, for example finishing the lesson by re-introducing the lesson starter and asking pupils to consolidate what they have (or not) learned in the lesson using lesson evaluation approaches such as exit passes (Part three section of Table 6.3), using washing line activity (see example in Chapter 11, p. 175), or asking pupils to write 'what went well' and 'what they (pupils) need support with', et cetera). Sharing and discussing how pupils' responses gained from the plenary activity can guide the planning for the next lesson
- Finally, discuss with the beginning teacher the benefits and drawbacks of: the planned plenary activity, the appropriateness of it, and its association with the key questions, learning outcomes and lesson starter.

In addition, it is possible to construct a lesson that has mini-plenaries that are introduced at different times in the lesson. You can, for example, ask the beginning teacher to use question and answer (Q&A) styled plenary to assess pupils. These Q&A periods could also include planning for extension questions (such as examination-style questions).

6.2.4 Participatory appropriation plane

At the start of this stage, a beginning science teacher should be independently planning and teaching full lessons. During this stage, they should be demonstrating a deeper level of reflection, which requires high support from you, especially to plan for differentiation and to produce long-term learning plans for pupils. Some suggestions for mentoring based on differentiation are presented below.

6.2.4.1 Planning for differentiation

To further reflect on the intended learning outcome, it is beneficial that a beginning teacher is aware of the different competency levels of pupils in the class. A beginning teacher can observe pupils' different individual competence levels by collecting evidence, such as pupils' written and/or verbal accounts, examination/test results, and classroom engagement with peers and material resources from all the pupils. You could perhaps ask the beginning teacher to focus on two or three pupils (ideally from the same class/year group), who they believe require differing learning support. Once some pupils are selected, you can then assist the beginning teacher in planning appropriate learning outcomes according to the needs of those selected pupils.

Table 6.4 can be used to record information about the pupils and how their data can be used to adopt the planned learning outcomes or to adapt them according to the learning needs of these pupils. In the first column of Table 6.4, initials of the selected pupils are inserted. Type of evidence (such as test results, field notes based on the selected pupils' behaviour with other pupils, et cetera) is included in the second column. Observations gained from the evidence is included in the third column, then some or all the learning outcomes in the fourth column and finally, the in last column some points from discussions with you regarding the competence levels of the selected pupils.

Table 6.4 Planning tasks according to pupil's different competence levels

Name initials	Evidence type	My observation	Learning outcomes	Discussion with the mentor
Pupil 1:				
Pupil 2:				
Pupil 3:				

6.2.4.2 Planning for differentiated questions

In supporting a beginning teacher in a pre-lesson discussion to plan a range of questions for pupils, you need to ensure that these questions address all expected learning outcomes for all pupils. This means that some questions could be targeted for the whole class, while other questions could only be for some pupils. As an extension to Table 6.1, Table 6.5 can be shared with the beginning teacher to initiate forming closed questions (which usually ask pupils for one-word answers or facts), guided questions (which ask pupils to think critically using some visible or hidden clues in the questions) and open-ended questions (which require pupils to analyse and self-evaluate their knowledge and skills) to promote pupils learning. Some examples of closed, guided and open-ended questions along with the learning outcomes for

Beginning teachers with lesson planning   87

the example of electricity are given in Table 6.5. Chapter 16 (p. 252), differentiates the three types of questioning (note: it refers to closed-ended questions as 'closed-guided', guided as 'closed-convergent' and open-ended questions as 'open-divergent'). Task 6.7 asks you to support the beginning teacher to plan for differentiated questions.

Task 6.7   Mentoring to support planning for differentiated questions

Encourage a beginning teacher to complete Table 6.5. In completing the table:

- Support the beginning teacher to complete the last three columns (closed, guided, open) with different types of questions they could ask pupils. Some example questions are presented in the table
- Ask the beginning teacher to signpost these closed, guided and open questions in relation to the potential ways they will be asked and answered. For example, signpost questions as classroom verbal (CV) if the beginning teacher is planning to ask some planned questions verbally in the classroom, or classroom written (CW) for questions that pupils will be asked to give written answers to either in the classroom (CW) or at home - signposted as homework written (HW)
- Instruct the beginning teacher to signpost initials of those pupils who will be individually approached to answer some particular questions
- Discuss the beginning teacher's justifications behind the signposting and suggest alternative strategies (if required) before these questions are practised in the classroom.

[You could use a different unit of work to complete Table 6.5].

6.2.4.3 Planning for differentiated tasks for the same activity

You also need to guide a beginning teacher in planning tasks for pupils that are supportive, yet at the same time challenging. You could encourage them to plan tasks for all the pupils by keeping the tasks open-ended so to give opportunities to pupils to take different routes to accomplish some learning outcomes (Bartlett, 2016). At this plane of development, it is important that the beginning teacher sees differentiation as a way to enable all pupils to learn as an integral part of the planning process rather than an "add on" after the lesson has been planned. Integrating differentiation into planning is an effective way to include all pupils in the lesson. For example, in a lesson plan on electricity (Table 6.3), all pupils will be able to carry out the practical work, possibly with some support. Most pupils will see, possibly with some guidance from the teacher, that roughly speaking as the current through the resistor doubles, so does the resistance across it. Some pupils may suggest calculating the value of the voltage divided by the current for their resistor, but all pupils can carry out this calculation using a calculator. Some pupils may have the skills to plot a graph of the results and know that the resulting straight-line graph shows that the ratio of voltage divided by the

Table 6.5 Using a range of questions to target the particular needs

Class	3A	Question type key:
Year group	Year 9 / Secondary 2	CV: Classroom - verbal
Date	XX.XX.XX	CW: Classroom - written
Lesson number	XX	HW: Homework - written

Unit of work	Electricity
Topic	'Current, resistance, voltage and Ohm's law', specifically on 'exploring current, resistance and voltage relationships for different circuit elements; including their graphical representations' (DfE, 2014, p. 15).

Learning outcomes (LO) and associated key questions (KQ) (from Tables 6.1 and 6.2)	Closed	Guided	Open
LO1: Set up a series electrical circuit to measure the current through a resistor and the voltage across it as the current in the circuit is varied **KQ1:** How can you design an electrical circuit to measure the current through a resistor and the voltage across it?			
LO2: Record the results in a table and calculate the ratio of the voltage across the resistor to the current through the resistor **KQ2:** Looking at the results table, what can pupils tell about the value of the voltage across the resistor as the current through it increases?	Has everyone completed their table? (CW)	What happens to the voltage across the resistor when the current through it increases? Does the voltage decrease, remain constant or increase? (CV)	What happens to the current through the resistor when the voltage across it decreases? (CV)
LO3: State that the value of voltage divided by current is approximately constant **KQ3:** What happens to the voltage across the resistor when the current through it doubles?	Tell me two or three values of voltage divided by current for your resistor. (CV)	What do you notice about the value you calculated for the voltage divided by the current? (CV)	Why does the value for voltage divided by current remain constant when the voltage changes? (CV)
LO4: State the formula for Ohm's law and explain the meaning of the symbols used **KQ4/6:** Describe the relationship between the current through the resistor and the voltage across it? What is the relationship between the voltage across a resistor and the current through it?	State the formula for Ohm's law. (CV)	If the voltage across a resistor is 10 V and the current through it is 2A, what is the resistance of the resistor? (CW)	If we increase the current through a resistor, what happens to the voltage across it? Explain why this happens. (CV)

Beginning teachers with lesson planning 89

Learning outcomes (LO) and associated key questions (KQ) (from Tables 6.1 and 6.2)	Closed	Guided	Open
LO5: Plot a graph of voltage against current *KQ5:* What sort of line can pupils draw on the graph? (Straight line or curve of best fit) *LO6:* State that the resultant straight-line graph shows that the voltage across a resistor is directly proportional to the current through it *KQ6/4:* What is the relationship between the current and the voltage for a resistor? What is the relationship between the voltage across a resistor and the current through it?			

current is constant. Then, all groups of pupils can be included in the discussion about the formula for Ohm's law: voltage equals current times resistance.

Planning for differentiated tasks could be a challenge for a beginning teacher, therefore initially at this participatory appropriation plane of development you could co-plan tasks with them and then jointly reflect on the impact of differentiated planning on teaching. While co-planning with the beginning teacher, you could ask them to answer questions indicated in Table 6.6. A useful mentoring strategy here is for you to take the lead in planning the

Table 6.6 Planning differentiated tasks

In this box, identify and describe the planned activity/task:

Questions ('I' refers to a beginning teacher)	A beginning teacher's response
What task(s) would I change to simplify this activity? What task(s) would I change to make this activity more challenging? What roles would I assign to individual pupils? How can I support all pupils to complete the activity? How can I vary the questions to include all the pupils? How can I support pupils to work with peers and in teams? Other questions to consider…	

90 *Bates et al.*

differentiated tasks initially and gradually letting the beginning teacher take more responsibility for incorporating differentiation in lessons. As the beginning teacher gains more experience, they could plan the lesson for you to teach. Sharing and swapping the planning and teaching roles in this way, especially at the participatory appropriation plane, is helpful for a beginning teacher's development.

6.2.4.4 Long-term planning

The next step for you is to support a beginning teacher in managing the transition in planning from individual lesson plans to long-term learning plans (i.e. interconnected multiple sequences of learning) for a specific unit of work or a combination of units of work. A long-term learning approach could support pupils' learning by adhering to the cognitive psychology perspective of learning as 'an alteration in long-term memory' (Sweller, 2005, p. 20). Given this definition, it stands to reason that planning pupils' learning should be focussed on making appropriate alterations to pupils' long-term memory through a series of lessons (Chapter 13). To support this, once the beginning teacher develops the ability to plan effective individual lessons focused on learning for all pupils, you could further support them in developing their planning for a sequence of lessons. Task 6.8 asks you to support a beginning teacher to develop a long-term plan based on a sequence of lessons using a unit of work and/or a combination of units of work.

Task 6.8   Long-term planning

Undertake the following steps:

1. Ask the beginning teacher to accumulate individual lesson plans from the last four to six series of lessons taught to a particular class of pupils from a specific unit of work (such as forces) or a combination (such as energy and forces).
2. Next, ask the beginning teacher to map common elements that these series of lessons present, such as:
    *   The overarching links
    *   The intended learning outcomes for the end of the sequence of lessons
    *   Some interlinking key scientific vocabularies
    *   The expected prior learning that is relevant to the unit of work
    *   Acknowledgements of common pre-conceptions/misconceptions and how to deal with them
    *   Types of assessment used across the sequence
    *   Resources and activities used across the sequence of learning.
3. Discuss the mapping of these lessons (obtained from a complete unit of work or a combination of two or three units of work) and offer the beginning teacher opportunities to develop it further for the next series of lessons.

---

4. Finally, ask the beginning teacher to reflect on planning the long-term plans (encompassing a complete unit of work or a combination of two or three units of work), rather than individual lesson plans by answering the below questions:
   - What does long-term planning of learning look like?
   - Are individual lesson plans good evidence of planning for learning?
   - What are the benefits and drawbacks to short and long-term planning (daily plans, weekly plans, monthly plans, half-term plans, and yearly plans)?
   - Based on the beginning teacher's thoughts about the above three questions consider how they would facilitate a shift in planning for individual lesson plans to a long-term planning.

Summary and key points

This chapter has explored how best to support a beginning teacher with lesson planning, highlighting:

- Self-reflection and mentoring strategies on lesson planning for pupils' long-term learning. The use of the experiential learning cycle to explore ways you can provide feedback and support a beginning teacher at different points in their journey and to grow as an autonomous teacher.
- Involvement of experienced teachers to support the beginning teacher's lesson planning practices.
- Ideas on how to support the beginning teacher in planning for learning outcomes, key questions, learning activities and associated tasks for a single lesson and how it can build further to incorporate differentiation to support learning progression for all pupils.
- The notion that the beginning teacher needs to progress from planning single lessons to planning a sequence of lessons, encompassing a complete unit of work or a combination of two or three units of work, in order to account for the development of pupils' long-term learning expectations.

Further resources

Fautley, M. and Savage, J. (2013) *Lesson Planning for Effective Learning*. Maidenhead: McGraw-Hill Education.
Fautley and Savage provide an overview of the stages of the lesson planning process and encourage beginning teachers to reflect on their practice. This book also considers lesson planning in the wider context of teaching and learning. In particular, Chapter 6 considers a number of different metaphors for teaching which you can use to encourage a beginning teacher to develop their pedagogy and become better teachers.

Savage, J. (2015) *Lesson Planning*. Abingdon: Routledge.
This book puts learning at the heart of planning, with step-by-step guidance on how and why lessons should be planned. This is a valuable tool for mentors to use to support a beginning teacher to plan lessons because it links theory to practice and provides exemplars for short and intermediate planning.

Appendix 6.1 Handout for pupils investigating the relationship between the voltage across a resistor and the current through it

Name _____   Class _____ Date _____

Title   Investigating the relationship between the voltage across a resistor and the current through it

Aim   To design an experiment to investigate the relationship between the voltage across a resistor and the current through it

Method   We designed the following circuit to investigate the relationship between current and voltage for a resistor:

Results

If you have time, plot your results on a voltage-current graph.

Conclusion

7 Supporting beginning science teachers to teach and evaluate their lessons

Morag Findlay, Saima Salehjee and Stavros A. Nikou

Introduction

This chapter aims to highlight some mentoring strategies when working with beginning teachers who are at different developmental stages of teaching. A beginning teacher you are mentoring might be observing and practising some basic teaching skills, but not yet teaching a full lesson, or they might have started to incorporate a range of teaching strategies in lessons, but these strategies are not specifically focusing on promoting pupils' learning and so on. Therefore, you should use your judgement and knowledge about the beginning teacher to identify the best mentoring strategy to use at any one time.

The chapter starts with a brief description of the stages of development using Maynard and Furlong's (1995) model of a beginning teacher's development concerning basic teaching skills, teaching strategies and teaching styles. Next, some characteristic behaviours of an effective teacher are presented. A range of mentoring steps to support the beginning teacher's journey of becoming an effective teacher, starting from early idealism then survival, recognising difficulties, hitting a plateau and finally to moving on stages of development are then given. The chapter closes with a discussion on how to support a beginning teacher to self-evaluate their lessons by using lesson debriefs (called post-lesson discussions in Chapter 8) and pupils' feedback.

Objectives

At the end of this chapter you should be able to:

- Recognise that it is a mentor's responsibility to identify a beginning teacher's stage of development and support them towards becoming an effective teacher
- Support a beginning teacher to develop the characteristic behaviours of an effective teacher
- Assist a beginning teacher to be able to identify and develop basic teaching skills, teaching strategies and a pupil-centred teaching style
- Encourage a beginning teacher to self-evaluate their lessons with the aid of lesson de-briefs and pupils' feedback.

7.1 Stages of development as a teacher

Maynard and Furlong (1995) suggested that a beginning teacher's professional development can be mapped by focusing on five-stages namely: early idealism, survival, recognising difficulties, hitting a plateau and moving on. In the early idealism stage of teacher development, a beginning teacher typically has an idealistic view of teaching and thinks that problems can be solved with goodwill. Reaching the survival stage is when the reality of teaching sets in and the beginning teacher's focus is on standing in front of a class and managing a lesson. As they gain more experience, a beginning teacher starts to recognise difficulties and anticipate these difficulties in the classroom and develop ways to teach a successful lesson. Beyond this, in the hitting a plateau stage, a beginning teacher begins to teach a short series of lessons, but does not always link their actions to their pedagogical content knowledge (PCK). In the moving on stage, a beginning teacher links their actions in the classroom to their PCK and is able to adapt their teaching strategies during a series of lessons, as appropriate. Some beginning teachers be able to utilise a pupil-centred style of teaching at the end of their initial teacher education (ITE) year, but the majority will take longer.

During Maynard and Furlong's (1995) five stages, a beginning teacher progressively develops their basic teaching skills and combines these into teaching strategies and teaching styles (Blair and Beaumont, 2020). A teaching strategy is the selection of appropriate basic teaching skills and pupil activities, such as explaining or questioning, managing classroom organisations and timings, to achieve the learning outcomes of a lesson. Over time, a beginning teacher begins to develop a range of teaching strategies that eventually leads to a pupil-centred teaching style.

Figure 7.1 depicts the relationship between basic teaching skills, teaching strategies and teaching styles. The evolving process of developing basic teaching skills, strategies and styles is dynamic, it develops as a beginning teacher takes greater responsibility and develops autonomy, but at the same time, it follows a linear progression in relation to the five-stages of development (Maynard and Furlong, 1995). These are shown on the left in Figure 7.1 and some different learning strategies applied at each level are on the right in Figure 7.1. This chapter discusses these evolving developmental stages and provides a range of mentoring strategies that can be adopted/adapted to support a beginning teacher's development as an effective teacher. [It is important to note that there is no fixed correlation between Maynard and Furlong's stages of development and the development of autonomy and responsibility by a beginning teacher].

As a mentor, your focus should be to facilitate the development and improvement of a beginning teacher's basic teaching skills and to build their teaching strategies to eventually develop their own teaching style. The level of support a beginning teacher needs from their mentor varies from considerable guidance to minimal guidance, depending on their experience, responsibility and autonomy about teaching science (Shea and Greenwood, 2007). Taking this into account, the effectiveness of different mentoring approaches is not the same at all stages of development. It also differs from beginning teacher to beginning teacher. Therefore, it is a mentor's responsibility to identify and support different aspects of a beginning teacher's teaching practices and provide differentiated levels of assistance.

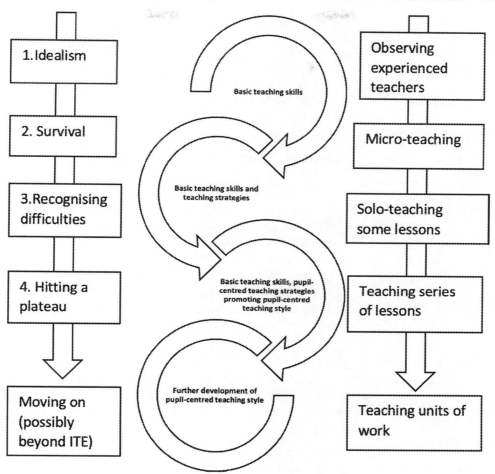

Figure 7.1 Stages of teacher development related to a beginning teacher's increasing responsibility and autonomy
(Source: Adapted from Maynard and Furlong (1995))

Before presenting some differentiated mentoring strategies to support the development of a beginning teacher's classroom-based teaching practices at different stages of development, the next section considers five characteristic behaviours of effective teachers. This guides further discussion on how to support the development of a beginning teacher's basic teaching skills, teaching strategies and pupil-centred teaching style, in all five-stages of teachers' development.

7.2 Characteristic behaviours of effective teachers

There are a variety of views about what constitutes an effective teacher. However, we believe that there is probably general agreement about five characteristics of effective teachers,

96 *Findlay et al.*

even if these characteristics can be viewed in different ways. These characteristics develop gradually from the early idealism to moving on stage of development (Maynard and Furlong, 1995). This gradual development varies from one beginning teacher to another, as mentioned above. Before presenting these five characteristics of an effective teacher, Task 7.1 asks you to list your top five characteristics of an effective teacher, then compare your characteristics with the five characteristics below.

Task 7.1 Characteristic behaviours of effective teachers

There are many characteristics of an effective teacher, therefore:

Step 1. List your top five characteristics of an effective teacher
Step 2. Next, read the suggested characteristics presented in this section of the chapter
Step 3. While reading the suggested characteristics of an effective teacher link/compare/ contrast them with the characteristics that you listed in Step 1
Step 4. Finally, using some guidance from the five characteristics identified in this section, identify some mentoring strategies you can use to support a beginning teacher to develop the characteristic behaviours of an effective teacher.

The five characteristics that we believe are necessary for a beginning teacher to develop as they move from Maynard and Furlong's (1995) idealism to moving on stages of development are calmness, clarity, consistency, care and confidence.

7.2.1 Calmness

Thinking back to your own experience, you might recall some of the beginning teachers you have observed, who tended to get flustered, were disorganised and probably shouted a lot, as well as blaming the class or individuals when things went wrong. You might consider that their classrooms were not calm environments that were conducive to learning! Therefore, from the period of initial idealism, you need to support a beginning teacher to understand that pupils appreciate teachers who are calm. Throughout the different stages of development, you need to encourage the beginning teacher to think carefully about ways they can develop themselves as a calm teacher by creating an atmosphere where pupils feel safe to learn. At first, probably during the early idealism and survival stages of development, you can model such calm environments with some of the classes you teach and discuss the approaches you use to promote calmness in the classrooms. The choice of classes could include lessons where the beginning teacher finds it difficult to keep the classroom environment calm. During later stages of development, when the beginning teacher is teaching some solo-lessons or a series of lessons, you could ask them to reflect and discuss their current classroom environments, focusing on ways they plan to keep calmness in their classrooms, what works and what support they need from you to make it better.

Teach and evaluate lessons 97

7.2.2 Clarity

From the time they first enter a classroom, a beginning teacher is talking to pupils individually, in groups and/or as a class. For a beginning teacher, in the early idealism stage of development, in particular, they need to ensure they are enunciating clearly (such as asking clear questions, explaining complicated ideas and giving clear instructions), among other things. Therefore, starting from the early stages of development, you need to encourage the beginning teacher to think about how they will explain concepts to pupils, what questions they will be asking the pupils, what questions they expect pupils to ask them and to plan their teaching accordingly. A key part of preparing clear instructions is to carry out activities in advance and identify key points that pupils may find difficult so that the instructions are clear for pupils. For example, a simple experiment might include asking pupils to use a burning splint to heat different volumes of water in a boiling tube and to record the rise in temperature. A beginning teacher will have some idea of the temperature rises expected. However, by carrying out the experiment in advance, they are able to think about conceptual difficulties pupils may have, such as calculating a change in temperature and why a burning splint is used to heat different volumes of water, et cetera.

7.2.3 Consistency

One of the characteristics of teachers that can really upset pupils is when they perceive a lack of fairness in a teacher's actions. It is worth discussing this at your weekly mentoring meetings with a beginning teacher you are mentoring, especially during the early stages of their development. For instance, John, a Year 8 pupil, calls out funny names to address other pupils in the class and is simply told by the beginning teacher 'not to do it again', but when James in the same class does the same thing, he receives a punishment exercise. Share this scenario with the beginning teacher and ask them to think about how these two incidents would be perceived by John, James and by the other pupils in the class and what, as a teacher, they could do differently so that all pupils are treated consistently. You could also share some of your experiences with the beginning teacher when pupils complain about lack of fairness in a teacher's actions. You should also discuss the importance of the beginning teacher learning about the school and departmental behaviour management policies so that they can apply them fairly and consistently. In addition, you should also encourage the beginning teacher to consider an approach to a variety of likely classroom scenarios so that they are prepared in advance for fairness and consistency. For example, what will they do if a pupil needs a pencil? What happens if a glass beaker is accidentally broken? We believe that when a beginning teacher thinks through likely classroom scenarios in this way, there is less need for ad hoc teachers' actions during the lesson. Developing these thinking processes during different stages of a beginning teacher's development could reduce the potential for perceived unfairness. It is also likely to increase the beginning teacher's ability to maintain a productive learning environment while dealing consistently with classroom issues according to the school's and/or science department's behaviour management policies.

98   *Findlay et al.*

7.2.4 Care

Encourage a beginning teacher to do simple things that demonstrate a caring relationship with their pupils. For example, when a beginning teacher is observing experienced teachers, they can start to learn pupils' names. Subsequently, addressing pupils by name can make a huge difference to their relationship with a class. You could also advise them to use a class map to learn pupils' names and share any techniques you use to learn pupils' names.

Beginning from the survival stage of development, a beginning teacher needs to start building a teacher–pupil relationship. This relationship can be built by chatting to pupils outside the classroom while they are lining up before they go into the classroom. For example, the beginning teacher might ask how their day has been so far or if they are in any after school clubs, et cetera. These chats could also take place during break time about things that interest pupils such as sports, television programmes, books they have read recently, the latest mobile phone/video game, et cetera. Chatting in this way can give a lot of information about what does or does not interest pupils and why, and how their interests can make its way in the science classrooms. These chats also make pupils feel that their (beginning) teacher cares about them as individuals. Therefore, you need to make the beginning teacher aware of the importance of these informal chats to help them plan lessons that reflect the pupils' interests where possible.

7.2.5 Confidence

Starting a teaching career can be challenging for a beginning teacher. Working with potentially dozens or hundreds of pupils is also a challenge, so it is not surprising that some beginning teachers feel that they lack confidence. At this point, the old adage 'fake it until you make it' can be useful. Therefore, if you find the beginning teacher you are mentoring working hard on planning how to teach a lesson in an interesting way but they are not teaching it this way due to their lack of confidence, then encourage them to act as if they are confident, by being calm and using confident body language in front of the class. We consider that acting in this way will gradually develop a beginning teacher's confidence, which could eventually result in confident teaching.

Another indicator of developing confidence is less teacher talk and more pupil talk in a lesson. A typical beginning teacher, because of lack in confidence, will give explanations or instructions by talking to the pupils themselves, thus adopting a teacher-centred approach. Therefore, to increase their confidence, you need to encourage the beginning teacher to plan how they give explanations or instructions by incorporating more questions and interactions with pupils. This has an additional benefit in that the less teacher talk there is in a classroom, the more the pupils talk about science (Figure 7.2), and so the more science they learn.

In supporting the development of confidence in this way, share the confidence graph (Figure 7.2) with a beginning teacher you are mentoring, ideally at the survival stage, when they are teaching a small number of lessons (or micro-teaching, see section on survival stage below). Review the lesson plan and accompanying lesson observations with them. Later, at the stages of recognising difficulties, hitting a plateau and moving on, i.e. probably when they are teaching a whole lesson or a series of lessons, revisit the graph and discuss the

Teach and evaluate lessons 99

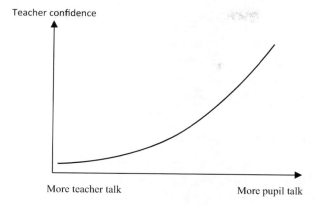

Figure 7.2 A schematic representation showing that as beginning teachers become more confident, they tend to talk less and the pupils tend to talk more

beginning teacher's confidence level. You need to support a beginning teacher in mapping their confidence levels, based on less teacher talk and more pupil talk. This confidence mapping requires you to ask and discuss some questions with the beginning teacher, such as where does the beginning teacher view themselves on the confidence graph and why? How much were teacher talk and pupil talk evident in the lesson? Did teacher talk decline and pupil talk increase over a series of lessons? How can the beginning teacher increase their confidence by accommodating more pupil talk about science and less teacher talk?

Task 7.2 asks you to allow a beginning teacher to develop their thoughts about their strengths and challenges in becoming an effective teacher. This task will also provide an opportunity for you to identify the beginning teacher's needs and your action points to support them in developing calmness, clarity, consistency, care and confidence in their teaching practices.

Task 7.2 Supporting a beginning teacher to identify strengths and areas of challenge in becoming an effective teacher

Complete the following:

- Encourage a beginning teacher to identify some teaching approaches they have observed or are already using in the classroom to be calm, clear, consistent, caring and confident.
- Then ask them to identify one challenge they face in each of these five characteristic areas mentioned above.
- Having identified the challenges, ask the beginning teacher to observe two or three other teachers and identify approaches the observed teachers use so that these challenges do not arise in their classes.
- Encourage the beginning teacher to discuss other teaching approaches with you and then plan to implement them in their classes.

The steps above can be repeated at three different intervals depending on the teaching load of the beginning teacher, such as, first, when they have started to plan and teach mini-sections of a lesson, such as starter activities only, then when they have begun to take on the responsibility of teaching a few lessons to one class or different classes. Third, when they are taking almost a full teaching load of solo-teaching sessions in your school.

7.3 A beginning teacher teaching lessons and mentor's support

As mentioned earlier in the chapter, the support you offer to a beginning teacher in their development into an effective teacher changes over time. This section considers practical steps in supporting a beginning teacher's development, starting from recommending they observe and practise basic teaching skills, developing teaching strategies to promote pupils learning and, finally developing a pupil-centred teaching style. These practical steps will be linked to Maynard and Furlong's (1995) stages of development and with a beginning teacher's increasing responsibility, from micro-teaching to teaching some solo-lessons, to teaching a series of lessons. However, as discussed above, different beginning teachers move through these developmental stages at different rates so there may be overlaps between different stages of a beginning teacher's development, and where they are in terms of their teaching timetable and responsibilities.

7.3.1 Early idealism stage of development

One of the most daunting experiences for many beginning teachers during the early idealism stage of development is standing in front of a class for the first time and learning to embed basic teaching skills in their day-to-day teaching. Thus, as a mentor you need to identify ways by which you can support the development of basic teaching skills by a beginning teacher in their early stages of development. Having said that, we believe that, depending on the performance and individual needs of a beginning teacher, sometimes you need to strengthen and/or recap these basic teaching skills even later in their developmental journey.

There are a wide range of basic teaching skills that beginning teachers need to develop, some of which will be stronger than others for any one beginning teacher (Kyriacou, 2018). In our view, these basic teaching skills incorporate teaching practices that align with the five characteristic behaviours for becoming an effective teacher, above. Some examples of these basic teaching skills are listed in Table 7.1, along with some possible characteristic behaviours of an effective teacher. Task 7.3 asks you to read and augment Table 7.1.

Task 7.3 Characteristic behaviours of an effective teacher and basic teaching skills

Follow the steps below:

Step 1. Look at Table 7.1. Do you agree with the examples of basic teaching skills?

Step 2. What other basic teaching skills would you add to the second column of the list? (Some characteristic behaviours and skills occur in more than one place in the table).

Teach and evaluate lessons 101

Table 7.1 Some examples of basic teaching skills (based on Bassett, Bowler and Newton, 2019, pp. 172–174; and Kyriacou, 2018) aligned with some characteristic behaviours of an effective teacher

Characteristic behaviours of an effective teacher	Some basic teaching skills
Calmness	Looking and sounding like a calm teacher.
	Managing a positive classroom environment.
Clarity	Embedding clear instructions (for themselves and for the pupils) to effectively carry out learning activities.
	Preparing classroom organisation and management in advance. Getting attention and providing instructions.
Consistency	Awareness of what is happening in the classroom ('eyes in the back of your head') and demonstrating fairness in their actions for all pupils.
	Following school and departmental procedures and routines.
Caring	Building positive relationships.
	Reinforcing expectations.
	Balanced use of praise.
Confidence	Looking and sounding like a confident teacher. Self-evaluation of strengths and development needs.

These basic teaching skills mainly start to develop in the early stages of a beginning teacher's development, namely during early idealism and survival stages, and require some reinforcement at the beginning of the recognising difficulties stages of development.

Now, referring to Table 7.1, your experiences both as a beginning teacher yourself and as a mentor, reflect on some of the challenges that a beginning teacher you are mentoring could face while standing in front of a class for the first time. So, how can you support the beginning teacher to deal with these challenges? Then using your accounts gained from Task 7.3, discuss some basic (day-to-day) teaching skills with the beginning teacher to help them identify areas of strength and areas for development. Since observation is very important in this stage of a teacher's development, in Task 7.4 you are asked to work with the beginning teacher to help them to identify some basic teaching skills that they have observed by viewing experienced teachers using certain basic skills and then to consider how they could develop such skills in their practice.

Task 7.4 Assisting a beginning teacher to develop their basic teaching skills at the early stages of development

1. When a beginning teacher you are mentoring is observing experienced teachers, ask them to fill in Table 7.2. They should note examples of basic teaching skills in column two and link these to one of the five characteristic behaviours of effective teachers presented in Table 7.1.
2. Next, during your weekly mentoring meetings, ask the beginning teacher to discuss the first two columns of Table 7.2. Then, support them to consider their next steps, drawn from their observations of experienced teachers and encourage them to complete column three of Table 7.1.

---

102 Findlay et al.

Table 7.2 Links between the characteristic behaviours of effective teachers, associated basic teaching skills and a beginning teacher's next steps in developing these skills

Characteristic behaviours of an effective teacher	Observed basic teaching skills	Next steps for beginning teacher

During the weekly mentoring meeting, as mentioned in Task 7.4, you may want to discuss the following points with the beginning teacher:

- The appearance of the experienced teachers – how do the teachers dress to present themselves as teachers? Smart/casual? Lab coat/no lab coat?
- Body language of the experienced teachers – open or closed. How do teachers demonstrate confidence?
- Experienced teachers' voice, tone, volume, pitch. How do the teachers manage their classes by using voice alone?
- Confidence of the experienced teachers – How do they show confidence in the classrooms?
- What strategies were they following for pupils' entrances and exits from the classroom?
- What were the teaching instructions during transitions between activities?
- What routines for collecting and returning equipment and homework were followed?

In addition to Task 7.4, you may want to encourage the beginning teacher to read relevant units from Capel, Leask and Younie (2019b), for example:

- Unit 2.3 Taking responsibility for whole lessons
- Unit 3.1 Communicating with pupils
- Unit 3.2 Motivating pupils
- Unit 3.3 Managing classroom behaviour.

You could discuss the tasks from these units with the beginning teacher to assist them to develop basic teaching skills, and also revisit and modify Table 7.1, during later stages of their development (ideally every month).

7.3.2 Survival stage of development

The survival stage is where you can reduce the number of observations made by a beginning teacher of experienced teachers (as in the early idealism stage of development) and offer opportunities to the beginning teacher to conduct some micro-teaching sessions.

Teach and evaluate lessons 103

Micro-teaching involves a beginning teacher planning (see Chapter 6) and then teaching part of a lesson, such as a lesson starter or a short demonstration of an activity. Now read Case study 7.1, where the mentor, Henry, is supporting a beginning teacher, Hanniyah. Task 7.5 asks you to plan questions that you would ask the beginning teacher to support their development.

Case study 7.1: Hanniyah and Henry

Hanniyah is planning a lesson about preparing different concentration of solutions. Henry, the mentor, suggests that the pupils have probably forgotten how to measure the volume of a liquid accurately and he suggests that Hanniyah plans and teaches a lesson starter about using a measuring cylinder before he takes the lead. Hanniyah researches information about different kinds of menisci and how to measure concave menisci for clear and coloured liquids (such as water and a solution of potassium permanganate) and a convex meniscus like mercury (Denby, 2018; Helmenstine, 2019). Hanniyah decides to remind pupils that the measuring cylinder should be on a level surface and that the pupil's eye must be level with the meniscus for an accurate reading. Hanniyah proposes that the learning outcome for the lesson starter is that pupils will be able to use a measuring cylinder accurately to measure the volume of clear liquids. Henry agrees, but asks Hanniyah to consider how to measure the achievement of the learning outcome. Hanniyah suggests using a series of multiple-choice questions using photographs or drawings of menisci in measuring cylinders. The pupils will use show-me-boards to record their answers and then explain their thinking via verbal questioning. Hanniyah also suggests that the pupils use measuring cylinders to measure 25 ml of water to show that they can measure liquids accurately.

In the discussion, they also decide that Hanniyah will line the pupils up outside the laboratory and then bring them in to begin the lesson starter. This will allow Hanniyah to establish herself as the teacher by using existing classroom routines and practising using her teacher's voice.

Task 7.5   Survival stage: Micro-teaching and mentoring support

Complete the following steps:

Step 1. Thinking about Table 7.1 and Case study 7.1, list questions that you could ask a beginning teacher, to support them to incorporate the basic teaching skills indicated below:

- Maintaining health and safety in the classroom
- Managing relationships and reinforcing expectations
- Gaining attention and providing instructions
- Maintaining classroom organisation and management

104   *Findlay et al.*

- Self-evaluating the strengths and weaknesses of their teaching
- Incorporating effective technology integration.

Step 2. Next, observe the beginning teacher's micro-teaching part of the lesson (you could use the lesson observation template from Chapter 8 (p. 126) to record your observations).

Step 3. If required, add further questions (during or after the observation) to the list of questions that you listed in Step 1.

Step 4. After the lesson, ask the beginning teacher to reflect on their micro-teaching session by asking them to answer and discuss the list of questions obtained from Steps 1 and 3.

Step 5. Finally, support the beginning teacher to plan next steps based on their reflections on the micro-teaching sessions.

Some sample reflective questions supporting Steps 4 and 5 of Task 7.5 could be (in this list 'I' refers to the beginning teacher):

- How will I pay attention to health and safety?
- What classroom routines will I follow for consistency?
- What instructions will I give the pupils? How I can make the instructions clearer? Should I repeat the instructions (or not)?
- What classroom management strategies will I adopt to engage all the pupils? How will I:
  o Spot and deal with low-level disruption effectively
  o Use praise and encouragement
  o Deal with wrong answers positively
  o Deal with unexpected events?
- How will I use my voice and body language to reinforce instructions?
- During group work, how frequently will I move from one group to another?
- Will I spend more or less time with particular group of pupils and why?
- How will I stick to the timings in the lesson plan or adapt appropriately?
- What are typical types of things that I should say at different points in a lesson?
- What are some of the teacher scripts I will use? such as:
  o Pens and pencils on the desk; bags under the desk and hang up your jackets
  o Start the activity
  o Stop
  o Eyes on the board
  o Pens down.

7.3.3 Recognising difficulties stage of development

After the survival stage, teachers usually start recognising numerous difficulties associated with their development as a teacher. By now, teachers are responsible for a whole lesson for

Teach and evaluate lessons   105

the first time; a milestone for any beginning teacher. Therefore, it is important to provide a beginning teacher you are mentoring with the support needed to overcome any perceived difficulties. During this stage of development, you need to encourage a beginning teacher to consider everything discussed in developmental stages one (idealism) and two (survival) for a whole lesson. Supporting the beginning teacher in this stage of development mainly requires you to encourage them to revisit some basic teaching skills and start considering a few teaching strategies that can promote pupils' learning. Some approaches to meet these mentoring requirements are presented below.

7.3.3.1 Revisiting basic teaching skills

In terms of lesson preparation and planning, the beginning teacher will plan an interesting and engaging lesson. However, at the start of the recognising difficulties stage, a beginning teacher may fail to recognise some basic skills, such as does the equipment need to be ordered from the technicians in advance? How do I encourage positive behaviour? How will I implement the school's behaviour management plan? What are foreseeable problems in the lesson, and how will I deal with them? Are there other basic teaching skills that I need to consider?

We believe that at the start of this developmental stage, you need to suggest to the beginning teacher that they keep revisiting and updating Table 7.1 to apply basic teaching skills consistently in their teaching practice, until these practices become part of their teaching routine. Next, you should observe at least one of their initial solo-taught lessons with a focus on the implementation of basic teaching skills. Task 7.6 asks you to do this.

Task 7.6   Recognising difficulties stage and mentoring support

Complete the following steps to guide a beginning teacher to develop some basic teaching skills:

1.   Observe a beginning teacher's lesson, focusing on a particular basic teaching skill or a combination of skills – see Table 7.1. Make sure you agree the main focus of the observation with the beginning teacher beforehand.
2.   In the post-lesson discussions listen to the beginning teachers' reflections on the lesson and give them your feedback gained from the lesson observation, encouraging the beginning teacher to reflect on the feedback provided.
3.   Use a copy of Table 7.2 to record some of your observations and further actions required.
4.   Next, following from the feedback and discussions, offer your support to the beginning teacher to strengthen their existing basic teaching skills or to initiate teaching skills that are essential but not yet a priority for them.

7.3.3.2 Teaching strategies

In addition to reinforcing some basic teaching skills, a beginning teacher needs to develop their teaching strategies. To this end, we recommend that you ask the beginning teacher to

106 *Findlay et al.*

read Mosston and Ashworth's continuum of teaching styles article (Mosston and Ashworth, 2002) (see further resources). However, it is important to note that what Mosston and Ashworth term teaching styles are usually referred to as teaching strategies, so we are using the term teaching strategies and not teaching styles when referring to Mosston and Ashworth's continuum.

During this developmental stage, a good starting point is to discuss some teaching strategies with the beginning teacher. One reason for this is that, at this stage, some beginning teachers feel that they must plan to control everything that happens in the classroom, resulting in a teacher-centred approach to learning (such as Mosston and Ashworth's (2002) command and practice strategies). Asking a beginning teacher to read Mosston and Ashworth's continuum supports them to consider moving to a more pupil-centred approach to learning. For example, rather than the beginning teacher giving instructions to pupils (exhibiting a direction-giving teaching strategy) for an activity, they could use questioning to develop the details of the activity with the class and have the pupils agree on how they would carry out the activity (exhibiting a collaborative problem-solving teaching strategy). In addition, you could discuss these different teaching strategies with the beginning teacher. You could model this for them in your practice and discuss the suitability of these teaching strategies for the lessons you have taught. Next, you can help the beginning teacher to suggest, recognise, choose and justify their choice of incorporating some specific teaching strategies, which they think are appropriate for two to three lessons that they are about to teach. This exercise should help the beginning teacher to understand that not all lessons should be teacher-led, nor can they be completely pupil-led: instead, it depends on the learning outcomes, safety issues and pupil needs. Some examples of teaching strategies are presented in the next part of this section (Hitting a plateau stage of development).

At this stage of development – or at a later stage – you could then support a beginning teacher to teach lessons using a pupil-centred approach to learning (linked to Mosston and Ashworth's continuum). You then need to observe the beginning teacher's lessons and provide feedback focusing on teaching strategies that promote (or not) pupil-centred teaching approaches to learning science.

7.3.4 *Hitting a plateau stage of development*

Another major milestone in a beginning teacher's development is moving from teaching one lesson at a time to planning and teaching a short series of three or four lessons within a unit of work for the same class of pupils (such as Year 9 pupils) included in the science curriculum, such as cell biology (a description of this unit of work can be seen Appendix 10.1). At this stage, the beginning teacher is beginning to know the class and can see how each lesson fits into the overarching unit of work. Teaching several consecutive lessons allows them to make their lessons more pupil-centred. They can build on their developing knowledge of teaching to make the most of their basic teaching skills (as part of their day-to-day teaching routine), incorporating observed and/or practised teaching strategies with an aim of promoting pupils' learning. Therefore, reaching this stage of development, a beginning teacher should spend more time considering the learning aspects of a unit of work, including how to help pupils to learn more effectively, taking account of the differentiated learning needs of individuals (see

Teach and evaluate lessons 107

Chapter 6). All these learning-oriented practices potentially require the beginning teacher to use a broader range of teaching strategies in their teaching.

One of the challenges mentors face supporting beginning teachers is to use a wide range of teaching strategies, as they (beginning teachers) start to rely too much on a few teaching strategies that work for them, and become reluctant to try new/different strategies. So, how can you encourage the beginning teacher you are mentoring to try a range of teaching strategies? A starting point could be to ask them to identify a variety of research-based teaching strategies (Muijs and Reynolds, 2018) and to include these strategies across a series of lessons they are about to teach. At this point, you need to encourage the beginning teacher to consider which teaching strategy is most pedagogically appropriate for each lesson (or a part of a lesson) and the pupils they are teaching. Through this encouragement, a beginning teacher will strengthen their PCK (see Chapter 10) and develop their pupil-centred teaching style in a research-informed way. Particularly at this stage of development, your focus should be to encourage the beginning teacher to use a variety of pupil-centred teaching strategies that could enable pupils to achieve the intended learning outcome(s) over a series of lessons (see Chapters 6 on planning learning outcomes). A variety of assessment for learning strategies can be helpful here. Chapter 12, section 4 presents some strategies to support the beginning teacher to develop formative use of rich questioning, comment-only marking, self- and peer-assessment and formative use of summative tests, et cetera, promoting the learning of science for all pupils. Next, some useful and varied teaching strategies for you to ask a beginning teacher you mentor to use are suggested. You can adopt/adapt as appropriate. In addition, there are many more teaching strategies a beginning teacher can try.

7.3.4.1 Use of questioning

Show-me-boards, for example, is a tool to allow all pupils to answer questions. They can be useful at any stage of a lesson. You can advise a beginning teacher to lay out a mini-whiteboard, a marker pen and a duster for every pupil before the lesson starts. You can then suggest ways to use these whiteboards so that all the pupils are engaged and show their answers at once and there is no copying. For example, the beginning teacher asks a closed question (such as what is the atomic number of the element chlorine) and then uses a countdown, 'three, two, one, show me'. Another use is to ask groups of pupils to construct a joint answer to an open question (such as what are the advantages and disadvantages of using chlorine in a swimming pool).

You must encourage the beginning teacher not only to check pupils' right and wrong answers but also to see what pupils think and how they reach those answers. This can be achieved by encouraging them to provide opportunities to the pupils to give a wide range of responses. Moreover, it is useful to discuss ways of using pupils' responses and misconceptions as a body of evidence to plan and teach their future lessons. Chapter 11 presents ways to cope and use unexpected questions and answers that arise in the teaching of science.

7.3.4.2 Incorporating group work

A beginning teacher needs to recognise that the aim of teaching is to promote pupils' learning and that learning is a social activity. Hence, using teaching strategies that require

108 *Findlay et al.*

pupils to work in pairs or groups can strengthen pupils' learning. You could ask a beginning teacher you are mentoring to choose groups for the pupils by matching pupils' strengths and weaknesses so that all pupils benefit from the group work. The beginning teacher should also realise that putting pupils into groups with different strengths could help pupils (with a range of learning needs) to develop their science skills and understanding. Next, ask the beginning teacher to select an appropriate group work strategy such as paired discussion in a think-pair-share activity, groups of pupils working together during experimental work in a discussion group or completing a longer-term project, et cetera. Once the beginning teacher has selected an appropriate strategy, you can ask them to reflect on why they think this particular group work-based activity is appropriate to boost pupils' learning. During this reflection, you can discuss how different group work strategies can be adapted, or differentiated, to cater for the needs of different pupils. In addition, you can allow the beginning teacher to allocate group roles to pupils and discuss the benefits of changing these roles regularly to develop pupils' science skills and understanding. Chapter 16 (pp. 253–254) suggests some mentoring suggestions on selecting group roles and responsibilities for the pupils.

7.3.4.3 *Use of texts*

Science textbooks provide textual and visual content for most of the science curriculum and can be supplemented with additional books or internet resources. In addition to using a science textbook, you may suggest that a beginning teacher uses a range of other text-related materials (for example, news items from *New Scientist* magazine, science mnemonics and word-pictures from TES website and abstracts/articles from student friendly magazines such as *BBC Science Focus*, et cetera) mainly because pupils find scientific text (from the textbook) challenging to read (SERP, 2020). Some examples of activities related to scientific texts are given below.

- You could model some of your lessons where you extend the use of written texts to promote pupils' learning of a scientific concept. For example, ask pupils to read a particular section of a book, such as the process of fractional distillation to distil different fractions from crude oil. Then, from their reading of the text and diagrams develop a flow chart, mind map or SWOT (strengths, weaknesses, opportunities or threats) analysis chart to present their understanding of distillation.
- A useful strategy for reading scientific texts is to introduce pupils to the Greek and Latin roots of many scientific words, such as photosynthesis, and the prefixes and suffixes used across the sciences (Feez and Quinn, 2017). For example, photosynthesis comes from the Greek word photos (light) and synthesis (making) and so means making with light – in this case making glucose from carbon dioxide and water in the presence of light. The word oxidation can be broken down into 'oxi' or related to oxygen and 'dation', which refers to a process. So, at an elementary level, oxidation occurs when an element reacts with oxygen or, more correctly, it is the process of losing electrons.
- You could also suggest using numbers as alphabetical codes to support learning scientific vocabulary. For example, which scientific process contains 15, 24, 9, 4, 1, 20, 9, 15 and 14? where the first letter 'o' is the fifteenth letter in the English alphabet (the answer is

Teach and evaluate lessons 109

oxidation). Alternatively, the letters of which chemical process add up to 111? or name the process where electrons are given away during a chemical reaction- hint – the code of the process adds up to 111.

- You could also advise the beginning teacher to incorporate newspaper articles and science magazines to stimulate critical dialogues in the classroom (McClune and Jarman, 2012). One way to do this is to use a discussion board, i.e. using the classroom whiteboard/smartboard to list evidence for and against pupils' ideas about a particular newspaper article, scientific discovery or scientific myth. Consider using mentoring approaches detailed in Chapter 15, which suggest some teaching strategies to use historical, contemporary and science fiction-based stories to stimulate pupils' critical thinking, raise awareness of societal issues, learning scientific vocabulary and awareness of misconceptions.

Task 7.7 asks you to reflect on your mentoring practices to support a beginning teacher who has moved on from teaching a solo-lesson to a series of lessons.

Task 7.7   Hitting a plateau – mentoring support

Answer the following questions to reflect on ways you can support a beginning teacher to teach a series of lessons:

1. How does your mentoring role change as a beginning teacher begins to plan a sequence of lessons?
2. How will you encourage the beginning teacher to reflect on a lesson and then use this reflection to inform the next lesson(s) in a sequence without starting to plan again from scratch?
3. How will you support the beginning teacher to use different teaching strategies by focusing on pupils' learning over the sequence of lessons rather than one lesson at a time?
4. Almost inevitably, in a sequence of lessons, some things will not go as well as expected or some teaching strategies may not work. So, what will you do to support the beginning teacher to come out of their comfort zone of using a particular teaching strategy that they believe works well and avoiding those that seem challenging? For example, if a particular strategy did not work in one lesson, it does not mean that it will never work. So, how will you support the beginning teacher to manage these aspects of learning to teach over days and weeks?

7.3.5 *Moving on*

This stage of development offers much more autonomy to a beginning teacher, as by now they should be independently teaching a series of lessons for a complete unit(s) of work using effective basic teaching skills and a wide variety of teaching strategies to promote

110   *Findlay et al.*

pupils learning. Therefore, as a mentor, you need to facilitate a beginning teacher to develop their teaching style by supporting them to develop a pupil-centred style of teaching. You can facilitate this by asking the beginning teacher to reflect on the actions they take to make their basic teaching skills and teaching strategies pupil-centred, and how these skills and strategies aligns with pupil-centred teaching style.

Most beginning teachers probably reach this stage after they have completed their ITE programme. However, we recommend you start supporting the beginning teacher to reflect on how basic teaching skills and teaching strategies align with pupil-centred teaching style while they are still in the ITE programme, as it will support them to achieve an effective pupil-centred teaching style before taking a full responsibility of teaching as a newly qualified teacher (NQT).

7.4 Evaluation of a beginning teacher's progress

A beginning science teacher's ability to self-evaluate their own teaching practice develops over time, aided by mentor/experienced teachers' feedbacks. In addition, part of the beginning teacher's self-evaluation requires feedback from pupils which they evaluate to improve the quality of teaching and learning. In this section of the chapter, we present some mentoring strategies that you can use to encourage a beginning teacher to evaluate their teaching effectively.

7.4.1 *Self-evaluations of lesson debrief*

A beginning teacher is regularly observed by you and/or by other experienced teachers to offer feedback during lesson debriefs, to strengthen their teaching practice. At the same time, it is necessary for the beginning teacher to self-evaluate their teaching practices, to enable them to develop their future practice. Therefore, you need to support a beginning teacher you are mentoring to self-evaluate their lessons, at all stages of development, such as after teaching: a micro-teaching lesson (probably during the survival stage of development), an individual lesson (probably during recognising difficulties stage of development), a series of lessons (probably during hitting a plateau stage of development) and teaching complete units of work (probably during moving on stage of development).

A discussion on self-evaluations based on a part/whole lesson debrief or a combination of lesson debriefs is ideally conducted every week in weekly mentoring meetings (Chapter 9, section 1, describes the difference between lesson debrief and weekly mentoring meetings). One of the skills that you need to support the beginning teacher to develop is to think of aspects of the lesson that went well (or not). This can be reinforced by initiating a discussion on lesson debriefs to talk about three things the beginning teacher did well and how these three things can be strengthened further and then talk about three things that did not go well and how they can develop this aspect. This evaluation process can be supported by using the WRAP (Wonder, Reinforce, Adjust, Plan) feedback framework (see Chapter 8, pp. 129–131). In addition, you could suggest to the

Teach and evaluate lessons 111

beginning teacher that they map their self-evaluations over time. Task 7.8 asks you to encourage a beginning teacher you are mentoring to self-evaluate their development along with some discussions with you progressively.

Task 7.8   Self-evaluation and mentor-mentee discussions

To support mentor-mentee discussions based on self-evaluations:

1. First share Appendix 7.1 with the beginning teacher and discuss the scope of the terms basic teaching skills, teaching strategies and pupil-centred teaching style. Some examples of basic teaching skills and teaching strategies are provided in the Appendix 7.1
2. Next, under the Week 1 part of the basic teaching skills and/or teaching strategies, ask the beginning teacher to identify and evaluate some specific basic teaching skills and/or teaching strategies, they practised during the week. They could mark these as (i) one of their best, (ii) one of their worst and (iii) a new basic teaching skill and/or strategy that they will be planning to develop in the following week

[To keep these evaluations concise, you could advise the beginning teacher to limit their evaluations to 100 words for each of the chosen basic teaching skill and/or teaching strategy, or use bullet points to make their notes brief.]

3. Next, encourage the beginning teacher to continue evaluating their lessons in a similar way for the next three weeks
4. Finally, arrange a meeting with the beginning teacher so that they can share the evaluations they have gathered over the four weeks. During this meeting you need to keep refocusing the beginning teacher's evaluations on basic teaching skills and teaching strategies and discuss how their effective use of some basic teaching skills and different teaching strategies can develop a pupil-centred teaching style. Encourage the beginning teacher to record these in the pupil-centred teaching style section of Appendix 7.1
5. You can repeat this cycle after every month or whenever you and/or the beginning teacher feel the need to reinforce some basic teaching skills and teaching strategies to strengthen pupil-centred teaching style.

7.4.2 Self-evaluations of pupils' feedback

Pupils' feedback on teaching strategies can be very useful, especially when a beginning teacher has started to teach a series of lessons. During this time, a beginning teacher has used a number of teaching strategies, so pupils have enough experience to provide feedback about the beginning teacher. This feedback should be formative for the beginning teacher to enable them to adjust their teaching strategies appropriately. The pupil feedback could be obtained via discussion or anonymously via sticky-notes or a class

112 *Findlay et al.*

representative. Some statements, along with feedback options, are given in brackets are given below. A beginning teacher could consider using these in order to gather pupils' feedback ('I' refers to pupils below):

- If I don't understand something, the teacher explains it to me (Never/sometimes/often/always).
- I understood today's lesson (Not at all/a little/a bit/a lot).
- Today's lesson was interesting (Not at all/a little/a bit/a lot).
- I can choose who I want to work with (Never/sometimes/often/always).
- The teacher helps me self-evaluate my learning (Never/sometimes/often/always).
- I can suggest a science topic that interests me (Never/sometimes/often/always).
- I like science (Not at all/a little/a bit/a lot).

These statements and feedback options can be extended by asking pupils to write the reasons for their choice of option given in brackets. For example, if the pupil chose 'a little bit' for the statement 'today's lesson was interesting' the beginning teacher can provide an opportunity to the pupil to write why they think that? and so on.

To gather pupils' feedback, you need to support the beginning teacher to use different tools to gather evidence of pupils' learning progression. In doing this, you can support them by modelling the use of some effective tools that you use to gather pupils' feedback. For example, asking pupils to: evaluate the lesson using traffic lights (red – I do not understand; amber – I understand some of the lesson; green – I understand the lesson), make a personal learning portfolio, design a concept map based on what they have learned (or not), use smartphones as polling devices to monitor pupils' engagement using apps such as Google Forms, Socrative, Kahoot, et cetera. After modelling from your own practice, you can ask the beginning teacher to practise using a few of these tools in their teaching. Task 7.9 asks you to support a beginning teacher to reflect on the use of selected tools to gather pupils' feedback.

Task 7.9 Supporting a beginning teacher to self-evaluate their practice based on pupils' feedback

Undertake the following actions to support a beginning teacher to self-evaluate their teaching practices:

1. Ask the beginning teacher to select a tool that they have used (or a tool they have observed someone else using) to evaluate pupils' feedback as a way to self-evaluate their teaching practices.
2. Encourage the beginning teacher to identify three merits and three limitations of using a particular tool. How can they use this tool more effectively?
3. Next, involve the beginning teacher in a discussion to evaluate:
    - The impact of pupils' feedback on their planning and teaching
    - The need for modification of some teaching strategies.

Summary and key points

This chapter has identified the following points:

- Different stages of teacher development require different mentoring approaches and it is your responsibility to modify your mentoring strategies according to a beginning teacher's developmental needs.
- Your support for a beginning teacher to demonstrate some characteristic features of becoming an effective teacher is vital at all the stages of development.
- You need to guide a beginning teacher to incorporate basic teaching skills, different teaching strategies and a pupil-centred teaching style so that they develop as an effective teacher.
- A beginning teacher needs your support to effectively self-evaluate their lessons by focusing on their reflections to promote pupils' progress.
- It is your responsibility to guide a beginning teacher to strengthen their teaching by self-evaluating their teaching practices. This includes the aggregation of evidence from lesson debriefs provided by you and/or experienced staff members, and pupils' feedback.

Further resources

Kind, V. and Taber, K. (2005) *Teaching School Subjects 11 - 19: Science*. Abingdon: Routledge.
This book is a wide-ranging introduction to beginning to teach science in secondary schools. It suggests and supports beginning teachers to plan teaching (part II) and evaluating (part III), and it offers support in many areas of learning to teach. In particular, Chapter 8 Acting to Teach Science offers useful suggestions about developing a beginning teacher's confidence in teaching science for pupils aged 11–19.

Mosston, M. and Ashworth, S. (2002) *Teaching Physical Education*. 5th edn. San Francisco, CA: Pearson.
Mosston and Ashworth's continuum – or spectrum – of teaching styles offers a useful conceptualisation of the amount of teacher or pupil input appropriate for different classroom activities. Although the continuum was derived in the context of physical education, it can be applied to any teaching subject including science. Mosston's teaching styles are referred to as teaching strategies in this chapter (see also pp. 105–109).

114 *Findlay et al.*

Appendix 7.1 Self-evaluation and mentor–mentee discussion template

1. **Basic teaching skills** (For example: building relationships, clarity of teacher talk, classroom awareness, et cetera)

Week 1
   • Your best
 	
   • Your worst
 	
   • Planning a new basic teaching skill to develop in the following weeks

Week 2
   • Your best
 	
   • Your worst
 	
   • Planning a new basic teaching skill to develop in the following weeks

Week 3
   • Your best
 	
   • Your worst
 	
   • Planning a new basic teaching skill to develop in the following weeks

Week 4
   • Your best
 	
   • Your worst
 	
   • Planning a new basic teaching skill to develop in the following weeks

2. **Teaching strategies** (For example: using questioning, incorporating group work, a combination of some teaching strategies   et cetera)

Teach and evaluate lessons 115

Week 1
- Your best

- Your worst

- Planning a new teaching strategy to develop in the following weeks

Week 2
- Your best

- Your worst

- Planning a new teaching strategy to develop in the following weeks

Week 3
- Your best

- Your worst

- Planning a new teaching strategy to develop in the following weeks

Week 4
- Your best

- Your worst

- Planning a new teaching strategy to develop in the following weeks

3.   **Pupil-centred teaching style**
[This section will act to consolidate the last four-weeks of evaluations. Discussing this section with the beginning teacher will potentially bring together the basic teaching skills and teaching strategies practised during one month, aiming towards developing pupil-centred teaching style.]

Mentor-mentee discussion points on the development of pupil-centred teaching style over a period of four weeks:

8 Pre-lesson discussions, lesson observation and post-lesson discussions in mentoring beginning science teachers

Morag Findlay

Introduction

Lesson observations of a beginning teacher and constructive feedback on that lesson are crucial for beginning teachers to develop as reflective teachers and to achieve the teacher standards that will enable them to acquire qualified teacher status (QTS). In this context, your mentoring role starts before the lesson observation. It does not end at the end of the lesson but continues (McNally, 2016) through discussion and feedback as part of a lesson and series of observed lessons. This is a cycle of pre-lesson discussion, lesson observation and post-lesson discussion, leading into the next cycle (note: post-lesson discussion is called lesson debrief in Chapters 7 and 9 in this book). Typically, mentoring discussions achieve more if they provide a safe space for dialogue (Bradley-Levine, Lee and Mosier, 2016, p. 80) and when they focus on agreed areas for a beginning teacher's development (Hudson, 2016b).

This chapter first addresses mentoring styles, focusing on lesson observation and feedback. It then presents three scenarios for a pre-lesson observation discussion about pedagogical content knowledge (PCK), teacher standards and focused aspects of the lesson for observation and feedback. Using the example of a practical lesson on the relationship between current and voltage in series circuits, this chapter presents Case studies of Brian and John to consider strategies and best practice before, during and after the lesson observation as part of the lesson observation cycle to develop pupils' conceptual understanding in science within the context of the Mentor Teacher Roles in Dialogues (MERID) model of mentoring (Hennissen, Crasborn, Brouwer, Korthagen and Bergen, 2008). Finally, the chapter considers how you could support a beginning teacher's teaching by encouraging them to become a reflective teacher and to use a mentoring checklist for the lesson observation cycle.

Objectives

At the end of this chapter you should be able to:

- Identify different mentoring styles and select appropriate skills to develop to be able to support the needs of a beginning teacher
- Manage mentoring conversations using the MERID framework
- Support a beginning teacher to achieve teacher standards by effectively coordinating the lesson observation cycle, from pre-lesson preparation to post-lesson follow-up and identifying focused dimensions of observation. Selecting from Hudson's dimensions, the praise sandwich and WRAP (Wonder, Reinforce, Adjust, Plan) feedback frameworks to support a beginning teacher's development
- Adapt a mentoring checklist according to the workplace context and the individual needs of a beginning teacher.

8.1 Mentoring style

We all have a preferred mentoring style, but being able to use different mentoring styles to adapt to the needs of a beginning teacher you are working with, is an important mentoring skill (Chapter 1). The Mentor (teacher) Roles In Dialogues (MERID) is one of a number of dialogue-oriented frameworks that you could adopt in working with beginning teachers (Hennissen, Crasborn, Brouwer, Korthagen and Bergen, 2008). MERID considers two main dimensions of mentoring: where you lie on a continuum from non-directive to directive and where you lie on an input continuum from reactive to active. The third dimension of mentoring is whether you talk for a long or a short time when you are giving feedback to a beginning teacher (Table 8.1).

Task 8.1 asks you to reflect on your mentoring style, using the MERID model, especially while giving feedback on a beginning teacher's approaches to teaching and learning science.

Task 8.1   What sort of mentor are you?

1. Where do you place yourself on the following scales?

   Non-directive ⟷ Directive

   Reactive ⟷ Active

   Talk a little ⟷ Talk a lot

2. Use your answers form the scales above, identify your preferred mentoring style in the MERID model (which identified four distinct mentoring roles), described in Table 8.1.

118 *Findlay*

Table 8.1 The MERID model

Dimensions	Active	Reactive
Non-directive	Initiator (little mentor talk)	Encourager (little mentor talk)
Directive	Instructor (a lot of mentor talk)	Advisor (a lot of mentor talk)

(*Source:* Adapted from Hennissen, Crasborn, Brouwer, Korthagen and Bergen (2008, p. 177))

More experienced mentors are generally non-directive, tend to talk less and encourage a beginning teacher to talk more during mentoring discussions. This allows a beginning teacher to reflect more on their teaching to develop their own understanding.

One of your most important mentoring roles is to establish a positive mentoring relationship with a beginning teacher you are working with, based on mutual respect and trust (Hudson, 2016a), along with a combination of emotional and instructional support (Hennissen Crasborn, Brouwer, Korthagen and Bergen, 2011, also Chapter 5). Another important role is observing a beginning teacher and giving feedback. As a mentor you also need to be flexible in your feedback approach because the nature of the mentoring relationship will vary depending on you and the beginning teacher's experience and personality (Chapter 1). Task 8.2 asks you to evaluate Case study 8.1 by maintaining a non-directive approach to mentoring.

Case study 8.1: Jane: Mentoring meeting targeting lesson observations

Jane is a beginning science teacher. It is her first placement in your school so she is feeling nervous about meeting you and her classes for the first time. You listen to Jane's concerns; one of which is about solo-teaching lessons and associated lesson observations. Jane is worried that she might make mistakes, and feels uncertain about the outcomes of observed lessons as a measure to achieve her teaching qualification.

Task 8.2   Mentoring approaches for Jane

Maintaining a non-directive approach to mentoring, answer the following questions:

1. How would you approach Jane's nervousness and encourage her to move on positively?
2. What mentoring strategies could you use to help Jane in overcoming her nervousness about being observed and making mistakes?
3. What strategies could you use to develop Jane's confidence in teaching? (You could consider some mentoring strategies identified in Chapter 7, pp. 98–99).

8.2 Lesson observation cycle

Lesson observation is an ongoing, complex and cyclical process that offers a consistent platform in which a constructive, professional mentor–mentee relationship allows a beginning teacher to develop as an effective teacher (Chapter 7, pp. 95–100 considers some overarching characteristic behaviours of an effective teacher). During this ongoing lesson observation cycle your role as a mentor is to first arrange a pre-lesson discussion with a beginning teacher about what will be observed in the observed lesson; the beginning teacher then teaches the lesson while you are observing the lesson; and, finally, you have a post-lesson discussion with the beginning teacher about what can be learned from the observed lesson and areas for their development. This then informs the next lesson observation cycle.

Your responsibility is to ensure that the lesson observation cycle links to the teacher standards towards which the beginning teacher is working and that you provide focused feedback to allow them to meet these standards by the end of their initial teacher education programme. This is similar to Bruner's (1960) idea of a spiral curriculum, where learners revisit areas of the curriculum, but each time they revisit an area it is at a more demanding level. Similarly, your reason for lesson observation might require you to encourage a beginning teacher to revisit components of the teacher standards and support them to demonstrate improved levels of mastery through each lesson observation cycle.

The beginning of each lesson observation cycle is the pre-lesson discussion to agree on areas of focus for the observed lesson. Although the observed lesson is at the heart of the lesson observation cycle, the beginning teacher teaches other lessons between observed lessons when they are also developing their teaching skills. The area of focus for an observed lesson can come from the previous observation cycle or be identified by the beginning teacher or by you as an area to address that has arisen in their ongoing teaching. You are ensuring that the area of focus links to the teacher standards to allow the beginning teacher to show progression in the components of these standards. This also allows you and the beginning teacher to ensure that they are developing across the whole breadth of the teacher standards.

What happens in any observed lesson in science is complex. One way to conceptualise your lesson observation of a beginning teacher is to use Hudson's (2016b) three dimensions of feedback (visual, auditory and conceptual) as a lens to view the area of focus on (see below). This is a valuable tool for conceptualising feedback, particularly if you are new to mentoring, because it offers some very clear elements of focus during lesson observation from the visual and auditory dimensions of practice to the conceptual understanding of both the beginning teacher's teaching practices and pupils' learning. This identification allows you to provide more focused feedback to the beginning teacher to help them develop their conceptual understanding of teaching and learning.

During the post-lesson discussion, the focus on the teacher standards through the auditory, visual and conceptual dimensions of the lesson observation can help both the beginning teacher and you to link the feedback discussion to particular events that happened during the lesson at the practical and conceptual levels, which can help the beginning teacher to reflect and create a more fruitful discussion. In addition, linking the teacher standards and

120   *Findlay*

the three dimensions of feedback in this way allows you and the beginning teacher to identify the areas of focus for the next lesson observation cycle more easily and gives you clear indicators of the areas where you are required to support them. The three stages of the lesson observation cycle are covered in more detail.

8.2.1 Pre-lesson discussions

Pre-lesson discussions with a beginning teacher involves you in supporting the development of their planning and teaching of the lesson and provides a platform for a constructive post-lesson discussion. Depending on you, the school and the beginning teacher, the pre-lesson discussions could include a number of different areas. Some areas are discussed below, i.e. PCK, teacher standards and focused dimensions of feedback.

8.2.1.1 Pedagogical content knowledge (PCK)

One of your main aims as a mentor is to support a beginning teacher in developing their PCK for teaching. This is a blend of the teacher's subject knowledge, knowledge of learners (pupils) and learning, the context (school and pupils) and the curriculum, as well as knowledge of the values, and purposes of education (Berry, Friedrichsen and Loughran, 2015). In Case study 8.2, John, a beginning science teacher, needs to transform his own subject knowledge into PCK, i.e. into a format that is suitable for pupils to understand the relationship between current and voltage in series circuits. Developing PCK can be difficult for a beginning teacher, but overcoming this and integrating it with an understanding of likely pupil difficulties results in more confident teachers and better lessons (Kind, 2009, see Chapter 10 on subject knowledge and PCK).

Case study 8.2: Brian and John (pre-lesson discussion)

John is the first beginning science teacher Brian is mentoring. John has prepared a draft lesson plan about teaching the relationship between current and voltage in series circuits to a class of 12-year-old pupils.

In the pre-lesson discussion, Brian took a non-directive mentoring approach, by asking John what subject knowledge he had about direct current and encouraged him to think through the conceptual problems and misconceptions that pupils might have in their understanding of this concept, and then how he would transform his subject knowledge into a form that it is suitable to teach 12-year-old pupils.

John was unsure about the conceptual problems the pupils might have. Instead of providing detailed teaching instructions and advice, Brian asked John to research possible pupil misconceptions as part of his lesson preparation.

Brian and John then decided to focus on the conceptual problems that pupils may have with the topic. John, with Brian's support, decided to plan a practical activity and a series of key questions (there is a description of key questions in Chapter 6, pp. 80–81) to address pupils' conceptual understanding of current and voltage.

8.2.1.2 Teacher standards

The pre-lesson discussion in the previous section focused on how John could develop his PCK for teaching about the relationship between current and voltage in series circuits. Brian could adopt a learning progression approach by mapping pre-lesson and post-lesson observation feedback focusing on PCK to link it with the teacher standards on developing effective teachers.

Task 8.3 provides an opportunity for you to make use of existing teacher standards to practise planning a discussion with the beginning teacher before a lesson.

Task 8.3   Pre-lesson discussions and teacher standards

Look at the teacher standards towards which a beginning teacher you are mentoring is working. Identify one or two standards or parts of these standards which focus on the following areas in the context of teaching and learning.

1.   Conceptual development needs of the beginning teacher.
2.   Inquiry (questioning) approaches during practical work.
3.   Linking science to pupils' everyday life.

Next plan pre-lesson discussion points using these areas of the teacher standards as indicators to link subject knowledge and PCK and to map the beginning teacher's progression over time.

8.2.1.3 Agreed on focused dimensions for feedback

To maximise a non-directive approach to mentoring, it is suggested that during pre-lesson discussions, you and the beginning teacher should agree on two or three areas of focus for lesson observation. These areas of focus can be seen through the lens of Hudson's (2016b) dimensions of feedback: the visual, auditory and conceptual aspects of a lesson. The visual, auditory and conceptual aspects cover everything that happens in the lesson; therefore, you and the beginning teacher need to agree on more specific areas of focus during the pre-lesson discussion.

Figure 8.1 provides a breakdown of each of the three dimensions of feedback. You and the beginning teacher could pre-plan to focus on some indicators of the visual (such as the use of boards, whether interactive or traditional), auditory (such as clarity of voice) and conceptual (such as pedagogical approaches) dimensions that they will use to demonstrate effective teaching strategies constituting the overlapping indicators (such as the various components of PCK) identified by Hudson (2016b).

You can also see from Figure 8.1 that the three dimensions of feedback overlap. For example, as an observer, as you look and listen to the beginning teacher and pupils, you will be able to tell if the timing and pacing of the lesson are going well. The written and spoken language of science can be challenging for both the beginning teacher and pupils, so for written texts or diagrams there is an overlap between the visual and conceptual dimensions of teaching, learning and feedback. Similarly, questioning depends on how a question

122 Findlay

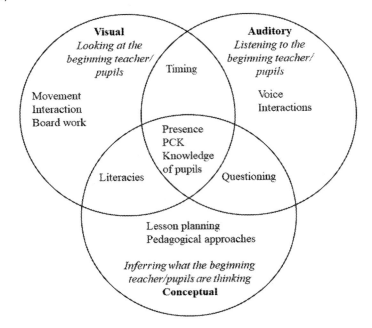

Figure 8.1 Three dimensions for providing lesson observation and feedback
(Source: Adapted from Hudson (2016b, p. 223))

is asked, which occurs at the overlap between the auditory and conceptual dimensions. And, finally, some aspects of teaching occur at the overlap of all three dimensions of teaching. For example, a beginning teacher's presence in the classroom is a combination of how they look and talk in the classroom as well as convincing pupils that they know what they are talking about conceptually. Task 8.4 asks you to reflect on how you could use Hudson's dimensions of feedback to inform the pre-lesson discussion presented in Case study 8.2 and Task 8.3.

Task 8.4 Focused feedback

Think about Case study 8.2 and the teacher standards you considered in Task 8.3. Next, focus on the visual, auditory and conceptual dimensions (Figure 8.1) of the lesson by listing:

- Appropriate indicators from the three dimensions that you generally draw on before a lesson observation
- Interlinking indicators (such as PCK or knowledge of pupils) you would focus on to incorporate Hudson's three broad dimensions
- Aspects of the dimensions the beginning teacher finds challenging to consider. Why does the beginning teacher find these aspects challenging? How will you help them deal with these aspects in practice?

Lesson observation and discussion   123

The next section presents some observation and feedback suggestions for you to practise during and after a lesson observation by extending the example of John and Brian's pre-lesson discussions (Case study 8.2).

8.2.2 Lesson observation

The lesson observation cycle is at the heart of supporting a beginning teacher's development and the observed lesson is at the heart of the lesson observation cycle. Although lesson observation has a summative assessment purpose in recording a beginning teacher's development, it has a more powerful formative assessment purpose in helping the beginning teacher to develop towards the relevant teacher standards, including developing their ability as a reflective practitioner to support their current and career-long professional development. It is important to record your observations of a lesson as this provides a source of evidence to support the development of a beginning teacher's competence. In the pre-lesson discussion, it is vital that you agree to a few aspects of lesson observation with the beginning teacher in advance (see above). These can be made against set teacher standards to assess the beginning teacher's achievement (see previous section) or targets set by the beginning teacher or school/department, but should sketch a true picture of the beginning teacher's development towards becoming an effective science teacher, especially, by demonstrating an ability to develop pupils' learning. During the lesson observation, your task is to make focused observations to form the basis for a developmental post-lesson discussion with the beginning teacher.

Your overall focus of lesson observations evolves over time. During the early stages of mentoring a particular beginning teacher, you might be focusing on the effectiveness of their basic teaching skills, whereas during the later stages you focus on their ability to support pupils' learning inclusively (Chapter 7, (Figure 7.1, p. 95) indicates a beginning teacher's developmental stages). Before you read about some mentoring practices during the lesson observation, Task 8.5 encourages you to reflect on one of your current lesson observations of a beginning teacher.

Task 8.5   Undertaking lesson observation

Consider a lesson that you have recently observed taught by a beginning teacher, and answer the below questions:

1. Identify what was discussed in the pre-lesson meeting and the agreed focus of the lesson observation you undertook.
2. Did you intervene while conducting the lesson observation? Did you guide the beginning teacher during the lesson? If yes then how, if not, then why not?
3. Did the agreed lesson observation foci change during the lesson and if so, how?
4. How did you record your observations? Did your recording style change during the lesson observation?
5. To what extent did you find your recorded observation helpful in providing feedback to the observed teacher? What would you do differently (or not) next time?

---

124 *Findlay*

The next section gives some suggestions about the two key ideas in Task 8.5. First whether or not a mentor intervenes while observing a beginning teacher and second about the style of recording and its usefulness of providing effective feedback to a beginning teacher.

8.2.2.1 When to intervene in an observed lesson?

One of the challenges for a mentor as a classroom observer is when – or whether – and how to intervene. It is important to allow a beginning teacher to develop their independence and teaching skills by making and correcting mistakes. It is also important for pupils to see the beginning teacher as the class teacher rather than always looking to the mentor (experienced teacher) for guidance. So, before conducting a lesson observation, it is important that you consider how you are going to support the beginning teacher during the lesson observation. Why, when and how would you intervene (or not) while they are teaching? How do you ensure that the pupils focus on the beginning teacher rather than on you while you are only observing the beginning teacher? Task 8.6 asks you to consider some situations and reflect on whether you should intervene during the lesson or wait until the post-lesson discussion.

Task 8.6 To intervene, or not to intervene, in a lesson

Below are possible circumstances that may call for intervention and questions for you to consider. You need to decide:

1. Why would you intervene during the lesson observation of the beginning teacher, if so, when and how?
2. Will you mention the issue immediately; at some point during the lesson; after the lesson; or not mention it?
3. Will you take control of the class temporarily; have a quiet word with the beginning teacher; have a quiet word with a small group of pupils; or something else?

In answering these overarching questions, consider the following circumstances:

*   Health and safety

All the pupils start to congregate around the side bench with the apparatus for the lesson.

*   Subject knowledge

During the lesson, the beginning teacher repeatedly uses incorrect scientific (subject) knowledge. For example, they talk about the current across the resistor and the voltage through it (sic) rather than the current through the resistor and the voltage across it.

*   Classroom routines

Arriving at the door – the pupils arrive late from their previous class and the beginning teacher waves them into the room.
Lesson starter – the lesson starter is not on the board when the pupils enter the room.

Body of lesson – the beginning teacher has given the class unclear instructions and you can see that the pupils are confused about what to do.

Plenary session – during the plenary session, it becomes obvious to you – but not the beginning teacher – that the pupils are confused by the beginning teacher's questions. Some pupils have noticed that as the current through the resistor increases so does the voltage across it, but they cannot articulate the relationship between the quantities.

- Technology problems

The beginning teacher has spent ten minutes before the lesson struggling to get the data projector to work and there is nowhere in the classroom to write anything.

- Behaviour management

You notice that one group of pupils are having an animated conversation about last night's 'must-see' television show, but that the beginning teacher is not aware of this.

- Formative assessment

The beginning teacher takes most of the answers from the small group of pupils who keep putting their hands up. The beginning teacher has written key questions in their lesson plan, but they are not used during the lesson.

- Timing

Slow start to the lesson, the pupils arrive late from their previous class.
Body of the lesson taking too much time.
The beginning teacher has become caught up in helping several groups of pupils to set up their circuit and is not checking that all the groups are recording their results. It becomes clear 15 minutes from the end of the lesson that only one or two groups have any results.

- Not enough time for a meaningful plenary session

The beginning teacher asks the pupils to put away their apparatus, which only leaves 2 minutes until the end of the lesson.

Unquestionably, when there is an urgent health and safety issue, the mentor must intervene immediately. However, other situations allow time for you to consider how to intervene in such a way as to support the beginning teacher and to reinforce their position as the class teacher. For example, in terms of subject knowledge, it is easy for the beginning teacher to say something like the atomic mass of carbon is 16. However, if the beginning teacher does not hear themselves say 16 instead of 12, it is not likely to be noticed by pupils and the beginning teacher will probably correct this statement at some point during the lesson. However, if the beginning teacher were to consistently confuse the atomic masses during the lesson, it is probably necessary for you to have a quiet word during the lesson so that the beginning teacher can correct their mistake while (still) remaining the teacher in the eyes of the pupils.

126 Findlay

8.2.2.2 Recording lesson observations

There are a number of approaches to recording lesson observations. These approaches range from a relatively unstructured chronological recording of what happened during the lesson or a recording of some significant incidents to focus attention on specific areas. Table 8.2 presents a lesson observation template that is divided into four sections. The first section asks for general information (name of the observed teacher, observer, et cetera). The second section provides space to record the agreed focus from the pre-lesson discussion, focused teacher standards and focused dimensions of feedback (such as WRAP feedback framework

Table 8.2 Lesson observation template

Observed teacher:

Observer:

Class:

Date:

Time:

Topic:

Pre-lesson discussion

Agreed focused professional teacher standards for feedback:

Agreed focused dimensions for feedback:

Lesson observation notes

Lesson observation feedback points and linked professional teacher standards:

Post-observation discussion

Strengths:

Further actions required:

Lesson observation and discussion 127

(see section 8.2.3). The third section gives space for you to make some observational points, mainly based on the agreed focused dimensions. The fourth/last section provides space for you to jot down some of your immediate evaluations of the lessons under the headings of strengths and further actions required. These can then be revisited and properly framed during the post-lesson discussion with the beginning teacher.

Appendix 8.1 provides a completed lesson observation template (using Table 8.2), on John's introductory lesson on direct current and voltage, where Brian used Hudson's (2016b) three dimensions and two specific teacher standards to structure the observation. After looking at Table 8.2 and Appendix 8.1, Task 8.7 is designed to enable you to evaluate the effectiveness of Table 8.2.

Task 8.7   Reflecting on John's lesson and Brian's observation

Answer the following questions to evaluate the effectiveness of the lesson observation recording template (Table 8.2 and Appendix 8.1):

1. Looking at Appendix 8.1, what role(s) does Brian take in the observed lesson? Are these similar to the roles you would adopt in an observed lesson?
2. What are the significant visual, auditory and conceptual notes Brian made during the lesson?
3. What other aspects are recorded by Brian that were not discussed with John during pre-lesson observation (Case study 8.2)?
4. Do you think that the recorded observation will offer constructive feedback to John?
5. Would you consider noting a detailed observation like (or unlike) Brain and record practices in chronological order? Why or why not?
6. What other ways of recording would you prefer to use in recording a similar science lesson observation?

You might prefer to record observations on the lesson plan itself rather than using any particular lesson observation template and after the lesson observation, write-up and aggregate feedback to be discussed with the beginning teacher. You can write this aggregated feedback from varying sources, including pre-lesson observation discussions, lesson plans, pupils' performances and lesson evaluations (verbal and/or written). You might also highlight strengths and areas for development to share with the beginning teacher (the WRAP method of feedback is covered below). You can give the beginning teacher the feedback prior to the post-lesson discussions. Giving them some extra time to reflect on the feedback can improve the post-lesson discussions further.

Whether you use a lesson observation template or not and whatever mode of recording you use (such as handwritten, typed on word document/excel sheet, and if your school permits audio and/or video recording of lessons, et cetera), your aim should be to record highlighted and focused features that can support the beginning teacher to progress their teaching practices.

128   *Findlay*

8.2.3 Post-lesson discussions

Referring back to the MERID model (Table 8.1), during post-lesson feedback, mentors were either:

*   Directive Advisor/Instructor (Active and/or Reactive) – focusing more on giving information, giving an opinion or assessing the beginning teacher and giving advice/instruction. These mentors tend to talk more, contradicting their mentoring role as an encourager; or
*   Non-directive Initiator/Encourager (Active and/or Reactive) – focusing on asking for concreteness, summarising what the beginning teacher said and helping to find and choose alternatives. These mentors tend to talk less than mentors taking on an advisor/ instructor role.

Task 8.8 asks you to revisit John's lesson observation and reflect on Brian's mentoring approaches to the post-lesson discussions (Case studies 8.3 and 8.4) by linking your reflections with the MERID model of mentoring (Table 8.1).

Case study 8.3: Brian's approach one

Brian: How do you feel the pupils got on in the lesson?

John: During the introduction they were good at designing the experiment to measure current in a series circuit and when I was talking with the groups, they all seemed to get the right answers.

Brian: Yes, they helped you to design the experiment, but during the practical work one of the groups struggled to understand that the different values of the current they measured were the same. It was difficult for pupils to understand that different readings are actually the same.

Case study 8.4: Brian's approach two

Brian: How do you feel the pupils got on in the lesson?

John: During the introduction they were good at designing the experiment to measure current in a series circuit and when I was talking with the groups, they all seemed to get the right answers.

Brian: Could you give me an example when they gave you the right answers?

John: Group A got good measurements and when I told them that the current is the same everywhere in a series circuit, they were happy with that.

Brian: So, you think Group A understood the point when you told them what happened? Could you have elicited the answer from them?

John: Maybe I could ask them why they think the current is the same in a series circuit...

Lesson observation and discussion 129

Task 8.8   Reflecting on mentoring approaches

Case studies 8.3 and 8.4 show two possible versions of a post-lesson discussion. Taking these two Case studies into account, answer the following questions:

1.   For each case study, decide the main style of mentoring. Use Table 8.1 to decide the mentoring style.
2.   In the light of your answers to question 1, what, if any, changes would you make to your approach to mentoring in future?

Post-lesson mentoring discussions can give rise to complex emotions for a beginning teacher and possibly also for the mentor. Some suggestions to take into consideration are:

- If the beginning teacher feels that the lesson went badly, it can be helpful to give them some time to collect their thoughts before the post-lesson discussion.
- Finding a quiet, neutral space for the meeting reduces the possible emotional impact on the beginning teacher (and you).
- Using the agreed pre-lesson discussion areas of focus, only feedback on the two or three main areas that will have the biggest impact on the beginning teacher's teaching.
- Help the beginning teacher to develop reflective skills to balance potential conflicting demands in a principled way.
- In addition to your feedback about the agreed areas of focus in the observed lesson, you also need to collate feedback about these areas from the other experienced teachers the beginning teacher is working with. It is worthwhile asking these experienced teachers to concentrate on the agreed focused areas to avoid the beginning teacher becoming overloaded.

One way to take account of the beginning teacher's emotions could be to use the praise sandwich feedback approach, where negative feedback is given between two pieces of positive feedback. However, there are two possible – and opposite – problems with this approach. One is that the beginning teacher only hears the positive feedback and discounts the negative feedback. The opposite problem is that the beginning teacher can dread the negative feedback and not hear positive feedback. A different and possibly more effective approach which could help a beginning teacher to develop their own reflective and professional skills and move them towards independent learning is the WRAP framework (Besse and Vogelsang, 2018). WRAP stands for Wonder, Reinforce, Adjust and Plan and is a framework for giving non-judgemental, constructive feedback. The difference to the praise sandwich feedback is that WRAP feedback explicitly encourages reflection and consideration of the next steps. A brief description of each of the WRAP framework stages is as follows:

1.   Wonder stage: you encourage the beginning teacher to reflect by wondering what went well during the lesson and what could be improved. This avoids the problem whereby the beginning teacher often only focuses on areas for development rather than considering the whole lesson.

130 *Findlay*

2. Reinforce stage: you reinforce the need for the beginning teacher to self-reflect/evaluate on areas where they did well and add any additional areas of strength.
3. Adjust stage: you and the beginning teacher mutually explore areas which the beginning teacher has identified as needing development (adjustment) in the wonder stage. During the adjust stage, you may also describe other areas that the beginning teacher did not identify but that also need development.
4. Planning stage: involves a discussion with the beginning teacher about specific teaching and learning strategies for moving forward.

Table 8.3 presents a post-lesson discussion chart using the WRAP feedback approach, which you could adapt/adopt/refine and use during post-lesson discussions with a beginning teacher. The first column of Table 8.3 identifies the four WRAP stages, the second column identifies some objectives for a beginning teacher to accomplish during the post-lesson discussion. For each of the four stages, the third column presents some objectives for both

Table 8.3 WRAP feedback chart for post-lesson discussion

WRAP stages	Objectives for the beginning teacher	Objectives for the mentor and beginning teacher	Facilitating roles of mentor
Wonder	To identify areas that went well and give evidence To identify areas that could be improved	Adhering to a balanced and reflective approach	Encourage the beginning teacher to identify positive aspects rather than only focus on areas for improvement. Refocus the beginning teacher to concentrate on the main areas for development by identifying practices that they would consider next time.
Reinforce	To self-evaluate	Adhering to a balanced and reflective approach	Start from the areas of strength identified by the beginning teacher. Reinforce the beginning teacher's capacity to self-evaluate. Add any additional major strengths.
Adjust	To consider the reasons why some areas were less successful	Take a factual approach focusing on specific actions rather than opinions	Give factual feedback about areas for improvement identified by the beginning teacher. Identify any additional significant areas for improvement.

WRAP stages	Objectives for the beginning teacher	Objectives for the mentor and beginning teacher	Facilitating roles of mentor
Planning	To take the lead in their own development	Consider: What are the next steps for the beginning teacher and for the mentor? What are the two or three focused areas of development for the next pre-lesson observation meeting?	Over time, give the responsibility for this step to the beginning teacher.

you and the beginning teacher and the fourth/final column identifies facilitating roles of the mentor for each of the WRAP stages.

8.3 Mentoring checklist

As mentioned above, mentoring a beginning teacher through the lesson observation cycle is a complex process. Table 8.4 provides a checklist of some topics that have been discussed in this chapter, which you can use to support a beginning teacher's progression. The list is not exhaustive and you should adapt this list to your own workplace and the needs of the beginning teacher.

Table 8.4 Mentoring checklist before, during and after a lesson observation

Before the lesson observation cycle begins, consider:
- What is your MERID mentoring style? (Initiator, encourager, instructor or advisor)
- How can you adapt your mentoring style for different situations or for an individual beginning teacher?
- How will you build a positive relationship with a beginning teacher?

Lesson observation cycle

Pre-lesson discussion
- Agreed areas of focus
    - Lesson planning
    - Classroom organisation and management
    - …
- Link the agreed areas of focus to the teacher standard towards which the beginning teacher is working.
- Agree which of Hudson's visual, auditory and conceptual dimensions of feedback to use. The list of dimensions is included in the observed lesson section.
- Over time as beginning science teacher progresses, encourage them to take the lead in the pre-lesson discussions.

(continued)

132 *Findlay*

Table 8.4 (Cont.)

During the lesson observations

- Decide on your role during the lesson (observation only or observation and some interaction with the pupils).
- Observe the agreed areas of focus and the dimensions of feedback. Some dimensions to consider (based on Hudson, 2016b, p. 223 and Figure 8.1) are given below.

Visual	*Auditory*	*Conceptual*
Teacher movement Preparation Monitoring Board work	Use of voice Using names Praise Clear instructions Rephrasing	Lesson planning Pedagogical approaches

Overlapping dimensions of feedback (Some examples are taken from Figure 8.1)

Visual/auditory	*Auditory/conceptual*	*Conceptual/visual*
Time management	Prior knowledge Checking for understanding Questioning	Use of text Literacy

Visual/auditory/conceptual

Aims Links to previous learning Classroom presence PCK Behaviour management Practical work

- If something unexpected happens, consider whether or not to include it in the post-lesson discussion.

Post-lesson discussion

- Arrange for a neutral venue where possible.
- If the lesson has gone badly, allow the beginning teacher time to recover before the discussion.
- Base the post-lesson discussion around the agreed areas of focus and dimensions of feedback.
- Make neutral statements of fact about the lesson rather than value judgements.
- Stick to the most important areas of feedback rather than trying to feedback on everything that happened.
- Encourage the beginning teacher to reflect on areas of strength as well as development needs.
- Decide whether to use the praise sandwich or WRAP approach to feedback.
- Over time as the beginning teacher develops, encourage them to take the lead in:
  - Identifying the areas of focus for the next lesson observation cycle
  - Planning how to address these areas.
- Encourage the beginning teacher to record their progress towards the teacher standards.

Summary and key points

This chapter has highlighted some mentoring approaches to support a beginning teacher in the lesson observation cycle, including pre-lesson discussion, lesson observation and post-lesson discussion. Specifically, it has highlighted the following points:

- Mentors need to be aware of the different mentoring styles and which style is appropriate for a given beginning teacher.
- Employ mentoring approaches to teaching and learning that give more opportunity to a beginning teacher to talk and reflect on their teaching and learning approaches.
- Plan your mentoring sessions by mapping teacher standards to support the gradual development of a beginning teacher.
- Before the lesson, agree to focus on a few areas of the teacher standards and then use the three dimensions of feedback (visual, auditory and conceptual) so that these can be incorporated into planning of the lesson.
- Structure your lesson observations and provide non-directive feedback to focus on agreed areas of the lesson observation.
- As part of the post-lesson discussion, agree with the beginning teacher the area(s) of the teacher standards that will be the focus for the next observed lesson cycle and/or a series of lessons.

Further resources

Ambrosetti, A., Rorrison, D. and Capeness, R. (2018) *Educating Future Teachers: Innovative Perspectives in Professional Experience*. Singapore: Springer.
This edited book considers recent changes in teacher education in an Australian context and has a section about changes in mentoring approaches – including approaches to lesson observation and feedback – which is relevant to thinking about mentoring in the UK. The focus of the mentoring section in this book is about reconceptualising mentoring in different ways, but in particular, ways in which beginning teachers and mentors can learn from the best mentoring experience.

Johnson, W.B. and Ridley, C.R. (2018) *The Elements of Mentoring: 75 Practices of Master Mentors*. 3rd edn. New York, NY: Macmillan USA.
This short, well-written and wide-ranging book gives an interesting introduction to the process of mentoring in general (including lesson observations) that can support a mentor and mentee development over time.

O'Leary, M. (2016) *Reclaiming Lesson Observation*. Abingdon, Oxon: Routledge.
This edited book looks at ways in which lesson observations can be used as a way to enable teachers to develop their professional practice and improve teaching and learning for themselves and their pupils. Although the mentoring section focuses on mentoring in further education, the focus on peer-mentoring as a means of professional development could be transferred to beginning science teachers supporting one another through mentoring.

134 *Findlay*

Appendix 8.1 Lesson observation template for John

Teacher: John

Observer: Brian

Class:

Date: XX.XX.XXXX

Time: XX:XX

Topic: The relationship between current and voltage in series circuits.

Agreed focused teacher standards (TS) for feedback:
1. Conceptual development needs of the pupils (TS1)
2. Inquiry (questioning) approaches during practical work (TS2).

Agreed focused dimensions for feedback:
1. *Explanation* of the direct current in series circuits (overlapping visual, auditory and conceptual dimensions)
    - Visual: use of boards, including interactive whiteboards; diagrams, physical circuits, et cetera.
    - Auditory and conceptual: direct current, flow, series circuit, single loop, ammeter, amperes (amps), ammeter connected in series (breaking into the circuit), current through a component, et cetera.
    - Conceptual: lesson planning, questioning strategies, et cetera.
    - All: linking subject knowledge, PCK and knowledge of the pupils.
2. *Questioning* (overlapping conceptual and auditory dimensions) to develop pupils' understanding.
    - Auditory and conceptual:
        - What do you notice about the circuit diagram for the series circuit? (One path for the current to flow or more than one path?)
        - As the current flows through a series circuit, does it increase, decrease or remain constant? Why does this happen?
        - Use of pupils' answers, et cetera.
        - Addressing the misconception that the current is 'used up' in a series circuit.

Lesson observation feedback points and linked teacher standards:

Brian made the following observations while he and John were waiting for the class to arrive.

- Before the lesson started, John had decided that he would elicit how to set up a series circuit with the class (TS2) and ask them to predict (TS1) what they thought would happen to the current in the series circuit before they carried out the experiment.
- He made sure that the equipment needed was set out around the side benches in the laboratory.

Extracts from Brian's observations during the lesson focusing on explanations (TS1) and questioning (TS2):

- At the beginning of the lesson, John questioned the pupils about how to set up a series circuit and together he and the pupils decided to connect two cells, a switch and two lamps in series (TS2).
- John drew the circuit diagram on the interactive whiteboard as the pupils made suggestions so that all the pupils could see the circuit (TS2).

Lesson observation and discussion

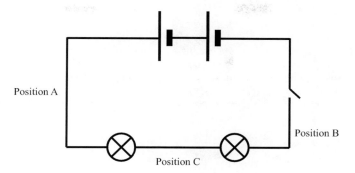

- As John led a question-based discussion about where and how to measure the current, the pupils decided to break into the circuit to connect an ammeter to measure the current before the first lamp (position A), between the two lamps (position B) and after the second lamp (position C) (TS2).
- Before the pupils carried out the experiment, John asked the pupils to use a think-pair-share approach to predict what they thought would happen to the current (TS1). He insisted that each group of pupils write down a shared prediction about what would happen to the current (increase/decrease/remain constant) (TS1).
- John moved round the laboratory interacting with the groups of pupils, questioning them about their results and whether or not they agreed with their predictions (TS1/2).

Brian paid particular attention to John's interactions with this group of pupils (Group A). The pupils' results are shown in the table:

Results for Group A	
Position	Current
A	0.27
B	0.26
C	0.25

John congratulated these pupils on completing the measurement of the current at each position and then asked the pupils what they had missed out of their table (TS2) before the following dialogue:

John: What do you notice about the current in the series circuit? (TS2)
Pupil: The current decreases by 0.01 amps as it goes through each lamp.
John: No, the current is the same at each point in a series circuit. (TS1)
Pupil: Why does that happen, sir?
John: Because a series circuit has one loop and the same number of electrons flow past each point so the current is the same everywhere. (TS1)

Does this result agree with your group's prediction? (TS2)
As John walks towards another group, Brian hears these pupils are arguing that the current 'does go down' as it goes through each lamp.
Brian made a note to ask John about this interaction in particular during the post-lesson discussion.

Strengths:
- You planned carefully and thought about how to address the misconception about the current being 'used up'. (TS1)
- At the beginning of the lesson, you worked hard with the pupils and used questioning effectively to help them to design the experiment and give them ownership of the ideas. (TS2)
- You encouraged the pupils to make predictions about what would happen to the current as it flowed through the series circuit. (TS1)
- During the lesson, you systematically asked each group if their results agreed with their predictions (TS2) and tried to use the answer to develop their thinking.

Further actions required:

Consider:

- As you saw, some of the pupils did notice (apparently) systematic changes in the current readings around the circuit. How can you help them to see that these readings are the same within the limitations of the ammeters they were using? Why is this important for conceptual learning? (TS1)
- What was different about the way you questioned the pupils effectively at the beginning of the lesson and the less effective questioning about Group A's results? (TS2).

9 Holding weekly mentoring meetings

Stephen P. Day

Introduction

Beginning teachers engage with a range of experiences while on their initial teacher education (ITE) programme, aimed at supporting their teaching practice in a progressive way. This can boost their sense of professional efficacy and aids their growing professional identity as a science teacher. Regular weekly meetings between a mentor and beginning teacher are an essential element of their developmental process and a requirement on most ITE programmes.

Weekly mentoring meetings are a critical component of mentoring in terms of providing the time and space necessary for a mentor and beginning teacher to engage constructively in collegial discussions. These discussions are required to facilitate the ongoing evaluation of a beginning teacher's practice against agreed developmental targets based around teacher standards. In addition, these meetings, when properly managed, help to develop and solidify a mentor-mentee (professional) relationship.

This chapter aims to give you some guidance on the purposes of weekly mentoring meetings as opposed to the purposes of lesson debriefs (in Chapter 8, lesson debrief is termed as post-lesson discussion). The first section details some external and internal drivers that can shape the purpose and structuring of these weekly meetings. The chapter then offers strategies to pre-plan the structure of these meetings to ensure that the beginning teacher feels able to speak freely and openly to you about their perceived and actual areas of development as well as being able to identify their strengths and areas of significant progress. A GROW (Goal, Reality, Obstacles/Options and Way forward) model is then introduced to support you in conducting weekly mentoring meetings effectively. Finally, the chapter asks you to reflect on your ability to hold weekly mentoring meetings effectively.

138 *S. P. Day*

Objectives

At the end of this chapter you should be able to:

- Understand the differences between the purposes of the weekly mentoring meetings and lesson debriefs
- Be cognisant of external and internal drivers which might impact upon how you organise and manage weekly meetings
- Practise some pre-planning routines to structure weekly mentoring meetings with a beginning teacher you are mentoring
- Use the GROW (Goal, Reality, Obstacles/Options and Way forward) model to stimulate directive but non-judgemental discussions within these weekly meetings
- Reflect upon your ability to organise and manage weekly mentoring meetings and to recognise some aspects of the mentoring process, which might need further development.

Before you start reading this chapter, Task 9.1 asks you to reflect on the effectiveness of weekly mentoring meetings.

Task 9.1   Running the weekly mentoring meetings – reflective questions

Use the questions below to reflect on the effectiveness of weekly meetings that you organise for a beginning teacher.

1. What aspect of the weekly meetings do you...
    - find most rewarding? Why is this the case?
    - find difficult? Why might this be so?
2. What element of the weekly meetings do you think is most supportive of a beginning science teacher? What evidence do you have that this is the case?
3. From a professional development perspective, what have you learnt from weekly mentoring meetings about your ability to successfully mentor a beginning science teacher?
4. What aspect of the weekly meetings do you think needs further development? What will you do to develop this aspect of the weekly meeting?

9.1 Purposes of a weekly mentoring meeting

Weekly mentoring meetings organised by you, as a mentor, play a vital role in supporting a beginning teacher's growing sense of professional efficacy because these meetings facilitate professional discussions regarding their progression as an effective teacher. These meetings provide a space where you and the beginning teacher make sense together of a range of learning experiences and affordances that might have occurred since the last meeting.

Holding weekly mentoring meetings 139

In discussing these learning experiences and affordances, most importantly, you need to consider that these discussions ought to look and feel differently to a lesson debrief.

Lesson debriefs (or post-lesson discussions) focus on the practicalities of an observed lesson in terms of the chosen pedagogies, management strategies, and critical incidents that may have occurred during a lesson. However, the purpose of a weekly meeting is to draw together both (i) feedback/evidence from lessons observed by you or another experienced teacher and (ii) to discuss ways the beginning teacher can develop effective teaching characteristics, such as understanding aspects of professionalism in the school environment, reaching consensus through reading literature on, for example, the theory of 'behaviourism' or discussing purposes/processes of including 'inquiry-based learning' approaches while planning, et cetera. Thus, weekly meetings support a beginning teacher to fit their reflections and discussions into their ITE journey by focusing on the 'bigger picture', as opposed to a detailed account of individual teaching episodes (lessons).

Both weekly meetings and lesson debriefs are essential elements of the mentoring process but serve different functions. Before reading further, Task 9.2 asks you to self-reflect on differences between weekly mentoring meetings and lesson debriefs.

Task 9.2   Weekly mentoring meetings verses the lesson debriefs

Reflecting on weekly mentoring meetings and lesson debriefs (or post-lesson discussions), consider how they differ by:

1. Listing the differing purposes of each in Table 9.1. The following questions might help with this list. Reflect on:
    *   Who (you and the beginning teacher) does what within weekly meetings and lesson debriefs.
    *   What might the focus of each activity (weekly meetings and lesson debriefs) be?
    *   What is learnt as a result of lesson debriefs (such as observing teaching and receiving feedback from lessons taught) and by whom (you, the beginning teacher and/or other experienced teachers)?
    *   What is learnt as a result of discussions on the ways the beginning teacher can develop effective teaching characteristics?
2. Table 9.2 provides some example purposes of weekly meetings and lesson debriefs. Where relevant, update Table 9.1, after reading Table 9.2.

Table 9.1 Weekly mentoring meetings versus the lesson debriefs

Purpose of the weekly meetings	*Purpose of the lesson debriefs*

140   S. P. Day

Table 9.2 Some example purposes of weekly mentoring meetings and lesson debriefs

Purpose of weekly mentoring meetings	*Purpose of lesson debriefs*
1. To discuss and evaluate progress overall.	1. To provide technical and professional feedback to a beginning teacher about aspects of teaching practice.
2. To provide space for professional dialogue and discussion on pupils learning that has occurred during teaching practice.	2. To provide an opportunity for a beginning teacher to discuss aspects of their teaching practice (such as lesson planning, enactment of the lesson and/or their professional judgements within and following a lesson) within a concentrated time frame with their mentor.
3. To plan the next lesson or series of lessons (pre-lesson discussions) aiming to improve pupils' learning.	
4. To focus development on teaching and set that against the wider professional context.	
5. To set developmental targets.	

9.2 External and internal drivers that guide the purpose of weekly mentoring meetings

There are a number of external and internal drivers that can shape the purpose of weekly mentoring meetings. Some of these drivers are identified below.

9.2.1 External divers

There are some available standards for mentor that act as an external driver to help you to tailor the purpose of your weekly mentoring meetings (for example, in England the Department for Education (DfE), 2016b). For example, in this document, mentoring standard 2 indicates 'teaching', which requires you to 'support trainees [beginning teachers] to develop their teaching practice in order to set high expectations and to meet the needs of all pupils', and mentoring standard 3 on 'professionalism', expects you to 'induct the trainee [beginning teacher] into professional norms and values, helping them to understand the importance of the role and responsibilities of teachers in society' (DfE, 2016b, p. 10). You can use these mentoring standards to help you think about how you can support a beginning teacher in terms of, for example, forming good relationships with pupils, in developing effective behaviour and classroom management strategies or promoting equality and diversity in their teaching, while at the same time encouraging them to participate in the life of the school and understand their role within the wider school community. By using these standards, you can focus weekly meetings in different ways to support a beginning teacher's learning journey as challenges arise, for example, if a beginning teacher does not appear to be making sufficient progress or they have simply plateaued in their practice. Thinking through these mentoring standards can enable you to explore the characteristics of effective mentoring and to be more impactful within the mentoring process.

Teacher standards towards which a beginning teacher is working also act as an external policy driver. Teacher standards are country specific (for example, the Department for Education (DfE) (2011) in England, the General Teaching Council for Northern Ireland (GTCNI) (2018a), GTCNI, 2018b), the General Teaching Council for Scotland (GTCS) Standards for Registration (2012) and the National Model of Professional Learning (Education Scotland, 2020), and the Education Workforce Council in Wales (EWC) (2018). Mapping these teacher standards against their continuing teaching practices also supports the ongoing development of a beginning teacher as they embark on their career as a newly qualified teacher (NQT).

A thorough discussion on teacher standards should be incorporated into weekly meeting discussions because these standards provide a clear frame of reference as to the expectations to attain qualified teacher status (QTS). This should support the beginning teacher to identify and integrate good teaching practices aligning with the teacher standards and where they have to channel their efforts further. Therefore in weekly meetings, you could encourage a beginning teacher you are mentoring to reflect on the ways their growing classroom experience confirms that they are meeting a specific teacher standard (or group of standards). Task 9.3 aims to support you with this.

Before completing Task 9.3, you need to consider that a beginning teacher undertaking an ITE programme could have already agreed some targets (to support their progression with respect to teacher standards) with their ITE tutor (frequently a university-based tutor) as a result of their previous school placement. In this case, these targets need to be taken into account while completing Task 9.3.

Task 9.3 Teacher standards: Professional developmental targets and strategies

In a weekly meeting:

1. Discuss with the beginning teacher the teacher standards they are working towards
2. Then ask the beginning teacher to complete Table 9.3 by identifying targets for their professional development on the current school placement against these teacher standards (and taking into account any targets set in a previous school placement). Encourage them to fill the second column of Table 9.3 by identifying:

- Some targets and strategies to develop each of the teacher standards in their practice
- Highlight any priorities which they feel have emerged since their first school placement, if any.

Share, as appropriate, Table 9.4, which shows a sample professional development plan filled by a beginning teacher in Scotland using the GTCS teacher standards (2012).

Table 9.3 A professional development plan adopting teacher standards

Teacher standards	Targets and strategies to be employed
Curriculum	
Teaching and learning	
Pupil assessment	
Professional Reflection and communication	
Any other teacher standards	

Table 9.4 A sample professional development plan to achieve teacher standards

Teacher standards	Targets and strategies to be employed
Curriculum	Target: 'Have knowledge and understanding of planning coherent and progressive teaching programmes'; 'know and understand how to justify what is taught within curricular areas in relation to the curriculum and the relevance to the needs of all learners' (GTCS, 2012, p. 8). Strategy: From experience during school placement one, I must develop my knowledge further in all areas of science within the (Scottish) science curriculum in order to be competent in teaching unfamiliar topics and be able to give enough background detail to improve learner understanding.
Pupil assessment	Target: 'Use assessment, recording and reporting as an integral part of the teaching process to support and enhance learning' (GTCS, 2012, p. 17). Strategy: I plan to further develop my skills in this domain from placement one through the use of various formative assessment strategies in my lessons as well as issuing relevant homework exercises, I will reflect on these techniques accordingly to better improve my classroom practice.
Professional reflection and communication	Target: 'Read and critically engage with professional literature, educational research and policy' (GTCS, 2012, p. 18). Strategy: During school placement one, I took a profound interest in improving and developing my teaching practice based on observation feedback from experienced teachers. Throughout school placement two, I plan on developing this even further to stand myself in good stead for school placement three and onto probation while developing my own pedagogical practice along the way.

Holding weekly mentoring meetings   143

Table 9.3 can be adapted to use to record weekly mentoring meeting records. See Appendix 9.1, which presents an example weekly meeting record document.

9.2.2 Internal drivers

Internal drivers such as the structure of the school day, the focus of the school and other roles and responsibilities held by the mentor may impact on the conduct of weekly mentoring meetings. In terms of the structure of the school day, some schools allow one period per week for a mentoring meeting, while others expect this meeting to take place after school working hours. In addition, some schools have a whole school agenda at a specific time, such as literacy, numeracy or health and wellbeing, which might impact the discussions held during weekly meetings. Task 9.4 asks you to discuss with colleagues internal drivers that impact on weekly meetings, ways these meetings are (should be) organised, and how school-based factors can have an impact (positive/negative) on these weekly meetings.

Task 9.4   What are the common internal drivers to consider when establishing the weekly meetings?

Discuss with experienced colleagues, other mentors and perhaps new members of staff what they think are the main internal factors within your school that could impact on your weekly meetings with a beginning teacher.

   You could consider asking the following reflective questions from your colleagues:

- Do you conduct the weekly mentoring meetings on a specific day/time and for a particular duration (or not)? During school working hours and/or after school working hours?
- Do you think that conducting meetings on a specific day/time and for a particular duration is (could be) helpful for the beginning teacher? Why/why not?
- What challenges do you face in making the time for planning and holding these meetings? How do you overcome these challenges?
- Do you (or would like to) use a set agenda for these meetings (such as numeracy and literacy, et cetera)? Are these meeting agendas provided by the school (or not)? Do you (or would you like to) let the beginning teacher to set the agenda? Why/why not?
- What challenges do you face in conducting these meetings focusing on set agenda? How do (would) you overcome these challenges?

Another internal driver affecting the ethos and dialogue of the weekly meetings could be the other roles and responsibilities you might have within the school. It is fair to suggest that these roles and responsibilities often colour the way a beginning teacher views their mentor. For example, if you hold a leadership role within the school such as head of science or principal teacher, a beginning teacher may see you differently than if you

144   *S. P. Day*

are an experienced science teacher or newly qualified yourself without additional roles and responsibilities. It is vital to ensure that as you establish a good working relationship with the beginning teacher, any other roles and responsibilities you undertake are acknowledged, but that these do not negatively impact on or overtake weekly meetings. Therefore, you need to be mindful of how your position within the school impacts on how a beginning teacher perceives you.

9.3 Pre-planning the structure of weekly mentoring meetings

During the early stages of your mentoring relationship with a beginning teacher, most of their concerns focus on logistics and expectations, such as: what a mentor/school and/or the ITE provider might be expecting from them. Therefore, in your first weekly mentoring meeting you need to set out your expectations in terms of how you would like to work with the beginning teacher such as how often will you meet them? Who takes responsibility for setting up the meeting? Where will the meeting take place and how long will the meeting last? You should also consider that these meetings provide a space where professional dialogue can flow, privacy (as far as possible) can be guaranteed in terms of not being overheard or interrupted, and is seen by you and the beginning science teacher as a safe space. The last point on safe space is vital because there might be times when a beginning teacher might be emotional, feel overwhelmed or upset and it is this safe space that allows them the time and space in which to reflect on their experiences. It is a place where professional learning ought to occur. Once these questions on logistics and expectations are achieved, you can then focus on outlining the structure of these weekly meetings.

The weekly meetings require reciprocity and explicitness in terms of clarity of expectations and actions, as well as a positive, empathetic and solution-focused ethos within the weekly meetings (Sears, 2018). That said, it is important to structure weekly meetings consistently so that the beginning teacher knows what to expect and can prepare for it. Therefore, in addition to safe space, some common pre-planning routines to conduct the weekly meetings are to:

- Establish a way of recording the meeting, for example providing the beginning teacher with a pro forma to use to formally capture the context, content and outcomes of the meeting
- Ensure that all paperwork is available and shared (either electronic or hard copy) and that both you and the beginning teacher are familiar with the paperwork. For example, lesson plans and accompanied units of work, agenda for the meeting, et cetera
- Prepare questions to open the meeting in a positive way, perhaps with a question that allow the beginning science teacher to respond positively. For example, by asking an opening question such as can you tell me what the highlights of your week were?
- Review targets set in the last meeting and prepare how you will systematically discuss these targets. What pieces of evidence will you ask the beginning teacher to present during the upcoming meetings, for example lesson plans, lesson evaluations, self-reflections on planning and teaching, assessment evidence from classes indicating pupil progress

Holding weekly mentoring meetings 145

and so on? Would you remind the beginning teacher about the pieces of evidence you will be discussing with them during the upcoming weekly meeting? If yes, then when? If not, then why not?

- Plan enough time to discuss further actions required (such as practising a variety of teaching strategies) and associated teacher standards (see Task 9.3)
- Consider any wider school or departmental practices you want to discuss with the beginning teacher, such as parents' evenings, whole school staff development days, extra-curricular activities (such as STEM ambassador work or science clubs) and school trips. Planning to talk about these practices is important as it avoids the notion that these experiences are ad hoc and unimportant in developmental terms and highlights that these practices are integral in developmental terms as they enable the beginning teacher to fit into the school's community
- Ensure you keep enough time to summarise the meeting so that the beginning teacher leaves the meeting with a clear understanding of what is going well, their targets that need to be developed, how they might develop those targets over the coming week(s), and what evidence they will need to gather and present in the next meeting.

9.4 The GROW (Goal, Reality, Obstacles/Options and Way forward) model

The weekly mentoring meetings naturally evolve with time as a beginning teacher develops and becomes more independent, particularly as their sense of professional efficacy grows. To best support a beginning teacher throughout their time with you, you need to recognise that your role must be flexible and adaptable. To begin with, you should take on the role of a facilitator during these weekly meetings. By using reflective questions, you can channel and focus discussion within a meeting in a directive but in a non-judgemental way.

While there are several different frameworks that are useful for supporting mentors to stimulate discussions within these weekly meetings, one evidence-based approach used within coaching and mentoring circles, which has been found to be effective is the GROW model (Whitmore, 2002). Table 9.5 outlines the GROW model.

Using the GROW model can be helpful during weekly meetings reviewing and identifying a beginning teacher's experiences, helping them to identify individual strengths and areas for development, discussing professional and work issues, agreeing on what support is required, exploring options open to the beginning teacher, and supporting them to set achievable, realistic yet developing targets.

It should be noted that the GROW model follows a non-linear process and discussion is iterative – with the meeting moving backwards and forwards between phases to refine and clarify the best course of action. It is important to recognise the non-linear nature of the model; this allows you maximum flexibility to move around the model according to your professional experience. Revisit each step as necessary, in any order, to ensure the beginning teacher remains motivated and that their goal fits with the schools aims, purpose and

146   S. P. Day

Table 9.5 The GROW model

Acronym	Description	Objective	Reflective questions (*A mentor asks the beginning teacher to answer*)
Goal (G)	• Determine the focus of mentoring by asking the beginning teacher to clarify what they want to achieve from each meeting	• Agree with the discussion topic • Agree with specific objectives for the session • Set a long-term goal or aim (if appropriate)	• What would you like to discuss? • What do you want to achieve in this session? • What differences would you like to see on leaving this session? • Do we have sufficient time for you to be able to attain this?
Reality (R)	• Raise awareness of present realities • Examine how current situation is impacting the beginning teachers' goals	• Invite self-assessment of topic or situation • Give specific examples of feedback • Check assumptions for validity • Discard irrelevant assumptions and history	• How do you know this is accurate? • How often does this occur? • What impact or effect does this have? • Are there other factors that are relevant? • What is X's perception of the situation? • What have you done or tried to date?
Obstacles (O) *Options (O)*	• Identify and assess challenges and obstacles • Identify and assess available options • Encourage solution-focused thinking and brainstorming	• Identify obstacles • Find out if the beginning teacher thinks there is more than one obstacle • Consider overcoming different obstacles such as: people, resources, environment, et cetera • Cover the full range of options open to the beginning teacher • Invite suggestions from the beginning teacher regarding their perspective on the options available to them • Offer suggestions carefully • Ensure that the beginning teacher makes choices	• What prevents you from achieving your goal? • What else could be preventing you? • What personal changes do you think you need to make to achieve your goal? • What is hindering you from changing? • Do any of your direct/indirect behaviours, attitudes, competencies, skills, et cetera contribute to or help the situation? • What alternatives are there to that approach? • Who might be able to help you? • Would you like me to make suggestions? • Can you identify the pros and cons for that option? • Do you have a preferred option you'd like to act on?
Way forward (W)	• Assist the beginning teacher to determine next steps • Develop an action plan and build motivation	• Get a commitment to act from the beginning teacher • Identify, together, the potential obstacles • Plan detailed actions within a set timeframe • Agree what and how support will be given to the beginning teacher	• What are your next steps? • What timeframe will you set? • Can you anticipate anything getting in your way? • How will you keep a log of your progress? • What support might you need? • How and when can you get that support?

(Source: Adapted from Spence and Grant (2007) and Brown and Grant (2010))

Holding weekly mentoring meetings 147

values as well as aligning with their professional purpose and values. If you were to follow this model, then each meeting should finish with clearly defined action steps or targets to be completed before the next meeting. Subsequent mentoring meetings begin by reviewing and evaluating the previous meeting's action steps before moving on to set a goal(s) for the current meeting.

Following the GROW model, it is important to recognise that overloading a beginning teacher with too many targets will overwhelm them so, as a mentor, you must filter and prioritise targets (no more than four every month) according to the needs of the beginning teacher. If the target is met in the following weekly meeting, remember to praise the beginning teacher as this will build a sense of achievement and progress. If a target is proving difficult to overcome then try to break it down into smaller, more specific and manageable sub-targets as this will aid the targets to be achieved.

The GROW model supports professional dialogue that should take place within the weekly meeting. The learning that emerges from the model is integral to the mentoring process as it is through this dialogue that progress is evidenced, targets are set, and the professional relationship between you and a beginning teacher is fostered and nurtured over time. The reflective questions identified in the last column of Table 9.5, could be used to support a professional dialogue that can challenge a beginning teacher's thinking in a supportive manner. Sometimes it is important to ask critical questions that relate to a beginning teacher's understanding of different policies and/or that probes their justification for pedagogical choices adopted within their teaching. To answer these reflective questions (mentioned in the last column of Table 9.5), documents such as lesson plans, examination questions and reflective reports can be used as sources of evidence. These documents can also be used to map the beginning teacher's development against teacher standards. Therefore, across a sequence of meetings, you need to support a beginning teacher to capture a pattern of growing evidence of their development, linking to the teacher standards, that can allow you and the beginning teacher to recognise the degree of development over time.

Finally, using the GROW model (or any other similar model) to conduct effective weekly mentoring meetings need to evolve over time. It evolves as a beginning teacher grows in confidence and gains experience. With this growth in confidence and experience, the nature and conduct of the weekly meetings evolve to the point that the control of the meetings swing towards the beginning teacher; where, gradually, they take more responsibility for the direction, context, content and conduct of the weekly meetings. As a result of this change, the way that weekly meetings are planned, conducted and evaluated must also change.

9.5 Reflection on your ability to hold weekly mentoring meetings

Mentors need to develop their self-reflection skills and knowledge about teachers' professional development. The ability to analyse and question your mentoring practice is an important element of your professional development. If the mentoring of a beginning teacher is viewed as an act of professional learning, then it is possible to argue that the

148   *S. P. Day*

mentoring process is similar to the learning process but that the 'learner' is not the pupil but the beginning teacher.

One way to engage in this reflection is to make judgements about your own developmental needs so that you can better support a beginning teacher to make steady progress. It is possible to explore your mentoring meetings from multiple perspectives. For example, you may wish to consider it from a structural perspective in terms of have you been given a timetabled period of time in which to carry out the weekly meetings? Or from the management perspective in terms of do you have adequate time and space in which to plan, conduct and evaluate the weekly meetings? Alternatively, you may wish to reflect on the effectiveness of the meetings from an outcome perspective by reflecting on the extent to which a beginning teacher is making progress in their classroom practice and more widely as a teacher (which may be, in part, as a consequence of the regular weekly meetings). Another way is to look at the effectiveness of the weekly meetings from the perspective of the impact that a beginning teacher is having on the attainment and achievement of pupils they are working with. Finally, you may wish to adopt a more personal development perspective in terms of how the experience of mentoring a beginning teacher generally and through weekly meetings have explicitly impacted on your own personal development by asking questions such as what characteristic of an effective mentor have I embodied this week? By engaging in such critical professional reflection, you might also see the development and growth of your mentoring skills in your relationship with a beginning teacher you are mentoring. Task 9.5 asks you to reflect on your mentoring skills and associated mentor-mentee relationship development.

Task 9.5   Mentor's reflection

Return to Task 9.1 and reflect on the questions again. Assess your answers in light of your reading of this chapter. Identify aspects of weekly meetings that have developed as you have interacted with this chapter and undertaken weekly meetings worked on the areas that require further development. As you do this, reflect further on the questions below:

- To what extent have you developed, within your weekly meeting practices, structural, managerial and professional development perspectives as you support the beginning teacher?
- How do you intend to tackle the dual role of a mentor and an assessor during weekly meetings, given that you will be building a close working relationship with the beginning teacher over time?
- What provision have you made for your own support in terms of a critical friend?

[A critical friend is ideally an experienced mentor who can act as a sounding board. They can help you to think through issues as they arise over the course of the mentoring process, provide friendly advice and pose critical questions to support your mentoring practice.]

Summary and key points

This chapter highlights the vital role of the weekly meetings in the mentoring process and in the development of a beginning teacher. It characterises weekly meetings as a safe space where reciprocal professional dialogue and reflection take place for the purpose of supporting a beginning teacher's professional growth in terms of their classroom practice, awareness of their specific role as a teacher and their wider roles and responsibilities to the school community. This part of the formal mentoring process ought to result in the growth and development of you as a mentor as well as the beginning teacher.

This chapter asked you to take into account the following points:

- Regular mentoring meetings are the prime conduit through which beginning teachers can effectively gauge their development and progress.
- A crucial aspect of these meetings is the building of a professional mentor-mentee relationship that is mutually respectful and trusting.
- The effectiveness of weekly meetings is underpinned by active listening and reflective questioning of the policy context (both internal and external) and how this impacts on classroom practice in general and the development of a beginning teacher's practice in particular.
- Critical professional reflection is the most useful tool used in the mentoring process as it acts as a conduit for professional dialogue between the mentor and beginning teacher.
- These mentoring meetings should evolve over time, in a way that a beginning teacher can evidence and feel that they are moving forward in their practice. They should be able to see that they are becoming less dependent on the mentor by taking more responsibility for the direction, context, content and conduct of the weekly meetings.

Further resources

Luft, J.A. (2009) 'Beginning secondary science teachers in different induction programmes: The first year of teaching', *International Journal of Science Education*, *31* (17), pp. 2355-2384. This article provides an insight into how different types of induction programme facilitate the development of beginning secondary science teacher's development over the course of one year. Some data informs the different styles of mentoring meetings and its application by the mentors, duration of meetings, effective and ineffective meetings from the beginning teacher's perspectives and the significance of meetings on a beginning teacher's performance. Reading this article could help you to understand the positive impact of science-specific mentor-mentee sessions (meetings) on a beginning teachers' classroom practices.

Wright, T. (ed) (2017) *How to be a Brilliant Teacher Mentor: Developing outstanding trainees.* Abingdon: Routledge.
This book is an informal and highly accessible guide to mentoring that provides ideas that could support your work as a mentor. The book offers advice on giving effective feedback, dealing with critical incidents, developing reflective practice and what to do if relationships break down. Chapter 2 of Wright's book titled 'inputs and outputs' (pp. 1-27) could extend your awareness of ways you could provide constructive, clear and timely feedback to a beginning teacher during a lesson de-brief and extend the discussions on effective pedagogical teaching methods during weekly mentoring meetings.

150 S. P. Day

Appendix 9.1 An example template of a weekly meeting record document

Week number Start time End time	This box needs to be completed by the beginning teacher before the meeting.		
Some developmental activities undertaken this week	This box needs to be completed by the beginning teacher before the meeting.		
1. Teacher standards: Professional developmental targets and strategies	Teacher standards	Reflecting on last week's targets and strategies employed This column needs to be completed by the beginning teacher before the meeting.	Reflecting on this week's targets and strategies employed This column needs to be completed by the beginning teacher during the meeting along with the mentor.
	Curriculum	Targets: Strategies:	Targets: Strategies:
	Teaching and learning	Targets: Strategies:	Targets: Strategies:
	Pupil assessment	Targets: Strategies:	Targets: Strategies:
	Professional reflection and communication	Targets: Strategies:	Targets: Strategies:
	Any other teacher standards	Targets: Strategies:	Targets: Strategies:

2. Further action required based on the previous week's targets.	This box needs to be completed by the beginning teacher before the meeting.	This box needs to be completed by the beginning teacher during the meeting along with the mentor.
3. Questions to be asked from the mentor.	This box needs to be completed by the beginning teacher before the meeting.	This box needs to be completed by the beginning teacher during the meeting along with the mentor.

(Source: Adapted from Golder, Arthur, Keyworth and Stevens (2019, p. 230) and from Table 9.3 above)

SECTION 3

Extending basic mentoring practices

10 Supporting beginning teachers to develop pedagogical content knowledge

Michael Allen and Simon Parry

Introduction

The teaching of knowledge in subjects is a core aim of schools and is at the centre of continuing debate about national and international standards in education. As mentioned in Chapter 1, in recent years changes to the Teachers' Standards in England (Department for Education (DfE), 2011) and the introduction of more knowledge-rich curricula have put greater emphasis on the importance of subject knowledge. Subject knowledge of science is full of conceptual difficulties, which has implications for pupils' learning. Therefore, our recommendation is that mentors instigate a learning progression approach for beginning teachers, initially developing subject knowledge and then focusing on enhancing their pedagogical content knowledge (PCK). PCK describes the ability to transform knowledge for the benefit of pupils' learning; it follows that having good subject knowledge is essential for developing beginning teachers' PCK.

In this chapter, we examine the link between the importance of a beginning teacher's subject knowledge and the learning outcomes of their pupils, how subject knowledge might be improved to solve the problems of teachers constructing erroneous concepts, the learning progression approach, and the interplay between the beginning science teacher's PCK and their subject knowledge.

Objectives

At the end of this chapter, you should be able to:

- Reflect on how you, as the mentor, can support the development of a beginning science teacher's subject knowledge
- Apply a three-step learning progression approach to develop a beginning teacher's PCK
- Support a beginning teacher's development from developing subject knowledge of science and PCK.

10.1 The importance of pedagogical content knowledge (PCK) in teaching science

It appears self-evident that a beginning teacher with a greater amount and depth of subject knowledge will be better at their job; pupils often identify this as a key characteristic of good teachers. However, the actual impact of a beginning teacher's subject knowledge on pupil outcomes often shows much less correlation than might be expected (DfE, 2016c). As a mentor, you might assume that by being in possession of a science degree, a beginning teacher's scientific knowledge will be sufficient to teach secondary school pupils. However, a degree is often quite narrowly focused, whereas the science taught in schools in the UK and beyond is wide-ranging. As a minimum requirement, a beginning teacher must be aware of the science content covered in the science curriculum and know the subject matter well enough to be able to teach it to their pupils. Therefore, it is your responsibility as a mentor to remind a beginning teacher to refresh their subject knowledge on a regular basis in accordance with the secondary science curriculum. You could ask a beginning teacher to record the names of books, internet resources and websites they are using to enhance their subject knowledge and keep evidence of any notes and solved examination-styled written/online questions in a folder. You can review this folder on a weekly or monthly basis, with the opportunity to discuss or share other resources.

Good subject knowledge is important for effective teaching when affiliated with good PCK. PCK is identified as having the strongest evidence of impact on pupils' learning outcomes (Coe, Aloisi, Higgins and Major, 2014) and evidence shows that it has a greater impact on learning than subject knowledge alone (Baumert, Kunter, Blum, Brunner, Voss, Jordan, Klusmann, Krauss, Neubrand and Tsai, 2010). To better understand the term PCK, we refer to the originator of the phrase, Shulman, who defined it as 'that special amalgam of content and pedagogy that is uniquely the province of teachers' (Shulman, 1987, p. 8). Therefore, not every beginning teacher with extensive subject knowledge can teach well, as 'there is a vast difference between knowing about a topic [subject knowledge] and knowing about the teaching and learning of that topic [PCK]' (Bucat, 2005, p. 2).

A beginning teacher needs careful mentoring to re-shape scientific knowledge from their own education, forming an altered version which can be used for teaching school science (Kind, 2009). PCK needed for teaching is complex and is difficult to measure. Despite the importance of PCK, it is not a commonly used term among beginning teachers. However, as a mentor of a beginning teacher you should recognise this powerful concept, which deserves to be fully explored during weekly mentoring meetings. As a mentor, you could initially ask a beginning teacher you are working with to differentiate a teacher from someone who is merely an expert in a subject and to explain why. A discussion with a beginning teacher on this broad question could support the assertion that a teacher having a degree in a specific subject is not necessarily an indicator of improved pupil outcomes – what is more significant is the ability to teach scientific knowledge to pupils (Kind, 2009; also see section below on Effective teaching: A journey from subject knowledge to PCK). Task 10.1 is designed to help you to discuss subject knowledge and PCK with a beginning teacher and to reflect on your mentoring practices in supporting a beginning teacher to develop PCK.

Developing pedagogical content knowledge   157

Task 10.1   What mentoring support is needed to develop PCK?

Complete the following steps:

1. From your prior experience with beginning teachers (if any), what subject knowledge, instructional skills and strategies in relation to PCK should a beginning teacher recognise – as a minimum requirement – to develop themselves as an effective teacher during their initial teacher education (ITE) programme? [If you do not have prior experience, discuss this with an experienced mentor.]
2. Ask a beginning teacher; (i) what they understand by the terms subject knowledge and PCK, and (ii) what subject knowledge, instructional skills and PCK strategies they recognise – as a minimum requirement – to develop themselves as an effective teacher during the ITE programme.
3. Working with the beginning teacher, categorise these PCK recognition indicators, rank them in order of importance and justify reasons for this ranking order.
4. Based on your responses to the questions, categories and justifications, reflect on your mentoring practices in supporting a beginning teacher to develop PCK. You could select a reflective practice (RP) model from Chapter 4 for this step.
5. Revisit steps 1 and 4, after reading this chapter.

10.2 A learning progression approach to the development of a beginning teacher's PCK

Using the Teachers' Standards in England (DfE, 2011) as a yardstick (or teaching standards towards which a beginning teacher you are mentoring is working), each beginning teacher's current stage of attainment in the different areas of competence can be determined (see Chapter 1 for a description of teachers' standards in shaping mentoring practices). This is, of course, normal practice during ITE. However, a learning progression approach assumes that complete competence in all the aspects within a specific teacher standard may not happen simultaneously. Instead, progress has to be mapped out in more detail, with partial competence being an acceptable staging post on the journey to complete capability of a standard.

Accordingly, a beginning teacher should recognise that their development as an effective teacher is a gradual process of accumulating experience and knowledge. Gaining a more sophisticated understanding of a particular area of the curriculum, or a pedagogical skill, can take several years (Schneider and Plasman, 2011). Moreover, as a mentor you need to encourage a beginning teacher to realise that each step in a learning progression does not necessarily happen autonomously, and might require your intervention, so they should not hesitate in asking for help and guidance from more experienced colleagues. As a mentor of a beginning teacher, you are ideally placed to fulfil this role of an experienced colleague or you can identify a few senior members of staff who can support a beginning teacher's learning progression in different aspects of science content.

Next, some mentoring strategies to support a beginning teacher in adopting the learning progression approach to developing PCK are outlined, using Figure 10.1.

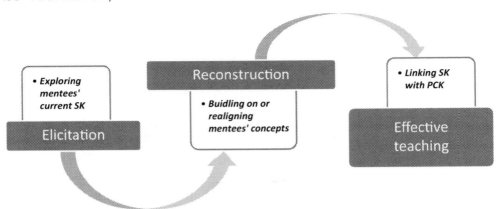

Figure 10.1 A learning progression approach to develop PCK [SK refers to subject knowledge]

Figure 10.1 identifies three-stages:

- Elicitation: A starting point for a mentor is to identify any parts of the science curriculum in which a beginning science teacher lacks knowledge and confidence of teaching
- Reconstruction: A mentor can then explore the beginning teacher's subject knowledge of science in detail to determine its limits and put plans in place to support progression of the beginning science teacher's conceptual journey.
- Effective teaching: A mentor can then emphasise the importance of the beginning teacher's PCK development, by guiding them to think about how pupils learn science (which includes their potential misconceptions) prior to planning and how they will teach it.

To put these principles into day-to-day mentoring practice, as a mentor, you need to consistently and effectively follow the following key steps throughout the time you are mentoring a beginning teacher:

- Refer to and discuss the relevant teachers' standards documents with the beginning teacher and find their position on the learning progression scale at the start of the mentoring period. This involves assessing which of the several competences contained within each standard have been reached and which are currently being worked towards. Try to repeat this exercise on a regular basis so that the beginning teacher can clearly track their progression over time (this can be done in weekly mentoring meetings – see Chapter 9).
- Emphasise the importance of learning to teach over time through conversations with the beginning teacher. Unlike a mastery method, with a learning progression approach to development, complete competence in a standard is an incremental process. As the beginning teacher passes along the progression, they will reach points that fall short of the required level.
- You can give some examples of your own progression approaches. These examples can help the beginning teacher to realise that their performance will not improve in great

Developing pedagogical content knowledge 159

leaps of advancement – rather, each individual competency within a teacher standard will be achieved one at a time. Therefore, encourage the beginning teacher to focus on only one/a few teachers' standards at a time with an awareness that some aspects of these standards can take longer to achieve than others and that they are operating at only partial competency within each standard.

We now discuss some mentoring strategies that you can adopt or adapt to support a beginning science teacher's subject knowledge development during their ITE programme, using the three interlinking learning progression approaches.

10.2.1 Elicitation leading to reconstruction stage of development

A common way to examine a beginning teacher's current science subject knowledge, based on the units of work recommended by the science curriculum, is by asking them to carry out a self-audit, which can identify gaps in their knowledge. An example of a subject knowledge audit is provided in Appendix 10.1. Task 10.2 asks you to consider a few steps to support a beginning teacher's development of subject knowledge using such an audit.

Task 10.2 Subject knowledge audit for a beginning science teacher

1. Ask a beginning science teacher to rate their subject knowledge on the list of units taught in your school, using the subject knowledge audit tool in Appendix 10.1 or another suitable tool.
2. Discuss their rating with the beginning teacher, identifying areas of strength and areas for development, focusing on how they can develop their subject knowledge of science (both strengths and aspects for development) and what support they might need from you in developing subject knowledge. As a result of this discussion, design an action plan including:
   a) *Agreed subject knowledge-based areas of strengths:*
      These areas of strengths will be consolidated by....
   b) *Subject knowledge development:*
      Areas for focused subject knowledge development: These will be addressed by....
3. Ensure that the action plan is discussed and monitored during weekly mentoring sessions and amended on a regular basis.

However, some beginning teachers may find the start of the placement not the most appropriate time for completing a subject knowledge audit, and may determine themselves that the best time for developing their subject knowledge is when they need to teach it (Lock, Salt and Soares, 2011, p. 36). In light of this, a different approach might be at the start of the placement to carry out a subject knowledge audit across the whole science department, with

160 *Allen and Parry*

an aim to highlight areas of expertise for sharing (Appendix 10.1 could be used by the whole science department).

10.2.2 *Reconstruction leading to PCK-mediated effective teaching*

In addition to monitoring a beginning science teacher's subject knowledge audit and subject knowledge action plan, to improve their science subject knowledge gradually, you can also recommend content-based materials to a beginning teacher, such as textbooks, revision guides, and internet resources.

The most common strategy for addressing deficits in subject knowledge is self-study. You could support a beginning teacher to adopt self-study by guiding them to read relevant texts summarising pupils' science misconceptions, the most well-known being Taber's two volumes summarising Chemistry Misconceptions in Secondary Schools (Taber, 2002a, 2002b), Driver, Squires, Rushworth, and Wood-Robinson's (1994) classic book Making Sense of Secondary Science and Allen's (2019) book on Misconceptions in Primary Science. In addition, you could organise an in-service training session on science misconceptions for science colleagues using the above texts as sources. In this session, you could ask teachers (including the beginning science teacher) to bring along some classroom scenarios based on their own and pupils' misconceptions and critique their teaching and learning practices using the above texts. After this session, you could ask the beginning teacher to evaluate the session based on the importance of understanding and acting on diminishing misconceptions that teachers and pupils can bring to the classroom.

You could advise the beginning teacher, especially when teaching a specific topic for the first time, for example enzymes from the unit of work cell biology (see Appendix 10.1), to read fully the relevant curriculum guidance on the expected levels of learning of most pupils for each of the units of work. This curriculum guidance could be an examination board specification for A-level or The General Certificate of Secondary Education (GCSE), the KS3/KS4 Science National Curriculum or equivalent, together with an appropriate textbook. Give support, if needed, so that the beginning teacher can answer all of the questions on the topic that are in the textbook. You can then challenge the beginning teacher further by asking them to think of three or four questions that they believe pupils might ask them, together with appropriate answers. You could also suggest they practise some past examination questions without looking at the mark-scheme, before teaching the specific unit of work. You and/or another experienced teacher could explain some of the answers more fully if needed; 5 minutes spent explaining could save a lot of a beginning teacher's time researching.

These suggestions might support a beginning teacher in reaching the minimum level of subject knowledge to aid them in developing their PCK. To help them develop PCK further, you need to practise some additional effective mentoring suggestions, for example:

- Setting aside some time in science departmental meetings to teach each other – this could be something new on the examination specifications, or just give a seminar on a specific unit of work that is of particular interest (it would be fair not to expect the beginning teacher to give the first presentation!).

Developing pedagogical content knowledge 161

- Making PCK an explicit part of your lesson observation feedback, and of weekly mentoring meetings. You can achieve this by asking the beginning teacher to keep updating the subject knowledge audit template alongside their lesson plans. You can then revisit the template on a regular basis.
- Encouraging the beginning teacher to join a subject association, such as the Association for Science Education (ASE), the Royal Society of Biology (RSB), Royal Society of Chemistry (RSC) or the Institute of Physics (IoP). You can then ask them to adopt/adapt some of these organisations' teaching and learning resources and associated PCK specific teaching notes in their practices.
- Suggesting to the beginning teacher that they read some popular science education books, for example, A Short History of Nearly Everything (Bryson, 2004), Bad Science (Goldacre, 2009), Astrophysics for People in a Hurry (Tyson, 2017), and many others. You can then discuss any changes in their perceptions and understanding after reading these books, and how it can help them to strengthen their subject knowledge and eventually PCK.
- Advising the beginning teacher to keep up with the latest science teaching and learning related research to reinforce PCK, by following some websites such as BBC News/BBC Science and Environment, or Science News. Encourage the beginning teacher to create a display board using interesting, pupil-friendly and curriculum-relevant science articles from newspapers and magazines, and guide them to involve pupils in this activity too. You could also provide them with opportunities to attend university-oriented free science lectures that are open to all teachers.

The third level of the learning progression stage, which advances from reconstruction of PCK to effective teaching, is explained in the next section.

10.3 Effective teaching: Linking subject knowledge with PCK

A beginning teacher needs your support in using PCK to, amongst other things:

- Develop and select appropriate activities for pupils.
- Choose a range of explanations and examples, including being able to explain in alternative ways if necessary.
- Use analogies and metaphors.
- Check pupils' understanding, and interpret their difficulties and misconceptions at the point of teaching.
- Facilitate productive discussion in class, knowing which ideas to pursue and which to let go.
- Adapt teaching in response to pupils' comments in class.
- Cope confidently with questions from pupils.
- Select purposeful practical work, to enhance scientific understanding.
- Make connections between the subject and the wider experience of pupils.

Before reading about some further ideas to support development of PCK, Task 10.3 asks you to co-plan a lesson with a beginning teacher you are working with to enhance pupils' learning.

Task 10.3 Mentoring a beginning teacher, with an emphasis on using PCK to enhance pupils' learning

Step 1. Ask a beginning teacher to discuss with you their lesson plan for an upcoming lesson, with a focus on planning for activities to evaluate pupils' learning.

Step 2. Working together, identify one or more activities for the pupils that might help to indicate that learning is taking place, beyond recall of information. During this co-planning, discuss not only the means or how the activity will be conducted but also the purpose and value of the activities. For example, allowing pupils to explain a scientific concept in their own words at the end of the lesson, in writing or verbally, with the purpose of allowing pupils to summarise their understanding of the learned scientific concept.

[This activity will help a beginning teacher to evaluate the impact of their teaching on pupils' learning, identify misconceptions among pupils more effectively and plan the next lesson accordingly.]

Step 3. The beginning teacher should then teach the planned activities, reflect on the taught activities focusing on their PCK approaches to teaching, and share their reflective comments during the post-lesson discussion with you. Such reflective accounts must include:
  • How did the lesson go?
  • What are the justifications of using a particular PCK approach(es) to teaching?
  • What were the important teaching points to aid pupils' learning and their development of scientific skills?
  • What might they do differently next time and why?

Step 4. This task could be repeated, using different PCK approaches; for example pupils having to explain ideas in their own words, applying their knowledge to a new situation, explaining their thinking, suggesting answers to more open-ended questions, asking questions of their own, or changing information from one form into another.

Used on regular basis, these suggestions could support a beginning teacher's journey towards developing PCK. A few useful resources and general strategies for you to consider while mentoring a beginning teacher during their gradual journey towards PCK competence are now suggested:

• Guide a beginning teacher to use online forums such as Times Educational Supplement (TES), TES community: Science (2017), encouraging them to find resources that can then be adapted to suit their particular classes.
• Accompany the beginning teacher on a professional development walk (PDW) based on lesson observations of experienced teachers, mainly focusing on aspects of PCK that they can develop. Then discuss the choices and reasons behind experienced teachers'

Developing pedagogical content knowledge   163

PCK-mediated actions and their implication on pupils' learning. You can adapt the PDW framework from Chapter 14 (Task 14.9, p. 225).

- Recommend continuing professional development (CPD) courses to the beginning teacher, to develop PCK, in and beyond the ITE programme (Evens, Elen and Depaepe, 2015). Suggest some courses that are outside of their specialist area of science. These may not be specifically referred to as PCK courses, but rather subject knowledge. Therefore, suggest they attend these courses to not only focus on subject knowledge acquisition but also focus on how subject knowledge can be best translated in their teaching practices.
- Discuss with the beginning teacher about the aspects of the unit(s) of work and accompanied pedagogical practices that they are about to teach. In addition, you could also pair a beginning teacher with a more experienced teacher, for the same purpose.
- Co-planning and reflecting with the beginning teacher during pre-lesson and post-lesson discussions may bring further gains. Reflecting on practice has been shown to be an effective way of developing PCK (Evens, Elen and Depaepe, 2015). But taking into consideration their workload, perhaps reflection in a group discussion might be better received than a written reflection task.
- Prioritise focused discussions on PCK during weekly mentoring meetings. These discussions should include reviewing some of their recently taught lessons, discussion on alternative strategies that could have been used, including ways of explaining, choice of practical work, progression of ideas, connections to everyday experiences, analogies and so on. You can also repeat Step 3 of Task 10.3 during these discussions.
- Consider using the Content Representation (CoRe) tool developed by Loughran, Berry, and Mulhall (2012), which aims to represent a teacher's understanding of a particular topic. Task 10.4 provides guidance for you to support an individual beginning teacher to develop subject knowledge on a particular topic using Appendix 10.2, and to make explicit links between knowledge, teaching, and learning of this topic, including possible misconceptions.

Task 10.4   Content Representation (CoRe) tool

Ask a beginning teacher you are mentoring to fill in the table in Appendix 10.2, by first identifying several 'big ideas' (or concepts) associated with the topic they are currently teaching. At first, you might need to collaboratively fill in the table with the beginning teacher. An example of a completed CoRe for the teaching of the topic 'enzymes' (under 'enzymes; factors affecting the rate of enzymatic reactions' (DfE, 2014, p. 8) in the unit of work cell biology) to 14-16-year-old pupils is given in Appendix 10.3.

You could encourage the beginning teacher to use this table independently to plan a CoRe matrix for other topics associated with a particular unit of work, i.e. plan activities/questions, then teach it, revise their accounts after the lesson and finally discuss the changes in their reflective accounts with you during their weekly mentoring meetings.

164   *Allen and Parry*

After reading this chapter, consider summarising the suggestions above, aimed at supporting a beginning teacher to develop PCK. Task 10.5 requires you to support a beginning teacher to construct an action plan to develop subject knowledge and PCK and link subject knowledge with PCK effectively.

Task 10.5   An action plan to help a beginning science teacher by developing subject knowledge and PCK and linking them effectively

Use the suggestions provided in this chapter to support a beginning teacher you are mentoring to draw up an action plan tailored to developing their subject knowledge and PCK and linking subject knowledge with PCK effectively, using the learning progression approach. You could adopt/adapt Appendix 10.4 as a template, which highlights some of the suggestions to elicit and improve PCK.

Ask the beginning teacher to reflect on their progress over time and discuss their progression with you on a weekly, monthly or termly basis.

Finally, revisit your answers from Task 10.1, and reflect, reconstruct and transform your mentoring practices in the future with the aim of supporting a beginning teacher to develop their PCK.

Summary and key points

A beginning teacher's PCK is a vital prerequisite for successful science teaching. In this chapter:

- We advised that one of your primary concerns as a mentor should be to ensure that a beginning teacher has a correct grasp and a broad appreciation of subject knowledge.
- With reference to the Teachers' Standards in England (DfE, 2011), we suggested a variety of approaches that a mentor can employ that might enhance a beginning teacher's subject knowledge and PCK.
- We acknowledged that linking a beginning teacher's subject knowledge with their PCK is frequently overlooked, but having one without the other means a science lesson is unlikely to be taught successfully.
- We took the position that nurturing a beginning teacher's PCK should be the overall aim of every aspect of mentoring, not merely actions concerning subject knowledge development.

Further resources

Allen, M. (2016) *The Best Ways to Teach Primary Science*, Maidenhead: Open University Press. Although originally written to help develop primary teachers' subject knowledge and PCK, this book has much to offer secondary specialists. Mentors can discuss, with a beginning teacher, some example misconceptions that are common across a wide age range, to support their learning progressions in a wide range of science content. This learning progression development can also be used by mentors to identify and rectify a beginning teacher's misconceptions while assessing their subject knowledge.

Association for Science Education (ASE) (undated) *School Science Review*, viewed 22 January 2020, from: www.ase.org.uk/resources/school-science-review
This quarterly journal is produced with secondary science teachers in mind. It comprises articles that focus on science teaching and learning for the 11–19 age range. Many articles are written by serving teachers, not researchers, and are a useful source of innovative lesson ideas to enhance a beginning teacher's PCK. Other articles are more academic and summarise the latest findings relating to how pupils learn science, and tried-and-tested approaches that have been found to be successful in helping them construct appropriate concepts, and develop their process skills.

Driver, R. (1983) *The Pupil as Scientist?* Milton Keynes: Open University Press.
This seminal book almost single-handedly triggered the emergence of the constructive view of science teaching and learning in UK schools and universities in the 1980s. Mentors can present this book to a beginning teacher to aid the development of PCK over a period of time, as the book highlights the basis of how contemporary school science has evolved to become what it is today. The easy-to-follow PCK ideas from this book can be discussed during weekly mentoring meetings to emphasise the need to elicit pupils' ideas prior to teaching, and how to use practical work effectively to help pupils reconstruct subject knowledge.

Goldacre, B. (2009) *Bad Science*, London: Harper Collins.
Not an academic text, but this popular science bestseller debunks 'dodgy' scientific claims in the media and elsewhere. Writing in a readable and amusing style, Goldacre calls into question how organisations such as advertisers and drug companies stretch the truth when trying to sell us their latest wares. The book could help a beginning science teacher to link their own critical faculties that they developed during their science studies with examples from the world at large.

Appendix 10.1 Subject knowledge audit for beginning teachers

Subject knowledge audit Rate your subject knowledge for each of the units of work in the curriculum using the three-point grading criteria					
Unit of work	**Grade**			**Next steps**
	Grade 1 **Outstanding knowledge**	Grade 2 **Good knowledge**	Grade 3 **Knowledge requires improvement**	
This column lists units of work, for Biology, Chemistry and Physics, which are taken directly from England's Key Stage 4 science curriculum for pupils aged 14-16 (DfE, 2014). The unit of work on cell biology is presented in this column. These are taken directly from the DfE (2014) curriculum guidance document. You could ask the beginning teacher to fill in the rest of this column, for the other units of work, in the similar way, using the curriculum guidance. You can adapt/adopt these units further according to your country's science curriculum. You could also use the same template to introduce the curriculum for age groups 11-14.				
Biology				
1. Cell biology Aspects of unit of work: • 'cells as the basic structural units of all organisms; adaptations of cells related to their functions; the main sub-cellular structures of eukaryotic and prokaryotic cells.' • 'stem cells in animals and meristems in plants.' • 'enzymes; factors affecting the rate of enzymatic reactions.' • 'the importance of cellular respiration; the processes of aerobic and anaerobic respiration' 'carbohydrates, proteins, nucleic acids and lipids as key biological molecules.' (DfE, 2014, p. 7 and 8).				

2. Transport systems				
3. Health and disease				
4. Photosynthesis				
5. Homeostasis and response				
6. Inheritance, variation and evolution				
7. Ecosystems				
Chemistry				
1. Atomic structure and the periodic table				
2. Bonding, structure, and the properties of matter				
3. Quantitative chemistry				
4. Chemical changes				
5. Energy changes				
6. The rate of chemical change				
7. Organic chemistry				

8. Chemical analysis				
9. Chemistry of the atmosphere				
10. Using resources				
Physics				
1. Energy				
2. Electricity				
3. Particle model of matter				
4. Atomic structure				
5. Forces				
6. Waves				
7. Magnetism and electromagnetism				
Other units of work				

Appendix 10.2 A CoRe matrix to develop PCK, adapted from Eames, Williams, Hume and Lockley (2011, p. 3)

CoRe matrix	Important idea 1	Important idea 2	Important idea 3
What do you intend the pupils to learn about this idea?			
Why is it important for the pupils to know this?			
What else is there about this idea that you do not intend pupils to know yet?			
What difficulties/limitations are connected with teaching this idea?			
What do you know about pupil thinking that influences teaching about this idea?			
Are there any other factors that influence your teaching of this idea?			
What teaching appoaches would you use, and why, for this idea?			
How would you ascertain pupil understanding of, or confusion about, this idea?			

Appendix 10.3 An example of a completed CoRe matrix, for teaching enzymes to 14-16-year-old pupils

CoRe matrix	Important idea 1	Important idea 2	Important idea 3
What do you intend the pupils to learn about this idea?	Enzymes catalyse specific reactions in living organisms	Enzyme activity is affected by a number of factors	Digestive enzymes convert food into smaller, more soluble products.
Why is it important for the pupils to know this?	Enzymes control the speed of chemical reactions in the body, without them reactions would be too slow for life to survive	Enzymes function correctly at optimum pH and temperature - link to homeostasis	Because it helps to explain what happens to the food we eat.
What else is there about this idea that you do not intend pupils to know yet?	Induced-fit hypothesis. Primary, secondary, tertiary structure	Enzyme inhibition	
What difficulties/limitations are connected with teaching this idea?	Particles are too small to see. Collision theory is an abstract idea	Can be difficult to relate to pupils' everyday experiences	

What do you know about pupil thinking that influences teaching about this idea?	Pupils may think enzymes are 'used up' in a reaction	Pupils may think enzymes are living, and can be 'killed' by high temperatures	Enzymes are involved in all metabolic processes, not just digestion. Pupils may think enzymes only break down molecules.
Are there any other factors that influence your teaching of this idea?	Maturity of pupils – are they able to work with abstract ideas? Pupil understanding of collision theory (links to chemistry)		
What teaching approaches would you use, and why, for this idea?	Analogies (lock and key), modelling (using plasticine, for example)	Practical work – consider if all factors would be taught through practical work (if not all, how many, and which ones?)	Creative writing – pupils write a story imagining they are a piece of food passing through the digestive system.
How would you ascertain pupil understanding of, or confusion about, this idea?	Translation activities – pupils draw pictures to show stages in enzyme and substrate combining, and formation of product.	POE (pupils predict, observe and explain). For example, teacher demonstration of raw and cooked liver added to hydrogen peroxide	Use of key words and ideas in the story could illustrate pupil understanding or misconceptions.

Appendix 10.4 A three-step process to help a beginning teacher to develop their subject knowledge and PCK [SK refers to subject knowledge]

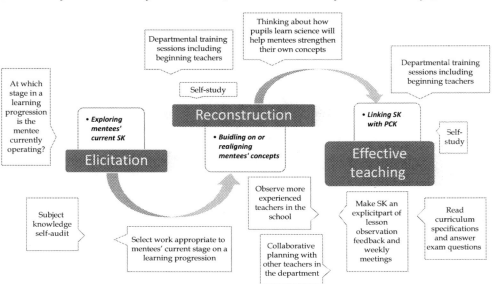

11 Supporting beginning teachers to cope with contingencies

Mike Watts

Introduction

Bozeman and Feeney (2007, p. 17) offer the following definition of mentoring:

> A process for the informal transmission of knowledge, social capital, and psycho-social support perceived by the recipient as relevant to work, career or professional development; mentoring entails informal communication, usually face-to-face and over a sustained period of time, between a person who is perceived to have greater relevant knowledge, wisdom or experience (the mentor), to a person who is perceived to have less (the protégé).

I pick up on a number of these points throughout this chapter. In my own long life of school teaching and university work, I have been blessed by the company of several key people, teachers and pupils, who have influenced and shaped both my general and particular life-course – mentors who are the silent co-authors of what I write here.

As a framework for the chapter, I trade on work by Rowland and colleagues (Rowland, Huckstep and Thwaites, 2005) to develop something they call the 'knowledge quartet'. In general terms, this quartet concerns teachers' subject knowledge and how this is deployed within classroom contexts. Although Rowland's work describes primary mathematics and mathematicians, I use it here to discuss secondary scientists. I want to articulate a sense of the 'mentoring self' – a sense of mentoring that incorporates a good deal of personal curiosity, questioning, guiding, explaining and answering. Alongside many other aspects of mentoring, I cast both the mentor and the beginning teacher as 'curious explainers of contextualised science'. Throughout the chapter, I ask a series of questions that focus on 'doing mentoring' and ways of 'being a mentor in action'.

Objectives

At the end of this chapter you should be able to:

- Understand some key issues involved in effectively supporting a beginning teacher's own learning in school science, enhancing and embellishing their subject knowledge to cope with unexpected and unplanned questions from the pupils

172 Watts

- Support a beginning teacher to become a better explainer as a way of answering contingent questions
- Support a beginning teacher to consider short- and long-term strategies to promote a productive and purposeful learning environment – not least in dealing with unexpected 'contingent' questions
- Support a beginning teacher to develop their own, and their pupils', science curiosity, and find ways in which to answer many unexpected and unsettling questions that arise in the teaching and learning of science.

11.1 Where does mentoring begin?

First, an example. The three states of matter is a fairly standard and useful explanatory story in science as a bare-bones summary of how materials might work. The science curriculum recommends that teachers teach 'the differences in arrangements, in motion and in closeness of particles explaining changes of state, shape and density' (Department for Education (DfE), 2013, p. 13). But is that it? The teacher differentiates the particularity of solids, liquids and gasses and then the science lesson is done and dusted? Well, not in the many lively classrooms of my own experience. Task 11.1 requires you to reflect on ways you could guide a beginning teacher towards going beyond one-off structured teaching of the three states of matter.

Task 11.1   A contingent moment for a beginning science teacher

The example below is a 'contingent moment', an unexpected, unplanned-for question from a 14-year-old Saima relating to the states of matter.

'Sir?' (David)
'Yes, Saima?'
'Why does a biscuit left out overnight go soft, but a piece of bread goes really, really hard?'

The beginning science teacher (David, in this case) is unsure how best to answer, how to construct an appropriate explanation within the specific confines of a lively lesson. Consider:

1. How would you advise David?
2. And what is the best way to tackle a question like that?

It is worth noting that advice proffered is commonly not the same as advice sought – what a mentor can offer by way of mentoring support and assistance may not match exactly what the beginning teacher needs or wants. Giving wise counsel, then, is an enormously uncertain business. Furthermore, one aspect of life is seldom discrete and separate from all of the other dimensions of personal or professional being. All this makes mentoring a distinctly inexact and tentative activity. One difficulty with the scenario above lies in the sensitivities involved. David does not want to blunt Saima's enthusiasm or dismiss her authentic question,

Supporting beginning teachers   173

but nor will there be many opportunities in a busy classroom to engage in extended discussions or explanations. Similarly, it may not be possible for you to probe David's subject knowledge in great detail, what science he actually knows about the issues involved, to know quite how best to mentor him.

Rowland, Thwaites and Jared's (2015) iteration of the subject 'knowledge quartet' has four dimensions: 'foundation' refers to teachers' subject-related knowledge and beliefs; 'transformation' concerns knowledge-in-action as shown both in the planning of teaching and in the act of teaching itself; 'connection' describes ways that teachers achieve coherence and connectivity both within and between lessons: it 'includes the sequencing of material for instruction, and an awareness of the relative cognitive demands of different topics and tasks' (p. 75) and, finally, 'contingency' captures the unpredictability in classroom events that were not planned for. This chapter focuses on supporting beginning teachers in dealing with contingency. An illustration of that is the beginning teacher's immediate search for an on-the-hoof answer to Saima's unexpected bread-and-biscuits question. Before reading further, Task 11.2 asks you to consider another example of a 'contingent moment', an unexpected question, asked by Aisha in the middle of a planned lesson linking to the topic of changes in the three states of matter and heat energy.

Task 11.2   A contingent moment in the middle of a planned lesson experienced by a beginning teacher

'Miss'? (Jenny Jones)

'Yes, Aisha?'

'You know when you eat a pizza, why does the cheese go all long and stringy?'

Beginning teacher Miss Jones approaches you, stung by her own inability to deal adequately with Aisha's perfectly reasonable question.

1.   How do you, her mentor, respond?
2.   What have you done in similar situations?
3.   How well have your teaching strategies worked in situations like this?

Both beginning teachers, David and Jenny, must see the support you offer and provide as being relevant to them and to their classroom situation. As you reflect on your advice, you will also be aware that:

- Teachers are encouraged to stimulate thinking through great questions, stimulate curiosity and open-mindedness and enthuse pupils to new learning.
- Genuine questions deserve genuine answers. Pedagogically, there needs to be time and space within school science that allows for answers and explanations to pupil's questions – both David and Jenny need to find appropriate ways to do this.
- School science, however, is but a tiny sliver of all the wealth of science that exists out there, and that its curriculum content is commonly ill-equipped to deal with many of the possible questions that pupils can ask.

174 *Watts*

- As beginning teachers, much rests on David's and Jenny's sense of confidence, their self-efficacy as teachers of science, their personal dispositions and their specialist scientific knowledge.
- That working with David and Jenny on their subject knowledge, on their approaches to teaching and learning, on their 'explanatory relationship' with their pupils, is both a sensitive, and a long-term process – there are few, if any, short-cuts.

11.2 Mentoring: What is scientific explanation?

To understand a phenomenon is to have it explained: explanations generate understanding, they help the question-asker to 'make sense' of something, satisfy their need to understand. In this way, explanation has its root in the practice of raising questions and giving answers, with the expectation of being answered genuinely in one way or the other so that it gives us strong psychological feelings of knowing, of having increased our grasp of the matter in question, of having constructed some sensible meaning for what is going on. Task 11.3 asks you to offer advice to a beginning teacher on the topic of the effect of temperature change on ice.

Task 11.3   Supporting a beginning teacher to build a scientific explanation for pupils

'Miss?' (Sally Smith)

'Yes, Tomas?'

'Why does your tongue stick to an ice lolly?'

In this contingent moment, Sally Smith needs to build an explanation around the temperature of an ice lolly and the freezing point of saliva.

1. How would you help here? Keeping in mind that there are many times when you realise that an explanation has not worked, that the person on the 'other end' has not grasped what you are explaining
2. Whose fault is it? Certainly, the explanation might be 'beyond' a particular audience (pupils), but is that the fault of the audience or of the explainer (teacher)?

The direction I follow is that explanation can best be understood in the general context of inter-personal communication: it is people who construct explanations. One thing is clear, there is a considerable degree of improvisation that happens in any lesson. Certainly, clear planning, good knowledge of the class, a solid understanding of beginning science teachers' ideas and misconceptions, an appreciation of the shape of the lesson, the shape of the day ahead, will reduce the number and level of uncertainty and surprises. It is possible to predict and plan for some of the contingency, but not to know in advance until events unfold. It is important to emphasise here that those surprises, those unexpected moments that disturb and unsettle beginning teachers, are not to be feared. They can galvanise the teacher to

Supporting beginning teachers   175

learn, to reflect, and to change ideas and plans for the following lesson. There is substantial empirical evidence, too, on how to manage and orchestrate such a classroom (for example, Pedrosa de Jesus, Leite and Watts, 2016). Over time, I have used each one of the following, with varying degrees of success. You could consider encouraging a beginning teacher you are mentoring to incorporate some of these into their planning and teaching practices:

- Put a cardboard post-box on one side of the classroom, rather like a ballot box, where pupils are encouraged to post their questions on slips of paper, anonymously if need be. Beginning teachers David, Jenny or Sally can then read the questions after the lesson, prepare answers and make time to deal with these at the start of the next lesson, as in 'We had a really interesting question from Saima in the last lesson, so let's see what to make of it...'
- A Year 8 class had a washing line along the wall on one side of the room; pupils were encouraged to 'hang' their questions on the line. The second class of the week ended with 10 minutes to spare and pupils were encouraged to take a question off the line and, working in groups, think of ways to answer it.
- For the teacher to deliberately build in question time into the lesson. This might be a 5 minute slot in the middle when pupils are encouraged to write and discuss questions, before the lesson 'proper' resumes again.
- One school had a science chat room on the school's online learning system, and pupils were encouraged to question and discuss issues raised in classes. The science teachers monitored the system and regularly interjected with questions – and answers – of their own.
- Some of the questions from the post-box, washing line or question time can be set for homework or holidays.

As David's mentor, you might also nudge David's own understanding of science. How much is he reading? What kinds of things is he reading? For example, reading Scientific American or even Reader's Digest regularly makes a considerable difference to one's breadth of knowledge.

You need to support the beginning teacher to develop their understanding about potential ways of addressing these questions, such as by sharing Aisha's contingent question and discussing what Jenny should do to answer her question. For example, Jenny needs to bring in her understanding that long-chain protein molecules 'curl' up in uncooked pizza cheese that separate more as the temperature rises and which, if pulled, can be extended into 'strings'. After sharing and discussing Aisha and Jenny's example with a beginning teacher, you could also discuss the use of analogy in science classrooms with them, such an analogy might be the long-chain molecules in a plastic shopping bag that, if heated or stretched, can be pulled into strings that are strong in the direction of the stretch (although they can split quite easily between the chains). Another example that you can share with a beginning teacher could be based on Tomas's question about licking ice lollies. You might make reference to the moisture on the tongue freezing and sticking to the ice crystals on the lollipop, that it is best to be gentle lest he (Tomas) rips a layer of skin off his tongue.

So, are these the 'right' explanations? The issue here is: What exactly is the right level of explanation for each of the pupils involved? So, in testing a beginning teacher's science, you

176 *Watts*

are also exploring their 'reading' of their audience, i.e. the appropriate level of explanation for the appropriate level of the pupil. Have they got it about, right? How would they gauge the listener's (pupil's) capabilities? How would they frame the explanation to a 13-year-old?

Moreover, do you think that beginning science teachers are expected to know all of the answers? No, that sort of explanatory knowledge is something that accrues over many years, is derived from a plethora of sources (television programmes, YouTube, friends, family, neighbours, magazines, books, DIY manuals, plumbing experts and so on). Such real-life multi-modal learning derived from a wide variety of sources has been termed 'complex learning' (Merrill, 2002; van Merrinboer, 2007; Davis and Sumara, 2009; Facer and Manchester, 2012). Complex learning theory (CLT) highlights the ways in which people accumulate and synthesise knowledge and understanding within everyday life. One of your roles as a mentor, then, is to emphasise the time span involved in becoming a science teacher: teaching can improve and be embellished year on year as teachers amass and incorporate new ideas, explanations, accumulate new science stories, contextual details, historical perspectives, industrial applications and much more.

It is important for a beginning teacher to be open to collecting as much incidental science as is possible. There are many ways they can do this. I began the chapter by emphasising curiosity, and there are few substitutes for marvelling and inquisitiveness in science. As a member of a large school science department, I was often engaged in convoluted break-time discussions of one current event or another. We were never afraid to ask each other questions or advice. For me, teaching biology for the first time, I was fairly constantly in the company of the resident biologist, asking awkward questions. As the mentor, you can encourage a beginning teacher to:

- Be honest about key strengths and real 'gaps in knowledge', and talk through upcoming lessons and subject areas. In this way, you can help a beginning teacher to 'know themselves', gain insight into their principles and values in relation to their knowledge and understanding
- Appreciate that a beginning teacher builds up specialist subject knowledge in a highly individualistic way, and that they must take the lead in developing their teaching. They need to know, too, that you are part of the resources they can call on for the appropriate use of subject knowledge in their teaching
- 'Buddy up' with another subject specialist, to observe their teaching, and to 'raid' their lessons for sources of ideas and answers.

11.3 Why can science learning be so difficult?

As an experienced science teacher, you know that contingent questions can 'come out of the blue', stimulated by pupils, often in an unexpected response to something that happens in the lesson. These questions are often oral, can come singly from a particular pupil or as the result of group activity. In their work Rowland, Huckstep and Thwaites (2005) described three kinds of pupil question: first in response to a question from the teacher; second in response to an activity or discussion, and third when a pupil gives an incorrect answer – to a question, or as a contribution to a discussion. Moreover, they said:

Supporting beginning teachers 177

Our data show that the teacher's response to unexpected ideas and suggestions from students [pupils] is one of three kinds: to ignore, to acknowledge but put aside, and to acknowledge and incorporate (p. 79).

Task 5.2 (p. 62), in Chapter 5, covered some aspects of mentoring to be judgmental (or not). Task 11.4 asks you to encourage a beginning teacher you are working with to reflect on their judgments when dealing with an unexpected question from a pupil, with the aid of Carla's scenario.

Task 11.4 Beginning teacher's judgment, explanation and contingent question

'Miss' (Carla)

'Yes, Jason?'

Jason: 'How come an ant can escape unharmed from heating in a microwave oven?'

Consider sharing this scenario with a beginning teacher you are mentoring and discuss the following:

1. Will the beginning teacher (Carla, in this instance) have an explanation to hand in a digestible form for Jason to feel satisfied?
2. One judgement Carla must make is the extent to which a pupil's question goes with – or against – the 'grain' of the lesson. Is Jason deliberately sowing 'red herrings'?
3. Is Jason mischievously trying to upset the rhythm and pace of Carla's lesson, or is his contingent question real and authentic?

While discussing these questions with the beginning teacher you could initiate a further discussion on the idea of teacher's implicit bias and equity gap.

You could elaborate the discussions in Task 11.4 by sharing and/or allowing the beginning teacher to share some similar instances. For example, the workings of household plumbing and appliances are common areas of non-knowledge or ignorance: how does a television remote control work? Is it possible to cool down the kitchen by leaving the fridge door open? How does a Wi-Fi system work? How come a car key-fob unlocks just your car and not any other of the millions of cars in the UK? When it's really windy outside, you can see the water in our toilet bowl move about. How does that happen? There are several mentoring points you might want to make here:

- Gaining a broad understanding of a range of topics should be seen as fun – the beginning teacher (all teachers, in my view) should 'browse for pleasure'. There is no obvious time span for this, it is on-going – there are numerous websites devoted to 'contextual' science information.
- Use pupils' questions as the basis for their own research and inquiry. Answering the 'ant question', for example, may take a few moments to problem-solve a response, not

just to Jason but the whole class. You could guide the beginning teacher to provide an explanation to a contingent question in small steps – ideally in three steps. Such as:

Step 1: Ants take advantage of the fact that microwaves in the oven are set to form a standing wave, with areas of low intensity and area of high

Step 2: Most ovens have a turntable to ensure that food is cooked evenly throughout

Step 3: As long as the ants resist riding the turntable, they will be able to detect and avoid areas of high intensity.

- Gaining subject-specialist knowledge is part of a teacher's responsibility: it is part of their work. As noted earlier, pupils' questions can be seen as challenges and opportunities for further study. For instance, in relation to the toilet question above, a toilet waste pipe is vented to the open air up at roof level, to help equalise the pressure in the drain system and prevent unwanted back siphoning and the like. When the wind blows, gusts can cause the water in the toilet bowl to move. You could share this example with the beginning teacher to understand how a good subject knowledge can support them in coping with contingent questions.

In some lessons the teacher is able to take some action in-the-moment in response to the relevant question, to incorporate this into the lesson. At other times, the teacher shelves the explanation – overtly or subtly – in the there-and-then and reflects on this at a later stage. The important issue for the mentor is to help a beginning teacher manage the lack of ready answer over time, and offer classroom management systems that allow pupils (such as Jason) to continue asking questions while generating sufficient time and capacity to enable themselves (such as beginning teacher Carla), and the pupil, to explore possible answers. Some ways of doing this (like the post-box) are listed above, but some more might be to:

- Encourage a beginning teacher to plan a time for questions (the question time) at the start of the lesson. This will give some insight into pupils' understandings and allow the teacher to indicate which questions will and will not be covered in the course of the lesson. Those questions that will not be dealt with can become 'open homework' tasks
- Suggest that a beginning teacher allows pupils to use Post-It notes to attach questions to a sheet on the wall as they leave the class at the end of the lesson. This allows time before the next lesson to answer relevant ones
- Suggest that a beginning teacher notes that, if the SAME questions keep appearing over time, then there is a key issue to be tackled. Thus, it is worth spending extra time with the class to ensure that the essential ideas are understood.

Hattie (2011), in a book called Visible Learning for Teachers, made the point that teachers with good subject knowledge can more easily respond to the needs of pupils, recognising those who are struggling and change the way that material is presented to make it more available. The 'bottom line' here is that complex learning is complex, not just because we derive learning from a multitude of sources, but because it is a-synchronous, serendipitous, and happens as small 'nudges of knowledge' (Salehjee and Watts, 2019) throughout life. As a good mentor you are party to this, offering relevant nuggets of advice, emphasising lifelong pedagogic learning, and giving the emotional support just as and when needed.

Supporting beginning teachers 179

So, some mentoring points of advice you could give beginning teachers, might be:

- To make contact with others on social media. There are many colleagues out there who are more than happy to share resources, experience, advice and answers to questions.
- Swap books and reading with others in the department – better – with those in the Technology or Religious Studies department.
- Keep contact with their current and old university for seminars, courses, lectures. If they can make time, even attend an evening course at a local college.
- Become engaged in external, industrial or commercial partnerships. Links with external concerns, from field study centres, to museums, businesses and factories, encourage a wide range of opportunities to expand knowledge and understanding.

11.4 Why are unexpected questions so unsettling for a beginning teacher?

It is rare to find a beginning teacher who can readily explain. They can be aware of key principles in science, but they often find it very difficult to apply those to specific problems. As Newton (2000) points out, understanding satisfies a number of personal needs:

> We often feel dissatisfied with merely knowing that event B followed event A. What we are curious about is why B followed A (p. 6).

The suggestion here is that puzzlement, curiosity, perplexity, doubt, challenge, wonder and incongruity are all forms of what Piaget (1971) called disequilibrium. It is clear that feelings of satisfaction, dissatisfaction, comfort or discomfort about thoughts or explanations, are emotional, affective issues and not just cognitive ones. So, dissatisfaction, or discomfort, with new incoming information is an emotional state. Task 11.5 asks you to consider how you can support a beginning teacher in building confidence of using these unexpected questions in building pupils' scientific concepts.

Task 11.5   Mentor's reflection: Building confidence of a beginning teacher

'Sir?' (Angus)
'Yes, Sarah?'
'Why do people keep a bucket of sand in case of fire?'

Sarah's question is a legitimate one despite being unpredictable in the context of a biology lesson. While the experienced teacher might have seen the opportunity for connectivity between 'choked respiration' and 'choked fires', it does take confidence and assuredness to take advantage of such opportunities, make those connections, and push pupils' thinking beyond the core focus of the lesson. So:

1. Where does confidence come from?
2. How can you support a beginning teacher (in this case, Angus) to develop confidence or self-assurance as they are working?

---

180 *Watts*

Harri-Augustein and Thomas's (1991) comment that 'learning embodies as much feeling as thought' (p. 17). A mentor's subject specific advice can certainly be helpful, especially if a hesitant beginning teacher is unsure of an appropriate science explanation (for example, about domestic plumbing), or have some idea but want a specialist to secure that knowledge for them. This can be effective for 'lighter' teaching-learning issues. However, beginning teachers like Carla, David and Jenny above, facing a series of more complicated professional challenges, probably want to know that the mentor can understand what they are going through, rather than seeking any 'quick classroom fix' that might miss the underlying issue altogether. In this sense, as mentioned in Chapter 5, a mentor's support involves the sensitive understanding of the beginning teacher's emotional experience. Therefore to understand and support any underlining issues a beginning teacher has, a mentor needs to actively listen, understand, and validate their emotions. Mentors might feel they simply must provide a solution because of their role when, in fact, there may be times when it is best not to proffer advice but stay quiet and simply listen.

If teaching only involved planning and teaching tightly prescribed lessons within a very specified curriculum, then it would probably be sufficient to know just enough subject matter for what is needed, just enough pedagogical knowledge to manage the session. But, from my perspective, that challenges perceptions of what teaching science is about.

There is, too, a great deal for pupils to learn in the ways that a teacher responds; how David, Jenny or Carla behave when confronted by science contingency, how they manage their own doubts and uncertainties, how sometimes they get stuck, how they reason their explanations. As Feynman (1985) famously said,

> A scientist has a lot of experience with ignorance and uncertainty... We have found it of paramount importance that in order to progress we must recognise our ignorance and leave room for doubt. It is our responsibility as scientists... to teach how doubt is not to be feared but welcomed and discussed (p. 175).

In addition, Wallace and Gravells (2005, p. 4) made the point that it is one of a mentor's responsibilities to support a beginning teacher's grasp of subject knowledge in terms of 'currency, breadth and appropriateness'. So, there is an important role for mentors in supporting a beginning teacher as they build this kind of subject knowledge to be effectively utilised in the classroom. Some supporting tasks you might use include:

- Sit with the beginning teacher and sketch a concept map of the immediate 'subject terrain', of 'threshold concepts', and give pointers as to where unexpected contingent questions might arise. Give some pointers to the kinds of resources and materials around that might support the teacher as he or she is working.
- Become an appreciative enquirer alongside the beginning teacher so that they feel supported empathetically in 'coming up to speed' on issues within their teaching.

Supporting beginning teachers   181

An effective one-to-one relationship is at the heart of mentoring, and the more effective this is, the more transformative that mentored learning can be.

- Encourage the beginning teacher to give presentations to other colleagues within and outside the science department. Reporting back on training sessions, organised outings or particular issues within the curriculum provides excellent opportunities for developing both sides of the subject spectrum – airing questions and reaping possible answers.

Summary and key points

Conceptualising teachers' subject knowledge is a complex issue. I have focused in this chapter on 'knowing that' rather than the procedural knowledge of 'knowing how' (of, say, setting up a practical demonstration). So, given the sense of contingency discussed here:

- Neither mentor nor beginning teacher should expect to have ready-made answers to everything. In the chapter, I have offered a range of practical approaches that can be used in mentoring for a beginning teacher using the five scenarios of David, Jenny, Sally, Carla and Angus. Important amongst these is the need to allow thinking time for rumination, to engage in inquiry, to improvise. A beginning teacher need to build their explanations, have a feel for the nature of explanation
- It is not uncommon for a beginning teacher to spend considerable time in planning pupil activities, but fail to plan themselves, their expositions, into their lesson plans. The best mentor helps a beginning teacher to plan their explanations carefully; understand that their own language needs planning. Whether in explaining new ideas, or in task setting, a beginning teacher needs to decide how explanations are going to sound. They have to prepare varied examples and anecdotes that will carry the lesson's meaning (Wright, 2012, p. 11)
- In the same vein, a beginning teacher needs your support to understand elements of scientific reasoning, ways of thinking and knowing in science. It is not surprising that many philosophers of science (for example, Hacking, 1983; Laudan, 1981) suggest that a 'useful' theory is one that has good explanatory depth and breadth, as well as some immediate social use. The essence here is that learning is a way of life, all should keep learning, keep reading, keep building analogies, metaphors, examples, stories
- A mentor needs to match the advice they give to the advice being sought. It is all too easy to say, 'Well I wouldn't actually start from here' but here is where the beginning teacher is 'at', and that must be the starting point. In subject terms, the mentor must consider how to support a beginning teacher's current subject knowledge, with an overall strategic view of developing a beginning teacher's ability to answer unexpected and unsettling questions that arise in the teaching and learning of science
- Following this sense of contingency would be to accept the accompanying vulnerability, not to close the door on opportunities.

Finally, it is important to feel the fun and delight of impromptu science and, to adapt Biesta's (2014) title, explore 'the beautiful risk of (science) education'.

Further resources

Alfred, G. and Garvey, R. (2010) *Mentoring in Schools Pocketbook*. 3rd edn. London: Management Pocketbooks.
The *Mentoring Pocketbook* helps in the design of a mentoring scheme, how to prepare to be a mentor, conducting mentoring sessions, and how to maintain the relationship through different stages of mentoring.

DfE (2016b) *National Standards for School-based Initial Teacher Training (ITT) Mentors*, London: DfE, viewed 19 April 2020, from: https://assets.publishing.service.gov.uk/government/uploads/system/uploads/attachment_data/file/536891/Mentor_standards_report_Final.pdf
This is a very comprehensive – and surprisingly useful – 'warts and all' look at mentoring in secondary education.

12 Supporting beginning teachers to develop their ability to assess pupils

Helen Gourlay

Introduction

It is important to support a beginning science teacher in developing assessment strategies by which they can begin to consider the effectiveness of their teaching and learning approaches. You will need to provide support for them in developing formative and summative assessments, and in understanding their responsibilities in relation to accountability for pupils' learning within the school system in which you work. In Chapter 1, Golder, Keyworth and Shaw pointed to Katz's (1995) model, in which beginning teachers experience an initial survival phase. The findings of my own EdD research with student science teachers in England are in line with Katz's suggestion of waiting to develop the advanced use of assessment until a beginning teacher has progressed beyond the survival stage.

This chapter is organised into four main sections. The first section introduces some mentoring suggestions to utilise the three dimensions of assessment (knowledge of assessment; understanding the context for assessment; recognising the impact of assessment) (Edwards, 2017) to determine what a beginning teacher knows about assessments and what they need to achieve over time. The next section includes suggestions for you to use to induct a beginning teacher into assessment policies and procedures in your school. The third section considers mentoring approaches to summative assessment, including alternatives to standardised testing. While a beginning teacher is involved in assessing pupils' work regularly, they need support in making their assessment truly formative. Therefore, the fourth section concerns mentoring strategies that you could use to support a beginning science teacher in developing formative assessment skills, such as the use of rich questioning and comment-only marking, facilitating self- and peer-assessment to support learning and using summative tests for formative analysis.

184 *Gourlay*

Objectives

At the end of this chapter, you should be able to:

- Utilise the three dimensions of assessment (Edwards, 2017) to support a beginning teacher's knowledge and practice of assessment procedures over time
- Induct a beginning teacher into assessment policies, procedures and practices in science in your school
- Support a beginning teacher in developing their understanding of some dimensions of summative assessments
- Support a beginning teacher in developing some important assessment strategies to incorporate formative assessments effectively.

12.1 Assessment dimensions development over time

Working with beginning teachers in New Zealand, Edwards (2017) developed a rubric for assessing their assessment literacy, in which she identified broadly three dimensions and ten subdivisions. These dimensions could provide a useful framework for describing the expertise that you would like a beginning teacher you are mentoring to develop over time. A summary of the dimensions is shown in Table 12.1.

Table 12.1 The three dimensions of assessment

Dimension	To what extent is the beginning teacher able to...
I. Knowledge of assessment	
1. Ability to describe assessment	...describe different types of assessment, for example formative, summative, diagnostic, showing an awareness of fairness, ethics and authenticity?
2. Knowledge of purposes of assessment	...articulate uses of assessment, for example reporting progress, accreditation, in-school evaluation of teaching, and national evaluation of teaching/schools?
3. Knowledge of what to assess	...integrate their knowledge of subject-specific content to be taught, with an understanding of pupils' progression through it, aligning this knowledge and understanding with assessments? (What is to be taught, when is it to be taught, and how is it to be assessed?)
4. Knowledge of assessment strategies and design	...design appropriate subject-specific assessment tasks or tests, with an appreciation of the need for validity and reliability?
5. Knowledge of assessment interpretation	...make accurate judgments of pupils' grades using mark schemes?
II. Understanding the context for assessment	
6. Knowledge of standards-based assessment in the relevant education system	...accurately assess pupils' work against teacher standards, including having an understanding of moderation processes?
7. Preparing pupils for standards-based assessment	...develop pupils' assessment literacy when preparing them for national tests and examinations, ensuring that they understand criteria of quality?
8. Using summative assessment formatively	...analyse summative data and use their findings to inform future teaching?

Dimension	To what extent is the beginning teacher able to...
III. Recognising the impact of assessment	
9. Understanding assessment consequences	...understand the impact of assessment on pupils, for example on their motivation and emotional wellbeing, and to use assessment in ways that promote the development of confidence and high self-esteem?
10. Fairness	...differentiate assessments to ensure that all pupils are able to access them, and to demonstrate what they have learned?

(*Source*: Adapted from Edwards (2017, pp. 213–215))

Table 12.1 provides quite a long list and you need to consider how a beginning teacher can be introduced to this material in a measured way over time. So, where do you start? It is important to start by finding out what a beginning teacher knows about assessment already, as this may enable you to identify strengths, areas for development and next steps. This information can inform your plans for supporting their professional development. Before reading further, Task 12.1 requires you to identify individual needs, in accordance with the dimensions listed in Table 12.1, by asking questions adapted from Lyon's (2013, p. 463) framework.

Task 12.1 Identifying what a beginning teacher knows about assessment

Ask a beginning teacher you are working with to answer the following questions (and any others you identify) and, with them, make a list of strengths, areas for improvement and next steps, which align with the dimensions indicated in Table 12.1 (in the below questions 'you' refers to the beginning teacher).

1. When you hear the word 'assessment' what are the first words or phrases that come to mind?
2. What experience have you had in learning about educational assessment?
3. How would you describe to a fellow science teacher what it means to assess learning?
4. Hypothetically, you are asked to construct an assessment of pupils' science learning. What are some things you would consider when constructing it and why?
5. What would you do with the assessment information you gathered about the pupils?
6. What does it mean to you to equitably assess pupils' learning?
7. What strategies have you used to assess pupils' learning?
8. How have other experienced teachers you have observed assessed pupils' learning?
9. What are your opinions about different strategies for assessing pupils' learning? What would be the impact of using different assessment strategies on pupils' learning?

[Where a beginning teacher has gaps in knowledge, you could refer them to some relevant literature, for example Chandler-Grevatt (2018) and readings in the further resources section].

12.2 A beginning teacher's induction to some assessment policies, procedures and practices in your school

Now moving from Dimension I (knowledge of assessment) towards Dimension II (understanding the context for assessment) (see Table 12.1), as a mentor, you are required to help a beginning teacher in understanding how assessment-based policies and procedures are implemented within your school's science department. In turn, these should fit into school assessment policies, procedures and practices. Thus, you should ensure that a beginning teacher has access to the school's assessment policies, marking procedures (which may also include homework procedures) and to relevant prior attainment data of the pupils they will be teaching.

To help with a gradual progression from Dimension I to II, you could collaboratively mark some pupils' work with the beginning teacher to model how to apply the school's and science department's assessment procedures. It would be beneficial to involve the beginning teacher when colleagues carry out cross-marking exercises to audit grading and the quality of the written feedback across the department (or the school). Within schools in England, for example, it is not uncommon for colleagues to carry out work scrutiny (sometimes called book scrutiny) to monitor teachers' work, and to provide feedback to improve teaching, learning and assessments. You could carry out book scrutiny of a beginning teacher's marking and provide them feedback using the questions below and/or ask the beginning teacher to self-scrutinise their marking using the similar questions, and discuss their answers with you. These questions are a selection from guidance for the Primary Science Quality Mark (PSQM, 2016, pp. 4–5), but are equally applicable to scrutinise marking in secondary school settings:

- Does marking give suitable feedback to pupils?
- Have pupils acted on feedback given?
- Are tasks marked to assessment criteria?
- Is marking accurate?
- Does written feedback reflect assessment criteria?

Similarly, where a beginning teacher is teaching examination classes, you should ensure that they are aware of key information about when and how their pupils will be assessed. The beginning teacher may need your support in accessing relevant materials, such as past examination papers and mark schemes. Some examination board's marking schemes are more detailed and specific than others, so you might consider carrying out a moderation exercise on a sample of marked papers, to support the beginning teacher in understanding the examiners' requirements. In some instances, training might be available from examination boards. At a later and relevant point in their development, you could encourage a beginning teacher to become a marker for an examination board, as this is an excellent way of developing a deep understanding of what is required for pupils to be successful in external examinations.

Supporting beginning teachers 187

In addition, in some countries, preparation for teaching examination classes might include inducting a beginning teacher about the examination board's assessment procedures and policies. As a mentor, you could work with a beginning teacher, ideally with the support of a laboratory technician, to enable them to familiarise themselves with core practical tasks assigned by the examination boards. A second strand to this preparation is to support the beginning teacher in recognising how the pupils' understanding of practical work will be assessed in written examinations and how might they prepare pupils to succeed.

At the time of writing (in England), it has become increasingly common for schools to have central databases of assessment information about their pupils, and to require departments to make regular (for example half-termly) data drops of pupils' scores or grades. If you are working within a system such as this, you need to ensure that a beginning teacher is aware of their responsibilities. My impression as a science teacher educator is that this whole school activity may have led to less recording of on-going assessment information lesson-by-lesson by the teacher themselves. It may be helpful to ensure that a beginning teacher has sufficient material recorded in their spreadsheet or mark book to prepare them for:

- Holding pupils to account for completing classwork and homework by having records of attendance, accompanied with records indicating pupils' attainment in each piece of marked work
- Monitoring pupils' progress so that action can be taken, where needed, rather than waiting for a whole school system to notice there is a problem once per half-term
- Being able to speak knowledgeably to parents or carers at parents' evenings (or equivalent) about pupils' strengths and areas for development in their science learning, rather than just reporting grades or levels
- Writing end-of-year school reports that give pupils meaningful targets about how they may improve in science.

Before reading further, Task 12.2 is designed to enable you to identify aspects of induction of a beginning teacher into your school's or department's assessment practices.

Task 12.2   A checklist for inducting beginning teachers into your school's or department's assessment practices

1. Adapt the checklist (Table 12.2), as needed, by considering the following steps:
   - Add any actions you are currently using that are not included in Table 12.2.
   - Align it with the context of your country and examination board(s).
2. Periodically return to the checklist with a beginning teacher you are mentoring, to monitor their induction into your school's and department's assessment practices.

Table 12.2 A checklist for inducting beginning teachers into your school's assessment policies and practices

Access to information and systems
Has the beginning teacher been given...   Tick ✓
- a copy of the school and department assessment and marking policies?
- relevant information about homework, for example policy, pupil planner, homework timetable?
- access to prior attainment data, and other relevant information, about their pupils?
- relevant information about the curriculum and assessment arrangements, including examination board specifications?
- access to end-of-unit of work tests and mark schemes?
- access to past examination papers and mark schemes of the examination board?
- access to systems for recording marks and grades, which might include a teacher planner or mark book?

Marking and record-keeping
Has the beginning teacher been given opportunity to...   Tick ✓
- see examples of work marked by experienced science colleagues?
- collaboratively mark work with an experienced science colleague?
- take part in a work scrutiny exercise?
- see how experienced teachers keep assessment records?
- take part in moderation of marking (especially external examination questions)?

Information about examination board's procedures and policies
Has the beginning teacher had an induction about the examination board's assessment procedures   Tick ✓
and policies, which might include...
- trying out core practical tasks with the support of an experienced teacher or laboratory technician?
- collaboratively marking assessed practical work?
- seeing associated recording systems?
- observing an experienced science teacher preparing pupils to carry out core practical tasks?
- observing an experienced science teacher preparing pupils for examination questions about practical work?
- opportunity to attend a continuing professional development (CPD) courses on effectively preparing pupils for assessment and on courses designed by the examination boards for teachers new to the role?

12.3 Supporting a beginning teacher to develop some dimensions of summative assessments

This section will support you to mentor a beginning teacher in developing summative assessments benefiting pupils' learning. It begins with an activity designed to support a beginning teacher to appreciate some criteria for quality in summative tests. It subsequently introduces some alternatives to standardised tests.

Task 12.3 is adapted from the Postgraduate Certificate in Education (PGCE) initial teacher education (ITE) programme used at King's College London (Harrison, 2013). Together with Table 12.1 (Dimensions I and II), this task will enable you to support a beginning teacher in understanding the construction and analysis of subject-specific standardised tests, emphasising:

- A range of marks for the pupils taking the test, distinguishing between candidates
- Well-designed questions and order of marks (higher-attaining pupils attain higher marks on each question than lower-attaining pupils)
- The order of questions (starting with easier questions in order to promote pupils' confidence).

Supporting beginning teachers 189

Task 12.3 Construction and analysis of summative tests

Follow the steps below during your mentoring sessions, using marks for a test which the beginning teacher you are working with has undertaken with one of their classes:

1. Access the pro forma provided on the companion website. [Web link to the spreadsheet – How good is your test?]
2. The spreadsheet assumes a test with ten questions, each with a maximum mark of 10, and a class of 30 pupils. You should change these numbers to match a test that is routinely used in your department, and which the beginning teacher has used with one of their classes.
3. The beginning teacher inputs the marks for each pupil, question by question, into the spreadsheet.
4. Sort the class into rank order in terms of their total percentage for the paper.
5. Select the top third of the class and the bottom third of the class and fill in the second table on the spreadsheet provided on the companion website, in rank order. [Web link to the spreadsheet – How good is your test?] This enables comparisons to be made between the highest attaining and lowest attaining pupils, question by question.
6. Discuss the following questions with the beginning teacher:
   - How well does your test meet the criteria suggested above?
   - Which questions may need to be replaced or adapted for the future?

In addition to the summative test papers mentioned above, pupils are assessed on their scientific inquiry skills (Archibald and Newman, 1988) including problem-solving and experimental skills. The practice of assessing pupils' scientific inquiry skills using rubrics is evident in many countries, where pupils produce portfolios of work that are assessed against rubrics describing national standards (see, for example, Qualifications and Curriculum Development Agency (QCDA), 2009; Queensland Curriculum & Assessment Authority (QCAA), 2017). Task 12.4 asks you to consider three steps in developing a set of instructions and rules to develop a beginning teacher's skills to assess scientific inquiry skills.

Task 12.4 Assessing pupils' scientific inquiry skills using summative styled rubrics

Step 1. Obtain the materials of the SAILS project 'Oranges: Will they sink or float? What's happening?' (Harrison (undated); see further resources).
Step 2. Use the materials to collaboratively plan an inquiry lesson with a beginning teacher (also see Chapter 16, Sections 2 and 4 on planning inquiry lessons).
Step 3. Support the beginning teacher in assessing their pupils' scientific inquiry skills using one or more of the rubrics provided in the material.

190   *Gourlay*

Learning from the above two tasks, Task 12.5 asks you to support a beginning teacher in reflecting on summative assessment of pupils' work by developing rubrics, marking and internally moderating together.

Task 12.5   Reflection on pupils' summative tests

Select a science topic that a beginning teacher is teaching. Next together with them develop an assessment task that could be used to assess an aspect of pupils' work. (See further resources for an example of a task from the QCAA (2014) paper, which assesses pupils' understanding of why we have seasons or practice on pupils' work used in Tasks 12.3 and 12.4). Then, follow the steps below:

1. Develop a rubric for forming judgments about quality, perhaps with reference to the rubrics from Queensland mentioned above.
2. Once pupils have completed the task, both of you should mark a sample of pupils' work against the criteria (rubric) you developed.
3. Meet to moderate your assessments and discuss the following questions:
    *   How do the assessments of pupils' work compare?
    *   If needed, how would they adapt the rubric for assessing pupils' work on another occasion?
    *   If needed, how would the beginning teacher adapt the assessment task for effective pupils' learning on another occasion?

12.4 Supporting a beginning teacher to develop some aspects of formative assessment

My professional experience as a teacher in schools over 17 years, as well as working with a range of schools as a teacher educator, suggests that science departments in schools in England may rely quite heavily on summative styled end-of-unit tests. This may be a difficulty internationally as well because we work in an increasingly globalised system, in which governments have tended to move education systems towards high-stakes and standardised testing. At its worst, this may create an environment in which it is difficult to resist instrumentalism, and teaching to the test (Broadfoot and Black, 2004). Research tends to suggest, however, that formative assessment (or assessment for learning (AfL)) is a means by which learning gains may genuinely be achieved (Black, Harrison and Lee, 2003). Formative assessment is not new, and as an experienced teacher you probably think that you are doing it already, but pressures that teachers (including beginning teachers) face in schools may militate against formative assessment practices developing to its fullest potential.

In England, for example, until recently, the Office for Standards in Education, Children's Services and Skills (Ofsted) published criteria for outstanding teaching, which included the

Supporting beginning teachers   191

requirement that pupils should make 'rapid and sustained progress' (National College for Teaching and Leadership (NCTL), 2012, p. 1). Anecdotally, this requirement was interpreted as suggesting that teachers needed to demonstrate that pupils made progress during an observed 20-minute lesson period. Understandably, in these circumstances, teachers may have found themselves focusing on producing summative evidence that pupils had progressed, rather than on applying the principles of genuine AfL. The Assessment Reform Group summarised formative principles as follows:

- AfL is any assessment for which the first priority in its design and practice is to serve the purpose of promoting pupils' learning. It thus differs from assessment designed primarily to serve the purposes of accountability, or of ranking, or of certifying competence.
- An assessment activity can help learning if it provides information to be used as feedback, by teachers and by their pupils, in assessing themselves and each other, to modify the teaching and learning activities in which they are engaged. Such assessment becomes 'formative assessment' when the evidence is actually used to adapt the teaching work to meet learning needs (Black, Harrison, Lee, Marshall and Wiliam, 2004, p. i).

Taking the above into consideration, findings from my ongoing research in England (Gourlay, 2019), suggests that beginning science teachers found it difficult to move beyond assessing what had been learned, to beginning to take formative action. For example, one of the beginning teachers (Zoe) made the following comment about assessment practice in her second placement school, in April of her ITE programme (which ran from September to June):

> I feel like – because we have this much data and we spend so much time doing tests, and marking tests, and [to improve a piece of written work, in response to teacher's feedback] 're-write a section' – and all of that... I feel like we should be doing something with it, because it's a lot of time invested in something to not use.

Zoe was showing concern about finding a way to make the large quantity of assessment information that she was gathering useful to guide subsequent teaching and learning practices. It is the act of putting the information to use that makes assessment formative – sometimes referred to as responsive teaching (Gotwals and Birmingham, 2016, p. 366).

A beginning teacher you are mentoring could be feeling like Zoe, and therefore needs your support to develop formative assessment for learning. So, what might formative assessment look like in practice? The King's-Medway-Oxfordshire-Formative Assessment Project (KMOFAP) (Black, Harrison, Lee, Marshall and Wiliam, 2004) worked with teachers to investigate how best to implement the findings of a literature review of international research about formative assessment and its general impact on pupils' learning, confidence, motivation; and on fairness for all pupils (Dimension III, Table 12.1). Broadly, the project suggested four areas of teachers' work in the classroom producing evidence of learning gains for pupils. These four areas of development are now discussed using some assessment strategies for you to share with beginning teachers.

192 *Gourlay*

12.4.1 *Rich questioning: Developing classroom dialogue and building confidence among pupils*

Chapter 11 specifically encouraged you to support a beginning teacher to embed channels of communication through rich questioning. Some other strategies include:

- Increasing the wait time (Rowe, 1986), giving pupils more time to think about their responses to the questions (see Chapter 13, Section 3 part on spacing effect).
- Using 'no hands up' policy, as a means of engaging the whole class in thinking about the answer, rather than relying on the most confident pupils (Black, Harrison, Lee, Marshall and Wiliam, 2004). Beginning teachers could, for example, write pupils' names on lollipop sticks and choose them at random to answer questions.
- Planning hinge point questions. These questions test understanding at a particular point in the lesson, and the teacher allows for the remainder of the lesson to take different paths depending on pupils' responses (Leahy, Lyon, Thompson and Wiliam, 2005).
- Asking pupils to produce questions (Black and Harrison, 2001).

These strategies for incorporating questioning can be presented to a beginning teacher by modelling a classroom scenario and sharing a lesson plan with them. For example, in a lesson on 'sedimentary rocks' (as part of a series of lessons on, 'the rock cycle and the formation of igneous, sedimentary and metamorphic rocks, under the unit of work 'earth and atmosphere' (DfE, 2013, p. 9)), the learning outcomes shared at the beginning of a lesson might be that pupils should know the properties of sedimentary rocks and how sedimentary rocks are formed and be able to draw a flow chart to show the order in which these processes occur when sedimentary rocks are formed. Towards the end of the lesson, the teacher could show an example examination question on the taught content, giving time for pupils to discuss their answers (increasing the wait time), gathering responses by randomly choosing pupils (using no hands up policy), before discussing the accepted answers. Pupils could then write their own questions (producing questions), followed by a class discussion of some of their examples. If the questions (hinge point questions) were introduced earlier in the lesson then the remainder of the lesson could be used for further teaching to address misunderstandings or misconceptions, if needed.

While a beginning teacher can undoubtedly learn much about teaching and learning from their experiences of teaching whole classes, there is some evidence that they may benefit from working with smaller groups of pupils to develop higher-order questioning (see Chapter 16 on group work and using higher order questions).

Task 12.6 looks at supporting a beginning teacher in using questioning strategies in the classroom to facilitate effective pupils' learning. It is based on the research of Weiland, Hudson and Amador (2014). Their intention was for beginning teachers to move away from questions demanding factual recall, or leading questions, and towards types of questions that supported the development of children's reasoning. Now complete Task 12.6, which asks you to support a beginning teacher you are mentoring in developing effective questioning practices.

Task 12.6 Developing effective questioning practices among beginning teachers

Undertake the following practical steps in supporting a beginning teacher in using questioning strategies effectively:

Step 1. Work with the beginning teacher to develop a protocol of questions they could ask a small group of pupils on a unit of work being taught. Inspiration for the questions could come from resources such as concept cartoons or published diagnostic questions (Moules, Horlock, Naylor and Keogh (2018) (see further resources section)).

Step 2. Familiarise the beginning teacher with some effective strategies for writing questions, such as using the language of Bloom's taxonomy. For a helpful guide to using Bloom's taxonomy to develop questions, which includes adaptable question stems, refer to Pedagogy and Practice Unit 7 (Department for Education and Skills (DfES), 2004, p. 13) (see further resources section).

Step 3. Video or audio record the beginning teacher interviewing a small group of pupils using the questions they have planned. Encourage them to ask follow-up questions (that are not included on the original list) to find out more about pupils' thinking. Afterwards, watch or listen to the recording with the beginning teacher, and, together, consider the following questions:

- What do the pupils' responses tell us about their understanding of the topic?
- What are the similarities and differences between the observations of the beginning teacher and yourself?
- How successful was the beginning teacher in asking questions that revealed pupils' reasoning?
- What could the beginning teacher do next to develop their questioning further?

12.4.2 Comment-only marking: Improving feedback and enhancing motivation among pupils

One of the underpinning arguments for comment-only marking is that where work is graded, many pupils do not pay attention to qualitative feedback in improving their work, but instead rely on the attained grades (Butler, 1988). It is also suggested that lower-attaining pupils make better progress in the absence of grades, since grading tends to be demotivating for them. Some examples of teachers' comments on pupils' science work are highlighted by Black, Harrison and Lee (2003, p. 45), such as:

Example 1. James, you have provided clear diagrams and recognised which chemicals are 'elements' and which are 'compounds'. Can you give a general explanation of the difference between elements and compounds?

Example 2. Richard, clear method, result table, and graph, but what does this tell you about the relationship?

194 *Gourlay*

You could share the above two examples with a beginning teacher you work with and ask them to make positive comments about what has been achieved by James and Richard and give feedback that guides what the pupil needs to do next (Wiliam, 2008). Before reading further, Task 12.7 looks at supporting a beginning teacher with comment-only marking.

Task 12.7 Developing comment-only marking

This task is adapted from one originally taught as part of the science PGCE programme at King's College London. Complete the following steps during weekly mentoring meetings:

Step 1. Support a beginning teacher in planning and teaching a lesson with clear learning outcomes, which includes a task in which pupils have the opportunity to demonstrate their understanding of the learning outcomes. For example, in a lesson on photosynthesis (associated with the topic: 'photosynthesis as the key process for food production and therefore biomass for life, the process of photosynthesis', and 'factors affecting the rate of photosynthesis' (DfE, 2013, p. 9)) with pupils in the 14–16 age range, learning outcomes are:
- To write the word equation showing the process of photosynthesis
- To explain how photosynthesis leads to growth
- To recognise the limiting factors in photosynthesis.

To accomplish these learning outcomes, pupils completed a piece of extended writing.

Step 2. Ask the beginning teacher to mark pupils' work and provide some written feedback on their extended writing on photosynthesis.
Step 3. Looking at the written feedback the beginning teacher has provided, you could consider the following questions by imagining yourself as a 15-year-old pupil, and discuss:
- How does the feedback make you feel?
- Does it help you see if you are on the right track?
- Does the feedback point out the work's limitations and encourage you to do something about it?
- Does it tell you how to improve the work?

Step 4. Now discuss the positive outcomes of planning, marking and providing feedback based on pupils' learning with the beginning teacher.

12.4.3 Self- and peer-assessment to support learning

As a mentor myself in various capacities, I have noticed that, during first attempts to include self- and peer-assessment, beginning teachers often involve pupils in marking their own or one another's work against a list of accepted answers. This is a good starting point, but the

Supporting beginning teachers 195

deeper point of self- and peer-assessment is to raise pupils' awareness of where they are in their learning; of what they can do to improve; and of the criteria for high quality work (Black and Harrison, 2001). So how can self- and peer-assessment be taken further? An example strategy for self-assessment is the use of traffic-lights against the planned learning outcomes. You can advise a beginning teacher to use this strategy as it can benefit pupils to think independently about what they have learned or not learned, which may act as a first step for them in becoming a self-regulated learner (Quigley, Muijs and Stringer, 2018). For example, you could guide the beginning teacher to teach a lesson on 'acids and alkalis' (linked to the unit of work 'chemical reactions' and particularly, 'the pH scale for measuring acidity/alkalinity; and indicators' (DfE, 2013, p. 8) for 12-year-old pupils, where pupils should be able to state that:

- Acids have a pH value less than 7
- Neutral solutions have a pH value of 7
- Alkalis have a pH value greater than 7
- Red litmus paper turns blue in alkaline solutions
- Soap solution is an everyday example of an alkali
- Lemon juice is an everyday example of an acid.

The beginning teacher then needs to facilitate pupils to use the traffic lights for each of the above learning outcomes – where green indicates good understanding, amber indicates partial understanding and red indicates little understanding. Items highlighted in red by pupils are the basis of further work, which may take different forms. You therefore need to support the beginning teacher to accommodate/change their planning and teaching for future lessons. For example, they might allow pupils to revise independently, or facilitate pupils to teach one another.

Next, to support a beginning teacher to include peer-assessment in their planning, requires you first to discuss the benefits of peer-assessment outlined by Black and Harrison (2001) with them, highlighting the fact that pupils may be more likely to pay attention to one another's feedback than to that of the teacher. You can then ask them to develop or re-use some pupil-friendly criteria for tasks, linked to planned learning outcomes. Next, you can encourage them to facilitate comment-only marking among pupils on one another's work, using, for example, the 'two stars and a wish' technique (Wiliam, 2008, p. 13). You may need to explain to the beginning teacher that this technique requires them to encourage pupils to write two positive comments on their peer's work and to identify one area for development. You can then support the beginning teacher to summarise the peer-assessed comments into two to three next steps for their next lessons and encourage them to plan the upcoming lesson(s) accordingly.

12.4.4 The formative use of summative tests and fairness for all pupils

Earlier, I raised a concern about science departments' over-reliance on end-of-unit tests. Further concerns are that these tests may not enable all pupils to demonstrate what they have learned to the same extent, since they are not all equally able to express themselves in writing; and that frequent testing may consume a lot of teaching time. These concerns may

196 *Gourlay*

be ameliorated to an extent by the assessment dimension of using the outcomes of summative tests formatively. An example of this approach, which you can share with a beginning teacher, is to ask pupils to mark one another's test papers without providing a mark scheme, but allowing them to consult one another, as well as their textbooks and exercise books (Black and Harrison, 2001).

Task 12.8 asks you to use step-by-step guidelines to develop a beginning teacher's understanding of using summative tests to inform teaching and learning formatively.

Task 12.8 A formative analysis of summative tests

The task is adapted from one suggested by Monk and Dillon (1995, pp. 188–189). The intention of this task is to consider how marking guidelines and lesson plans can be used to analyse summative assessments formatively.

Undertake the following steps:

1. Support a beginning teacher you are mentoring in selecting the marked test papers of three higher-attaining pupils, three middle-attaining pupils, and three lower-attaining pupils.
2. The beginning teacher then reads through the papers to:
   - Identify questions or topic areas that pupils have answered well
   - Look for questions or topic areas that pupils found more difficult
   - Evaluate why some questions and topic areas were answered well or not (you could provide prompts in helping the beginning teacher to answer these questions, for example: a question not matching up well with what was taught; the wording of the question, et cetera)
   - Consider how the teaching/assessment strategies and lesson plans could be adapted before teaching the same topic to another class
   - Consider how any gaps in knowledge, misunderstandings or misconceptions could be addressed in future teaching with the current class.
3. Discuss what they have found out from this activity. What were the positive outcomes and limitations and what will be your and the beginning teacher's next steps?

After the beginning teacher has developed and practised some of the formative assessment skills, the next step is to master it. So, how can you support them to master their formative assessment practices? You can replicate an example way of doing that which is highlighted in the KMOFAP project (Black, Harrison and Lee, 2003), where the teachers involved in the research were (i) initially provided with some training about formative assessment, (ii) then given the opportunity to try out different strategies in the classrooms, (iii) then asked to produce action plans identifying an area of their practice that they wished to develop, (iv)

Supporting beginning teachers 197

after attaining support on the specific identified area, they returned to their classrooms to implement these assessment driven plans. In addition to these steps, teachers also had the opportunity to attend further in-service education and training (INSET) sessions at which they were able to receive support from the researchers, and to share their ideas with other teachers. These approaches appear to have been effective because they enabled (beginning) teachers to work flexibly to find strategies that worked within their own subject specialisms which were adaptations of their usual assessment approaches and took into account their own teaching contexts. Task 12.9 asks you to support a beginning teacher in using an adapted version of the KMOFAP project, to enable them to master formative assessments.

Task 12.9   The KMOFAP approach

Follow the steps below:

1. You and the beginning teacher read one of the following pamphlets about formative assessment: 'Inside the black box' (Black and Wiliam, 2006); 'Assessment for learning: Beyond the black box' (Broadfoot, Daugherty, Gardner, Gipps, Harlen, James and Stobart, 1999); 'Working inside the black box' (Black, Harrison, Lee, Marshall and Wiliam, 2004); or 'Science inside the black box' (Black and Harrison, 2006).
2. Next, ask the beginning teacher to select a new assessment strategy they will try in their teaching practice over an agreed period of time, and support them in producing an action plan about how they will do so (see Appendix 12.1).
3. Where relevant, observe the beginning teacher teaching a lesson (or a sequence of lessons) in which they apply the chosen assessment strategy.
4. Review the success of the assessment strategy in supporting pupils' learning. How has teaching been adapted in response to the assessment information gathered?
5. Identify with the beginning teacher, the next steps in the development of their formative assessment practices.

Summary and key points

This chapter has considered how you might support a beginning teacher in developing effective assessment strategies. Specifically,

*   As a mentor, you need to induct a beginning teacher into the assessment policies and practices of your school and department.
*   You should support a beginning teacher to construct, record and analyse summative test papers.

198 *Gourlay*

- You should support a beginning teacher in developing rubrics for summative assessment, as an alternative to standardised testing.
- Research evidence suggests that an emphasis on the development of formative assessment provides the best environment for learning.
- Employ mentoring strategies to support a beginning teacher to develop their formative assessment practices, enabling them to develop genuinely responsive teaching, and support their pupils' learning.
- You could give a beginning teacher a choice in deciding which aspect(s) of their formative assessment practices they might wish to develop. This approach has the potential to enable them to embed assessment strategies into their teaching practices that work for them in the context of the nature of the groups of pupils they work with in the school, and within the constraints of the curriculum they teach.

Further resources

Chandler-Grevatt, A. (2018b) *How to Assess Your Students: Making Assessment Work for You*. Oxford: Oxford University Press.
This book is a practical guide that can be used by beginning teachers independently, as it explains the principles of assessment and suggests how assessment data can be used by teachers to support pupils' learning.

Department of Education, University of York (2018b) Developing diagnostic assessment, Department of Education, University of York, viewed 1 December 2018, from: www.york.ac.uk/education/research/uyseg/projects/developingdiagnosticassessments/
The Science Education Group at the University of York developed diagnostic tests for a range of science topics as part of the Evidence-Based Practice in Science Education (EPSE) project. Beginning teachers can use the sample questions from this website to design diagnostic assessments. These questions may help a beginning teacher to assess pupils' understanding of key scientific ideas, and to consider how they might modify teaching to support learning.

Department for Education and Skills (DfES) (2004) *Pedagogy and Practice: Teaching and Learning in Secondary School, Unit 7: Questioning*. London: DfES. Viewed 1 December 2018, from: http://dera.ioe.ac.uk/5671/8/cea27fdd968639560cb245efafd9c2ff_Redacted.pdf
This document was produced as part of the National Strategies in England. It makes a range of practical suggestions to support the development of questioning practices, including many which are informed by research. Task 12.6 has referred to the section suggesting question stems based on Bloom's taxonomy.

Harrison, C. (undated-b) Oranges: Will they sink or float? What's happening?, Strategies for Assessment of Inquiry Learning in Science, viewed 23 November 2019, from: http://www.sails-project.eu/units/floating-orange.html
This science activity was developed as part of the Strategies for Assessment Inquiry Learning in Science (SAILS) EU project. Task 12.4 suggests using this activity to support a beginning teacher in developing their assessment of science inquiry.

Monk, M. and Dillon, J. (eds) (1995b) *Learning to Teach Science: Activities for Student Teachers and Mentors*. London and Washington, DC: Routledge Falmer.
This book contains a large number of professional learning activities that could readily be used/adapted for use with a beginning teacher you mentor.

Moules, J., Horlock, J., Naylor, S. and Keogh, B. (2018b) *Science Concept Cartoons Set 2.* England & Wales: Millgate House Education Ltd, viewed 17 January 2020, from: https://www.millgatehouse.co.uk/product/science-concept-cartoons-set-2/
A concept cartoon could form the focus of discussion for a beginning teacher to develop effective questioning practice with a small group of pupils (see Task 12.6). This focus may support a beginning teacher in developing their understanding of pupils' alternative conceptions in science, as well as how to elicit this information from their classes. This assessment information may support their teaching as diSessa (2014) suggests that pupils make better progress where teachers are aware of their preconceptions.

QCAA (Queensland Curriculum & Assessment Authority) (2014b) Why do the seasons change? Australian Curriculum Year 7 Science sample assessment, QCAA, viewed 28 March 2019, from: https://www.qcaa.qld.edu.au/downloads/p_10/ac_sa_sci_yr7_why_do_seasons_change.pdf
This resource can be considered as an example approach during mentoring sessions to discuss with a beginning teacher how teachers could assess pupils' understanding of science against national standards, as an alternative to standardised summative testing.

Teachers TV (2010b) Teachers TV: Secondary formative assessment, TES, viewed 1 December 2018, from: https://www.tes.com/teaching-resource/teachers-tv-secondary-formative-assessment-6039026
This video could be used with a beginning teacher as an introduction to formative assessment. It includes material about questioning, self and peer-assessment and feedback, presented by Paul Black and Christine Harrison.

Appendix 12.1 Action plan template

Your name:				
Area for development	Successs criteria	Actions (including timescales)	Support arrangements	Monitoring (evidence)

Evaluation

Reflection (continue on another sheet if needed)

13 Supporting beginning teachers to link learning, memory and inquiry

Jonathan Firth

Introduction

An effective teacher needs more than just a repertoire of teaching strategies and pupils' activities – they also need to understand and be able to justify their choice of activities to promote pupils learning. One area of professional learning that underpins justification of choices is an understanding of human memory.

Memory processes are at work when pupils process new information, when they form it into a coherent understanding, and when they later recall and use what they have learned. Teachers aim to ensure that these processes proceed successfully, and an understanding of memory therefore affects both the moment-to-moment running of a class and the planning of lessons or activities. However, a beginning teacher's professional understanding of memory is likely to be restricted or flawed without suitable guidance, and is subject to popular misconceptions. Gauging learning as it happens is a diagnostic process, and requires an accurate analysis of classroom evidence in a way that takes account of factors such as practice and forgetting.

This chapter explains some fundamental memory principles that can be applied to help a beginning science teacher make more successful teaching decisions. It also looks at some misconceptions that a beginning teacher may have about memory and learning, and at how to address them. Finally, it discusses how mentoring can help to set a beginning teacher upon a path of inquiry to make their practice more effective.

Objectives

At the end of this chapter you should be able to:

- Understand the importance of placing a focus on effective teaching and successful learning during mentoring meetings with a beginning teacher
- Guide a beginning teacher to discuss their own beliefs about memory and learning
- Support a beginning teacher to incorporate memory and learning-related processes of desirable difficulties in their practice
- Guide a beginning teacher to inquire into memory and learning processes using classroom evidence.

202 *Firth*

13.1 Effective teaching and successful learning in science classrooms

Professional knowledge underlies effective, evidence-based practice. In the same way that doctors need technical knowledge of principles such as infection and the immune response, so teachers must have a knowledge base that underpins their classroom actions. For science teachers – indeed, for any educator – a vital aspect of this knowledge is an understanding of how learning works, such that they can make optimal decisions on issues such as what information to present, and when and how to present it.

Placing the focus on learning processes during mentoring meetings makes it easier for a beginning teacher to think systematically about effective teaching. Any classroom action or decision taken by a beginning teacher could have either a positive effect or a negative effect; it could be beneficial over the short term, the long term, or not at all. For example, a task that aims to review ionic bonding could be carried out too soon or too late to have the maximum benefit for pupils as learners, while a mathematics practice exercise could be either too short or too long in terms of time efficiency (Rohrer and Taylor, 2006). Some classroom activities might not affect pupils' understanding at all.

Teachers' thinking and decisions about pupils' learning is a form of metacognition, i.e., thinking about thinking. More specifically, it draws on beliefs about the cognitive processes that underpin learning. Metacognitive beliefs have consequences for a beginning teacher because they guide minute-by-minute decisions both during planning and when in the classroom. An understanding of learning processes can, therefore, be seen as a key part of a beginning teacher's professional toolkit (Firth, 2017). As a mentor, you can share some classroom examples with a beginning teacher to help them recognise that immediate performance is not the same thing as learning, and that learning cannot be judged on a pupil's performance in a single lesson (Soderstrom and Bjork, 2015). For example, a pupil may leave the room full of confidence after a lesson on electrical circuits, but two weeks later be unable to explain the difference between series and parallel circuits.

It is safe to say that one aim for a beginning teacher is to ensure that pupils remember the material they have been taught, and that they will already have some awareness of the risk of forgetting. However, this professional understanding is still at an early stage and will be characterised by misconceptions. Case study 13.1 presents one example of this issue. The broader state of a beginning teacher's understanding of learning and memory is discussed in the next section.

Case study 13.1: Paul's mentoring meeting

Paul is a deputy head teacher of a large secondary school and has responsibility for running weekly meetings with beginning science teachers. These beginning teachers are given a short academic article about the psychology of memory to read in advance of each week's mentoring meeting, which is then discussed at the beginning of the meeting. The focus of each meeting is an aspect of learning that is commonly neglected or misunderstood.

Link learning, memory and inquiry   203

This week, beginning science teachers are looking at the timing of written practice tasks which are used to consolidate laboratory work. After discussing the research article, Paul asks the beginning teachers to briefly explain how and when they would carry out written consolidation of practical experiments in Chemistry.

Paul has noticed that even confident and capable beginning teachers have misconceptions about how and when pupils should consolidate learning, and about how quickly forgetting takes place. In their planning processes, most of the beginning teachers suggest that reviewing at the end of a lesson and via an immediate homework task would be optimal, and that further review of the taught topic could then be left until examination time.

Instead, Paul recommends that reviews are delayed beyond the individual lesson and that consolidation is built in regularly during the academic year, with older material being explicitly linked to newly learned concepts. Paul says, 'It is difficult to judge how quickly pupils will forget information they appear to have mastered in a single lesson.'

Task 13.1 asks you to reflect on Case study 13.1.

Task 13.1   Mentor's reflection on effective learning

Having read Case study 13.1, consider the following:

1. Do you agree with the points made by Paul?
2. What other advice would you give to a beginning teacher?
3. What misconceptions about learning have you noticed?
4. As an experienced teacher and mentor, how can you be sure that you do not have your own misconceptions about how memory works?

13.2 What are beginning science teachers' beliefs and understandings about memory and learning?

From a psychological perspective, learning involves long-term changes in what people think or what they can do. Such changes rely on the formation or strengthening of long-lasting memory traces, which can then be transferred, i.e. flexibly applied to novel situations (Bjork, 1994). An event that leads to a pupil improving their skills, understanding or knowledge can be linked to changes that are both neural and psychological, i.e. affecting the structure of brain cells in a way that is reflected in what the pupil can think, do and understand. Of course, such learning cannot be reduced to memorising separate pieces of information; memory is based around a set of meaningful, interconnected schemas (Bransford, Brown and Cocking, 2000).

204 *Firth*

Unfortunately, many features of memory can be counterintuitive, and are not easily understood through life experience alone. This was demonstrated in a survey of the general public by Simons and Chabris (2011), who found that most people, including teachers, endorsed a set of false statements about memory (for example, that memory works like a video camera in that it accurately records the events we see and hear for later inspection), none of which were accepted by memory researchers. This finding shows that many common assumptions about memory conflict with the scientific consensus.

Task 13.2 asks you to support a beginning teacher to analyse their own beliefs and understanding of memory, then to facilitate their thinking about these issues.

Task 13.2   A beginning teacher's beliefs and understanding about memory and learning

With a beginning teacher you are mentoring, discuss the idea raised by Simons and Chabris (2011) that the general public often have flawed beliefs about how memory works.

Next, ask the beginning teacher to consider the following questions:
Which of these things are true?

1.   Human memory works like a computer hard drive.
2.   New terminology does not enter memory unless you pay attention to it.
3.   Revision for a science examination mainly involves short-term memory.
4.   Memorisation of new ideas primarily depends on the rapid repetition of information.
5.   Learning a new science fact involves creating a file in long-term memory which is new and separate from existing knowledge.

After they have considered the questions, discuss their answers along with the suggested answers at the end (Appendix 13.1) in a weekly meeting.

You may discover from the discussion in Task 13.2 that the beginning teacher has considerable flaws in their understanding of memory, leading to misjudgements of how best to promote learning among pupils. If this is the case, you should help them to recognise that several aspects of learning are not obvious. Such misconceptions start early; pupils' self-directed learning tends to be characterised by a preference for flawed study strategies such as re-reading and highlighting texts. In addition, therefore, it would be beneficial for a beginning teacher if you could have a conversation with them regarding effective study guidance for their classes, with an awareness that pupils do not spontaneously come to perceive the limitations of flawed study strategies, or begin to adopt better strategies without guidance (Rohrer and Pashler, 2010).

You may ask a beginning teacher to list what they think are advantageous strategies for learning among pupils and what they think are not, and why. You can then extend the discussion in relation to what pupils believe are advantageous learning strategies. This kind of professional dialogue can be supported by relevant literature that demonstrates metacognitive flaws in how we understand learning. For instance, in an experiment that presented sets of images to learn, Kornell and Bjork (2008) found that 85% of learners did as well or even better when different categories of images were mixed (or 'interleaved'; see below) rather than separated into blocks of the same type, but 83% of the participants incorrectly believed they had done at least as well in the blocked condition. Discussing such research with a beginning teacher will help to make them aware of a striking mismatch between beliefs about learning and the reality of how well pupils, as learners, actually do in tasks, as well as showing the limited effects of direct experience.

It would be helpful for a beginning teacher if such flawed ideas about effective pupil learning strategies were corrected during initial teacher education. However, given the considerable variability in what is taught to beginning teachers (Carter, 2015), it is unlikely that the profession can rely on this. There is no guarantee that what beginning teachers have previously been told about learning, for example by university tutors, will concur with the scientific consensus, because even experienced teachers seem to be prone to errors. For example, Morehead, Rhodes and DeLozier (2016) found that while university tutors held slightly more accurate views of learning and memory than did their students, the difference was small and the overall pattern was broadly similar.

Therefore, through dialogue, you will need to encourage a beginning teacher to analyse memory and learning processes in their teaching and learning practices, with an awareness that metacognitive flaws are common and widespread. The next section looks in more detail at some of the classroom-relevant memory processes that you might choose to focus on.

13.3 Supporting beginning teachers to optimise learning by embedding the memory phenomenon of desirable difficulties in their classrooms

One group of important and particularly counterintuitive learning phenomena are known as desirable difficulties. These are a range of factors that increase the challenge level of a study (learning) task – often slowing down performance during practice and causing more errors – but which improve learning over the longer term. Contrary to the typical subjective perception that learning tasks that feel easier are desirable (Rhodes and Castel, 2008), interventions that increase a learner's sense of difficulty can actually lead to more effective and durable learning. As Bjork and Bjork (2011) put it, 'Conditions that create challenges and slow the rate of apparent learning often optimize long-term retention and transfer' (p. 57).

Three major desirable difficulties (the spacing effect, interleaved practice and retrieval practice) are presented below, along with some mentoring strategies which you can use to promote their use by a beginning teacher.

13.3.1 The spacing effect

As suggested by Paul in Case study 13.1, a delay between initial learning and later practice work results in a boost to retention (Rohrer, 2015), a phenomenon known as the spacing effect. This can apply to any type of learning, although the benefit may not be apparent

206 *Firth*

immediately – it is best judged at the point of a later test. For example, if a teacher spaced out the teaching of kidney dialysis by reviewing this concept a fortnight after the initial lesson, pupils may find this more difficult than if the review were to happen straight away, but the payoff is that their eventual test scores would be better. In your mentoring meetings, you can:

- Emphasise to a beginning teacher that the spacing effect is counterintuitive; because it implies that an element of forgetting is helpful, in comparison to practising when items are still well remembered by a class
- Advise the beginning teacher that when spacing out practice, a longer gap is better than a short one (Cepeda, Vul, Rohrer, Wixted and Pashler, 2008), though it is important to emphasise that the information or skills need to be well learned in the first teaching session. As Rawson and Dunlosky (2011) put it, 'our prescriptive conclusion for students [pupils] is to practice recalling concepts to an initial criterion of 3 correct recalls and then to relearn them 3 times at widely spaced intervals' (p. 283)
- Raise the beginning teacher's awareness that many popular learning strategies fail to take account of spacing. Most notably, any benefits of overlearning – i.e. continuing to practise beyond the point of mastery – seem to be short-lived, and this technique can therefore be seen as an inefficient use of learning time (Rohrer and Taylor, 2006). Such additional practice would be of more benefit if delayed, in keeping with the spacing effect
- You could then ask the beginning teacher to attempt Task 13.3, which asks them to reflect on their teaching and invites you to support the beginning teacher in embedding spacing into their professional practice.

Task 13.3 Supporting beginning teachers to use the spacing effect in the school context

Complete the steps below:

1. Ask a beginning teacher to identify one area of content that pupils often find difficult in science, such as the electrochemical series.
2. Then encourage them to think of two or more practice tasks relating to this content, such as lab demonstrations, workbook exercises, homework, and so forth.
3. Next, discuss with the beginning teacher how these are commonly scheduled in your department, and think of ways that the practice could be spaced out more. For example, could review/consolidation tasks be delayed by a week or so, and homework on a new concept completed a couple of weeks or a month later?

13.3.2 Interleaved practice

The term interleaving refers to varying the order of a set of tasks or examples such that each item is immediately followed and preceded by an example of a different category or concept;

Link learning, memory and inquiry 207

for example, item types A, B and C would be presented in the order: ABCABCABC. Teaching plant cells to a class might involve alternating images of one type of cell (for example, a root hair cell) with images of a different type of cell and tissues (for example, xylem tissue), rather than showing the class several examples or illustrations of the same type of cell/tissue at one time (which is termed a 'blocked' arrangement).

Eglington and Kang (2017) found significant benefits of using interleaving when learning about the molecules of different hydrocarbon categories. They found that learners demonstrated better recall of these molecules, and their ability to categorise previously unseen examples was also improved.

To help introduce a beginning teacher to the benefits of interleaving you could:

- Ask the beginning teacher to think of the scientific concepts they teach that could be presented either blocked by category or interleaved (different categories mixed together)
- Then encourage them to plan interleaved questions or problems for practice tasks These help pupils to notice and understand the differences between contrasting items
- Next, complete Task 13.4, which focuses on the ways you can support a beginning teacher to reflect and incorporate interleaving in their classrooms.

Task 13.4 Supporting beginning teachers to use interleaving

Ask a beginning teacher you are mentoring to review the PowerPoint slides of a lesson they have recently taught and/or a worksheet prepared for the lesson. This self-review could focus on questions such as:

- Are multiple scientific concepts included in the materials?
- If so, are the concepts presented together (allowing for contrast) or within different sections/tasks?
- Are all of the questions in a worksheet on similar concepts?
- In future, how could the beginning teacher increase the extent to which different types of question are mixed together?

Discuss the answers to the above questions with the beginning teacher, and support them to embed interleaving in their planning. For example, you could consider supporting them in planning contrasting and contingent cases to teach energy using differential concepts, such as the stringy cheese and sticky ice lolly (Chapter 11, pp. 173-175) examples.

13.3.3 Retrieval practice

The technique known as retrieval practice involves asking pupils to effortfully retrieve things from memory, for example using a short quiz. This is more likely to boost and consolidate learning than the provision of information via a lecture or reading, even though retrieval is more difficult and can lead to more errors than simply listening or copying (Agarwal, Bain

208 *Firth*

and Chamberlain, 2012). This means, for example, that it would be preferable for pupils to listen to a teacher explaining acids and alkalis and then subsequently summarise these concepts into their notes, rather than taking down notes during the teacher's talk.

As with other desirable difficulties, the benefits are only obvious after a number of days, not after an immediate test (Roediger and Karpicke, 2006), and therefore performance during the class itself may mislead teachers and pupils alike into thinking that retrieval is ineffective, and that easier strategies such as copying or re-reading are preferable. In Task 13.5 you are asked to invite a beginning teacher to reflect on lesson planning and to analyse whether or not retrieval practice was adequately included. You could first encourage the beginning teacher to complete Table 13.1, which asks them to reflect on their current views about retrieval practice.

Next, using the answers from Table 13.1, discuss the beginning teacher's understanding of retrieval practice. During this discussion and/or from their recent observed classroom practices, you might realise that although the beginning teacher acknowledges the importance of retrieval practice, they exhibit some reluctance to use it in their classrooms, and prefer to plan and implement easier strategies such as asking pupils to copy texts from the whiteboard or repeat verbal explanations of scientific concepts. Therefore, in Task 13.5, you are asked to support a beginning teacher to self-reflect on one of their lesson plans and to analyse whether (or not) retrieval practice was adequately included.

Task 13.5   Supporting beginning teachers to use retrieval practice

Follow the steps below:

1. With a beginning teacher, find one example from one of their recent lesson plans where pupils were asked to take notes, copy from a screen or books, or listen to an explanation.
2. Now ask the beginning teacher to think of an alternative method of completing this section of the lesson, such that the lesson aims would still be met but the pupils would be required to actively retrieve information from memory.
3. Prompt the beginning teacher to consider not just quizzes but also strategies such as summarising, oral questioning or class discussion (all of which require retrieval).
4. Ask them to try out this approach in a similar situation in a future lesson and discuss their evaluation of its effectiveness with you in the lesson debrief and/or during the weekly meeting.

All the strategies mentioned above have potential benefits if applied in the classroom, but as highlighted in the previous section, it is very likely that a beginning teacher will have misconceptions about them. Therefore, the next section encourages you to take an approach to mentoring that will help them to overcome misconceptions via professional inquiry.

Link learning, memory and inquiry 209

Table 13.1 A beginning teacher's views on retrieval practice

Teaching example	My view
Pupils are instructed by the teacher to listen to a brief explanation of a new concept, and then to summarise this new concept in their jotters, using a textbook to help.	This approach does/does not make use of retrieval practice because... I could increase the level of retrieval required by...
Pupils are allowed to take down notes while the teacher is reviewing a recent sub-topic (such as drug addictions under the topic of 'use and abuse of drugs') using verbal explanations and a PowerPoint.	This approach does/does not make use of retrieval practice because... I could increase the level of retrieval required by...

13.4 Beginning teachers' inquiry into misconceptions about learning and memory

From the points made so far, it may seem to be an obvious conclusion that mentors should correct erroneous misconceptions and beliefs about learning held by beginning science teachers. However, there are problems with such a simplistic solution. Researchers who study metacognition have increasingly come to recognise that it is difficult to tackle misconceptions about learning and memory directly, as merely being told about techniques such as spacing and interleaving does not necessarily work. However, a theoretical explanation combined with practical experience may be more beneficial (Yan, Bjork and Bjork, 2016). You can see an example of a theoretical explanation along with a practical solution in Case study 13.2.

Case study 13.2: Dorothy and Viktoria

Dorothy is a science head of department who is mentoring Viktoria, a beginning teacher, during a five-week school placement. Viktoria has frequently expressed the view that pupils need to be told things four times during a single lesson in order to remember them.

Dorothy chooses to take a coaching approach, asking questions such as 'How can you be sure that this works?' and 'What evidence is there for that idea?'

Dorothy writes down all the conversations with Viktoria. They then access a research study by Soderstrom and Bjork (2015) on the difference between performance and learning, before returning in subsequent weeks to discuss the notes on their earlier conversations on learning and memory.

Through these discussions, Viktoria has recognised that while pupils may appear to learn something well by repeating it within a single lesson, it is possible that they may remember the facts and skills better if repetitions are spaced out over separate weeks and are combined with quizzes. In order to put this to the test, with the support from Dorothy, she agrees to try this approach with half of her classes, while continuing her current approach with the others.

---

210 *Firth*

As can be seen in Dorothy and Viktoria's Case, a non-directive approach through probing questions empowered Viktoria to analyse and interrogate her previous assumptions. While there may sometimes be advantages to providing direct instructions to a beginning teacher you are mentoring, this can serve to discourage their self-directed development (Ehrich, Hansford and Tennent, 2004).

Case study 13.2 also demonstrates an empowering way to correct misconceptions about learning through engagement in research activities. In such an arrangement, as a mentor you can guide the process of inquiry without mandating particular changes to practice. This moves the mentor–mentee relationship towards a collaborative inquiry, facilitates autonomy on the part of the beginning teacher, and is more effective in promoting professional learning over the long-term (Sachs, 2016).

Moreover, such research-led classroom projects in schools can also take the form of shared inquiry carried out by a group of teachers, including beginning teachers. You could discuss with a beginning teacher the potential benefits of such inquiry-based group projects, for instance:

- Doing such work collectively is less challenging for the beginning teacher and allows for the pooling of both research skills and findings.
- A group of inquiry-focused teachers at any stage of their careers could be established in a school or cluster of school settings.
- This group may constitute what researchers call a 'community of practice'; there is a genuine real-world context, shared goals, and a framework where they can learn from more experienced peers without the need for formal instruction (Lave, 1991; see Chapter 17).
- Such projects allow the beginning teacher to test evidence-based techniques in a collaborative environment.

Having a research mentor to guide a group of research-engaged teachers can provide a useful stimulus. As exemplified in Case studies 13.1 and 13.2, sharing relevant literature can be a good starting point when encouraging a beginning teacher to become research-engaged. The 'Teacher ready research review' format found in the Scholarship of Teaching and Learning in Psychology is a good example of research papers written to be accessible, while many teacher organisations provide access to research journals.

As mentioned in previous sections, the mentoring process can highlight metacognitive flaws in a beginning teacher's beliefs and understanding about pupils' learning, and can then push them beyond their comfort zone and away from their early assumptions that they may have developed, as exemplified in Case study 13.2. Accurate feedback on a beginning teacher's classroom performance based on metacognitive flaws about pupils learning – something that is difficult for the beginning teacher to achieve alone (see above) – can be obtained from the mentor, the peer-group, and indeed from the outcome of the inquiry itself, reducing the chance that a beginning teacher confuses immediate classroom performance for long-term learning.

Finally, Task 13.6 asks you to reflect on mentoring strategies to support a beginning teacher to develop their beliefs and understanding of memory, learning, misconceptions and inquiry practices.

Link learning, memory and inquiry 211

Task 13.6   Mentor's reflection on strategies to support a beginning teacher in developing learning, memory and inquiry

Reflect and review the ideas covered in this chapter by doing the following:

1. Summarise misconceptions about learning and memory that you are likely to encounter when mentoring a beginning teacher.
2. Identify one 'desirable difficulty' that you feel would be especially useful for a beginning teacher to focus on in their planning and teaching.
3. Plan a process of mentored inquiry, either for an individual beginning teacher or for a group of teachers. This mentored inquiry could be focused on one of the desirable difficulties mentioned in the last point.
4. Identify one or more sources of information that a beginning teacher could draw on for background reading about learning and memory.
5. Follow up the classroom inquiry with collaborative reflection on a recent lesson. This could be informed by the beginning teacher's reflective account and pupils' or mentor's feedback, and will help in identifying areas to be further investigated and/or changed.

Summary and key points

This chapter has highlighted ways to support a beginning science teacher in understanding and applying memory processes to promote effective learning among pupils. Specifically,

- An understanding of learning is vital for successful teaching.
- Pupils' learning of science is based on memory, and the counterintuitive nature of memory – in particular desirable difficulties – means that a beginning teacher is likely to have misconceptions about its functioning.
- A mentored research and inquiry approach can motivate a beginning teacher to engage with evidence and provide opportunities to build their professional expertise.

Further resources

Gilchrist, G. (2018b) *Practitioner Enquiry: Professional Development with Impact for Teachers, Schools and Systems*. Abingdon, Oxon: David Fulton Books.
This is a highly readable guide to mentoring teachers through the process of conducting their own research and inquiry.

Horvath, F.J., Lodge, J. and Hattie, J. (2016b) *From the Laboratory to the Classroom: Translating Science of Learning for Teachers*. Abingdon, Oxon: Routledge.
A comprehensive edited volume with chapters on topics ranging from memory to dyslexia, providing a gateway into the research background on a beginning teacher's educational area(s) of interest.

Smith, M. and Firth, J. (2018b) *Psychology in the Classroom: A Teacher's Guide to What Works*. Abingdon, Oxon: Routledge.
An accessible guide to applying psychological concepts in teaching, including memory, understanding, creativity and emotion. This can be used to find out more about desirable difficulties or as recommended reading ahead of the weekly mentoring meetings.

CCT (The Chartered College for Teaching) (undated-b) *The Charted College of Teaching (CCT)*, London: College of Teaching Limited, viewed 19 January 2020, from: https://chartered.college
The CCT's easy to follow website focuses on applying learning in a science classroom, with access to their journal's impact, which has numerous articles on memory, evidence-based professional practice, and ways for beginning teachers to engage with research.

Link learning, memory and inquiry 213

Appendix 13.1 Task 13.2 suggested answers (based on Firth, 2018)

1. False – there are many important ways that your memory differs from a computer – not least the effort required in taking in new information.
2. True – learners need to focus attention in order for the new term to enter memory and be successfully linked to other knowledge.
3. False – short-term memory (or 'working memory') only holds information for a matter of seconds or minutes, so your pupils' learning for their examination is based on long-term memory.
4. False – repetition is not the best means of ensuring learning (see the section on retrieval practice).
5. False – memories link together into meaningful and organised 'schemas'.

14 Supporting a beginning teacher to apply features of the nature of science

Nqobile Nkala

Introduction

The main distinguishing features of science are the nature of its knowledge and the methods it uses to generate knowledge (its epistemology). Several schemes have been suggested to help classify knowledge within any subject. Of particular relevance here is Schwab's scheme (Furlong and Maynard, 1995), which distinguishes syntactic and substantive knowledge. These find some correspondence with views of science as both process (the nature of science) and product (subject knowledge of science) respectively (Millar, 2004). Along these lines, science consists of a body of knowledge that represents current understanding of natural systems and the processes whereby that body of knowledge has been established and is being continually extended, refined, and revised (Duschl, Schweingruber and Shouse, 2007). Science education not only aims to convey subject knowledge of science but also attempts to induct pupils into the ways of doing science, including skills, dispositions, knowledge generation and refinement processes, encompassed under the term nature of science (NoS).

This chapter focuses on how a mentor can support a beginning teacher to grapple with elements of the NoS, especially in planning practical activities found in the secondary school curriculum. It also suggests mentoring strategies to support a beginning teacher to incorporate health and safety procedures in practical-based science lessons.

Objectives

At the end of this chapter, you should be able to:

- Support a beginning teacher to understand the importance of elements of the NoS in their teaching practices
- Support a beginning teacher to reflect on the best ways to teach NoS by auditing the presence of NoS elements in the science curriculum
- Support a beginning teacher to reflect on their current approaches to practical work by using the nine elements of the NoS
- Incorporate health and safety training for a beginning science teacher to establish safe and effective laboratory procedures
- Organise a professional development walk (PDW) for a beginning teacher to allow them to observe other science teachers and evaluate the relationship between subject knowledge, practical activities and health and safety procedures

Applying features of the nature of science 215

- Supporting a beginning teacher to use, revisit, adopt/adapt a NoS focused lesson plan pro forma to plan practical lessons incorporating the nine elements of the NoS, practical work and health and safety.

Your role as a science mentor is likely to involve responsibilities to equip a beginning science teacher with the theory of education, specifically science education with respect to the concept of NoS, by developing teaching and learning skills that help them plan and conduct science lessons effectively. Task 14.1 asks you to reflect on mentoring strategies that you think are particularly relevant to science to support a beginning teacher in developing their teaching and learning skills.

Task 14.1   Aspects of science teaching and mentoring

Reflect on your current and most recent mentoring role (if any), by responding to the following questions:

1. What aspects of mentoring are particularly relevant to science and why?
2. Reconsider your answers from Task 1.8, to link your general understanding of mentoring to science specific teaching and mentoring processes. Signpost relevant policy and guidance documents, effective mentoring strategies and reflective models introduced in Chapter 1.

One aspect of mentoring which you might have identified as particularly relevant is supporting a beginning teacher to understand the importance of the NoS. This is considered next.

14.1 Mentoring to support a beginning teacher's understanding of the importance of the nature of science (NoS)

Research suggests a complex relationship between a beginning teacher's understanding of the NoS and their practice. Some beginning teachers' views may be overly inclined towards subject knowledge to teach a specific curriculum; adopting transmission pedagogies that may result in skewed views of science by their pupils. This chapter highlights the importance of an inquiry-based approach to planning and teaching. Inquiry-based teaching approaches incorporate elements of the NoS as part of effective pedagogy. This chapter provides some inquiry mediated mentoring approaches linked to practical activities that can support a beginning teacher to embed elements of the NoS in the science classrooms. Before reading about such approaches in the next section, you need to recognise and identify a beginning teacher's existing views about the role of elements of NoS in their teaching. This awareness of a beginning teacher's current knowledge and/or gap in their understanding about the role of NoS in conveying scientific knowledge will help you to target your mentoring support in the right direction. To this end, Tasks 14.2 and 14.3 help you to check a beginning teacher's knowledge of and views on the NoS and support them to reflect on the implications of this on their teaching practices.

Task 14.2 Articulating a beginning teacher's views about NoS

In order to establish a beginning teacher's view about NoS, ask them to answer the questions below:

1. How is scientific knowledge generated?
2. Is scientific knowledge subjective or objective?
3. Is scientific knowledge immutable or changeable? In what circumstances is it changeable?
4. What are the differences between observations and inferences? What examples can they give of where scientific knowledge or theories were generated through observations or inferences?
5. What are the differences between scientific laws, theories, predictions and hypotheses?
6. What is uncertainty in science? Why is it important?
7. What is the point of teaching all pupils science?

Then discuss the beginning teacher's answers to the questions with you. You could make notes using the second column of Table 14.1, and then, together with the beginning teacher, elaborate this discussion based on your notes by filling in the next three columns (strengths, gaps and requires improvement).

During this discussion with the beginning teacher you can share some of your classroom-based examples, linked to the subject knowledge in the curriculum and highlighting NoS elements, to strengthen their understanding of the pedagogical implications of the NoS.

Table 14.1 Articulating a beginning teacher's views about NoS

NoS implications to accommodate scientific knowledge	A beginning teacher's viewpoints/examples	Strengths	Gaps	Requires improvement
Subjective or objective				
Immutable or changeable				
Observations or inferences				
Uncertainty in science				
Teaching science to all				
Other				

Applying features of the nature of science 217

Task 14.3 Supporting a beginning teacher to exemplify the elements of NoS

After completing Task 14.2, in the next weekly mentoring meeting, ask the beginning teacher to exemplify elements of the NoS and how they can effectively implement NoS in the science classroom. You could share the following examples with a beginning teacher to discuss about the elements of NoS and its implementation in the science classrooms:

- Albert Einstein's theory of relativity.
- Darwin's theory of evolution by natural selection.
- Kekulé's discovery of, and explanation of the bonding in benzene.

You may also ask the beginning teacher to come up with other examples, which you then discuss with them. Table 14.1 can be used to record these discussions.

14.2 Is there a best way of teaching the NoS in the curriculum?

The inclusion of the NoS in the curriculum has a long history in science education, but there have always been arguments about the best way to teach it. Research documents early attempts to teach it using hands-on approaches, real-life experiments and incorporating inquiry-based pedagogies (Abd-El-Khalick, Bell and Lederman, 1998). However, it appears that many of these approaches achieved limited success as they assumed that pupils would passively assimilate elements of the NoS through engagement in these activities (Abd-El-Khalick, 1998). As an intervention strategy, some science curricula (for example the Office for Qualifications and Examinations Regulation (Ofqual, 2015) in England), are increasingly integrating the assessment of pupils' understanding of elements of the NoS with the assessment of content. How Science Works is the term commonly used in England to refer to learning and assessment activities related to the NoS, i.e. activities allied to the collection and processing of data, and making conclusions (Abd-El-Khalick, Bell and Lederman, 1998). Some elements of the NoS included in England's 11–16 Science National Curriculum are:

1. Scientific attitudes, for example objectivity and concern for accuracy and precision
2. Experimental skills and investigations, including making observations, predictions, identifying variables and the correct use of equipment
3. Analysing and evaluating, including identifying patterns, sources of error, applying mathematical concepts and drawing conclusions (Department for Education (DfE), 2015, p. 43).

Tasks 14.2 and 14.3 identify some specific views of a beginning teacher that can support them in focusing on NoS in their teaching. Moreover, as a mentor, it is important to ensure that a beginning teacher has a clear understanding of the elements of the NoS that are in the curriculum that they teach in your country. Task 14.4 asks you to support a beginning teacher to audit the NoS in the science curriculum.

Task 14.4 An audit on the presence of NoS in the science curriculum

Ask a beginning teacher to conduct an audit of the presence of NoS elements (such as: scientific attitudes, experimental skills and investigations, analysis, evaluations and conclusions) in the curriculum they are teaching (or planning to teach) by answering the questions below:

1. Which elements of the NoS and its practices are included in the curriculum?
2. What elements of the NoS do they (beginning teacher) think should be included in the curriculum and why?
3. How do they approach teaching the NoS in their lessons? What has influenced this approach? What practical-based lessons would they include to embed elements of the NoS?
4. How do they assess pupils' understanding of these elements of the NoS?

In answering the above questions, encourage the beginning teacher to highlight NoS elements provided in the science curriculum's recommended units of work. You could support them in mapping these elements to different units of work in order to ensure a comprehensive coverage of the NoS with their pupils.

The discussion points in Task 14.4 would probably help a beginning teacher to acknowledge the significance of practical work as one of the effective ways of promoting the inclusion of NoS elements in science lessons. You then need to support the beginning teacher to incorporate these into their lessons. The next section provides you with some mentoring strategies that can support a beginning teacher to teach NoS elements using practical work.

14.3 Supporting a beginning teacher to reflect on their existing practical work mediated teaching practices using the nine elements of the NoS

Practical work is an important aspect of teaching and learning science. It offers many opportunities to develop pupils' understanding of the NoS, such as the reliance of science on empirical data, testing predictions and hypotheses, and fair testing. As a mentor, it is important to help a beginning teacher with building their attitudes by thoroughly reflecting on what elements of the NoS can be conveyed within certain practical activities, and demonstrating their wider applications. You need to support a beginning teacher to plan practical work in their lessons that not only promotes enjoyment among pupils but also enhances pupils' learning and scientific skills development, for example, by focusing on reasons why scientific concepts are continuously tested and validated. The beginning teacher should include the nine elements of the NoS in planning for a practical activity, that is:

- Making hypotheses
- Making predictions

Applying features of the nature of science 219

- Identifying variables
- Accurate use and handling of equipment
- Making careful observations
- Making inferences
- Tables and graphs
- Drawing conclusions
- Evaluations.

You could ask the beginning teacher to first evaluate their current lesson plans by mapping these nine NoS elements. This can be achieved by asking them to complete Task 14.5, which invites a beginning teacher to reflect on the elements of the NoS and its implication for a classroom-based practical activity.

Task 14.5   Reflecting on what aspects of the NoS can be taught through a given practical activity

Ask a beginning teacher you are mentoring to plan an investigation for 13-year-olds on either whether or not a sample painting by Frida Kahlo is genuine or fake using the technique of chromatography or any topic they are about to teach.

After teaching the lesson, ask the beginning teacher to reflect on the nine elements of the NoS that were covered (or not) and why (or why not).

Then ask them to answer the following questions:

1. How can they more effectively address NoS elements during this lesson?
2. What other considerations can they make before deciding which elements to cover?
3. What are the positive outcomes for pupils?

Then discuss the answers to these questions with the beginning teacher and mutually agree on the next steps.

One of the next steps from Task 14.5, could be to encourage and support the beginning teacher to use, revisit, adopt/adapt Table 14.3, which presents a NoS mediated lesson plan pro forma, before they teach future practical lessons. Moreover, it is desirable that you keep monitoring and supporting the beginning teacher's (practical-based) lesson plan and teaching gains/setbacks throughout their time with you in order to develop their pedagogical practices, utilising the NoS elements, in a gradual and sustained manner.

As this chapter advocates the use of practical work to teach NoS elements, the associated feature for planning and performing practical work is the consideration of health and safety. The next section identifies mentoring support you can give to promote health and safety training for a beginning teacher you mentor.

14.4 Incorporating health and safety training as part of beginning teacher development

Health and safety issues cannot be ignored while planning and incorporating NoS elements into practical activities. The history of school science is replete with examples of accidents that have occurred when adequate assessments of risk were not carried out. Hazard identification and risk assessment are some of the main reasons for a beginning teacher's reluctance to carry out practical activities in science lessons, which leads to reduced enjoyment of, and engagement in lessons by pupils. The increasing diversity of entrants into science teaching includes newly qualified science graduates and career changers, some of whom may not be familiar with the hazards associated with certain experiments and practical activities that are part of school science. As a mentor, you have a responsibility for providing a beginning teacher with a thorough induction on health and safety procedures for conducting practical lessons – both generally and for a specific practical activity – and for offering continued guidance throughout the early years of their teaching career. For a start, ask the beginning teacher to complete Task 14.6 below to reflect on some health and safety procedures and issues.

Task 14.6 'A matter of terms'

Hazard and risk are terms that are commonly used as if their meanings are commonly understood. During a weekly mentoring meeting, discuss with a beginning teacher the following questions, to help them develop clarity about the terms; hence, ensuring precision in their presentation of these terms to pupils in their lessons.

1. What is a hazard?
2. What is a risk?
3. What guidance is commonly used in schools to identify hazards associated with certain materials and equipment?
4. Are there practical activities that can be considered 'hazard free'?

During these discussions, ask the beginning teacher to make notes on the best ways to appraise hazards and risks while planning for practical activities (and ensuring the inclusion of the NoS elements discussed above).

To enable a beginning teacher to embed health and safety issues in planning for practical lessons, this chapter suggests three vital ways, which are: sources of guidance, induction to the laboratory and risk assessment for every practical activity.

14.4.1 Sources of guidance

It is important for you to make sure a beginning teacher has access to sources of guidance regarding health and safety matters. In England, for example, the Department for

Applying features of the nature of science 221

Education (DfE), has provided some guidance for schools that can be adopted and/or modified in accordance with the school's context.

As a start, you could share the list below of weblinks or equivalent references of organisations used in your country with the beginning teacher:

- Consortium of Local Education Authorities for the Provision of Science Equipment (CLEAPSS) website: http://science.cleapss.org.uk/resources/resource-search.aspx?search=health%20 and%20safety
- DfE guidance: Asbestos management in schools' website: www.gov.uk/government/ publications/asbestos-management-in-schools--2
- DfE guidance: Emergency planning and response' website: www.gov.uk/guidance/ emergencies-and-severe-weather-schools-and-early-years-settings
- Health and Safety Executive' (HSE) website: 'Identify the hazards' www.hse.gov.uk/risk/ identify-the-hazards.htm
- Outdoor Education Advisers Panel for school trips' website: www.diverseschooltravel. co.uk/destinations/?gclid=CjOKCQjwpLfzBRCRARIsAHuj6qVilhyZZU3obd 61PJunQwoOxHDd2DpHWCz9g68grYPYV5Ryt-dg7VQaAjmWEALw_wcB

As a mentor, you are the primary source of support for a beginning teacher, so you could provide a general overview on health and safety practices based on some of the above (or similar) list of resources. However, for continued, all-round development of a beginning teacher and to hand over some of this responsibility to them, instead of you giving them a general overview, you could direct them to the above (or similar) resources, which they can access as the need arises. To facilitate this practice appropriately, ask the beginning teacher to complete Task 14.7, which allows them to identify and reflect on resources they could use to gain guidance on health and safety procedures regarding specific practical activities.

Task 14.7   Sources of guidance

Follow the steps below:

1. Ask a beginning teacher to reflect on where they would get advice from, for each of the practical activities indicated in Table 14.2 and any others they will be teaching in the near future.
2. Then discuss with the beginning teacher some of their learning gains from the documents and ask them to identify some of the sources that helped them the most, as well as those which were not helpful.
3. Encourage them to keep updating Table 14.2 in future by adding and reflecting on additional health and safety documents regarding these four examples as well as other practical activities.

Table 14.2 Sources of guidance for practical activities

Activity	Sources of guidance associated with required materials and equipment	Sources of guidance regarding associated hazards
1 Using chemical reagents		
2 Using radioactive sources		
3 Dissecting animal organs		
4 A field trip to a nature reserve		
5 Others – add as appropriate		

14.4.2 Induction to the laboratory

Science mentors should provide a thorough laboratory induction for a beginning teacher. This not only involves the beginning teacher thinking through practicalities, for instance seating plans, equipment distribution and collection but more serious contingency issues, such as:

- Considering how to evacuate the laboratory in case of incidents
- Location of gas and electricity cut-off switches
- Location of eye washes and watering stations
- Availability and location of fire extinguishers and blankets
- Availability and location of sharps buckets
- Procedures for cleaning up spills and breakages
- Dealing with burns and scalds.

To facilitate discussion, during one of your weekly mentoring meetings ask the beginning teacher to complete Task 14.8.

Task 14.8   Induction to the laboratory on dealing with serious contingency issues

Ask the beginning teacher to:

1. Go through the list of serious contingency issues (above) and identify where they need more guidance
2. Include other issues that they can add to the list of contingency issues
3. Reflect on incidents they have encountered in their practice so far and how they (or the teacher) dealt with them
4. Recall and revisit laboratory hazard and safety symbols for equipment and materials that are commonly used in practical activities. For any they are not aware of, ask them to research them and record them in their diaries
5. Propose ways to develop their understanding of health and safety in planning for practical activities.

Applying features of the nature of science 223

> To strengthen this laboratory induction further, you can probe by asking the beginning teacher questions such as:
>
> - How has reflecting on the above points supported their understanding, knowledge, awareness and even confidence of conducting practical work to embed NoS in their practices?
> - What further support do they need in this particular area of development?

14.4.3 Risk assessment for every experiment

It is good practice to require a beginning teacher to do a risk assessment for any practical activity they are planning to teach. This should be monitored by you, a laboratory technician and/or by a health and safety officer. This will make the practice of risk assessment habitual for a beginning teacher. For older pupils (aged 15 and above), a beginning teacher can be encouraged to jointly do the risk assessment with them, so as to reinforce its importance among pupils. For more serious risks, such as handling radioactive sources, as a mentor, you should organise specific training for the beginning teacher with a designated person or external bodies (such as CLEAPSS in the UK context) who offer such training. It is equally important to ensure that risk assessment becomes part of weekly meetings where you can:

- Discuss every practical activity that the beginning teacher aims to teach in the following week and its associated hazards
- Provide guidance on the availability of chemicals, materials and equipment to use and possible safer alternatives and quantities
- Encourage the beginning teacher to reflect on the availability of written and verbal instructions to the pupils before and during the practical exercise
- Provide some trustworthy written and/or video-based resources on health and safety specific to particular practical requirements.

Health and safety can be documented for every practical lesson by adding a column titled health and safety considerations to the lesson plan pro forma containing the nine NoS elements mentioned above (see Table 14.3, row two, column two). These steps are particularly important in the early stages of initial teacher education in order to (i) identify learning gaps in the beginning teacher's practice, (ii) give them guidance where they find difficulty in anticipating hazards and risks or they find problems in planning to support pupils who they think will experience difficulty in adhering to health and safety procedures, and (iii) recognise that health and safety considerations start from the first element of the NoS, i.e. making a hypothesis and not always from the elements which involve handling of equipment or observations or while pupils/teacher are doing the experiment (Table 14.3).

Table 14.3 A lesson plan pro forma to include the elements of the NoS in the planning and teaching of practical work (including health and safety)

Date:

Unit of work:

Learning outcomes:

Practical lesson title:

Elements of the NoS	Health and safety considerations	Practical work	
		Pupils' activities	Teacher's activities
Making hypotheses			
Making predictions			
Identifying variables			
Accurate use and handling of equipment			
Making careful observations			
Making inferences			
Tables and graphs			
Drawing conclusions			
Evaluations			

[See description on the terms used for unit of work and learning outcomes in Chapter 6]

14.5 A professional development walk (PDW)

The focus of PDWs is on a beginning teacher's development - through them observing peers' practices alongside their mentor in order to unravel reasons behind some 'expert teacher' (experienced science teacher) actions that may seem intuitive and automated. It can be followed up by a conversation where the beginning teacher asks the experienced science teacher reasons for particular actions and the experienced teacher articulates the thinking behind some skills they demonstrate. This is an excellent opportunity for the beginning teacher to understand the relationship between the NoS, subject knowledge highlighted in the curriculum, practical activities and health and safety procedures, from the experiences of experienced teachers.

Applying features of the nature of science 225

Task 14.9 asks you to carry out a PDW on a practical-based science lesson with a beginning teacher you are mentoring, so that they get a feel of how experienced teachers teach practical activities, encompassing the learning and assessment of elements of the NoS and ensuring health and safety procedures are observed in their classrooms.

Task 14.9   PDW to unravel NoS elements and health and safety procedures in practical science lessons

Ask a beginning teacher to observe a practical-based science lesson taught by an experienced science teacher. Next, arrange a post-lesson discussion meeting between the beginning teacher and the observed (experienced) teacher. This discussion would allow the beginning teacher to ask the experienced teacher questions about the ways the experienced teacher has implemented the elements of NoS and health and safety procedures in the lesson.

For this post-lesson discussion, you could provide a set of questions to the beginning teacher, such as the following:

1. How was the practical activity organised, i.e. in groups, pairs or individually? and why?
2. How were equipment and materials distributed? and why?
3. What was the teacher doing during practical activities? and why?
4. What elements of the NoS were being taught and emphasised?
5. How were theories presented to pupils?
6. To what extent were hypothesising and theory generation encouraged? How were they linked (or could be linked) to practical activities?
7. What health and safety protocols were administered?
8. What were the health and safety instructions given to the pupils before the practical activity? Were these instructions given to the pupils once? Or these instructions for the pupils were revisited by the teacher in the lesson?
9. What hazards were being dealt with?
10. What else have they noted in the lesson that indicates the use of elements of the NoS and health and safety procedures in a science practical-based lesson?

14.6 NoS focused lesson plans

After carrying out Task 14.9, Task 14.10 enables you to support a beginning teacher to practise planning practical lessons that focus on elements of the NoS, practical work and health and safety. This is an important activity for a beginning teacher's pedagogical knowledge development. In planning these practical-based lessons, as a mentor, support the beginning teacher with their planning. This can help the beginning teacher to map their progression in teaching practical lessons.

Task 14.10   Lesson planning to incorporate practical activities, along with the elements of the NoS and instruction on health and safety

Ask a beginning teacher to plan a few lessons, for example, the next ones they are going to teach, or the ones below. Table 14.3 can be used as a template.

- Heat transfer with a group of 13-year-olds.
- Titration with a group of 16-year-olds.

Annotate these lessons plans, then discuss them with the beginning teacher.

As a beginning teacher develops their ability to plan practical lessons, you may encourage them to reflect on the questions below while planning and teaching the lessons to incorporate best practice in their classrooms:

1. Which elements of the NoS could be covered in this lesson?
2. How can they be approached and assessed?
3. What are their next steps in developing these skills, knowledge and understanding (progression of skills)?

Summary and key points

This chapter has addressed aspects of teaching, learning and mentoring the NoS. Key points that have emerged from this chapter:

- A beginning teacher needs a thorough understanding of the elements of the NoS and interlinked subject knowledge in science. Mentors need to support a beginning science teacher to develop specific science teaching and learning strategies and to gain expertise in teaching effective practical science lessons.
- Mentors need to support a beginning teacher to articulate their views about the NoS and carry out suggested activities for its articulation.
- A beginning teacher needs an understanding of the role of practical work as one of the important components of the NoS. Your responsibility is to enable them to maximise the use of NoS elements while planning and teaching practical activities.
- Health and safety must be an integral aspect of a beginning teacher's development. To facilitate that, as a mentor, you need a way to demonstrate some seemingly complex and intuitive elements of their practice. A professional development walk (PDW) is suggested as a way to demystify expert practice.

Further resources

Abd-El-Khalick, F., Bell, R.L. and Lederman, N.G. (1998) 'The nature of science and instructional practice: Making the unnatural natural', *Science Education*, *82* (4), pp. 417–436.
In light of the extensive discussion about making pedagogies of elements of the NoS in the curriculum explicit, Abd-El-Khalick's paper is a useful introduction and refresher about 'what

exactly is the NoS?' As a mentor, you could set a task for a beginning teacher related to reading and analysing the paper (or another similar one) and identifying implications for their practice. As nomenclature of the elements of the NoS differs from one country to another, the paper would also be useful to help a beginning teacher to understand where the relevant aspects from the curriculum they are teaching sit within the larger framework.

Millar, R. and Abrahams, I. (2009) 'Practical work: Making it more effective', *School Science Review*, *91* (334), pp. 59-64.

In this paper, Millar and Abrahams underscore the importance of practical work in school science. They advocate 'hands-on' and 'minds-on' practical work that beginning teachers need to develop to make practical work more effective and enjoyable. Millar and Abraham also introduce two domains (lenses) through which to view practical work, corresponding to domains of objects and observables on one side and on the other; the domain of ideas – useful concepts and exercises for the beginning teacher to carry out and embed elements of the NoS. The paper would form a sound grounding for a mentor to read in order to support a beginning teacher understand the wider role of practical activities in school science.

15 Supporting beginning teachers in embedding scientific literacy

Saima Salehjee and Mike Watts

Introduction

The National Curriculum for Science in England aims to equip all pupils with 'the scientific knowledge required to understand the uses and implications of science, today and for the future' (Department for Education (DfE), 2013, p. 3). Indeed, there is considerable research available that shows the need for scientifically literate citizens in the world. But what exactly constitutes a scientifically literate citizen? Is it, for example, a person who 'applies scientific habits of minds' (Huxley, 1882, p. 4); one who develops scientific attitudes and exhibits 'open-mindedness, intellectual integrity, observation, and interest in testing their opinions and beliefs' (Dewey, 1934, p. 3); who can communicate between two cultures – science and arts – that results in an understanding and learning of science among families, cultures and societies (Snow, 1959); or is it someone who can engage in self-directed learning in science and technology beyond the school years (Rennie, Stocklmayer and Gilbert, 2019)? We see scientifically literate citizens as people who may not be working in any science specialist fields (such as marine biology or astrophysics), but who can accumulate and grasp aspects of science while solving everyday problems. They can, for instance, exhibit abilities to research and critique facts on social media, acquire scientific vocabulary, listen and understand BBC Radio 5 science podcasts, and appreciate science content in the daily news et cetera.

As a framework for this chapter, we consider first how you can introduce some pedagogical practices associated with developing scientific literacy to a beginning teacher. We then consider how you can support them to embed scientific literacy in planning and teaching lessons by focusing on the four dimensions of scientific literacy identified by Brickhouse (2007) (civic, personal, cultural and critical). The next, and longer, part of the chapter identifies some mentoring ideas, encompassing Brickhouse's (2007) dimensions along with Toth and Graham's (2016) scientific literacy elements. You can use these dimensions and elements to

Embedding scientific literacy 229

support and empower a beginning teacher as they embed scientific literacy in their planning, teaching and evaluations.

Objectives

At the end of this chapter you should be able to:

- Encourage a beginning teacher to plan scientific literacy enriched lessons
- Support a beginning teacher to outline teaching and learning practices using Brickhouse's dimensions of scientific literacy (civic, personal, cultural and critical)
- Assist a beginning teacher in incorporating these scientific literacy dimensions, along with Toth and Graham's (2016) four elements, as integral parts of their lesson planning, teaching and evaluations
- Support a beginning teacher to self-reflect on their teaching strategies to implement scientific literacy in their day-to-day practices.

15.1 Mentoring a beginning teacher to incorporate some pedagogical practices associated with scientific literacy

Toth and Graham (2016) maintain that science teachers – especially beginning science teachers – find difficulty in implementing work linked to scientific literacy in their classrooms, even though the science curriculum requires every teacher, no matter how experienced, to include elements of scientific literacy in their work. This leads to questions such as: (i) How often does scientific literacy actually make an appearance in classrooms? (ii) How well do beginning teachers manage this in lessons? and (iii) How do you prepare and support a beginning teacher to adopt scientific literacy oriented pedagogical practices that can improve their planning and teaching? To support a beginning teacher, make progress here, you need:

- Knowledge and understanding of your own beliefs about the use of scientific literacy in planning and teaching the science curriculum
- Ways of supporting a beginning teacher to gain knowledge and understanding beyond their subject knowledge of the science curriculum
- Skills such as analysing and critiquing social issues as well as ways of supporting a beginning teacher to achieve these skills
- Attributes such as flexibility and resourcefulness around science issues.

Task 15.1 asks you to introduce some pedagogical practices associated with scientific literacy to a beginning teacher for planning a science lesson. The example used in this task concerns 'coastal erosion' (specifically: 'evidence, and uncertainties in evidence, for additional anthropogenic causes of climate change' under the unit of work 'earth and atmospheric science' (DfE, 2014, p. 13). Alternatively, you could use another unit of work that a beginning teacher will teach in the near future.

Task 15.1 An introduction to pedagogical practices associated with scientific literacy

1. In one of your weekly mentoring meetings, raise the contemporary issue of coastal erosion (or another topic) and ask the beginning teacher to start planning a lesson around this. They will need to take account of:
   - Coastal erosion is increasing. A beginning teacher should be aware of the impact of changing weather patterns and rises in sea-level on costal populations. Ask them to contribute their own knowledge and experience of this issue, identifying some key aspects causing erosion in general. A beginning teacher might 'spider diagram' these issues at the start of a possible lesson plan. [If required, you can ask a beginning teacher to read the section on constructing a spider diagram from Shaw (2019, pp. 316–317).]
   - Coastal erosion causes people to lose their land and homes. Here you can suggest that a beginning teacher may use a story of a fictional family with their pupils. For example: The Baker family live in Happisburgh, Norfolk. A recent storm brought a sea-cliff landslide that has taken many square metres off their land into the sea, not just depriving them of valuable grazing for animals, but also bringing the cliff edge ever closer to their farmhouse.

   [Your support in planning lessons in this way allows a beginning teacher to critically assess and analyse both the science issues, and the social impact on lives.]

2. Your questions could support the beginning teacher in planning a lesson on a social issue, like coastal erosion, and should act as a model for the questions they then ask a class, for example:
   - How can the beginning teacher find out more about coastal erosion?

   [The answer here is relatively straightforward through a simple Google search. Coastal erosion, however, is a complex interdisciplinary issue and demands some clarity of thinking to shape answers to major questions about, for example, sustainability, land use, housing, food production, population mobility and local employment patterns.]
   - What examples is the beginning teacher using? What measures could be taken to minimise coastal erosion? Can the beginning teacher identify and explore some of the measures already taken by local and national government in this area?

   [Again, there is no one single answer for these questions, but you are asking a beginning teacher to be flexible and resourceful in their work with pupils.]

3. Encourage the beginning teacher to discuss similar environmental issues with geography and geology teachers at the school. What work are they doing with pupils? and how it can be associated with the work being undertaken in science lessons?

15.2 Supporting beginning teachers to embed scientific literacy dimensions in their teaching practices

Once a beginning teacher is able to articulate the use of some pedagogical practices related to scientific literacy, the next step is to ask them to identify some scientific literacy-based teaching approaches from their own classroom practices and/or observed practices of other teachers. This could be achieved by asking the beginning teacher to read, and then discussing with them, the article by Brickhouse (2007). Brickhouse generated four dimensions of scientific literacy from her evaluations of the broad field, and her belief is that these interlink to portray some important characteristics of scientifically literate citizens. Below, her ideology is adapted to be appropriate for secondary pupils:

1. Civic dimension – pupils who demonstrate a level of understanding and are able to critique professional science and scientists for the betterment of public life. For example, such a pupil has the ability to critique contemporary issues on poverty, global warming, health and so on.
2. Personal dimension – pupils who can draw upon scientific knowledge and skills in order to make personal choices for a better lifestyle. For example, having the capacity to make an informed decision on whether to use a home remedy to cure a cough and cold and/or to use cough syrups or antibiotics and other medications.
3. Cultural dimension – pupils who are able to appreciate and understand scientific ideas in relation to their own interests. For example, reading and discussing with friends and family issues behind having plastic surgery, laser treatment for acne, a high protein diet to build muscles, use of video games or the implications of a gluten-free diet.
4. Critical dimension – pupils who can critically analyse written, oral and/or visual texts to make scientifically informed decisions. They are able to challenge claims made in advertisements; for instance, to evaluate the statements made for the use of electronic cigarettes as a popular alternative to avoid the use of tobacco smoking.

Task 15.2 asks a beginning teacher to recall experiences in order to link it with Brickhouse's (2007) four dimensions.

Task 15.2 A beginning teacher outlining scientific literacy-mediated events and experiences

Ask a beginning teacher to answer the following questions in detail:

1. As a science graduate, what civic, personal, cultural and critical understanding can you bring to teaching the science curriculum to secondary pupils?
2. What civic, personal, cultural and critical understanding have you witnessed during observed and/or team-taught science lessons?
3. What are the merits or demerits of including these dimensions in science classrooms?

The next step is to discuss their detailed answers to clarify any misconceptions and to support them to plan effective teaching and learning strategies that cover civic, personal, cultural and critical dimensions.

---

232 Salehjee and Watts

Following Task 15.2, you could support the beginning teacher to introduce Brickhouse's (2007) dimensions in teaching the science curriculum, preferably by choosing a specific unit of work they will be teaching in a few weeks. This activity will support the beginning teacher in exploring different ways subject knowledge locks with scientific literacy dimensions. It would be ideal to discuss one unit of work at a time, which can later be split into a series of lessons and/or merge with the next or the same unit of work. During these scaffolded mentoring discussions, you should encourage the beginning teacher to develop innovative ideas to implement scientific literacy in the classroom. Equally, you need to encourage them to self-reflect on the planning and teaching of these innovative ideas in the classrooms. This balance in the discussions can be achieved by mutual agreement on what can or cannot be incorporated into lesson plans.

Case study 15.1 provides a scenario of Sarah and exhibits some mentor-mentee discussion points. Task 15.3 asks you to recall similar mentor-mentee discussions from your own mentoring experiences.

Case study 15.1: Sarah: Mentor-mentee discussion points

Sarah, a beginning science teacher, planned to teach the physical and chemical properties of iron (Fe) and the process of rusting, using some visuals of Iron Man (a super hero character) and the Tin Man character (from the film Wizard of Oz). Some of the mentor-mentee discussion points included:

- The potential of using these story characters to incorporate cultural and critical dimensions.
- Possibilities of drawing scientific misconceptions such as tin (Sn) is an element that does not rust, unlike the Tin Man in the story.
- Opportunities for pupils to critique media-based (visual) texts using scientific evidence.
- Opportunities to discuss some other aspects of characters with pupils, for example gender-neutral choice of characters.
- Some possible ways Iron Man and Tin Man characters can (or not) incorporate civic and personal dimensions of scientific literacy in science lessons.

Task 15.3 Mentor's reflection on prior mentoring in relation to scientific literacy

From prior experiences similar to the example in Case study 15.1, recall and evaluate:

- Ideas you have discussed with a beginning teacher to implement scientific literacy in relation to civic, personal, cultural and critical dimensions

Embedding scientific literacy

- Mentoring strategies you have incorporated during these discussions that had positive or negative impact on a beginning teacher's practices towards implementing innovative ideas
- Mentoring strategies to set specific targets for a beginning teacher as next steps and the next steps you took to refine your mentoring skills?

You can record your answers in Table 15.1.

Table 15.1 Mentor's reflection in relation to scientific literacy

Beginning teacher's innovative ideas to implement scientific literacy	Mentoring strategies			Next steps
	Resultant targets agreed by you with the beginning teacher	Positive impact on the beginning teacher's practices	Negative impact on the beginning teacher's practices	

15.3 Assisting beginning teachers in planning lessons to highlight a pedagogical view of scientific literacy

The next steps are for you to support a beginning teacher in incorporating Brickhouse's (2007) four dimensions within their lesson planning. A beginning teacher will already be co-planning lessons with you (see Chapter 6) and many of them may find lesson planning time-consuming (and anxiety-inducing). You should carefully and critically evaluate their lesson plans. This gives you opportunities to explore a beginning teacher's thinking and

234 *Salehjee and Watts*

planning processes and give an indication as to how you can offer further support. You could ask the beginning teacher, for example, to develop individual lesson plans or ask them to prepare one master plan per unit of work, and later split this into a series of lessons. We recommend the latter because, in this way, the beginning teacher will be able to plan the breadth of scientific literacy dimensions and can then devise adaptable ways to section them into a series of progressive and fluid lessons.

You may want to share the lesson planning template with the beginning teacher. This lesson planning template can be divided into three columns encompassing learning outcomes and scientific literacy elements, associated activities and assessments– see Appendix 15.1. Some mentoring points to support the beginning teacher in planning the three columns of Appendix 15.1 are as follows:

15.3.1 Column one: Learning outcomes and scientific literacy elements

Learning outcomes need to exhibit a clear relationship with pupils learning (Chapter 6, pp. 78-85). You need to support a beginning teacher in constructing specific, measurable and pupil-friendly learning outcomes. These outcomes can be drawn from the curriculum's units of work by using Brickhouse's (2007) dimensions mentioned above. For example, Sarah's Case study 15.1, involving detailed reflections on the use of story characters to incorporate scientific literacy, can be related with 'properties of elements arranged in order of atomic number' (aspect of the unit of work – 'Atomic structure and the Periodic Table') (DfE, 2014, p. 11). The beginning teacher can plan expected learning outcomes for pupils in this vein. The starting point for you is to support a beginning teacher in planning learning outcomes. These learning outcomes should connect pupils' learning with scientific literacy-based dimensions (civic, personal, cultural and critical) related with a particular unit of work (a list of units of work can be seen in Appendix 10.1). You can use the following Toth and Graham (2016) elements to make these connections, for example by:

1. Identifying the scientific claim taught in the lessons
2. Searching for evidence by using prior knowledge to investigate further
3. Warranting and expressing limitations for evidence
4. Communicating qualifiers of the claim based on the evaluated evidence (see Figure 15.1).

In addition, ask a beginning teacher to use Table 15.2, which provides some example verbs that can initiate the writing of learning outcomes using Brockhouse's (2007) four elements as indicators of scientific literacy.

Moving forward, these learning outcomes are used to plan and assess an individual pupil's learning. A beginning teacher might find this kind of planning quite intimidating and, therefore, you could first support them in dividing the learning outcomes into three broad expected levels (such as: all pupils must, most pupils should and some pupils could – see Chapter 6, example on current, resistance, voltage and Ohm's law, Table 6.3 (p. 82) second row). This will support the beginning teacher to devise strategies to support pupils at all three levels. Then, later, it is essential to support the beginning teacher in planning to unpick individual pupil's learning needs.

Embedding scientific literacy 235

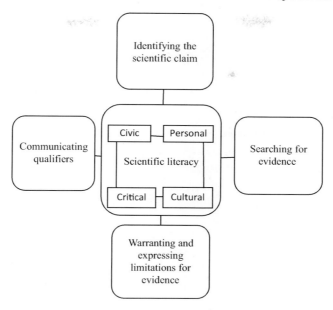

Figure 15.1 Connecting scientific literacy dimensions and scientific literacy elements to form learning outcomes

Table 15.2 Verbs for writing learning outcomes to incorporate scientific literacy in lesson planning

Toth and Graham (2016) elements	Identifying the scientific claim(s)	Searching for evidence		Warranting and expressing limitations for evidence	Communicating qualifiers
		Prior knowledge	Investigation		
Additional verbs: (Shabatura, 2013)	Engage	Elicit	Explore	Evaluate	Elaborate
	Ask questions	Predict	Observe	Explain	Extend and reflect on conclusions
		Compare	Experiment	Justify	
		Classify	Interpret	Infer	Ask extended questions drawn through discussions
			Find answers	Suggest answers gained from the data.	
			Measure and use appropriate tools to investigate and record data		Answer questions with a recognition that it can be answered in different ways

15.3.2 Column two: Activities

Once the beginning teacher has firmly established the aim of highlighting pupils' scientific literacy, lesson activities can then be shaped to develop this. Throughout the process of constructing activities, you need to support the beginning teacher in planning activities that connect with the intended learning outcomes. This column can be further broken down into three interlinking sections, that is:

(i) Pupils' activity, which covers what pupils will be doing and learning from these activities. Your support in planning these activities would need to:
   - Direct the beginning teacher's planning to focus on pupils' learning for the future. That is, not just aiming for a one-off scientific literacy-based knowledge and skills development lesson, but aiming for continuing development that can be polished and advanced in future science lessons, non-science lessons, out-of-school contexts and also later in life
   - Revisit their activities to make them increasingly pupil-friendly, precise and manageable within the allotted timeframe. You need also to check that the planned activities involve all pupils in the classroom, and are not only focused on a particular group of pupils
   - Encourage the beginning teacher to plan and use a range of teaching and learning strategies that elicit skills among pupils, so that pupils can identify, evidence, evaluate and communicate scientific or pseudo-scientific claims
   - Support them in planning questions for pupils that can be asked before, during and after the lesson. You need to review the questions and suggest changes to ensure that they align with the scientific literacy dimensions, learning outcomes, and align as much as possible with individual pupil's learning needs
   - Encourage and support the beginning teacher in planning activities that resonate with their own scientific literacy skills, gained through their science degrees which can then be adapted for secondary aged pupils.
(ii) Group activity, which covers the essential scientific literacy skill of critical thinking through argumentation and communication. This makes group activities an essential requirement of developing scientific literacy in the classrooms. Despite being an essential requirement, some beginning teachers avoid group activities due to lack of confidence in organising and managing groups. Therefore, you could support a beginning teacher to plan for group work by working with them to complete Task 15.4.

Task 15.4   Supporting a beginning teacher to plan for group work

Ask a beginning teacher to organise small groups, keeping in mind the learning needs of each member of the group. You could assist them in organising these small groups (see Chapter 16, pp. 253–254, on one way of organising group roles).

- Encourage the beginning teacher to name the groups, in Table 15.3. The names given are A, B and C, but these could be changed. Then, complete the first column by using the initials of all pupils under their respective group names.

- The second column includes a description of the activity, such as practical work to test for purity of water from the nearby river, or from the school's water fountain. These could be problem-solving activities using a news item on health hazards of drinking polluted water in rural areas of some countries, et cetera.
- Next, ask the beginning teacher to fill in the third column: What scientific knowledge and skills will pupils gain from the activity, and how? and the fourth: How can the activity be connected with scientific literacy dimensions? in as much detail as they can, and then discuss their answers with you.
- Finally, ask the beginning teacher to complete the last three columns on strengths, weaknesses and next steps, based on their articulation of your comments, suggestions and recommendations.

Throughout the discussions, you need to ensure that the beginning teacher's focus remains on pupil's development of scientific literacy, by allowing pupils in groups to identify claim(s), search for evidence, warrant and articulate limitations for evidence and communicate qualifier of the evaluated evidence.

Table 15.3 Supporting a beginning teacher to plan for group work

Choice of pupils for each group	Group work description	What scientific knowledge and skills pupils will gain from the activity and how?	How can the activity be connected with scientific literacy dimensions?	What are the strengths?	What are the weaknesses?	What to do when an individual pupil's learning within the group is not meeting the desired outcomes?
Group A, pupils:						
Group B, pupils:						
Group C pupils:						

(iii) Teacher's activity (part of the Appendix 15.1 column on activities) includes teaching strategies to promote pupils' scientific learning. As many beginning teachers tend to focus more on what they will do rather than on what pupils will do in the classroom, this can lead to an overly didactic teacher-centric approach, contradicting the principles of scientific literacy-based teaching and learning. To move the beginning teacher from teacher-centric to pupil-centric approaches, you need to encourage them to plan pupil activities first – and then plan teacher activities after to facilitate the planned pupil activities. At this point, you could also share some recent examples of pupil activities associated with specific learning

238 *Salehjee and Watts*

outcomes, for example where pupils have been asked to select some reliable evidence from both newspapers and documentary programmes in order to evaluate the impact of climate change. You can then support the beginning teacher in planning teacher activities focused on keeping all pupils on task by giving them freedom to research, search, evaluate and voice evidence in the light of scientific knowledge and skills. This focus would support the beginning teacher in increasing individual and/or group work, and make the teacher's activities effective in achieving the learning outcomes.

We believe that teachers-as-facilitators can foster a rich scientific literacy-oriented learning environment for pupils, by using questioning as a tool to increase pupils' participation level. A beginning teacher will need your guidance to increase pupils' voice and to appreciate that there can be more than one correct response, to promote critical thinking, incorporate positive presuppositions, support pupils in developing and refining responses, paraphrasing judgements and evaluations gained from scientific or pseudoscientific evidence. A beginning teacher can use Table 15.4 (adapted from Costa and Kallick, 2000) as a prompt to plan and write their questions in the teacher's activities column of Appendix 15.1. Once the beginning teacher has planned these questions, you need to comment on/discuss these before the lesson – to ensure that the questions tie in well with pupils' activities (individual and/or group), learning outcomes and the time available to achieve these outcomes.

Table 15.4 Enhancing scientific literacy by maximising a pupil's participation (Costa and Kallick, 2000)

Promoting pupil's voice	Openness for different responses	Encouraging critical thinking among pupils	Using positive presuppositions	Refining and developing pupil's responses	Using paraphrasing prompts to elaborate evaluations
What are some of your ideas?	What are your conclusions?	As you consider ...	What are the merits and demerits of using this strategy to justify the claim?	Why do you think in this way?	You are indicating...
What predictions did you make?	What limitations and warrants make you come to this conclusion?	As you evaluated...		Please elaborate/ clarify your point about ...?	You are suggesting ...
What are your observations?		As you inferred...	What are some of the chosen parameters that will keep you on track and progressing?		You are justifying...
What would you do differently?		As you proceeded...		What do you mean by ...?	You evidenced...
					You concluded...

[The terms 'you' and 'your' in this table refer to the beginning teacher]

15.3.3 *Column three: Assessment*

You could support a beginning teacher in using the questions from the teacher's activity column two, as a baseline for assessing pupils' learning encompassing scientific literacy. You can then provide suggestions to the beginning teacher to advance these literacy-styled questions, track and record them formatively and/or adopt them to form summative assessment-styled

Embedding scientific literacy 239

questions. These records can then shape future lesson activities and inform new teaching and learning strategies. You could also support the beginning teacher in recording pupil progression that links with the learning outcomes. Chapter 12, on assessment, provides some helpful strategies on recording pupils' progression, which can be adapted here as well.

15.4 Mentor and beginning teacher's evaluations

A beginning teacher's evaluations are key evidence in tracking their progression and as indicators of areas for future development. As a mentor, you should encourage a beginning teacher to spend time in reflecting on the planning and teaching of lessons and base their evaluations on pupil progression in relation to intended learning outcomes. Some beginning teachers write 'what activities they did' in the classroom rather than evaluating what went well and what needs to be worked on in future. Therefore, you should not accept 'what activities they did' as evaluations and, instead, ask the beginning teacher to use the points from the pupils' activity and teacher's activity parts of Appendix 15.1 to reflect on the suitability, effectiveness, strengths and weaknesses of pupils' learning and their teaching.

Lesson observations of a beginning teacher by you and/or other experienced teachers provide a range of opportunities to understand their strengths and areas for improvement. Documenting these observations is essential to reflect on the feedback given to a beginning teacher, even after several weeks/months. You might use the lesson observation/evaluation template provided by their initial teacher education provider, the school's recording system or use Table 8.2 (p. 126), to observe the beginning teacher for a complete lesson or part of a lesson. These templates can be adapted to provide focused feedback, based on scientific literacy. Table 15.5 provides an example lesson evaluation template based on a planned and taught lesson (learning outcomes and associated scientific literacy elements, activities and assessments), its strengths and weaknesses, and identifies areas where further actions are required. These evaluations could be focused on Toth and Graham's (2016) four elements of scientific literacy in order to embed Brickhouse's (2007) four scientific literacy dimensions in teaching and learning of science. Task 15.5 asks you and a beginning teacher you are mentoring to evaluate taught lessons.

Task 15.5   Mentor-mentee evaluations

You and a beginning teacher separately evaluate a lesson taught by the beginning teacher and observed by you. At first, a beginning teacher is likely to find difficulty in conducting an in-depth self-evaluation on their own teaching. Therefore, it is advisable that you support them by filling in the same lesson evaluation template, such as Table 15.5, where you complete the sheet as an active observer and the beginning teacher completes it as an active reflector of their own teaching. The evaluation should:

- Analyse the extent to which scientific literacy dimensions are achieved in relation to pupils' learning, based on developing scientific literacy associated knowledge and skills

- Highlight the presence or possibility of embedding suitable scientific literacy dimensions (civic, personal, cultural and critical).

Then compare and discuss each other's evaluations to identify the next steps for the beginning teacher.

Table 15.5 Lesson evaluation template focused on planning and teaching scientific literacy dimensions

1. Learning outcomes and associated scientific literacy elements	• Strengths
	• Further action required
2. Activities	• Strengths
	• Further action required
3. Assessment	• Strengths
	• Further action required

These in-depth, mentor and mentee evaluations are beneficial for the beginning teacher to enable them to outline their progression in imparting scientific literacy in their teaching. They also help build the beginning teacher's professional reflection capacity in developing scientifically literate pupils for the future. Another benefit of completing the evaluation sheet separately and then comparing them together is that it enables identification of similarities and differences in a mentor's and beginning teacher's evaluations, which will support the beginning teacher to understand different perspectives and identify next steps. For example, some beginning teachers might believe that – for a group work activity – it is essential for them to move around from one group to another as quickly as possible to make sure that all pupils are on task. However, a mentor might view this rapid movement as a distraction for pupils and observe that the beginning teacher gave insufficient time to each group to discuss and communicate their thoughts effectively. Such differences are very common and need to be discussed and documented in the lesson evaluation template for future reference.

Summary and key points

This chapter has highlighted some mentoring strategies to support a beginning teacher in developing scientifically literate pupils. Specifically,

- Mentoring strategies should encourage a beginning teacher to use their graduate skills to implement scientific literacy in the classroom. This can be achieved by giving them examples of how they might cascade their graduate skills to pupils.
- Supporting a beginning teacher in producing scientifically literate pupils for a lifetime. This entails incorporating discussions and outlining teaching and learning strategies to teach the science curriculum using civic, personal, cultural and critical dimensions of scientific literacy.
- Assisting a beginning teacher to outline the four scientific literacy dimensions on the curriculum, and to plan learning outcomes along with scientific literacy elements, activities, and assessments.
- Mentoring to evaluate a beginning teacher's progression as an active observer and encouraging them to become active reflectors of their own teaching aimed to implement scientific literacy for all pupils.

Further resources

Brickhouse, N.W. (2007) 'Scientific literates: What do they do? Who are they?', in *Proceedings of the Linnaeus Tercentenary Symposium at Promoting Scientific Literacy: Science Education Research in Transaction*, Uppsala University, Uppsala, Sweden, 28-29 May 2007, pp. 90-94, viewed 10 December 2019, from: https://eprints.qut.edu.au/12883/1/Linnaeus_Tercentenary_Symposium.pdf#page=88
This short conference paper describes a scientifically literate everyday person. This comprehensive account could be shared with a beginning teacher to help them realise that a goal for them as science teachers is to plan and teach science lessons with a view that pupils learning of science encompasses the making of scientifically literate citizens.

Hodson, D. (2009) *Towards Scientific Literacy: A Teachers' Guide to the History, Philosophy and Sociology of Science*. Rotterdam, the Netherlands: Sense Publishers.
This book can act as a guide for beginning teachers, school mentors and university-based tutors, to implement the complexity of scientific literacy in the education of pupils by focusing on the history, philosophy and sociology of science.

Toth, E.E. and Graham, M.S. (2016) 'Preparing scientifically literate citizens: Pre-service teacher candidates' use of normative and logical thinking for critically examining news-media', *Electronic Journal of Science Education*, 20 (1), pp. 1-17.
This paper provides you with practical techniques and models by which you can engage beginning teachers to utilise their graduate skills to advance their scientific literacy knowledge and skills and some methods to model scientific literacy-based planning in secondary science classrooms.

242 *Salehjee and Watts*

Appendix 15.1 A lesson plan template: Scientific literacy dimensions

Scientific literacy dimensions				
Learning outcomes and associated scientific literacy elements	*Activities*	*Assessments*		
		Formative	*Summative*	*Diagnostic*
Identifying claims	Pupils' activity			
	Group activity			
	Teacher's activity			
Searching for evidence: Prior knowledge	Pupils' activity			
	Group activity			
	Teacher's activity			
Searching for evidence: Investigation	Pupils' activity			
	Group activity			
	Teacher's activity			

Embedding scientific literacy   243

Warranting and expressing limitations for evidence	Pupils' activity			
	Group activity			
	Teacher's activity			
Communicating qualifiers	Pupils' activity			
	Group activity			
	Teacher's activity			

16 Mentoring beginning teachers in implementing process-oriented guided inquiry learning: An example of an inquiry-based pedagogical approach of teaching science

Sheila S. Qureshi, Adam H. Larson and Venkat Rao Vishnumolakala

Introduction

As a mentor, you are vital to the success of beginning teachers. You introduce them to new pedagogical strategies for creating stimulating, pupil-centred classrooms and, for this reason, you should remain current in the latest trends in science pedagogy. Increasingly, science educators have employed pupil-centred, collaborative learning approaches to foster significant learning (Eberlein, Kampmeier, Minderhout, Moog, Platt, Varma-Nelson and White, 2008). In this chapter, we describe how to mentor beginning teachers using one such approach: process-oriented guided inquiry learning (POGIL). POGIL works by developing pupils' subject knowledge and process skills through structured small-group learning and has proven effective at boosting achievement in diverse school contexts (Qureshi, Bradley, Vishnumolakala, Treagust, Southam, Mocerino and Ojei, 2016). Mentoring beginning teachers to use the POGIL approach involves equipping them with teaching and learning strategies for enhancing pupil interaction and critical thinking in the science classroom (Moog, 2014).

This chapter provides an overview of POGIL, situates it within a spectrum of inquiry-based science pedagogies and offers a sequence of tasks for mentoring beginning science teachers in using the POGIL approach.

Objectives

By the end of this chapter you should be able to:

- Understand POGIL as an effective inquiry-based pedagogical approach
- Support a beginning teacher to understand the benefits of inquiry-based science teaching and evaluate pupil activities at four increasingly complex levels of inquiry (confirmation, structured, guided and open)

Process-Oriented Guided Inquiry Learning 245

- Support a beginning teacher to develop a POGIL plan, by incorporating three steps (exploration, invention and application) adopted from the POGIL learning cycle
- Encourage a beginning teacher to incorporate POGIL process skills in their lesson plans and suggest practical ways to implement inquiry questions and group work in classrooms
- Support a beginning teacher to plan and implement a series of POGIL lesson plans.

16.1 POGIL: An inquiry-based, experiential learning approach

POGIL is an inquiry-based, experiential learning approach that enables small groups of pupils to solve carefully designed activities that adhere to a well-formulated cycle of learning (Moog, 2014). Inquiry-based, pupil-centred learning approaches like POGIL are grounded in constructivist and progressive educational theories that emphasise conscious reflection on experience (Dewey, 1938; Piaget, 1973; Vygotsky, 1978; Kolb, 1984). For constructivists, learners 'construct their understanding of the world as a product of their actions in the world' (Mascolo, 2009, p. 4). This point is crucial, as learning depends on active construction of understanding from concrete experience. As a mentor, you can support beginning teachers to adopt constructivist approaches by modelling inquiry-based teaching strategies in your classroom, which they can then adopt and/or adapt. Then, discuss your modelled teaching strategies to encourage them to plan, teach and reflect on their own practices grounded in inquiry-based pedagogical approaches.

Many beginning teachers value traditional teaching styles and associated teaching strategies, as they impart information quickly and efficiently. However, these classroom practices reduce interactions between teachers and pupils, and among pupils (Moog and Spencer, 2008). Inquiry-based approaches, including the POGIL approach, address the drawbacks of traditional teaching by discouraging passivity. By shifting emphasis from teacher presentation to pupil activity, beginning teachers can, with your support, recognise the importance of pupil-centred activities and become 'facilitator[s] of learning, asking probing questions to help guide the students to develop understanding, and addressing misconceptions and misunderstandings' (Moog and Spencer, 2008, p. 2). Along these lines, Task 16.1 asks you to support a beginning teacher you are mentoring to self-reflect on their personal values and understanding of effective pedagogical approaches. They then discuss these reflections with you so you can suggest ways they can employ inquiry-oriented pupil-centred pedagogies in their practices.

Task 16.1 Self-reflection of inquiry-based and experiential science education

Ask a beginning teacher to:

1. Write a personal teaching philosophy

   After the beginning teacher has written a teaching philosophy, you should read and discuss it. During your discussion, guide the beginning teacher to reflect critically on their assumptions and beliefs about what 'works' in science teaching

2. Discuss general views on effective inquiry-based pedagogical approaches

   While discussing the beginning teacher's general positive and/or negative views on inquiry-based pedagogical approaches, ask them to elaborate on their motivation for becoming a science teacher and how this can support their pupils' learning

3. Discuss the theoretical relevance of teaching and learning science

   In further discussion, elicit the benefits and drawbacks of different learning theories (such as behaviourist and constructivist approaches) to reflect on effective teaching and learning strategies. This discussion should extend from the suggestions above, based on the beginning teacher's teaching philosophy and views on inquiry-based pedagogical approaches.

The discussions/beginning teacher's self-reflections in Task 16.1, can be documented in Table 16.1. In this table, the left-hand column presents the three points from the discussion outlined in Task 16.1. The second and third columns record a beginning teacher's self-reflections (strengths and limitations). These recorded strengths and limitations on the three discussion points presented in the first column of Table 16.1 can then be discussed with you. You could ask them 'why', 'why not', and 'how' questions, while they are discussing their strengths and limitations with you. The last column includes your suggestions for possible next steps to support the beginning teacher to adopt inquiry-oriented pupil-centred pedagogies. Revisit Table 16.1 by arranging at least three weekly meetings with the beginning teacher at different time intervals to support their self-reflection on philosophical orientation towards teaching and learning science (for example, at the beginning of their school placement/year, mid-placement/year and near the end of the school placement/year). In addition to these designated weekly meetings, ask the beginning teacher to update Table 16.1

Table 16.1 A beginning teacher's self-reflections on philosophical orientation towards teaching and learning science

Discussion points	Strengths	Limitations	Next steps
My personal teaching philosophy			
My general views on effective inquiry-based pedagogical approaches			
My understanding of the theoretical relevance of teaching and learning science			

[In this table 'my' refers to the beginning teacher.]

Process-Oriented Guided Inquiry Learning   247

every month and allow them to discuss their development and/or concerns with you at any point during the school placement/year.

16.2 Mentoring science as inquiry

Inquiry is an important way of teaching and learning science, however, inquiry-based learning remains loosely defined – a fact that challenges even the most devoted beginning teachers and mentors. The National Research Council in the United States (1996) defines inquiry as 'multifaceted activity' involving diverse knowledge and skills, such as 'making observations', 'posing questions' and 'using tools to gather, analyse and interpret data' (p. 23). Fitzgerald, Danaia and McKinnon (2019) build on this multifaceted notion of inquiry to identify four levels of inquiry: confirmation, structured, guided and open. You could encourage a beginning teacher to understand the benefits of Fitzgerald, Danaia and McKinnon's (2019) four levels of inquiry by asking them to complete Task 16.2. Task 16.2 asks the beginning teacher to classify pupil activities and plan lessons based on the four increasingly complex levels of inquiry (confirmation, structured, guided and open).

Task 16.2   Classifying pupil activities using Fitzgerald, Danaia and McKinnon's (2019) four levels of inquiry

Consider following the below steps:

1. Ask the beginning teacher to read Fitzgerald, Danaia and McKinnon's (2019) paper.
2. Give them a sample lesson plan to choose at least three different activities (such as practical activity, writing activity, discussion-based activity, et cetera).
3. Ask them to classify the chosen activities, according to the four different levels of inquiry identified by Fitzgerald, Danaia and McKinnon (2019), and record these classifications in Table 16.2.
4. Once the beginning teacher has completed Table 16.2, discuss their classification of activities and support them to understand the four levels of inquiry-based pedagogical approaches to teaching and learning of science further.
5. Finally, ask them to develop a lesson plan with your support on a topic that comes under a specific unit of work in the science curriculum guidance they are about to teach. Encourage them to record a minimum of three inquiry-based activities (linking to the four levels of inquiry: confirmation, structured, guided and open) in Table 16.2.

You can use Task 16.1 and Tables 16.1 and 16.2 to support a beginning teacher with developing an appreciation for the diversity and flexibility of inquiry-based pedagogical approaches. However, once the beginning teacher is planning and teaching lessons, they may face a number of obstacles to implementing 'science as inquiry' practices in their teaching. Most significantly, local policy and curricula may emphasise standardised benchmarks of science achievement which discourage beginning teachers from experimenting with new approaches,

Table 16.2 Analysing and/or planning different lesson activities according to the four levels of inquiry

Unit of work:

Topic:

Learning outcomes:

Class:

Levels of inquiry (adapted from Fitzgerald, Danaia and McKinnon (2019))	Activity 1	Activity 2	Activity 3
Level 1: Confirmation inquiry Provide research questions, procedures and results. Pupils confirm how the experiment or phenomena works.			
Level 2: Structured inquiry Remove results, so pupils formulate evidence-based explanations for specific scientific phenomena.			
Level 3: Guided inquiry Provide informational models. Pupils design procedures and explain results. (POGIL is a form of guided inquiry.)			
Level 4: Open inquiry Pupils develop research questions, conduct investigations and communicate results.			

(Source: Adapted from Fitzgerald, Danaia and McKinnon (2019))

despite research which has demonstrated the transformative potential of pupil-centred collaborative learning (Bryce, Wilmes and Bellino, 2016). Another potential obstacle could be lack of support for professional development that aims to foster 'inquiry identity' (professional identities grounded in inquiry-based pedagogical approaches). Instead, teachers may be expected to cover an overcrowded science curriculum within a limited time period, engage in excessive administrative duties, and use suggested and/or restricted readymade teaching resources (Crawford, 2007, Bryce, Wilmes and Bellino, 2016; Fitzgerald, Danaia and McKinnon, 2019).

These challenges are quite real, so you must consistently encourage a beginning teacher to continue developing their skills in inquiry-based pedagogical approaches. As a 'seasoned traveller', you accompany them on their journey by modelling competent inquiry-based instructions, providing space for exploration and identity development, and deepening relationships through dialogue and inclusion in a professional community of practice

Process-Oriented Guided Inquiry Learning 249

(Awaya, McEwan, Heyler, Linsky, Lum and Wakukawa, 2003; Luehmann, 2007; Melville and Bartley, 2010). To begin supporting a beginning teacher with implementing inquiry-based pedagogical approaches in their teaching practices, complete Task 16.3, which asks you to work with a beginning teacher to identify and discuss important challenges and reflect on possible solutions for implementing inquiry-based pupil-centred learning in their lessons.

Task 16.3 Challenges to implementing inquiry-based pedagogical approaches

With a beginning teacher you are mentoring:

1. Discuss challenges to implementing inquiry-based pedagogical approaches in their lessons
2. Support them to reflect on how to overcome these challenges.

Based on your discussions in Task 16.3, you could design a POGIL plan with the beginning teacher. This plan would support them to develop inquiry-based pupil-centred learning approaches teaching skills and construct inquiry identity. To develop this plan, you may link beginning teachers to POGIL's resources and thriving worldwide community of practitioners who model and share their approaches (see www.pogil.org). The rest of this chapter introduces you to POGIL philosophy and practice, and offers several concrete teaching strategies and reflections for implementing a well-validated, evidence-based approach to inquiry-based science teaching.

16.3 The POGIL learning cycle: Understanding the link between theory and practice

Before supporting a beginning teacher to develop a plan, you must discuss with them the steps involved in the POGIL learning cycle (Figure 16.1) following the mentoring suggestions presented below. The learning cycle includes three-phases: (1) exploration, (2) invention (or term introduction), and (3) application:

1. Exploration
   The exploration phase is where pupils accumulate information and search for meaningful patterns to draw evidence-based conclusions. During this phase you can guide a beginning teacher to POGIL activities that offer carefully constructed models and data sets that illustrate key concepts (Moog, 2014). Pupils can use such models and data sets to identify valuable information and construct a coherent explanatory framework.
2. Invention
   During the invention phase, pupils develop concepts to account for the patterns they noticed during the exploration phase. For this phase, you can guide the beginning teacher to identify and provide key terminologies related to the scientific concepts

250 S. Qureshi et al.

they are planning to teach. The activity sequence enables pupils to learn the key terms after concept development.

3. Application

During the application phase, pupils apply their concepts to new situations, which gives them an opportunity 'to strengthen the concept, show how it can be used, and/or test its generalisability' (Moog, 2014, p. 158). During this phase, you can support the beginning teacher to plan and implement open-ended 'divergent' questions to stimulate critical thinking and involve pupils in engaging scientific content at a deeper level.

Before reading further, Task 16.4 facilitates discussion with a beginning teacher about the three-phases of the POGIL learning cycle and enables you to support them to develop a POGIL plan.

Task 16.4 The POGIL learning cycle: Developing a POGIL plan

Follow the steps below:

1. Discuss and explore with a beginning teacher examples of the three main phases of the POGIL learning cycle presented in Figure 16.1. The detailed description of the phases can be found on the POGIL website (www.pogil.org).
2. Next, encourage the beginning teacher to complete Table 16.3:
   - First, in the first row, identify the unit of work and in the second row the topic they are going to teach next week.

[Or they can use the sample unit of work ('energy changes in chemistry'; including 'measurement of energy changes in chemical reactions (qualitative)' (DfE, 2014, p. 12)), and associated topic (rates of reaction) provided in Appendix 16.1.]

   - Second, in the third row, write a minimum of three learning outcomes. You could support the beginning teacher with writing learning outcomes (some mentoring suggestions on writing learning outcomes are provided in Chapter 6, pp. 78–79).
   - Third, fill in the pupils' activity and teachers' activity columns linked to the three-phases of the POGIL cycle (exploration, invention (or term introduction), and application).
   - Fourth, in the column titled required support from the mentor, identify any required support they want from the mentor in planning/teaching some or all of the planned pupil and/or teacher activities.
3. Finally, arrange a mentoring meeting to discuss the completed parts of Table 16.3. During this discussion, you need to support the beginning teacher by:
   - Appreciating their effort in completing the POGIL plan
   - Refining their learning outcomes and pupil/teacher activities where needed (see also suggestion 1 and 2 below on planning for pupil/teacher activities)
   - Giving them support based on the support identified by the beginning teacher in the required support from the mentor column

Process-Oriented Guided Inquiry Learning 251

> - Allowing the beginning teacher to record your suggestions in the mentor's suggestion column.
>
> You could repeat the above steps to support a beginning teacher planning lessons using the POGIL plan for the next couple of weeks.

Figure 16.1 The POGIL learning cycle
(Source: Courtesy of Daniel Southam, Curtin University)

Table 16.3 A POGIL plan

Unit of work				
Topic				
Learning outcomes	1. 2. 3.			
POGIL cycle	Pupils' activities	Teacher's activities	Required support from the mentor	Mentor's suggestions
Exploration	Pupils use model and data sets to accumulate information and search for meaningful patterns to draw evidence-based conclusions.			
Invention	Pupils develop concepts to account for patterns they noticed during the exploration phase. They learn key terminology related to concept development.			
Application	Pupils apply concepts in new situations to strengthen the concepts and test their generalisability.			

252   *S. Qureshi et al.*

Next, we recommend some mentoring suggestions that you can use to support a beginning teacher in planning for pupils' and teacher's activities.

16.3.1 *Inquiry questions*

To master guided inquiry approaches like POGIL, a beginning teacher must become an effective questioner incorporating both written and oral questions in their lesson plans to facilitate inquiry. The POGIL project offers numerous lesson plans and templates you can use as exemplars to support a beginning teacher, focussing on three main types of questions:

- Directed questions, which address the exploration phase of the POGIL learning cycle. While pupils explore the models and data sets, a beginning teacher asks targeted questions to guide pupils' inquiry and conceptualisation. The beginning teacher should emphasise 'fact-based' questions that encourage pupils to think deeply about the data.
- Convergent questions, which are more suitable to the invention phase. You can support a beginning teacher in constructing questions that draw attention to key trends in the data and enable pupils to reach consensus on a concept. The beginning teacher may ask about specific features of a graph or data set to test pupils' concepts and explanations.
- Divergent questions, which are appropriate to the application phase. These questions aim to stimulate pupils' critical thinking and involve them in engaging with the scientific content at a deeper level. In planning divergent questions, a beginning teacher should consider how pupils could apply their learning to new contexts and build connections to related concepts.

Task 16.5 asks you to guide a beginning teacher through the three-phases of POGIL learning cycle. Support them to identify the three types of questions using the sample POGIL worksheet on rates of reaction (see Appendix 16.1). Alternatively, you may choose to explore a different topic more relevant to the beginning teacher's teaching context.

Task 16.5   The POGIL learning cycle: Analysing a POGIL activity

Using an example POGIL modelled worksheet (such as Appendix 16.1), ask a beginning teacher to:

- Identify the different phases of the learning cycle
- Label each phase as E (exploration), I (invention) or A (application)
- Label each question as D (directed), C (convergent) or V (divergent)
- Discuss their results with you.

For additional practice, ask the beginning teacher to write their own questions for each phase of the model, or develop questions for a new model addressing topics associated with the same or different unit of work, they plan to teach in the next four weeks.

Process-Oriented Guided Inquiry Learning   253

16.3.2 Group roles and responsibilities

Another important aspect you need to focus on with a beginning teacher is group work. A beginning teacher may be anxious about conducting group work, especially regarding behavioural issues. However, group interactions can improve both disciplinary knowledge and key process skills (Farrell, Moog and Spencer, 1999). During POGIL activities, teachers are encouraged to allow pupils to work in groups of three or four, and each member has a role (manager, recorder, presenter and reflector) with specific responsibilities. These include the following:

1. The manager is the pupil who directs group dynamics and keeps members focussed and on task as they move through the activity. This pupil ensures that all members of the group reach consensus on each question and record the answers on their own activity sheet. Moreover, the manager is the group's spokesperson, responsible for informing the teacher about group questions and concerns.
2. The recorder is the pupil who logs group responses to each question, and may write a 'recorder's report' summarising key concepts that the group developed. This report serves as an important study guide that condenses group learning and concept development.
3. The presenter is the pupil who communicates the group's reports, both oral and written, to the rest of the class. The presenter also explains how the group arrived at each answer.
4. The reflector is the pupil who provides feedback to the group about its internal functioning, including; 'what the group is doing well, what needs improvement, and how that improvement might be achieved' (Moog, 2014, p. 150). Typically, reflectors offer their insights at regular intervals determined by the teacher.

Task 16.6 asks you to support a beginning teacher to plan an activity using the group members roles.

Task 16.6   Considering group roles

Ask a beginning teacher to follow the suggestions below:

1. For a lesson they are teaching, establish groups of four pupils and assign individual roles to pupils (manager, recorder, presenter and reflector). The recorder should record the group members' names and any questions and also summarise the findings.
2. Use the sample lesson plan model on rates of reaction in Appendix 16.1 (or a lesson plan on a topic they are about to teach), and act as a facilitator while teaching the lesson. Explain the group roles to pupils. Tell the group that the activity takes about 30 minutes and designate the time intervals as follows:
   - Read the information in Appendix 16.1 and answer Questions 1-2 (5 minutes).
   - Answer Questions 3-9 (10 minutes).

254   *S. Qureshi et al.*

- Answer Questions 10–11 (10 minutes).
- Orally communicate their findings with the other groups (10 minutes).

In addition to these instructions, the beginning teacher should provide an additional 10 minutes for the group to reflect on (1) their individual role and the roles of other group members, and (2) the opportunities and challenges of implementing these group roles in the classroom.

While these roles are recommended to maintain optimal participation, they are quite flexible. As Moog (2014, p. 149) points out, 'the roles that are assigned may vary from day to day, depending on the nature of the activity, the instructor's preferences, and the process-skill goals for that day'. The beginning teacher should be advised to rotate the roles for different activities so that all pupils experience different responsibilities. This will enable the beginning teacher to adapt POGIL to different instructional objectives and diverse classroom contexts.

16.4 Implementing POGIL process skills

With each lesson, POGIL aims to integrate seven process skills. As a mentor, you play an important role in supporting a beginning teacher to effectively incorporate process skills into their instructional activities. The seven process skills are described below.

1. Oral and written communication

Encourage a beginning teacher to initiate oral communications between pupils by creating opportunities to (i) exchange information and understanding through speaking, listening and non-verbal behaviours during group activities and (ii) communicate their ideas by persuading, negotiating and resolving differences. Encourage the beginning teacher to facilitate written communication by asking pupils to convey information and understanding to an intended audience through written accounts, laboratory reports and answers to questions, as well as predictions, explanations, inferences and conclusions.

2. Teamwork

Encourage the beginning teacher to develop pupils' teamworking skills by facilitating interaction with peers to build on strengths and competencies and accomplish common goals. Support them in planning and teaching interactive and small-group activities.

3. Problem solving

Model for the beginning teacher how to include problem-solving activities in their lessons. For instance, develop interesting, challenging problems that puzzle pupils and capture their interest. You should demonstrate some teaching strategies for guiding pupils to identify

Process-Oriented Guided Inquiry Learning 255

extension activities (see Case study 18.1, p. 280). Encourage the beginning teacher to assist pupils to work inductively from small data sets provided to develop solutions and explanatory frameworks before giving direct instructions on the taught topic.

4. Critical thinking

Coach the beginning teacher to facilitate pupils critical thinking by incorporating activities that ask pupils to analyse, evaluate and synthesise relevant information to form an argument and reach justifiable conclusions supported with appropriate scientific evidence.

5. Management

Support the beginning teacher in helping small groups of pupils to progress through the stages of planning, organising and conducting a task, as well as efficiently directing and coordinating their own and others' efforts. The beginning teacher might struggle to move pupils through the stages, as some might proceed more slowly than others. For this reason, both the beginning teacher and pupils need management skills to maintain awareness of the time and effort needed to complete a task. For instance, you could advise the beginning teacher to use cue cards, timers or a timed-station-rotation model to achieve smooth progression from one stage of the task to the next or from one task to the other task.

6. Information processing

First, ask the beginning teacher to reflect on their personal experiences in school, college and university in which they had to process information (evaluate, interpret, manipulate or transform) using charts, graphs, diagrams, models, calculations, and written representations of experimental findings. Next, have them consider ways of incorporating these skills into their teaching practice, such as: asking pupils to represent their research findings using charts and graphs, using diagrammatic representations to model the microscopic structures (for example, of a water molecule) or use MolyMod molecular models to demonstrate chemical bondings, et cetera.

7. Assessment

Encourage the beginning teacher to include self- and peer-assessment in their classrooms. For instance, pupils can write short reflective journals after completing a learning task. Additionally, pupils can debrief one another after an activity to think deeply about their interpersonal interactions and how they can improve. Advise the beginning teacher to observe and record how pupils learn, and how their knowledge adapts and changes over time.

It is important that you support a beginning teacher to teach planned POGIL activities that include one or more of the seven process skills to facilitate attainment, knowledge and understanding. The accumulation of these process skills promotes learning and offers

256   *S. Qureshi et al.*

'great value in the workplace and in life' (Moog, 2014, p. 148). For instance, a POGIL modelled worksheet and associated activities may ask pupils to assess data quality (critical thinking), cooperate with group members (teamwork), interpret a chart or graph (information processing), or identify the most important features of a problem (problem solving). Task 16.7 asks you to support a beginning teacher to incorporate POGIL process skills in their lesson planning.

Task 16.7   Incorporating POGIL process skills in science lessons

Ask a beginning teacher to identify process skills in the sample modelled worksheet on a topic they are about to teach or on rates of reaction (see Appendix 16.1), then support them to:

1.   Develop a series of science lessons that employ strategies for including one or more of the seven process skills (see also next section, 16.5).
2.   List potential challenges and opportunities for both the teacher and pupils.

16.5 Developing a series of POGIL lesson plans

Successful POGIL activities need sufficient advanced planning. After working through the sample task on a topic of their choice, or rates of reaction, guide a beginning teacher through the process of developing a sequence of POGIL lessons on a particular unit of work (a list of units of work can be seen in Appendix 10.1, p. 166). As the beginning teacher plans, or co-plans, support critical reflection aspects of their planning by asking what, why, when, who and how questions, ensuring that each activity is pupil-centred, inquiry-based, and contributing to pupils' learning. Table 16.4, provides a template to support a beginning teacher's POGIL lesson planning for a series of lessons in a unit of work recommended in the science curriculum. The different aspects of the POGIL plan in Table 16.4 are explained below.

The first three rows of Table 16.4 include (1) the curriculum's unit of work and topics to be explored with a group of pupils, (2) the learning outcomes and (3) the number of lessons it will take to complete a particular unit of work. In the columns that follow, ask the beginning teacher to specify (1) inquiry questions (directed, convergent and divergent) for each of the POGIL learning cycle phases (exploration, invention and application) in column two and, (2) pupils' activities in column three. Encourage the beginning teacher to develop some group activities, and specify how they are going to make transitions between group and individual activities, (3) teacher's activities in column four and (4) highlight POGIL process skills which link with teacher and/or pupil activities in the last column. The final two rows of Table 16.4 provide space for the beginning teacher to describe any additional support they need to implement POGIL in the science classroom in light of suggestions made by you as their mentor. Next, some questions that you can ask a beginning teacher in completing the POGIL lesson plan for a series of lessons are given in Table 16.4.

Process-Oriented Guided Inquiry Learning

Table 16.4 A POGIL lesson plan for a series of lessons

Unit of work

Topics

Learning outcomes

Lessons

POGIL learning cycle phases	Inquiry questions	Pupils' activities (might include group work)	Teacher's activities	POGIL process skills
Exploration				
Intervention				
Application				
Additional support				
Next steps				

16.5.1 Mentoring questions to facilitate planning, teaching and evaluation

Some questions that you can use to support a beginning teacher in completing a POGIL lesson plan for a series of lessons (Table 16.4) during pre-lesson discussions, lesson observation and post-lesson discussions, are below:

1. Pre-lesson discussions

During the pre-lesson discussions, as you co-construct the learning outcomes for a series of lessons, you could ask the beginning teacher the following questions:

- What learning outcomes they plan for unit of work (such as 'Coordination and Control', and specifically 'the relationship between structure and function in a reflex arc', the 'principles of hormonal coordination and control in humans'), including topics such as: 'structure and functions of Central Nervous System', 'Peripheral Nervous System', 'voluntary and involuntary control', 'hormones', 'differences between hormonal and nervous control', et cetera) (Department for Education (DfE), 2014, p. 8).
- How can they use these learning outcomes to assess learning over a series of lessons?
- Ask the beginning teacher to indicate the appropriateness of the series of lessons.
- Ask them to stimulate critical reflection with questions such as:
  o Why do they think X number of lessons is appropriate?
  o How does this lesson relate to the one before it and/or after it in the sequence?
  o How will they ensure a smooth transition from one lesson to the next?

258   S. Qureshi et al.

Next, while reviewing the inquiry questions the beginning teacher has planned, frame your discussion around questions like:

- What is the purpose of the planned inquiry questions?
- How does it relate with the POGIL learning cycle phase(s)?
- Do the planned inquiry questions meet the criteria of directed, convergent and divergent questions?
- When would they ask these inquiry questions in the lesson and in the series of lessons?
- Is the time allocated for each of the inquiry questions set appropriate?
- Could they rephrase the inquiry questions to improve clarity and focus learning?

Next, ask the beginning teacher to include group work as part of pupils' activities. As in Task 16.6, during the pre-lesson discussion, support the beginning teacher to plan group activities in some of the lessons by asking them questions such as:

- How have they planned to distribute group roles to the pupils and why have they planned the distribution in this way?
- How have they planned to ensure that all the pupils contribute to the group?
- What strategies have they planned to employ if group dynamics do not work according to plan?

2. Lesson observation

Observe a beginning teacher's teaching (of all or some of the series of lessons) for the above POGIL lessons. During these lesson observations you need to look for the following:

- Were any/all of the seven process skills incorporated in the lessons?
- How well did the beginning teacher integrate process skills into each teacher and/or pupil activities?
- Where does the beginning teacher need further support and development?

Next, observe the ways inquiry questions were incorporated during the lesson by the beginning teacher. You could look for:

- Did the beginning teacher include all the planned inquiry questions (directed, convergent and divergent) in the classroom (or not)?
- Did they give enough time to the pupils to answer the questions?
- How did they support pupils who were struggling to answer some/all the questions?
- How did they support pupils who found these questions very easy and finished answering them before the rest of the class?

If the beginning teacher has planned group work then you should look for:

- Does the beginning teacher ensure that pupils perform their roles appropriately?
- Were the instructions and explanation of group roles clear?
- Was enough time allotted to complete each task? Did the amount of time for each activity minimise behaviour issues? Was the lesson well-paced?
- How often did the beginning teacher visit each group to provide support?

3. Post-lesson discussions

During the post-lesson discussions, after all or some of the series of lessons, ask the beginning teacher the same questions that you used to observe their lesson(s), then discuss their answers further by sharing your observation focused on group dynamics. In your discussions, highlight the beginning teacher's strengths while identifying where you can support their further development.

Finally, in relation to POGIL process skills, during post-lesson discussions, support the beginning teacher to evaluate their teaching by asking questions such as:

- How well was the indicated POGIL process skill(s) integrated in the series of lessons?
- How did the pupils respond to the planned inquiry questions? Did the inquiry questions successfully guide the pupils to complete each task? Why or why not?
- If they were to teach this lesson (or these lessons) again, would they change anything? Why or why not? If yes then how would they change it?
- Were the (pupils' and teacher's) learning activities appropriate for all pupils? Do they need to rephrase some to accommodate all learning needs? How would they accomplish this?

Summary and key points

This chapter has introduced inquiry-based pupil-centred learning specifically POGIL, a guided pedagogical approach to inquiry-based pupil-centred learning. It has offered suggestions for how, as a mentor, you can assist a beginning teacher with teaching 'science as inquiry'. More specifically, it highlighted the following points:

- POGIL provides a beginning science teacher with a concrete strategy for implementing inquiry-based pedagogical approaches, and helps them understand the benefits of such approaches in teaching.
- Mentoring a beginning science teacher through the POGIL learning cycle equips them to plan and teach inquiry-based pupil-centred pedagogies.
- Mentoring a beginning science teacher in designing and implementing POGIL activities raises awareness of important POGIL-associated process skills, enhances appreciation of collaborative learning and promotes willingness to employ such approaches in the classroom.

Further resources

POGIL (Process-Oriented Guided Inquiry Learning) (2019) The POGIL project, POGIL, viewed 20 January 2020, from: https://pogil.org/about-the-pogil-project
This website provides resources that mentors can use to support a beginning teacher to gain deeper insight into the implementation of inquiry-based pedagogical approaches in their classrooms.

POGIL (undated) POGIL: High school implementation guide, POGIL, viewed 20 January 2020, from: https://pogil.org/uploads/attachments/cj5mtm1x501moekx4n3zhh6zu-pogil-high-school-imp-guide-for-web.pdf
This comprehensive POGIL implementation guide can be used by mentors to assist a beginning teacher with transitioning from teacher-centred learning to pupil-centred learning. This document contains useful links, video clips, group work templates and many other useful resources that can be adapted to support a beginning teacher in constructing their POGIL plan.

Appendix 16.1 Rates of reaction

Qatar is one of the world's largest producers of ammonia (NH_3). Ammonia is in such demand globally it must be produced fast and in large quantities. The equation below presents the industrial way of ammonia formation:

$$N_2(g) + 2H_2(g) \rightarrow 2NH_3(g)$$

But how fast is fast? For instance, the chemical weathering of rocks is a very slow reaction, so we say it has a **low rate of reaction**. By contrast, the combustion of rocket fuel is a very fast reaction, so we say it has a **high rate of reaction**. The production of ammonia would be a very slow reaction but scientists have used their knowledge of collision theory to speed the reaction up and make the production of ammonia a profitable industry.

Unit of work
'Energy changes in chemistry' (DfE, 2014, p. 12)

Topic
Rates of reaction

Learning outcomes
Pupils should be able to explore the main factors that affect the rate of reaction and learn about some of the different experimental techniques used to measure the rate of reaction by:

- Describing how the concentration, temperature, surface area and catalyst affect the rate of reaction
- Applying collision theory and the kinetic particle model in order to explain the changes in rate of reaction.

Prior knowledge
It is assumed that this lesson builds upon an introduction to collision theory and the kinetic particle model.

Model 1: Effect of concentration on rate of reaction
Maryam and Fatima perform an experiment with thin magnesium strips in 50 cm³ 1 M hydrochloric acid at 20°C. They measure the volume of hydrogen gas given off using a syringe. They plot the volume of hydrogen gas generated over time and annotate it with key observations.

The chemical equation for the reaction is:

$$Mg_{(s)} + 2HCl_{(aq)} \rightarrow MgCl_{2(aq)} + H_{2(g)}$$

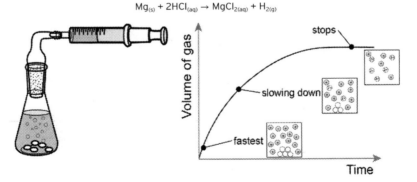

Exploring Model 1
1. Consider the reaction described in Model 1.
   a. Name the reactants

   b. Name the products

2. Write the correct chemical species (molecule, ion or atom) under each of these diagrams
   - Hydrogen molecule [$H_{2(g)}$], Hydrogen [$H^+_{(aq)}$],
   - Magnesium [$Mg_{(s)}$], Magnesium ion [$Mg^{2+}_{(aq)}$]

3. The particle diagrams in Model 1 represent the solution in the conical flask. Why do you think the hydrogen molecules are not depicted? Hint look at its state.
4. Would the mass of the conical flask and reaction mixture *increase/decrease/stay* the same as reaction progresses? Explain your answer.
5. What is the relationship between the gradient of the graph and the speed of the reaction?
6. Use particle diagrams in Model 1 to describe what happens to concentration (i.e. number of particles) as reaction progresses for:
   a. Magnesium (Mg)
   b. Hydrogen ions (H^+)
   c. Magnesium ions (Mg^{2+})
7. Use observations from Q6 to explain why you think rate of hydrogen gas evolution was:
   a. Fastest at the beginning?
   b. Slower as time progressed?
8. Why does the line of the graph plateau (level off)?
9. How could you tell by looking at the flask if the reaction has stopped?
10. Collision theory states that anything that increases the chance of an effective collision increases the speed of the reaction. If we doubled the concentration of the acid (H^+ ions) to 2M, what would happen to:
    a. The rate of the reaction? Explain your answer.
    b. The amount of hydrogen produced?
11. What other everyday examples involve the concept of 'rates of reaction'?

> This is an extension question. Hint: look at particle diagram and decide whether the magnesium or hydrogen ions gets used up first.

(Source: Adapted from Qureshi, Bradley, Vishnumolakala, Treagust, Southam, Mocerino and Ojeil (2016))

SECTION 4
Moving beyond

17 Supporting a beginning teacher to become autonomous

Gareth Bates and Ralph Littler

Introduction

Starting by linking with a beginning teacher's development over time, considered in other chapters (for example Chapters 6 and 7), this chapter unpicks the need for mentoring to support the development of a beginning teacher to become an autonomous teacher. As seasoned professionals, we have learned how to reflect on our classroom practices, change or transform our teaching strategies and resolve issues in the next lesson and beyond. This develops with experience, and hence a beginning teacher has not yet developed the ability to do this. Chapter 4 introduced various reflective practice models, indicating that you should support a beginning teacher to value the reflective process and also to recognise that experienced teachers continue reflecting and are always looking to improve their teaching.

The importance of the relationship of a beginning teacher with their mentor, the department and the wider school community is discussed in this chapter using the term 'community of practice' (Lave and Wenger, 1991) as a lens to look at how you, as a mentor, can introduce a beginning teacher to different communities that operate in a school. We have found during our time either as mentors or working with mentors that considering communities of practice can support beginning teachers in their development, helping to remove the silo or isolation that some beginning teachers can experience. After discussing some ideas concerning communities of practice, ways of mentoring can effectively facilitate the journey of a beginning teacher towards becoming an autonomous teacher are explored. Similar to the ideas of Daloz (2012), Katz (1995) and Clutterbuck (2004) (see Chapter 1), Rogoff's (1995) three planes and Wenger, McDermott and Snyder's (2002) communities of practice towards the development of an autonomous teacher, from an apprenticeship plane to guided participation and ultimately to the participatory appropriation plane (Hall, Murphy and Soler, 2008) are explored.

266 *Bates and Littler*

Objectives

At the end of this chapter you should be able to:

- Reflect on your mentoring strategies to develop, retain and sustain a mentoring relationship to promote a beginning teacher's autonomy and provide opportunities for them to learn about teacher's autonomy from you and other experienced staff members
- Adopt mentoring strategies to introduce a beginning teacher to the wider school community
- Consider the incorporation of some mentoring strategies to strengthen your support in transitioning a beginning teacher between the three developmental planes (apprenticeship, guided participation and participatory appropriation) to develop teacher's autonomy.

17.1 Mentor's self-reflection and a beginning teacher's peer-discussions to support the development of an autonomous teacher

As mentioned in Chapter 1, in abiding by government policies and guidance documents, the ultimate goal of a mentor is to ensure that a beginning teacher reaches the specified teacher standards at the end of their initial teacher education (ITE) programme, as this determines if they are then able to continue a career in teaching (or not). During the final stages of ITE, it is expected that a beginning teacher progresses to a point where they are able to work as an autonomous teacher. However, if a mentor takes an approach of making a beginning teacher a carbon-copy of themselves, this would hinder the beginning teacher's progress to becoming an autonomous teacher. If a mentor dictates particular teaching approaches to a beginning teacher, this could be because such approaches have worked for them and, thus, they are convinced that it will work for the beginning teacher as well. Self-reflection on your mentoring support and intentions is an essential component of your practices that should remind you to avoid providing directive support to a beginning teacher that can result in them copying what you do and/or performing for you in their lessons, rather than presenting an authentic account of themselves as a teacher.

Rogoff (1995), in describing the development of autonomy among teachers, indicated three transitional planes; 'apprenticeship', 'guided participation' and 'participatory appropriation' (see also Chapter 6). These three transitional planes accommodate a 'process by which individuals transform their understanding of and responsibility for activities through their own participation' (p. 150). Therefore, as a mentor, you need to reflect on how your mentoring style can have an impact on a beginning teacher's transition from apprenticeship to participatory appropriation plane and how the support you give can support or impede them in transforming their teaching and learning practices to become an autonomous teacher.

Some of strategies on lesson planning (Chapter 6) and on teaching (Chapter 7) can support a beginning teacher to develop their autonomy. The next sections of this chapter provide further strategies to support a beginning teacher in understanding the need of school communities to support their development as an autonomous teacher. Before reading

Becoming autonomous 267

further, Task 17.1 asks you to reflect on your mentoring strategies and its potential to impact on a beginning teacher's development towards autonomy.

Task 17.1   Mentor's reflection: Mentoring strategies related to supporting the development of an autonomous teacher

Reflect on your mentoring strategies in supporting the development of an autonomous beginning teacher, by answering the following questions:

1. What mentoring strategies do you incorporate to support a beginning teacher to develop as an autonomous teacher? What influenced you to establish these strategies?
2. What situations have you had where a beginning teacher found difficulty in planning and teaching autonomously? How did you support them?
    Did you involve other colleagues (experienced teachers) to support this development? If so, how?
3. What would you do differently in future to support a beginning teacher in becoming autonomous?

After finish reading this chapter, consider completing this task again to reflect on any changes.

Now consider reading Andrew's scenario (Case study 17.1) and complete Task 17.2, which asks you to reflect on the case study and suggest strategies to strengthen Andrew's autonomy as a teacher, further.

Case study 17.1: Andrew (a beginning science teacher)

Andrew is a career change beginning teacher in his late 30's with a PhD in chemistry. He recently worked in a large pharmaceutical company as a manager. Prior to embarking on the ITE programme, he volunteered in a number of different school settings and displayed a good understanding of the role of a teacher.

Mrs McCormack, his school mentor, views him taking the lead in his development by suggesting and rationalising his own developmental targets. Andrew is popular in the school and pupils respond positively to his well-developed teaching style. He uses school policies, in particular the behaviour policy, to his advantage without exhibiting stress or lack of confidence in implementing certain behaviour rules, such as removal of a pupil from class to cool them down or following the school's rewards and sanctions policies. Some of Andrew's recent reflections included that scientific knowledge was never a challenge, and the support and freedom provided by his chemistry mentor (specifically) have been very beneficial for him to progress as a teacher.

---

268   *Bates and Littler*

Task 17.2   Supporting Andrew in increasing autonomy

Read Case study 17.1 and answer the following questions:

1.   What targeted mentoring strategies should Andrew expect from Mrs McCormack to progress further?
2.   What expectations would Mrs McCormack have from Andrew?
3.   How could communities of practice assist a beginning teacher like Andrew, to progress as an autonomous teacher, further?

Mrs McCormack viewed Andrew to be moving rapidly towards becoming an autonomous teacher and enlisted some targeted mentoring strategies to support him. For example:

- In one of their weekly mentoring meetings Mrs McCormack asked Andrew how quickly he wanted to start delivering solo-teaching lessons. Andrew was keen to start teaching full lessons as soon as possible. He was not particularly interested in teaching other science subjects (i.e. biology and physics), and expressed determination to teach as many chemistry lessons as he could. Through a three-way negotiation between Andrew, the mentor and the head of science, it was felt he should teach full chemistry lessons and arrangements were put in place for him to teach above the number of specified lessons in week two of his school placement.
- Then, Mrs McCormack made sure she observed Andrew's three full lessons per week. During feedback on the first observed lesson, she encouraged Andrew to lead the post-lesson discussion (lesson de-brief). Andrew was reflective of the methods he used to assess the progress of pupils and the strategies he used that needed small adjustments to be more effective and was very receptive to his mentor's feedback. Mrs McCormack provided Andrew with a list of tactics that could be employed to strengthen the strategies to develop pupils' learning and chart pupils' progress against the learning outcomes, some linking to the observed lesson, but many for future lessons.

Next, read Liam's Case study 17.2, which exhibits a contrasting scenario to Andrew's Case study 17.1. Task 17.3 enables you to read Case study 17.2 and suggest mentoring support that can support Liam's development as an autonomous teacher.

Case study 17.2: Liam

Liam is a career change beginning teacher with over 30 years' experience of working in an Information Technology (IT) company. Prior to entering ITE, Liam undertook two days of classroom observations in his children's school.

His first school placement review indicated that there was a lot of developmental work to be done, such as introducing a variety of activities and teaching practices to the classroom. Moving to a second placement school did not seem to be an issue for

Liam. In fact, during a pre-placement visit to the school, he commented that the children were about the same (in behaviour) as the first placement.

Early negotiations with his mentor regarding what Liam would be teaching in the second school placement did not go well as he wanted to follow some prescribed developmental process set out in the university handbook, which he believed were suitable for him. He insisted on observing classes that he would teach for two lessons prior to taking over and seemed relieved when he was informed that he could teach physics because it was a strength but he was not confident in teaching biology.

Liam ensconced himself in the science preparation room for most of his extended school placement and his reflection at the end of this placement was that he should have made more use of the wider school community, building connections with teachers in other departments.

Liam had established himself as a lecturer and this became his default. Initially, he would plan activities for the class but revert to the lecture style of teaching to 'ensure they (pupils) all understood the detail', indicating a lack of confidence or an understanding of learning pedagogy.

The head of science and Liam's mentor both provided lots of ideas on how to make lessons more engaging, and over a series of weekly meetings it became evident that Liam was not really engaging to improve teaching, but more with keeping behaviour under control.

With school placement two being extended to include school placement three, Liam started to make the transition to understanding that lessons needed a hook for the pupils (as learners) to engage.

Task 17.3 Supporting Liam in increasing autonomy

Read Case study 17.2 and answer the following questions:

1. What do you consider are the priorities that Liam needs to be aware of so that he can increase his autonomous control in the right direction?
2. In the next school placement, how should a mentor introduce higher challenge in order for him to make progress?
3. How could the mentor divert Liam's isolation from the staff members?

In a nutshell, Liam's transition could be viewed as meandering. The main reasons for this meandering transition, included Liam's extensive focus on behaviour management and less on pupils' learning needs, lack of confidence in using different pedagogical approaches, making autonomous but unsuccessful decisions, not listening to his mentor's advice, and having limited interaction with the other school staff members.

A beginning teacher you are mentoring might be experiencing problems similar to those being experienced by Liam. In this case, you could discuss some targeted strategies

270 *Bates and Littler*

with them with respect to their concerns, for example, on behaviour management and its impact on pupils' learning. One of the targeted strategies for this concern could be that you can encourage the beginning teacher to shadow a particular pupil, for a week, who exhibits some behavioural issues in the classroom. And advise them to focus on the pupil's learning progression gains during these shadowed observations. You can also discuss the benefits of the shadowing process with the beginning teacher. For instance, this shadowing process could help them to see how a particular pupil's learning and behaviour changes from one teacher and subject to another. This pupil shadowing strategy is not limited to supporting a beginning teacher to deal with behaviour management issues only. It can be useful to target other developmental areas of the beginning teacher. For example, Chapter 19 encourages a mentor to support a beginning teacher to shadow special educational needs and disability (SEND) pupils to improve their planning for pupils with learning disabilities. Tasks 19.5 and 19.6 (pp. 301–303) provide step-by-step guidance on pupil shadowing; these tasks are specifically designed for SEND pupils, but can be adopted for pupils without SEND as well.

In the process of supporting a beginning teacher to become autonomous, this chapter looks through the lens of Wenger, McDermott and Snyder's (2002) communities of practice in teacher education, which states that,

> Communities of practice are groups of people who share a concern or a passion for something they do and learn how to do it better as they interact regularly.
>
> (Wenger McDermott and Snyder, 2002, p. 4)

As a mentor you aim for a beginning teacher to be able to negotiate teaching and learning strategies, and participate, adapt and develop activities with people (such as new and experienced teachers, laboratory assistants, teaching assistants, management and leadership members of the school staff) to establish their involvement with the school's communities of practice. Before reading further, Task 17.4 asks you to share some of your personal autonomy-associated practices with a beginning teacher you are mentoring.

Task 17.4   Sharing practices that makes an autonomous teacher

Consider the following questions:

1. What attributes or characteristics do you currently possess that exhibit autonomy in your teaching and learning practices?
2. How did these attributes and characteristics develop over time?
3. How did the wider school community help you in becoming an independent, reflective and self-directed teacher, and how?

Share the attributes, characteristics, and experiences identified by considering these questions with a beginning teacher to help them to understand some qualities of an autonomous teacher and identify ways in which they can collaborate with the wider school community to become an autonomous teacher.

Becoming autonomous 271

After sharing your practices, you can next involve the beginning teacher in peer-based discussions with other experienced staff member(s), ideally from other subject areas and/or from the senior management team, as this can enable them to gather a range of experiences from the wider school community – see Task 17.5.

Task 17.5 My peer's autonomous development as a teacher

Encourage a beginning teacher you are mentoring to ask the following questions from at least two experienced members of the staff and note down some points from these discussions:

- What attributes or characteristics do you currently possess that exhibit autonomy in your teaching and learning practices?
- How did these attributes and characteristics develop over time?
- How did the wider school community help you in becoming an independent, reflective and self-directed teacher?

You can then arrange a meeting with the beginning teacher to discuss their notes and consider opportunities by which they can collaborate with the wider school community (for example, subject department, year recreational and professional development communities).

17.2 Introducing a beginning teacher to the wider school community

Introducing a beginning teacher to the wider school community involves a negotiation about who (mentor, a beginning teacher and other staff members) is going to do what and when. This introduction could start from your first weekly meeting with a beginning teacher. You could adapt the Personal Record of Progress (PRoP) form, provided in Appendix 3.1(p. 46), to facilitate a discussion identifying a beginning teacher's viewpoints and targeted support, involving:

1. Expectations of a beginning teacher by you, other colleagues and school
2. School and departmental expectations of a beginning teacher
3. Agreed ways of mentor and beginning teacher communicating with each other, along with clear expectations on when a reply is required.

Once you have established a trusting relationship you will want to quickly situate a beginning teacher in various communities across the school. Therefore, you should have a well-designed induction programme for the beginning teacher that outlines:

1. Who they will meet?
2. What different types of meeting they should attend (such as science subject meetings, pastoral, child protection, weekly briefings, et cetera)?
3. What is the purpose and output of the meetings mentioned above?

272 *Bates and Littler*

In Task 17.3, you considered ways to support Liam to build interactions with the other staff members (i.e. members of the school community), but then you also need to consider what happens if the members of the school community do not interact with the beginning teacher appropriately, especially when the beginning teacher is not making progress as expected. In our experience, this usually results in poor outcomes for a beginning teacher and a breakdown in relationships between them and the different communities within the school. You therefore need to consider how to hit the reset button to enable the beginning teacher to make progress. Some strategies that you could consider to reset such situations are:

- If there are specific aspects of a beginning teacher's practice that members of the community of practice find challenging, then you need to talk to the beginning teacher about these practices. Next, agree on some action points, along with the beginning teacher, to deal with the issues that the members of the community find challenging while working with them.
- If there are specific members of the community that are hindering the progress of a beginning teacher then you may wish to limit their interaction.
- You need to be prepared for the fact that it may be your mentoring approach that is hindering a beginning teacher's progress and therefore revisit and readdress your mentoring strategies to support the transition between Rogoff's (1995) three planes and Wenger, McDermott and Snyder's (2002) communities of practice. In readdressing your mentoring strategies, Chapter 5 (pp. 69-70) presents five steps (be aware of your own emotions, practice, using appreciative comments, the cause of negative feelings and resolving issues) and Task 5.6 (p. 68-69) asks you to follow these five steps to bring the mentor-mentee relationship back on track.
- Offer peer support to the beginning teacher by finding two (or at least one) experienced staff members, as mediators, with whom the beginning teacher feels comfortable conversing, then ask these experienced staff members if they are willing to devote additional support to the beginning teacher. Task 17.5 could help a beginning teacher to facilitate their conversation with the mediating staff members.
- In addition to peer discussions, you can encourage the beginning teacher to complete Table 17.1 every week to record (i) what role and responsibilities they have (or would like to have) as a valuable member of the wider school community, (ii) how often they attend (or should attend) wider school community's offered meetings, and whether they should be involved with social media chats, workshops, lecturers, et cetera offered by the wider school community, and (iii) how these interactions (through these meetings, chats, workshops and lectures) with the wider school community are helping or not helping (or could help or not help) them to establish their autonomy. You, or the mediating staff member, could monitor the beginning teacher's recordings weekly and provide them with feedback on how effectively they are developing their autonomy and support them by discussing what they can do next to strengthen their interactions further.

Becoming autonomous 273

Table 17.1 A weekly log to record my involvement with the wider school community to enhance teacher's autonomy

Week number:
Date:
My current roles and responsibilities as a member of the school's community are:
The date and time of physical/media associated meetings, chats, et cetera with one or more than one experienced members of staff: 1. 2. 3. 4.
The benefits I have gained (or not) from these above interactions within the school communities to develop my autonomy as a teacher: 1. 2. 3. 4.
A discussion with the mentor (or other staff members) based on my next steps to advance my teacher's autonomy further.

[In this table 'my' refers to the beginning teacher.]

17.3 The continued transition between the three planes to develop teacher's autonomy

As a mentor you need to continue to provide high challenge and high support (Daloz, 2012; Chapter 1) to support a beginning teacher to transition between the three planes, apprenticeship to guided participation to participatory appropriation. This section of the chapter presents some potential mentoring suggestions to support this transition.

17.3.1 Apprenticeship plane: Inducting a beginning teacher into the wider school community

In the apprenticeship plane, a beginning teacher is less autonomous as they are mainly shadowing you and familiarising themselves with the school/science department. This plane requires you to induct a beginning teacher into the wider school community. Ways you can do this are as follows:

- Organise a pre-school placement visit (if one is not already arranged by the beginning teacher). This enables security checks to be processed and access to online systems and policy documents to be made. Introduce the beginning teacher to key members of staff: subject leader/head of department and department staff, members of the senior

274 Bates and Littler

leadership team (SLT) and the wider teaching community. A tour of the school site can be useful, particularly if it includes lunch and/or break times, as this allows the beginning teacher to observe how you and other teaching and/or non-teaching staff members interact with pupils. Emphasise to the beginning teacher that they do not need to remember all the staff they meet but can ask questions as they come up, ideally during weekly mentoring meetings.

- Explain to the beginning teacher institutional rules and routines that need to be understood from the outset: accessing the car park or where to put their bike; staffroom etiquette (don't sit in that person's chair!); paying for tea and coffee if appropriate; whose mug is whose and when to buy cakes. Some schools have breakfast meetings or clubs; when and where meetings are held and for how long; if there is a club, how the beginning teacher can get involved and the benefits of membership. Expectations for being at the school – do all teachers need to start work at 08:00 and stay until 16:30? Does the beginning teacher have a supervisory duty to perform, if so where, how long for and what to look for?

- Provide modelling of the general classroom routine for the beginning teacher wherever possible as this helps them understand and integrate with school routines. This could be demonstrating how to let a group of pupils enter a classroom by meeting them at the door, using names and reminding, where necessary, about behaviour expectations. The mentor could use this moment to check on a pupil they are concerned about, have a quick chat about a recent sporting fixture or share a joke or two. If the modelling is by someone other than yourself, ask the beginning teacher how they have got on with it. This is an avenue to start interacting with the wider school community and probably extending their agentic (personal) viewpoint of the classroom and school context and practices. By extending their agentic viewpoint they will move from the prescriptive, doing as told environment of apprenticeship, through to participatory appropriation.

- It would be best if you encourage the beginning teacher to ask questions from those around them, themselves and friends outside of school, to negotiate a new way of being. Answers to these questions will inform their practice and lead them being able to offer solutions to dilemmas that other people express.

17.3.2 Guided participation plane: Introduce the concept of negotiation of meaning

A beginning teacher can be constrained to apprenticeship through reading/completing documentation and interpreting school practices, so it is your role to support their transition to a guided participation plane.

Some suggestions are:

- Ask staff members (SLT, other teachers, laboratory assistants, librarians and other staff, as appropriate) about their relationship with the beginning science teacher. You could ask questions such as: Have working relationships started to build with you? Do you see any positive and/or negative emotional and/or professional changes in the beginning teacher?

Becoming autonomous 275

- Reflect on your mentoring support by considering questions such as: Am I aware of any changes in the beginning teacher? If so, what changes have I made to my mentoring practices or style? Consider making notes to evidence progression in the beginning teacher and when appropriate discuss their progression with them. Additionally, ask the beginning teacher to make notes of their self-progression, as this will aid a discussion on their progression from both yours and their perspectives.
- You could also record and annotate a beginning teacher's practices in a diary about their effective (or ineffective) involvement with various school communities and guide them with next steps.
- Boost a beginning teacher's confidence by explaining that their constructive involvement with the wider school community are recognised and valued (Hall, Murphy and Soler, 2008).

17.3.3 *Participatory appropriation plane: Characteristic changes in exhibiting personalised teacher's identity*

A beginning teacher who is operating in the participatory appropriation plane has made the transition towards becoming an autonomous teacher with a personalised teacher identity. Some indications that a beginning teacher has made this transition are that:

- They connect with varied communities both within school (such as board of studies, child protection, health and wellbeing, religious communities, et cetera) and beyond the physical structure of the school's establishment within their city/country (becoming an active member of external communities of practice such as the Royal Society of Biology (RSB), Royal Society of Chemistry (RSC) and/or Institute of Physics (IoP) or Association for Science Education (ASE), et cetera)
- They have started to make a valuable contribution to the science department and school, and use their interpersonal skills to influence school community-based practices as well as practices influencing themselves
- Their observations and formal meetings are leading to meaningful discussions and practices locally within the school and regionally with various external communities.

Reaching this stage of development, you generally need to support practices that require a longer-term consistent involvement with the community. For example, you could:

- Introduce a beginning teacher to research practices such as practitioner inquiry practices (Gilchrist, 2018)
- Involve the beginning teacher with aspects of the school's development plan to aid their continuing professional development (CPD). Specific foci could include, for example, improving scientific literacy among pupils, pupil's assessment procedures, implementing practices to enhance health and wellbeing among pupils and staff or monitoring of equality among ethnicity, race, gender, et cetera.

Task 17.6 asks you to list, describe and evaluate some effective mentoring strategies used with beginning teachers who have reached the participatory appropriation plane.

Task 17.6 Mentoring support to strengthen participatory appropriation plane

1. List and describe at least three mentoring strategies (your own or strategies you have observed others using) that you believe have supported some beginning teachers to reach a participatory appropriation plane.
2. List and describe at least three mentoring strategies (your own or strategies you have observed others using) that you believe have hindered the progression of some beginning teachers to reach a participatory appropriation plane.
3. How would you modify these strategies in the future?

Summary and key points

This chapter has explored ways to support the development of an autonomous teacher. The most important relationship in supporting the transition of a beginning teacher towards becoming an autonomous teacher begins with their introduction to the wider school communities that exist within your setting. This chapter specifically suggests the following points. You need to:

- Discuss and evaluate the starting point of a beginning teacher and establish a relationship by sharing experiences that helped you and other experienced teachers to be autonomous in your/their teaching practices
- Offer varying levels of challenge and support for a beginning teacher to maintain their growth towards being autonomous
- Introduce a beginning teacher to different local (school) and regional (city/country), as well as professional communities and continue to support them to become a valuable member of these communities.

Further resources

Bambrick-Santoyo, P. (2018) *Leverage Leadership 2.0. A Practical Guide to Building Exceptional Schools*. San Francisco, CA: Jossey-Bass.
This US focused book is popular with some ITE providers in the UK and some secondary schools as it looks at a whole school approach to development. As a mentor, you will need to be selective about which elements to use and when to use them to support a beginning teacher to develop autonomy. The author of this book is mindful of teachers' developmental routes and guides readers (mentors) to specific chapters. There are also exemplars of paperwork, how to set out observation and feedback schedules, so that both a mentor and beginning teacher can maintain a productive relationship to promote autonomy of a beginning teacher.

Department for Education (DfE) (2018) Respectful school communities self-review and signposting tool, DfE, viewed 20 December 2019, from: HL11980_Respectful_School_Communities_publication_attachment.pdf

This DfE document is useful to share with a beginning teacher at all three planes of their development. It includes discussions to promote respect and discipline in school by enhancing the communities of practice culture beyond the science department. This document also highlights the benefits of engaging beginning teachers with the wider school community to prevent the silo syndrome developing.

Kell, E. (2018) *How to Survive in Teaching: Without Imploding, Exploding or Walking Away*. London: Bloomsbury Publishing PLC.

This short book, written by a highly experienced educator who is fully aware of the need to support a beginning teacher, is based on research. Some of the data presented should be concerning to all within education, but within the book there is plenty to feel positive about. Kell presents some easy-to-use reflection tools for both mentors and beginning teachers so that they can develop their mentoring or teaching practices autonomously. It also gives some strategies for use at key moments of the school day, referred to as, 'at the chalk face'.

18 Supporting a beginning teacher to implement extension and enrichment

Jane Essex

Introduction

When beginning teachers commence teaching in a classroom in initial teacher education (ITE), they commonly find it a challenge simply to plan basic lessons. They are likely to give pupils access to all learning outcomes but are unlikely to respond to individual pupils or to offer rich learning experiences (see Chapter 6). Instead, beginning teachers are likely to focus on teaching essential content and establishing classroom routines. The next phase of practice involves planning and teaching lessons that are differentiated to meet the needs of the full range of pupils, learning that is stimulating and achieves diverse outcomes, underpinned by confident classroom management (Chapter 7). This transition gives a beginning teacher rewarding new insights into their ability to support high-quality learning and enables them to witness the full capabilities of their pupils.

How a mentor might support this post-basic professional growth further is considered in this chapter. A set of practical mentoring strategies to support a beginning teacher to use differentiated forms of extension practices and to enrich their planning practices are presented in the context of two Case studies. The process of helping a beginning teacher to implement enrichment practices is discussed, in detail, against current models of mentoring (Maynard and Furlong, 1995; Clutterbuck, 2004; Katz, 1995; outlined in some detail in Chapter 1).

Objectives

At the end of this chapter you should be able to:

- Support a beginning teacher to understand the link between differentiation and extension, and how these approaches can meet pupils' learning needs
- Support a beginning teacher to understand the term enrichment and consider how to incorporate planning for enrichment activities
- Use a five-step framework to guide a beginning teacher to select some suitable strategies to implement enrichment in their practices. The five-steps are: eliciting reflection; targeted planning; modelling good practice; external expertise support; review; and plan for the future.

18.1 Differentiation and extension

The notion of differentiation to teach different pupils in a range of ways to meet their different learning needs is almost universally accepted by teachers. A scrutiny of teacher's standards for meeting this notion in the UK's four nations (England, Northern Ireland, Scotland and Wales) specifies the relevant governments' requirement. Previously in this book, teacher standards have been discussed. In this chapter, teacher standards are discussed explicitly in relation to learning for all the pupils, for example, the Teachers' Standards for England (Department for Education (DfE), 2016d) explicitly require teachers to adapt teaching to respond to the strengths and needs of all pupils and specify differentiation as a mechanism for achieving this. By the same token, the Northern Irish Teacher Competences (General Teaching Council of Northern Ireland (GTCNI), 2018b), specify the need for challenge, and a related quality and pace (of learning) for all pupils. The Professional Standards in Scotland (General Teaching Council of Scotland (GTCS), 2012) call, in two different pre-registration teachers' standards, for teachers to meet the needs of all learners. Similarly, the Professional Standards for school practitioners in Wales (Welsh Government, 2017) state that teachers should 'exhibit high expectations and commitment to the achievement of each learner' (p. 25).

One element of differentiation is scaffolding for those pupils who may have difficulty in learning, which ensures access to the curriculum. For other pupils, extension activities offer enhanced access to the curriculum implementation of differentiation. Discussing differentiation in this way can be controversial because a beginning teacher working in a specific context might then set low expectations, which can cap progression for some pupils, whilst they commonly reserve extension work for the gifted and talented (G and T), or most able, pupils. Therefore, before you move on to the next section, Task 18.1 asks you to reflect on the context in which a beginning teacher you are mentoring is operating differentiation to include learning for all the pupils.

Task 18.1   Mentor's reflection: Looking at the context of differentiation

Answer the following questions:

1. What expectations of different teaching for different pupils are set out in the assessment framework you use in mentoring the beginning teacher?
2. How did a beginning teacher you have worked with respond to the expectation of differentiation? and How did you support their teaching and learning practices?

The notion of extension, or stretch and challenge, as a way of providing differentiation is far from an uncontroversial practice, being widely driven by notions of ability as a fixed attribute of pupils. Therefore, you should continuously guide a beginning teacher to not just give 'more able' pupils more to do, whilst giving their 'less able' peers less to do. This mentoring guidance could begin with co-planning learning outcomes for a proposed lesson/series of

280   *Essex*

lessons, as it would offer an opportunity for you and the beginning teacher to think about the purposes of extension and differentiation to promote science learning for all the pupils. In doing so, you can encourage the beginning teacher to consider both specific and immediate, but also extensive and transferable outcomes so that the purpose is elevated beyond simple content acquisition. Now read Case study 18.1, which presents a beginning teacher, Zarah, who is prompted to make her learning outcomes effective by considering ways to set rich learning environments for all the pupils.

Case study 18.1: Zarah: Reach for the stars

Zarah is a beginning teacher specialising in chemistry. She is coming to the end of her post-graduate teacher education year having undertaken her second school placement with you. Her subject knowledge is excellent, and her classroom management is secure, but you feel that what she teaches is often devoid of context, so pupils sometimes complain that it is dull or seems irrelevant. She is still working on making her lessons suitably stimulating for the full range of pupils and is seeking her mentor's support. She is about to start teaching Year 8 (age 12 and 13) pupils a topic on the solar system and has written the following learning outcomes:

* Be able to list the planets in the solar system in order.
* Be able to describe differences in the surface temperature, size, gravity and composition of the planets.
* Be able to explain why life only exists on earth.

Zarah's mentor wants her to re-write her learning outcomes by introducing differentiated yet extended aspects of learning.

Before I present some mentoring suggestions that Zarah's mentor used to support her, complete Task 18.2. Task 18.2 asks you to indicate ways you, as Zarah's mentor, would use to support her in differentiating and extending the learning outcomes for her Year 8 pupils.

Task 18.2   Mentoring strategies for Zarah

Consider the following questions:

1. Based on what you have been told about the beginning teacher Zarah (Case study 18.1), plus any relevant mentoring experience you may have, what types of support do you anticipate you would need to give Zarah?
2. How could your support facilitate Zarah to implement differentiated yet extended aspects of learning in her planning of the topic solar system, catering learning for all pupils?

Implementing extension and enrichment 281

Zarah was asked by her mentor to encompass differentiated forms of extension, which show progression through the use of higher order thinking skills (HOTS). The mentor considered supporting Zarah by using Bloom's taxonomy framework as a way to employ differentiated use of HOTS in planning the learning outcomes and associated activities for pupils. [You could share Shabatura's (2013) online resource with a beginning teacher you are mentoring. This suggests using Bloom's taxonomy to write learning outcomes and plan activities. Shabatura (2013) presents differentiated 'action verbs' that align with each of the progressive (HOTS) levels of Bloom's taxonomy (see further resources section), to help the teachers write differentiated learning outcomes.]

The three learning outcomes presented in Case study 18.1 used action verbs – list, describe and explain – though differentiated but pitching at the lower thinking levels of 'remembering' (list) and 'understanding' (describe and explain), and lack higher levels thinking skills of 'applying' (such as model, calculate, predict, apply, solve), 'analysing' (such as classify, break down, categorise, criticise, simplify), 'evaluating' (such as choose, support, relate, determine, judge) and 'creating' (such as design, create, derive, modify, develop). Therefore, Zarah's mentor took the following steps:

1. First, the mentor suggested a broad question as the title of the lesson, which is not conclusively agreed upon by everyone so that different answers could be accommodated with validity, for example, could there be life on other planets in our solar system? This extended question accommodated the 'evaluation' level of higher thinking order in planning the learning outcomes.
2. The mentor then suggested to Zarah that she look again at the learning outcomes (Case study 18.1) in light of using the 'action verbs' from Bloom's taxonomy framework aiming at the higher thinking levels of 'apply', 'analyse', 'evaluate' and 'create'
3. Next, Zarah's mentor reviewed the re-written learning outcomes, which included the extension element of HOTS:
    * 'Classify' patterns in the surface temperature, size, gravity and composition of the planets.
    * 'Predict' planet measurements using given data.
    * 'State', with 'reasons', an answer to the question, could there be life on other planets in our solar system?
4. The mentor then encouraged Zarah to plan pupils' activities that provide more time to pupils for exploratory talk about the subject matter by making use of other forms of pupils' accounts to assess their learning. Such as differentiation by:
    * Including 'analyse' – a higher thinking level, by asking pupils to 'classify' the characteristics of the planets by recording the characteristics on an incomplete table with the missing answers supplied separately
    * Providing additional support for pupils who might struggle, for example, to whom a completed copy of the table could be available
    * Incorporating higher thinking level of 'evaluate', to capture pupils' evaluation of the data without a lot of writing, such as drawing a sketch of each planet in a box on the table and give each one a suitable user name, for example Mercury might be the hot one.

282 *Essex*

In addition to these steps, a mentor can incorporate further discussions with a beginning teacher about differentiated forms of extension practices by sharing ways the mentor (and other science teachers – if any) manage class learning when setting challenging and open-ended tasks. The beginning teacher could then undertake two/three lesson observations of the mentor and/or other experienced science teacher and focus observations on ways in which pupils are facilitated to achieve more than the core learning recommended in the science curriculum, without setting low standards for pupils who are not expected to achieve any more than the core learning. The next step, for the beginning teacher, after observing the experienced teacher's lessons, might be to report back their observations to the mentor at the next weekly mentor meeting. Then, a beginning teacher could be guided by the mentor, to try out some extension focused strategies that they have observed in the observed classes.

18.2 Enrichment

Enrichment refers to the incorporation of material beyond the core curriculum, which is essential for teaching the lesson content. It equates to what is termed inter-disciplinarity, but specifically from the perspective of the target discipline, in this case science. You need to build a beginning teacher's awareness that enrichment activities, unlike extension activities, are drawn from another discipline(s), usually bringing a cultural dimension to bear on the content. You could provide some examples to a beginning teacher, such as: connecting a particular topic/concept of science to a story of the history of science; a trip to a relevant visitor attraction, a comparison of appropriate technologies relying on a scientific principle taken from different parts of the world; or using poetry to explore a science concept. You could provide some examples of enrichment activities, from your teaching or practices you have observed, for example making links between the science content and a relevant societal or cultural context (Chapter 15, pp. 229-230).

Before supporting a beginning teacher to plan lessons to embed enrichment activities, you could ask them to read Godec, King and Archer's (2017) article and then discuss their understanding of planning for enrichment with you. You can elaborate this discussion by engaging the beginning teacher with the benefits and limitations of including culturally driven enrichment activities in their classrooms as a way to engage all pupils. After the beginning teacher has discussed the potential benefits of including enrichment activities, Task 18.3 encourages you to discuss with the beginning teacher whether they would categorise a field trip activity as an enrichment activity (or not), and why. This task will not only help a beginning teacher you are mentoring, to be able to start thinking about planning some enrichment activities for all the pupils, but will also be helpful for you to target support, by carefully listening to the beginning teacher's motivations or hesitations to implement enrichment-oriented activities in their teaching.

Task 18.3   Supporting a beginning teacher to start thinking about planning enrichment activities

1. Ask a beginning teacher to list the names of at least two field trips that they would like to organise for their pupils. Discuss how these field trips could cater to the learning of all pupils.

Implementing extension and enrichment **283**

2. Then, discuss the following questions with the beginning teacher:
   - To what extent do these proposed field trips constitute an extension of the demands of the science curriculum, and to what extent is it enrichment, through the introduction of other disciplines that relate to the topic?
   - How would you introduce the relevant scientific content and how would you introduce other daily life knowledge to pupils (if appropriate)?

The discussions from Task 18.3 will support you in employing a range of mentoring practices to involve a beginning teacher in diverse approaches to teaching science. The five steps of the framework (eliciting reflection; targeted planning; modelling good practice; external expertise support; review; and plan for the future) could broaden a beginning teacher's ability and in turn enrich learning – see below. The framework focuses on a mentor supporting a beginning teacher, Chen, to reflect on the notion that 'doing more' is much less helpful than the notion of 'doing differently' to provide enrichment. Before presenting the framework, read Chen's scenario (Case study 18.2), which presents a beginning teacher who is planning to incorporate enrichment activities in his practice and is asking for mentor's support in planning a field trip to a waste recycling plant. And complete Task 18.4, which asks you to indicate mentoring strategies for a beginning teacher, Chen.

Case study 18.2: Chen: Field trip

Chen has undertaken a school-based teacher education route in your school and is now undertaking his induction year. He studied environmental science as an undergraduate and has been actively involved in the Ecology Club, which runs weekly in the school. He now wants to take the participating pupils, who range in age from 11 to 14 years old, with two sixth form helpers, on a field trip to a waste recycling facility in the region. He has mentioned the possibility to the pupils who were very enthusiastic and he now feels under pressure to meet their expectations. However, the demands of this apparently simple task are beginning to dawn on him. He asks you for advice, including whether it is worth running the trip in the first place.

Task 18.4 Mentor's strategies for Chen

Consider the following questions:

1. Based on what you have been told about the beginning teacher, Chen (Case study 18.2), plus any relevant mentoring experience you may have, what types of support do you anticipate you would need to give Chen?
2. How could your support facilitate their implementation of enrichment practices, with the aim of catering for all pupils.

284 *Essex*

18.3 Framework for supporting the ability of a beginning teacher to enrich pupils' learning

The five steps set out below (i.e. eliciting reflection; targeted planning; modelling good practice; external expertise support; review; and plan for the future) provide a suggested framework for you to use to support a beginning teacher to develop their ability to enrich pupils learning. The stages correspond closely to different elements described in the three models, namely Maynard and Furlong (1995), Clutterbuck (2004) and Katz (1995), of mentoring as set out in Chapter 1, and the five steps are illustrated by reference to the case study of Chen.

18.3.1 Mentoring to elicit reflection

Eliciting reflection by a beginning teacher is one of the important, if not the most important, things that a mentor does (Maynard and Furlong, 1995). This is as true when working towards the introduction of enrichment, as with any other aspect of practice. Therefore, as a mentor, you need to support a beginning teacher to reflect on prior and existing experiences and beliefs which bear upon their undertaking. Failure to do so will prevent the beginning teacher from identifying some inappropriate insights. For example, Chen a recent graduate in environmental studies, needs to reflect more deeply on differences between how a field trip activity for undergraduate students would differ from a field trip activity for school-aged pupils. Chen needs to be helped by the mentor to recognise that the context in which he saw the enrichment activity undertaken (such as in his graduate life) is significantly different from the one in which he is working. It may seem unnecessary, or even time-wasting, for you to explore which aspects of teaching a beginning teacher finds challenging, why they find them so, and what relevant prior experience they may have. However, this shared understanding of a beginning teacher's perception enables you to offer truly personalised guidance for them. This process fulfils the Chartered Institute of Personnel and Development (CIPD, 2012) criterion for mentoring, which states that some personal matters should be discussed, where it is relevant to the achievement of the professional tasks. The process also corresponds to the counselling element described in Clutterbuck's (2004) model. This may seem off-putting – and you may feel unqualified for such a role; if so, you may find it easier to think of it as simply an exploratory opening conversation. For example, you could support the beginning teacher to start by looking to how science can be applied in real-world contexts, asking questions, such as:

- Are there local employers whose businesses use some aspect of the science content?
- Is the content related to a recent news item?
- What planning strategies might be suited to an activity where a broad range of responses are acceptable, such as strategies to increase recycling rates?

Next, once the beginning teacher has provisionally decided to undertake a field trip to a specific venue, it will be helpful to ask them to list the reasons that they were initially enthusiastic about the trip, what obstacles they now perceive and what support would help them to negotiate these obstacles. This supported analysis would help a beginning teacher, like Chen, to evaluate the merits of proceeding, or not, with the trip.

Implementing extension and enrichment 285

18.3.2 Mentoring to support Chen's learning outcomes

Chen's 'headline' learning outcome is to evaluate the risks and benefits of the trip. If the balance lies in favour of proceeding with the trip, the next step will be to run a successful trip to the waste recycling plant. Therefore, Chen's learning outcome embodies several constituent criteria:

- To have researched and evaluated opportunities to learn about waste management at a relevant venue.
- To have researched the procedures for running a trip out of school, including the associated administrative processes.
- To have determined appropriate learning from the trip, incorporating wider learning benefits than purely scientific ones, such as technology, engineering and citizenship.

To this end, the three criteria mentioned above have been set out in the chronological order in which learning outcomes would be expected to be achieved. The first learning outcome will require a beginning teacher, like Chen, to undertake independent research on waste recycling venues, where his findings and evaluations could be monitored by the mentor. You will notice that these learning outcomes are unlikely to be completed rapidly so the beginning teacher will need a mentor's support to construct a medium-term agenda that can be monitored over several weeks until the trip has been conducted. However, individual components of the activity, and the corresponding learning outcomes, can be assessed by the beginning teacher and the mentor at different review points, for example fortnightly until three weeks before the date of the trip and, thereafter weekly until the post-trip evaluation is completed.

In accomplishing the second learning outcome, a mentor's task is to signpost Chen to colleagues who may be able to help them in the research part, such as colleagues teaching Geography, local environmental education groups and people with relevant specialist knowledge in the local educational council. With the procedural elements of the trip, administrative staff in school will be able to guide Chen as to the current procedures for running an off-site visit, including health and safety requirements, to make transport arrangements et cetera.

Undertaking the third learning outcome can start once the venue has been decided. At this point, Chen will need guidance from the mentor on arranging a pre-visit. It is possible that the focus of the visit is likely to be on enrichment, possibly focusing on how social and economic factors affect waste handling practice. Since these areas may be unfamiliar to Chen, given their science background, a mentor's 'sponsorship' in meeting other colleagues will be important. Chen can usefully be introduced to colleagues in suitable curriculum areas to discuss how the trip could fit with other aspects of the school curriculum and to draw on their subject expertise. In addition, Chen will also need guidance from the mentor on how a field trip to the waste recycling venue could enhance the development of transferable skills among pupils (such as making observations, testing hypothesis, exploring phenomenon, et cetera).

18.3.3 Using the modelling of good practice to provide support and challenge

Working collaboratively with a more experienced colleague and getting the chance to observe how they undertake a targeted activity, such as enrichment, can be invaluable support for

286   *Essex*

a beginning teacher's development. The scope of this modelled observation of experienced teachers is commonly focused on teaching but can cover a host of related activities, including lesson planning, assessment and evaluation of lessons. All of these observations would be relevant to a beginning teacher seeking to broaden their understanding of how to implement enrichment in their practices.

For Chen, it would be helpful for him to talk to other teachers who have arranged opportunities for learning outside the classroom successfully, in order to understand both why and how they undertook the activities. Next, Chen could shadow an experienced teacher who is conducting a trip in the near future. This would enable him to see at first hand the 'mechanics' of organising a trip and to learn 'how to' run one. In supporting this activity, Chen's mentor might help him by identifying a colleague, irrespective of their subject. For example, a colleague from the English department could be asked about the practicalities of leading a non-residential trip, because they regularly arrange theatre trips. Then the mentor needs to facilitate an arrangement to shadow the colleague who is organising the next trip, to find out the practicalities of the process. The mentor might want to make the planning of the trip a running agenda item for forthcoming weekly mentor meetings, thus ensuring that it does not get forgotten as the term gets busier. Once Chen has gathered further information from colleagues and others with relevant expertise such as education officers at potential venues, the mentor could prompt him to re-consider the pluses, minuses and interesting things about the trip, so that he can start to reach his own decision as to whether it is a worthwhile undertaking this enrichment activity further.

One of the supportive things that a mentor can very usefully do, during weekly mentoring meetings, is to encourage a beginning teacher to try out small enrichment activities, at first, in their lessons as early as possible during their ITE programme. If a mentor helps the beginning teacher to see that larger enrichment activities are composed of small steps of the sort that they have already been doing, it should give them confidence to attempt more ambitious activities. This gradualised approach is in keeping with Maynard and Furlong's (1995) competency model of mentoring, which sees a holistic 'performance' as being composed of a set of smaller competences. The atomisation of a task is likely to help the mentor and beginning teacher to monitor progress in planning enrichment activities. It also provides scaffolded development; during which the mentor can lessen the support they provide to facilitate the transition to implementing enrichment activities. This can, therefore, contribute to a mentor's endeavours to support a beginning teacher to 'manage their career and improve skills' (CIPD, 2012, p. 1).

18.3.4 *Draw on external expertise to develop relevant knowledge-based enrichment activities*

At every stage of a (beginning) teacher's career, they benefit from engagement with appropriate sources of external support to broaden and enrich their knowledge of the curriculum and approaches to planning and teaching it. External organisations can offer valuable guidance and specialist expertise that complement the help provided by the mentor. Collectively, such guidance contributes to the overall mentoring process as

Implementing extension and enrichment 287

shown by Clutterbuck (2004) (see Chapter 1). What is notable about this stage of the framework is that it has a dual purpose under Clutterbuck's model, offering an important opportunity for networking. The networking may take the form of direct personal contact or engagement with external organisations. For example, during any pre-visit, a mentor can encourage a beginning teacher to draw on the expertise of staff at the venue. Professional bodies, such as the Council for Learning Outside the Classroom, Consortium of Local Education Authorities for the Provision of Science Services (CLEAPSS) and Scottish School Education Research Centre (SSERC), can be an invaluable source of guidance and ideas.

For Chen, there is likely to be suitable guidance on leading a field trip already published. However, Chen is unlikely to find an 'off the shelf' solution to his specific proposal. In this instance, he may need to be signposted to suitable outside agencies (see further resources) and then helped to apply the guidelines to the specific trip that is being planned. Likewise, Chen, should be directed to liaise with staff at the site of a proposed visit, as they will have extensive knowledge of the site. Chen could be asked, as part of his preparation, to evaluate, for example, four resources and identify the relevance of the advice given about the proposed trip. Based on this, he should be able to estimate both the plausibility of running such a trip and its desirability. A beginning teacher may, like Chen, however, need further guidance with selecting the best external materials to help them to achieve their aims. Since the scrutiny of resources prior to the development of enrichment tasks further increases the time taken for planning, they may need support with this from the mentor, including the adjustment of other demands being placed upon them. Task 18.5 encourages you to reflect on sources of support available to a beginning teacher you are working with.

Task 18.5 Signposting the beginning teacher to sources of support

Having read step 4 of the framework, drawing on external expertise, answer the following questions:

1. What resources and expertise, formal or informal, are available that could be helpful for a beginning teacher you are mentoring when planning for an enrichment activity? You might find it useful to look at the website of the external bodies Association for Science Education (ASE), CLEAPSS and STEM Learning mentioned in the further resources section.
2. How would you support the beginning teacher to broaden their networking with external organisations?
3. How is, or could, the beginning teacher be helped to make best use of these resources?
4. Discuss any specific needs the beginning teacher has identified with the senior teacher/senior leadership team member who oversees staff development.

288 *Essex*

18.3.5 Step 5. Review and plan for the future

A beginning teacher should be engaged in reviewing their achievements and setting future targets, in processes akin to Katz's (1995) consolidation and renewal stages (see Chapter 1). Where specific aspirations have been identified for the beginning teacher, as they have been for Chen, and feedback is available from multiple sources (teachers, technicians, directly from pupils, indirect evidence from pupils), the format can be akin to that of a solutions-focused coaching approach (Allen and Sims, 2018). In solutions-focused coaching, successive peer supported evaluation, target setting, and implementation of teaching strategies form the basis for future plans. At this stage of the planning, execution and review cycle, the reflective model of mentoring (Maynard and Furlong, 1995) should dominate over the apprenticeship or competency models (see Chapter 1). The focus on specified outcomes at this stage of the framework corresponds to Clutterbuck's (2004) component of coaching; this is not, however, a discrepancy of the models, but a salient reminder that mentoring is a complex and multi-faceted process.

Returning to Chen to present what impact the mentoring process might have had:

- Chen demonstrated that he had reached the consolidation phase of his development (Katz, 1995) by being able to justify his decision about the value of the trip. Having evaluated it, he still thought it should proceed. A successful outcome would be to have devised a detailed and plausible plan, which is accepted by the senior leadership team
- At this stage of his career, where he is on the brink of the renewal phase (Katz, 1995), this activity will help Chen's progress to reflect on the applicability of both planning and running a trip for other classes he teaches.

Having considered the five-step framework, you are now aware of some mentoring strategies by which a beginning teacher can develop enrichment activities. You have been reminded of your important role in signposting a beginning teacher to suitable sources of support, both to achieve their immediate goals, but also in developing their sense of themselves as a collaborative member of the education community. You have considered the benefits of introducing enrichment to the beginning teacher's impact upon learning and have identified some obstacles to their implementation. Task 18.6 asks you to reflect on the five steps of the framework for supporting the ability of a beginning teacher to enrich pupils' learning.

Task 18.6 Reflection and review of the five-steps of the framework

Review the five steps of the framework set out in this chapter and reflect upon:

1. How many of the mentoring strategies mentioned in this chapter have you already used?
2. How comfortable do you feel about implementing each of these steps with a beginning teacher you are currently mentoring? What would help you to feel more able to use any strategies that you are currently not using?

3. Do you think that some of the steps are more essential than others? If so, which ones, and why?
4. What will be the next practical step(s) you take to promote the use of enrichment with the beginning teacher with whom you work?

Summary and key points

In this chapter, consideration has been given to the importance and practical implications of developing the ability of a beginning teacher to introduce differentiation with extension and enrichment into their teaching. The key points made are as follows:

- Developing the ability to incorporate differentiated forms of extension and enrichment practices during lessons, which is key for a beginning teacher's professional development.
- One of your roles as a mentor is to judge the point at which a beginning teacher is ready to introduce extension and enrichment dimensions into their lessons.
- Using the five steps framework to support beginning teachers in incorporating enrichment activities in their planning.
- Signpost a beginning teacher to appropriate additional support and helping them to form relevant professional relationships.

Further resources

ASE (Association for Science Education) (2018) Best practice guidance, ASE, viewed 16 March 2020, from: https://www.ase.org.uk/bestpractice
This website provides best practice guidance for a series of key aspects of the teaching and learning of science. One of the key aspects is outdoor learning which you can share with a beginning teacher. The outdoor learning file provides short and easily accessible guidelines for teachers along with some useful further support weblinks.

CLEAPSS (Consortium of Local Education Authorities for the Provision of Science Services) (2019) Student safety sheets: Fieldwork including any science work outside the laboratory, CLEAPSS, viewed 16 March 2020, from: http://science.cleapss.org.uk/Resource/SSS075-Fieldwork.pdf
This one-page pupil safety sheet can be used by the teachers as a checklist for pupils prior to the outing and for reference during the trip.

DfE (Department for Education) (2018) Health and safety on educational visits, DfE, viewed 16 March 2020, from: www.gov.uk/government/publications/health-and-safety-on-educational-visits
This website provides guidance to help schools understand their roles and responsibilities when undertaking school visits. It would be a good resource for a beginning teacher to read before planning any field trips for pupils.

HSE (The Health and Safety Executive) (2011) School trips and outdoor learning activities: Tackling the health and safety myths, HSE, viewed 16 March 2020, from: www.hse.gov.uk/services/education/school-trips.pdf

290   *Essex*

This short document encourages teachers to recognise the benefits of out-of-school learning. It outlines some health and safety procedures that the school, staff, parents and pupils should be following.

Institute of Education (IoE) (2020) ASPIRES 2: Longitudinal research project studying young people's science and career aspirations. IoE, viewed 2 April 2020, from: www.ucl.ac.uk/ioe/departments-and-centres/departments/education-practice-and-society/aspires-2
Through the site you can download the PDF, 'The Science Capital Teaching Approach', which gives numerous practical suggestions for enrichment strategies that may enhance the uptake of science by pupils, especially by under-represented groups. You may find the suggestions useful to share with a beginning teacher who is considering how to enrich science lessons.

Light, D. (2017) Stretch and challenge in your classroom, SecEd, viewed 9 June 2019, from: www.sec-ed.co.uk/best-practice/stretch-and-challenge-in-your-classroom/
This account of stretch and challenge (extension) is not science-specific but is valuable because it describes approaches that will help extend all pupils, not just the few most highly attaining in the class. The top ten list provides a helpful summary and all could be put into practice without difficulty. You might wish to jointly select one or more of the strategies for a beginning teacher you are mentoring to implement and you to jointly evaluate afterwards.

Shabatura, J. (2013) Using Bloom's taxonomy to write effective learning objectives, TIPS, viewed 15 April 2020, from: https://tips.uark.edu/using-blooms-taxonomy/
This online resource provides a verb table including some key 'action verbs' and example learning outcomes for each of the six levels of learning identified in Bloom's taxonomy. The author uses the term 'learning objectives' instead of learning outcomes, but this means the same. These verbs and example learning (outcomes) objectives could support a beginning teacher to write learning outcomes which presents differentiation using HOTS approach.

STEM Learning (2020) Enrichment, STEM Learning, viewed 19 March 2020, from: www.stem.org.uk/enrichment
This area of the STEM learning website brings together a wealth of resources from a range of external agencies, which could be used to enrich the science curriculum. It also enables you to request specialist support from STEM ambassadors whose contributions would enrich the science curriculum by showing 'real-life' applications. (Note that you need to be registered as a user, but there is no charge for registration.)

19 Supporting beginning teachers to work with pupils with special educational needs and disability

Darren Moore and Alison Black

Introduction

It is said that 'there is very little in the way of dedicated subject-specific continuing professional development (CPD) provision for science teachers in special schools, nor for those who work in the mainstream but have children with special educational needs [SEN] in their classes' (Bullough and Booth, 2013, p. 12). This chapter draws upon available information about special educational needs and disabilities (SEND) in secondary schools applied to science teaching, as well as a broader examination of inclusion in science, which often has direct application to teaching pupils with special needs (Piggott, 2002). A focus on SEND in science can move beyond differentiation in terms of groups of pupils and can also provide recognition of the importance of teacher–pupil relationships (Lawson, Norwich and Nash, 2013). Therefore, supporting beginning teachers with the inclusion of pupils with SEND is inextricably linked with teaching and learning for wider diversity (Black, Lawson and Norwich, 2018).

This chapter recognises some of the SEND, and individual differences amongst those pupils diagnosed with some learning difficulties, that a secondary school teacher is likely to encounter, even in their beginning years. It aims to encourage consideration of how you, as a mentor, might offer practical advice to a beginning teacher about how to plan for these pupils in lessons. Particular emphasis is placed on the need for a beginning teacher to work collaboratively with you and relevant colleagues to plan and teach lessons which can enhance science learning and scientific skills development of pupils with SEND. The suggestions highlighted in this chapter are drawn from our previous experience as teachers, but in particular our work over the last ten-years both with secondary science beginning teachers and the provision of focused training on SEND across subjects with secondary and primary beginning teachers.

292 *Moore et al.*

Objectives

At the end of this chapter you should be able to:

- Support a beginning teacher to reflect on their knowledge, understanding, assumptions, and perceptions about SEND and how the needs of such pupils may impact on their science lessons
- Assist a beginning teacher to implement some teaching strategies, identified in some recent research, to implement experiential learning, scientific literacy, and inquiry-based learning for pupils with SEND
- Support a beginning teacher to use case study and in-depth discussion approaches as overarching activities to identify, anticipate, and contemplate the impact of teaching and learning practices on pupils with SEND on a one-to-one basis.

19.1 What do we mean by special educational needs and disabilities (SEND)?

There is a global agreement that all children have the right to be formally educated, including children who have SEND. This agreement is formalised in the Convention on the Rights of the Child (United Nations, 1989), as well as the Convention on the Rights of Persons with Disabilities (United Nations, 2008). In England, for example, SEND is recognised as a key priority by the Carter Review of Initial Teacher Training (Carter, 2015) and continues to be a prominent feature of successive inspection frameworks by the Office for Standards in Education, Children's Services and Skills (Ofsted, 2015, 2019).

So, what do we mean by SEND? Definitions vary widely across the world. Some countries define SEND using a general definition that might refer to disabled pupils or those with significant learning difficulties. Other countries, such as Japan, define it by categorising pupils with SEND into more than ten different categories (see Organisation for Economic Cooperation and Development (OECD), 2012). Our simplified definition is:

> A pupil who is not able to make progress in the education made generally available for all learners (pupils) of the same age, without additional support or adaptation.

Countries apply different conceptual frameworks in identifying teacher standards related to SEND. Some countries (for example, the Czech Republic and Italy) include pupils with medical disabilities in what they refer to as special education, Turkey includes gifted and talented amongst SEND, Switzerland includes a foreign first language and, since 2015, England has clearly organised SEND provision under four categories (Department for Education (DfE) and Department of Health (DoH), 2015), which are:

- Communication and interaction such as: Autism Spectrum Disorder (ASD); speech language and communication needs.
- Cognition and learning such as dyslexia; moderate learning difficulty.

Work with pupils with SEND 293

- Social, emotional and mental health difficulties such as: Attention Deficit Hyperactivity Disorder (ADHD); anxiety.
- Sensory and/or physical needs such as visual impairment; cerebral palsy.

It is important that you familiarise a beginning teacher you are mentoring with your country's documents and teacher standards relevant to SEND. Before sharing this overview about SEND with the beginning teacher, Task 19.1 allows a beginning teacher, with your support, to reflect on the view of the relative importance of SEND to planning science lessons, and what SEND information/provision it would be valuable to know to plan and teach lessons.

Task 19.1 A beginning teacher's reflection on SEND information and provision

Ask a beginning teacher to answer the following reflective questions. Support the beginning teacher in elaborating their reflections on their teaching practices (by, for example, probing and/or providing example practices from your own teaching practices).

1. What are the implications of having a class with more or fewer pupils with SEND? What difference does it make?
2. What information is it critical to know beyond the number of pupils with SEND?
3. What broader teacher standards or aspect of pedagogy should they consider relevant to pupils with SEND (for example, differentiation, diversity, individual needs, lower attainment)? Would the answer to this question make a difference to how SEND is planned for?

A takeaway message from Task 19.1 is the viewpoint that teaching pupils with SEND does not need to be seen as a separate aspect of science teaching itself. We anticipate question 2 from Task 19.1 is likely to lead to responses in terms of more specific learning needs and the necessity to respond to these individual needs when planning a lesson. However, McGinnis (2002) identified reluctance among beginning science teachers to teach pupils with SEND, due to the complex nature of planning and teaching to ensure individual pupil needs are met. It is often reported by beginning teachers that they would like more training on behaviour management and associated planning for pupils with SEND to feel confident in teaching them, along with other pupils, i.e. within the context of a full class. Therefore, it is important that you discuss behavioural management issues with the beginning teacher, taking into account the full class context. You can then support the beginning teacher to understand that behaviour management for pupils with SEND should not be different, instead it requires reasonable adjustments to be made, where necessary, for some pupils with SEND. Task 19.2 asks you to question preconceptions and knowledge of a beginning teacher about managing the behaviour of pupils with SEND, and to share the case study of Jo to extend the discussion on reasonable adjustments for pupils with SEND.

Task 19.2   A beginning teacher's preconceptions and knowledge on managing pupils with SEND

Step 1: Discuss perceptions/assumptions that a beginning teacher has about teaching pupils with SEND in their lessons. Ask them to think about this by answering the questions below:

1.   What do they think are the challenges?
2.   What are some differences between the behaviour/misbehaviour of some pupils with SEND that are symptomatic of a range of individual needs?

[You could prompt the beginning teacher by sharing some example of pupils from your school or Case studies readily available online of pupils with SEND like autism, ADHD, dyspraxia or hearing impairment.]

Step 2: Share the following case study of Jo with the beginning teacher you are working with:

Jo is a beginning science teacher who has just received a timetable for the next school term. New to the school, she looks up information about each of the classes. Jo is struck by a Year 7 (age 11-12, first year of secondary school) class where a quarter of the pupils have SEND. Jo is a very capable science teacher and has progressed very well, but shows reluctance to teach this group. Jo considers that:

*   The Year 7 class would be difficult to manage because of the high number of pupils with SEND. Behaviour management is something that Jo perceives as a challenge while teaching pupils with SEND
*   In comparison to the Year 7 class, a Year 9 class will be easier to manage as only 10% of pupils have SEND, and there are also two teaching assistants assigned to pupils in that class
*   She should ask the head of science if it would be possible to take Year 9 and a more experienced teacher could take Year 7
*   It would be beneficial to meet with the SEND coordinator to seek advice.

Step 3: Next, discuss the case study with the beginning teacher, ask them to list some reasonable adjustments Jo should make in teaching Year 7 and discuss this list. Moreover, during these discussions:

*   It is worth discussing other challenges of starting to teach new classes and sharing anecdotal examples of successes with previous pupils with SEND. [We can remember vividly some pupils with SEND who really loved science.]
*   Introduce the beginning teacher to your school's SEND coordinator and teaching assistants, and discuss the range of support these staff members can provide to the beginning teacher
*   Discuss the complexity of reasonable adjustments for a range of pupils. For instance, some will have a severity of needs such that a teaching assistant or

other resources are provided perhaps through an Education and Health Care Plan (EHCP). Others have SEND support needs identified by their school as part of a graduated response that may lead to an EHCP (DfE and DoH, 2015)

- Revisit answers from step 1 and extend the discussion focusing on any preconceptions, reluctance or lack of confidence that the beginning teacher has in managing pupils with SEND, and identify targeted mentoring support for them.

After completing Task 19.2, the beginning teacher could co-plan science lessons with specialist SEND teachers (Swanson and Bianchini, 2015) and/or science teachers who have experience in planning lessons for the particular classes and particular pupils with SEND they are going to teach. While we have taken care not to recommend anything that would be very challenging to implement (for example, co-teaching and the use of video games), we think that the messages from Swanson and Bianchini's (2015) article regarding the benefit of collaboration with SEND experts, or those who know particular pupils with SEND, would enhance the beginning teacher's planning for pupils with SEND. Moreover, you could signpost the beginning teacher towards further reading about types of SEND, readily available documents on pupils with SEND, and documents on teacher's reflection on reasonable adjustments for pupils with SEND (see further resources).

19.2 What does research say about SEND classroom practices and how can you support a beginning teacher to implement best practice?

In this section, we consider more specific research about working with pupils with SEND in science lessons. It is important for a beginning teacher to consider planning for pupils with SEND more broadly, because (i) being prepared for every individual SEND would be challenging, and arguably an unnecessary task, since (ii) there will be individual differences amongst pupils with a similar conditions and (iii) suggestions for teaching pupils with SEND share many features with high-quality teaching for all pupils. Moreover, Davis, Florian and Ainscow (2004) conducted a literature review and concluded that there was no single strategy for teaching pupils with SEND, nor were there recommended methods for particular groups of pupils with SEND. Therefore, it would be beneficial to support a beginning teacher you are mentoring to adopt a manageable number of teaching strategies in their planning to have an effective impact on pupils' learning across the different categories of SEND in a full class context. Three useful strategies are discussed below.

19.2.1 Experiential learning

Kang and Martin (2018) investigated the impact of engaging beginning science teachers in experiential learning to improve learning opportunities for pupils with SEND. They suggested that any opportunity that can be given to the beginning teacher to teach science to pupils with SEND outside the classroom not only helps them to see that experiential learning

296 *Moore et al.*

improves attitudes towards the learning of science by pupils with a wide range of learning needs, but also enhances pupils' interest in science and their feeling of competency in the subject. The beginning teacher could adapt/adopt an experiential learning context, highlighted by Kang and Martin (2018), such as a visit to a science fair, including activities tailored to specific needs. While supporting planning an experiential learning context, in this way, you need to remind the beginning teacher that embedding experiential learning could be a challenge for them, but it is important to embed in their practice, as it provides opportunity to connect all pupils with science without the challenges that a traditional classroom setting may pose them and can be of benefit to the full range of pupils, not just those with SEND. You might like to revisit Chapter 18, which provides some useful mentoring steps in supporting a beginning teacher (Chen) to plan and conduct a science field trip as an enrichment activity. The mentoring steps mentioned in Chapter 18 could be tailored to make reasonable adjustments for pupils with SEND.

19.2.2 Scientific literacy

Villanueva and Hand (2011) focused on scientific literacy as an intrinsic goal of science education to overcome potential challenges, especially when working with pupils with a range of learning needs, in particular processing and cognition difficulties exhibited by learners with dyslexia. Along these lines, you could share the points below about dyslexia with the beginning teacher:

- Dyslexia is characterised by difficulties in literacy. It can affect areas of cognition such as memory, speed of processing, time management, coordination and directional aspects. There can also be visual and phonological difficulties. Therefore, supporting literacy and cognitive load can help pupils with dyslexia.
- The negative effects of dyslexia on a pupil can be profound, including relationships with peers. It is important therefore to select groups with care and provide support for pupils to contribute.
- Learned helplessness may be an issue for pupils with dyslexia, particularly when they have not been recognised. Therefore, teachers should be mindful that avoidance of academic work may be because pupils believe that they cannot achieve, rather than actual skill deficits.

After sharing these points with the beginning teacher, you can discuss that such difficulties and recommendations are not exclusive for pupils with dyslexia only, but can also be useful for other pupils with SEND.

Another suggestion to improve scientific literacy is to encourage the beginning teacher to read the Education Endowment Foundation (2018) guidance report Improving Secondary Science – particularly the section on developing scientific vocabulary to support pupils to read and write about science. Next, you can support them by pinpointing literacy interventions that are more likely to help with language and cognition difficulties faced by some pupils with SEND. For instance, identifying key words that are already used in familiar contexts that can create confusion for pupils with SEND, such as:

- Keyword 1: Boiling point
  Common confusion: That it is a fixed temperature when water boils or subjective in terms of when someone thinks it is too hot.
- Keyword 2: Photosynthesis
  Common confusion: 'Photo' creates confusion as it is considered to relate to a picture rather than light.

To plan reasonable adjustments for confusions such as those above, support the beginning teacher to use writing frames as scaffolds for scientific writing, by helping pupils structure their writing and providing prompts to include certain features in sections. For instance, a writing frame for a conclusion written after practical work on boiling point could include:

> My results show that as water is heated using a Bunsen the temperature .... A sign of water boiling is when .... This (does/does not) agree with my hypothesis as I predicted that the water would boil at .... degrees Celsius. This may be because ....

Moreover, you could introduce Hand and Key's (1999), recommended framework for using writing prompts to promote scientific literacy, support inquiry, argumentation and scientific language, as a guide for a beginning teacher to incorporate science investigation and reasoning for pupils with different learning needs. Along these lines, Villanueva and Hand (2011) (Table 19.1) provided evidence of the positive impact of using a writing framework approach to promote scientific literacy with a range of pupils with SEND, demonstrating that it can improve critical thinking, use of scientific language and science attainment scores. Table 19.1 can be

Table 19.1 A template to promote scientific literacy

	Teacher designed activities to promote scientific literacy	Writing frame prompts for pupils
1	Exploration of existing understanding through individual or group concept mapping.	Beginning ideas: What questions do I have about this topic?
2	Pre-practical activities, including informal writing, brainstorming, posing questions and planning.	Tests: What will I do and why?
3	Pupils' participation in practical activity.	Observations: What did I see?
4	Negotiation phase 1: writing personal meanings for laboratory activity (for example writing journals).	Claims: What can I claim?
5	Negotiation phase 2: sharing and comparing data interpretations in small groups (for example making group charts).	Evidence: How do I know? Why am I making these claims?
6	Negotiation phase 3: comparing science ideas to textbooks or other printed resources (for example, writing group notes in response to focus questions).	Reading: How do my ideas compare with other ideas?
7	Negotiation phase 4: individual reflection and writing (for example, creating a presentation such as a poster or report for a larger audience).	Reflection: How have my ideas changed?
8	Exploration of post-teaching understanding through concept mapping.	Communication: How can I communicate my claims, evidence, readings, findings and evaluations with my peers/class/teacher?

(Source: Adapted from Villanueva and Hand (2011, p. 236))

298 *Moore et al.*

used to support a beginning teacher in developing scientific literacy in their lessons by explicitly promoting laboratory understanding and scientific skills development. The first column highlights eight laboratory-based understanding and skill development activities to promote scientific literacy and the second column indicates writing frame prompts, in the form of some questions for pupils that could support the beginning teacher to incorporate each of the eight laboratory-based activities in a science classroom. Task 19.3 asks you so use Table 19.1 with a beginning teacher to plan a lesson and reflect on the impact of the planned lesson on pupils' learning.

Task 19.3   A template to promote scientific literacy among pupils with SEND

Step 1:   Give Table 19.1 to a beginning teacher (you are working with).

Step 2:   Encourage the beginning teacher to consider ways to include the eight laboratory-based understanding and skills development activities in their lesson planning.

Step 3:   Make a point of suggesting to the beginning teacher that they add prompts (questions and/or key words) in column two of Table 19.1. Then, discuss whether or not these prompts would be useful for pupils with various types of SEND.

Step 4:   Support the beginning teacher to plan and teach a lesson using the template for a whole class.

Step 5:   After they have taught the lesson, discuss its effectiveness with the beginning teacher and how they can develop its use in future lessons.

Moreover, you can adapt mentoring suggestions from Chapter 15 on embedding scientific literacy for all the pupils and assessing pupils' scientific literacy-based learning gains from Chapter 12 (p. 189) to support a beginning teacher in planning and teaching pupils with SEND.

19.2.3 *Inquiry-based learning*

After conducting a review of inquiry-based learning approaches in science lessons for pupils with SEND, Rizzo and Taylor (2016) concluded that these approaches can improve science achievement for pupils with SEND as much as for pupils without SEND. This may not be too surprising for you as an experienced teacher, particularly given the implication that often pedagogy for pupils with SEND does not differ from high-quality teaching for all pupils. However, for a beginning teacher it could be surprising because they might consider that inquiry-based pedagogical approaches or practices are too advanced for pupils with SEND. Therefore, you need to encourage the beginning teacher to plan inquiry-based

Work with pupils with SEND 299

learning approaches for all pupils, giving explicit consideration to the needs of pupils with SEND. You could support the beginning teacher to plan inquiry-based learning instructions by first asking them to read and discuss some research work based on making some adjustments to incorporate inquiry-based learning in their teaching for pupils with SEND, such as:

- Rizzo and Taylor (2016), who noted that direct instructions are needed alongside inquiry-based learning instruction for pupils with SEND.
- Starling, Lo and Rivera (2015), who found that a combination of inquiry-based practical activities and direct instructions improved performance among pupils with learning disabilities or ADHD, as compared to using either method alone.
- Szyjka and Mumba (2009), who suggested that pupils with SEND are often given a very structured form of one-to-one instructions, which can limit these pupils' participation in inquiry-based learning style of (guided/open-ended) instructions and group work.

Szyjka and Mumba (2009) suggest that limiting pupils' inquiry-based learning opportunities is something that needs to be discussed in detail with the (beginning) teacher, so that as a mentor you can support them in planning for active and inclusive learning approaches in teaching science. During this discussion, you could highlight the use of scaffolding approaches for all pupils to engage more inquiry-based learning practices in their science lessons. Some examples of using scaffolding approaches to incorporate inquiry-based learning practices for pupils with SEND can be discussed with the beginning teacher, such as pupils with ASD, two specific areas warrant consideration:

1. Group work is frequently included in inquiry-based learning practices, ranging from peer-discussions to practical work (see Chapter 16). Therefore, a beginning teacher should give careful consideration to group work activities by (i) clearly communicating the group work activities with the pupils with SEND, (ii) appropriately allocating group roles to them, and (iii) considering group dynamics during lesson planning, aided by discussions with experienced colleagues.
2. Encourage the beginning teacher to anticipate difficulties that can arise, particularly for pupils with SEND in inquiry-based learning designed science lessons. Difficulties could involve various transitions, for example: seated work, planning an investigation in groups, preparatory work, performing practical work in groups and writing up a laboratory report with peers. Therefore, the beginning teacher should always plan ahead to minimise such difficulties and provide plenty of notice about planned activities to pupils and/or perhaps ask a teaching assistant working with pupils with SEND to give a pre-lesson explanation on the structure of the inquiry-based learning designed science lesson.

Task 19.4 is aimed at enabling you to support a beginning teacher to incorporate inquiry-based learning practices into teaching pupils with SEND in their own context.

Task 19.4   Incorporating inquiry-based learning practices for pupils with SEND

Ask the beginning teacher to:

1. Read the Nuffield Foundation Practical Work for Learning project (www.nuffield-foundation.org/practical-work-learning)
2. Select one of the three pedagogical approaches, argumentation, model-based inquiry or science in the workplace to practical work. Then highlight reasonable adjustments, on the selected practical lesson from the Nuffield website, needed for pupils with SEND
3. Plan a lesson using pedagogical approaches to practical work, mentioned above, and during the pre-lesson discussion with the mentor, discuss the choice of reasonable adjustments for pupils with SEND in lesson planning
4. Evaluate the use of inquiry-based learning practices and associated adjustments during the post-lesson discussion with the mentor, to inform future use of inquiry-based learning practices in their lessons.

19.3 Overarching activities for beginning teachers

Finally, this section introduces two tasks (Tasks 19.5 and 19.6) that we have used with beginning teachers across subjects for several years. Completing Tasks 19.5 and 19.6 has provided considerable benefits to beginning teachers teaching pupils with SEND, as it allows them to (i) reflect on their teaching practices by comparing and contrasting responses across subjects, (ii) conclude what is key to science teaching in comparison with other subjects, and (iii) collaborate to share observations with other teachers (beginning and/or experienced). You could use Tasks 19.5 and 19.6 with a beginning teacher you are mentoring using a similar format, or adapt it according to your school's context, individual needs of beginning teachers and pupils with SEND.

19.3.1 Case study

You could introduce an intensive case study task (Task 19.5) to a beginning teacher to help them in addressing feedback about lack of planning for an individual pupil. Task 19.5 asks the beginning teacher to select a pupil with SEND, assess the selected pupil's learning needs, plan, teach, evaluate pupil's progress and review their teaching approaches. This allows the beginning teacher to understand the needs of an individual pupil. In turn, it supports them in recognising that their approach to teaching and learning varies when a different pupil with different needs is encountered in the future. Moreover, you can support the beginning teacher with their thinking about differentiation more generally and how teaching and learning might be adapted to meet the needs of an individual pupil.

Work with pupils with SEND 301

Task 19.5   A case study task

1. Ask the beginning teacher to select a pupil with SEND in one of the classes they teach, and through whom they will be able to learn more about the SEND needs and its impact on science learning.
2. Next, ask them to follow the four steps below:

Step 1 – Assess the pupil's individual needs

Gather the following information about the pupil:

- Relevant history (for example school attendance, previous specialist reports).
- Nature of SEND and action plan they have.
- Strengths and weaknesses (in science specifically if applicable).
- Current factors supporting learning and barriers to learning.
- Current support provision available to the pupil.
- Current targets and relevant progress – how do these translate to science?

Step 2 – Planning and teaching

Ask the beginning teacher to plan and teach lessons, promoting specific teaching approaches for the pupil commensurate with the information gathered in Step 1 and which respond to the pupil's needs (such as experiential learning, scientific literacy, inquiry-based learning et cetera). Make sure that the beginning teacher discusses the planned teaching approaches with you, before teaching the lesson. Then you could observe these lessons.

Step 3 – Assess the pupil's progress

Encourage the beginning teacher to use assessment data to measure the pupil's progress with an awareness that this data is unlikely to provide strong evidence for the effectiveness of the teaching and learning (due to factors such as different topic, different classroom space and novelty of new approaches).

Step 4 – Review the approaches used

Ask the beginning teacher to collate information gathered from these three steps and reflect on them.

3. Finally, evaluate with the beginning teacher in the post-lesson discussion, the effectiveness of their planning, teaching and pupil's learning. This might include:

- How they planned and undertook the work with the selected pupil.
- Did they promote learning broadly along the lines of the pupil's support plan or equivalent targets or did they examine how the pupil's targets might be reviewed?
- What did they do? What setting? How often? What teaching strategies did they use? From where did they gain ideas for teaching (for example, websites, school

302   *Moore et al.*

materials, discussion with the SEND coordinator, reading relevant literature et cetera)? How did they monitor the pupil's progress? What records did they keep?

- Did they evaluate the impact of the strategies they used on the pupil's progress against the target/s set? Discuss any difficulties they encountered in teaching and learning and reasons why.
- What recommendations do they suggest for the next steps in teaching this pupil in science? Give reasons for these.
- What have they learned from the task – knowledge, understanding, skills, and attitudes?
- How can they use this knowledge in future?

19.3.2 In-depth discussion

An in-depth discussion (as in Task 19.6) has been found to be a valuable activity when beginning teachers have undertaken Task 19.5. Task 19.6 is designed to be completed with one beginning teacher, although it can be adapted to include more than one beginning teacher (could be across subjects). If Task 19.5 has not been completed, steps 1–3 of Task 19.6 could be completed focused on a pupil with SEND whom the beginning teacher is familiar.

Task 19.6   In-depth discussion

Step 1 – Sharing information

Ask the beginning teacher to spend 2 minutes sharing the following information with you about the pupil they focused on in Task 19.5:

- A description of the chosen pupil WITHOUT mentioning their SEND or their 'ability'/attainment.
- A description of the pupil's STRENGTHS (What are they good at? What do they do well?).
- A description of the pupil's attainment (again, WITHOUT reference to SEND), for science, and compare it with literacy, numeracy and other subjects.

As their mentor, encourage the beginning teacher to share factual and respectful descriptions with you.

Step 2 – Describing barriers to learning

Ask the beginning teacher to spend 2 minutes describing barriers to learning that the selected pupil faces. The following can be used as a prompt:

- Attention span/lack of focus
- Motivation

Work with pupils with SEND 303

- Working memory
- Observational learning
- Generalisation (transfer of learning and skills across settings)
- Interpersonal skills
- Physical use of equipment.

As their mentor, during these discussions try to steer the beginning teacher's focus away from the SEND label and onto pupils learning.

Step 3 - Sharing SEND details

Next, ask the beginning teacher to spend 2 minutes sharing details about their observed pupil by answering the following questions:

- What level of support do they have (for example SEN support, EHCP provision)?
- What category of SEND are they in (for example, communication and interaction difficulties; cognition and learning difficulties; social, emotional and mental health difficulties; sensory and/or physical needs)? Do they have a diagnosed SEND? (for example, dyslexia, cerebral palsy, Down's syndrome?)
- What impact does their SEND have on learning in science?

Step 4 - Reflecting on teaching and learning practices

Finally, spend the remaining time discussing teaching and learning of the pupil they worked with, reflecting on the following:

- What are the targets for teaching the pupil in future and more generally for teaching according to pupils' individual needs?
- Would any of the teaching strategies be beneficial for others/all learners?
- Would the teaching described be relevant for other teachers (beginning and/or experienced)?

Summary and key points

This chapter concludes with five main points for you to consider:

- Beginning teachers often report a lack of training in relation to SEND teaching. As a mentor you can take responsibility for supporting them and address any lack of confidence in teaching pupils with SEND within the context of a full class. You can also stress that teaching pupils with SEND can be no different from high quality teaching for all pupils generally.
- As a mentor you should aim to instil an understanding in a beginning teacher that individual pupils with SEND vary in terms of the severity of need and type of learning difficulty. Therefore, there is no one strategy for teaching pupils with SEND or for particular groups of pupils with SEND, rather a range of strategies are effective.

304 *Moore et al.*

- Scientific literacy can be a challenge for a range of pupils with SEND, including those with dyslexia. But supporting a beginning teacher with ways they can include scientific literacy for pupils with SEND is needed.
- Some pupils with SEND may need guided inquiry-based associated learning instructions and support for group work to achieve it. So, you need to support the beginning teacher to plan required learning instructions and group work activities for these pupils.
- Case study and in-depth discussion tasks focusing on barriers to learning and needs of specific pupils can be a highly beneficial exercise for a beginning teacher. Such activities will help a beginning teacher to chart a SEND pupil's learning needs. This charting exercise will, in turn, support them to plan required planning and teaching adjustments for the pupils, self-reflect on their teaching practices, and develop a better understanding of pupils with SEND.

Further resources

Cheminais, R. (2015) *SEN for Qualified and Trainee Teachers*. 3rd edn, Abingdon, Oxon: Routledge.
This book can be shared with a beginning teacher to provide a comprehensive introduction to SEND to help them to build knowledge and confidence in teaching pupils with SEND. It also places emphasis on barriers to learning rather than an individual deficit, which can be discussed during weekly mentoring meetings.

Education Endowment Foundation (2020) Special educational needs in mainstream schools, viewed 28 May 2020, from: https://educationendowmentfoundation.org.uk/tools/guidance-reports/special-educational-needs-disabilities/
This guidance report for schools and teachers offers five evidence-based recommendations to support pupils with SEND in mainstream schools, including practical ideas that can be implemented in teaching pupils with SEND.

Nuffield Foundation (undated) Practical work for learning, Nuffield Foundation, viewed 7 June 2019, from: www.nuffieldfoundation.org/practical-work-learning
This website forms the first step in the steps involved in completing Task 19.4. It is a very useful website for you to use to support a beginning teacher in planning lessons as it includes example resources for different SEND needs, which are easily accessed by using SEND terms in the search box, such as autism. In addition, it provides a useful basis for you to engage a beginning teacher in reflecting on how pupils with SEND might need support in accessing inquiry-based practical learning in science.

Sheffield Hallam University/Sheffield Institute for Education (undated) Science for all, Sheffield Hallam University/Sheffield Institute for Education, viewed 7 June 2019, from: https://scienceforall.shu.ac.uk/about.html
This globally accepted project can be shared with a beginning teacher to provide inspiration for teaching science to pupils with SEND. It provides successful case studies, scenarios and examples of work with pupils with SEND in science, including in a secondary school context. In addition, you can use some of these case studies, scenarios and examples of pupils' accounts to adopt/adapt and compare/contrast according to the beginning teacher's developmental needs.

20 To conclude

Saima Salehjee

To become an effective science teacher is not straightforward; there is satisfaction, enjoyment, passion and determination, but also bumps, hurdles, disappointments and challenges. Therefore, in this non-linear and complex journey of becoming a teacher, the role of a mentor is essential, no matter at which stage of the journey a teacher resides.

This book has looked at mentoring beginning teachers, including not only student teachers who are currently completing their initial teacher education (ITE) programme to qualify as a teacher, but also newly qualified teachers (NQTs) and early career teachers. Hence a mentor's roles and responsibilities do not end once a teacher has achieved qualified teacher status (QTS). Rather, it continues beyond the provision of ITE. Therefore, to support you, as a mentor, of a beginning science teacher, this book has highlighted various mentoring approaches, strategies and resources to facilitate your mentoring practices. Your practice should be based on the beginning teacher's developmental needs rather than aligning mentoring support based on a beginning teacher's years of experience.

The suggested mentoring practices presented in this book are drawn from the mentoring experiences of 25 authors. The focus of all authors in this book is firmly on strengthening mentoring practices to support the development of effective beginning science teachers. There is a lot to say in conclusion, but I will highlight some aspects that this book has offered to support you in embracing effective mentoring practices.

Chapters have repeatedly suggested that mentors view and support each beginning teacher as an individual and to acknowledge that there is no one-size-fits-all mentoring style for all beginning teachers. Hence, generalising mentoring styles and associated strategies for all beginning teachers is imprecise and uncertain. Therefore, you need to accept a beginning teacher as an individual and focus on their specific developmental needs/their own point of departure, rather than where you think they should begin from. To accomplish an individualistic approach to viewing a beginning teacher, you must become self-reflective about your mentoring practices on a regular basis, such as what style of mentoring you are comfortable with. Does a beginning teacher respond well to your specific mentoring style? How effectively are chosen mentoring strategies supporting the beginning teacher's development? What mentoring strategies are you using (or should be using) to develop a beginning teacher's autonomy? et cetera.

306 *Salehjee*

Effective mentor–mentee discussions form the basis of a strong mentor–mentee relationship and provide waypoints to support a beginning teacher's developmental journey of becoming an effective teacher. Therefore, you need to ensure that these discussions do not only rely on lesson-debriefs on a lesson taught by the beginning teacher and/or discussions on some topics needed to be taught in the upcoming lessons. Rather, they should also involve a range of conversations. Such conversations could range from home- and work-life balance to pupil-related issues inside and outside the science classrooms to attaining teacher standards to pedagogical-oriented discussion and discussion of issues and solutions related to making science learning accessible for all the pupils. One way of establishing effective discussions is by recounting your own experiences and listening to a beginning teacher's real-life experiences as scenarios or stories. Sharing experiences in this way could allow you and the beginning teacher to incorporate reflective talks on prior learning, teaching, and evaluating practices by discussing the impact of such practices in their current and upcoming teaching lives. Thus, some tasks in the book ask mentors and beginning teachers to share their real-life experiences with each other and with other staff members. In addition, this book offers some example scenarios or stories as Case studies, for a mentor to reflect on their mentoring strategies and styles, some of which is suggested to be shared with a beginning teacher. These Case studies are from within school settings, including accounts from the anonymised science mentors, beginning science teachers and pupils.

It is important that a mentor acknowledges that becoming a teacher is an emotional business. Therefore, you need to maintain a positive mentor–mentee relationship. For example, listening to a beginning teacher more and talking less boosts their confidence and provides a source of positive energy through appreciating their effort and employing constructive discussions. It could be an emotional business for the mentor too. So, it is vital that you do not overwhelm yourself and the beginning teacher you are mentoring by committing to unrealistic expectations from each other. Further, it is essential that you reflect on your impact on the beginning teacher and simultaneously encourage them to share positive and/or negative emotions with you when they arise rather than leaving it far too long to be appreciated and/or to be dealt with.

Modelling best practices is one of the essential aspects of a mentor, as a beginning teacher tends to follow in their mentor's footsteps to develop their planning and teaching practices. So, as a science mentor, you should model yourself as a scientific activist promoting scientific literacy for all the pupils. You can achieve this by not only displaying ways of planning and teaching science to pupils within the recommended science curriculum, but also incorporating sources other than the science curriculum, such as using pedagogical strategies used in the (science) education-based secondary literature in your country and beyond, including exciting discoveries presented in science-based podcasts and introducing news items in the classroom related to science et cetera. Further, you need to model these best practices by allowing a beginning teacher to co-plan and co-teach lessons with you.

Additionally, this modelling of best practices by the mentor should not be one-off as the development of a beginning teacher is a gradual process. Therefore, you need to reflect and model ways by which you build your knowledge, skills and understanding regularly. For example: How do you bring, and use, innovation into science classrooms? Do you regularly reflect on your teaching practices based on pupils learning? Do you regularly modify your

To conclude   307

plans according to the learning needs of pupils? Do you keep a reflective journal like your beginning teacher? What continuing professional development (CPD) courses do you attend? What other leadership roles do you practice? What role do you play in establishing partnerships with other local schools, university, museums, industry and with local/regional science-bodies (such as the Royal Society of Biology, Royal Society of Chemistry and Institute of Physics)? and how do you seek to develop the issues/solutions of science education at a global level? et cetera.

It is important that you keep a growth-oriented approach to mentoring a beginning teacher, with a mindset of developing an autonomous teacher over time. This approach and associated mindset require you to initially give more support to a beginning teacher in planning, teaching and evaluating their classroom practices, and then gradually lowering your support over time, with an increase in a beginning teacher's responsibility and autonomy in their classroom practices. For example, you provide more support when a beginning teacher is planning and teaching parts of the lessons (micro-planning and micro-teaching). You then lower your support when a beginning teacher is planning and teaching a series of solo-lessons. The support lowers further when they are planning and teaching parts of the science curriculum's units of work. To achieve this growth-oriented approach, it is also important that you help a beginning teacher to extend their ability to evaluate their practices based on self-reflections, feedback from lesson observations from you and other experienced teachers and pupils' feedback. Moreover, using your professional judgement and expertise, you support a beginning teacher in setting their developmental targets during their early stages of development. However, over time with more autonomous control, a beginning teacher should be allowed to set their developmental targets themselves with less support from you.

A growth-oriented outlook of a mentor needs you to not only support a beginning teacher to achieve the teacher standards to attain a QTS, but it is also be aimed to develop a beginning teacher as a life-long learner. Therefore, you need to direct the beginning teacher to extend their development by getting involved with CPD opportunities to upskill their learning and teaching practices. Moreover, you need to consider supportive ways to make a beginning teacher part of the school community, such as by establishing relationships, team-working skills and leadership activities with the other staff members of the school beyond their usual day-to-day practices in the science classroom/laboratory. This can be achieved by involving a beginning teacher in the school's community to create inclusive teaching, learning and leadership practices, in accordance with the school's developmental plans, for example, to improve the school's learning and teaching procedures to cater to all the pupils with varying learning needs. An inquiry could involve the beginning teacher observing and shadowing teachers and individual pupils, making field notes and reviewing reflections to be discussed with staff members on, for example, how misconceptions among pupils have risen from the subject knowledge taught in the classrooms. How do experienced science teachers tailor needs for special education needs and disability (SEND) pupils, within a full class context? How do teachers, as leaders and staff with leadership roles, contribute to the need for education for all pupils?

Finally, I will end this book by saying that the support given in this book would potentially develop you to recognise yourself and be known by a beginning teacher as a teacher educator rather than a classroom-teacher. The difference is that a classroom-teacher with mentoring responsibilities helps a beginning teacher with routine practices, assists in mirroring some teaching exercises, shares pre-planned lessons and resources, and provides some emotional support. On the other hand, a teacher educator-oriented mentor sometimes does what a classroom-teacher would do, but primarily acts as a developmental advocate of a beginning teacher, who can converse and model the how and why of teaching interwoven with a growth-mediated outlook of developing an autonomous and effective science teacher with a lifelong learning attitude.

REFERENCES

Abd-El-Khalick, F., Bell, R.L. and Lederman, N.G. (1998) 'The nature of science and instructional practice: Making the unnatural natural', *Science Education*, *82* (4), pp. 417–436.

ACAS (The Advisory, Conciliation and Arbitration Service) (undated) Challenging conversations and how to manage them, ACAS, viewed 28 April 2020, from: https://archive.acas.org.uk/conversations

Agarwal, P.K., Bain, P.M. and Chamberlain, R.W. (2012) 'The value of applied research: Retrieval practice improves classroom learning and recommendations from a teacher, a principal, and a scientist', *Educational Psychology Review*, *24* (3), pp. 437–448.

AITSL (Australian Professional Standards for Teachers) (2011) *The Australian Professional Standards for Teachers*. Melbourne: AITSL. Viewed 19 April 2020 from: www.aitsl.edu.au/teach/standards

Alfred, G. and Garvey, R. (2010) *Mentoring in Schools Pocketbook*. 3rd edn. London: Management Pocketbooks.

Allen, M. (2019) *Misconceptions in Primary Science*. 3rd edn. London: Open University Press.

Allen, M. (2016) *The Best Ways to Teach Primary Science: Research into Practice*. Maidenhead: Open University Press.

Allen, R. and Sims, S. (2018) *The Teacher Gap*. London: Routledge.

Ambrosetti, A., Rorrison, D. and Capeness, R. (2018) *Educating Future Teachers: Innovative Perspectives in Professional Experience*. Singapore: Springer.

Anderson, L. (2011) 'A learning resource for developing effective mentorship in practice', *Nursing Standard*, *25* (51), pp. 48–56.

Archibald, D.A. and Newman, F.M. (1988) *Beyond Standardized Testing: Assessing Authentic Academic Achievement in Secondary Schools*. Washington, DC: National Association of Secondary Principals.

ASE (Association for Science Education) (2018) Best Practice Guidance, viewed 16 March 2020, from: www.ase.org.uk/bestpractice

ASE (undated) School Science Review, viewed 22 January 2020, from: www.ase.org.uk/resources/school-science-review

Awaya, A., McEwan, H., Heyler, D., Linsky, S., Lum, D. and Wakukawa, P. (2003) 'Mentoring as a journey', *Teaching and Teacher Education*, *19* (1), pp. 45–56.

Bambrick-Santoyo, P. (2018) *Leverage Leadership 2.0. A Practical Guide to Building Exceptional Schools*. San Francisco, CA: Jossey-Bass.

Bartlett, J. (2016) *Outstanding Differentiation for Learning in the Classroom*. London: Routledge.

310   *References*

Bassett, S., Bowler, M. and Newton, A. (2019) 'Supporting beginning physical education teachers to deliver and evaluate their lessons', in Capel, S. and Lawrence, J. (eds), *Mentoring Physical Education Teachers in the Secondary School*. London and New York: Routledge, pp. 169-182.

Baumert, J., Kunter, M., Blum, W., Brunner, M., Voss, T., Jordan, A., Klusmann, U., Krauss, S., Neubrand, M. and Tsai, Y. (2010) 'Teachers' mathematical knowledge, cognitive activation in the classroom, and student progress', *American Educational Research Journal*, *47* (1), pp. 133-180.

Beauchamp, C. and Thomas, L. (2009) 'Understanding teacher identity: An overview of issues in the literature and implications for teacher education', *Cambridge Journal of Education*, *39* (2), pp. 175-189.

Berry, A., Friedrichsen, P.J. and Loughran, J. (eds) (2015) *Re-Examining Pedagogical Content Knowledge in Science Education*. New York and London: Routledge.

Besse, C. and Vogelsang, L. (2018) 'The WRAP: An alternative to Sandwich feedback in clinical nursing education', *The Journal of Nursing Education*, *57* (9), pp. 570-570.

Biesta, G.J.J. (2014) *The Beautiful Risk of Education*. Boulder, CO: Paradigm Publishers.

Binney, J., Barrett, D., Green, S., Pocknell, L. and Smart, W. (2019) 'How to mentor beginning physical education teachers through the lesson planning process', in Capel, S. and Lawrence, J. (eds), *Mentoring Physical Education Teachers in the Secondary School*. London and New York: Routledge, pp. 151-168.

Bjork, E.L. and Bjork, R.A. (2011) 'Making things hard on yourself, but in a good way: Creating desirable difficulties to enhance learning', in Gernsbacher, M.A., Pew, R.W., Hough, L.M. and Pomerantz, J.R. (eds), *Psychology and the Real World: Essays Illustrating Fundamental Contributions to Society*. New York: Worth Publishers, pp. 56-64.

Bjork, R.A. (1994) 'Memory and metamemory considerations in the training of human beings', in Metcalfe, J. and Shimamura, A. (eds), *Metacognition: Knowing about Knowing*. Cambridge, MA: MIT Press, pp. 185-205.

Black, A., Lawson, H. and Norwich, B. (2018) 'Lesson planning for diversity', *Journal of Research in Special Educational Needs*, *19* (2), pp. 115-125, doi: https://doi.org/10.1111/1471-3802.12433

Black, P. and Harrison, C. (2001) 'Self-and peer-assessment and taking responsibility: The science student's role in formative assessment', *School Science Review*, *83* (302), pp. 43-50.

Black, P., Harrison, C. and Lee, C. (2003) *Assessment for Learning: Putting It into Practice*. Maidenhead, England: McGraw-Hill Education.

Black, P., Harrison, C., Lee, C., Marshall, B. and Wiliam, D. (2004) 'Working inside the black box: Assessment for learning in the classroom', *Phi Delta Kappan*, *86* (1), pp. 8-21.

Black, P.J. and Harrison, C. (2006) *Science inside the Black Box: Assessment for Learning in the Science Classroom*. London: Kings College/GL Assessment Limited.

Black, P.J. and Wiliam, D. (2006) *Inside the Black Box: Raising Standards through Classroom Assessment*. London: NferNelson.

Blair, R. and Beaumont, L. (2020, in press) 'Designing teaching approaches to align with intended learning in physical education', in Capel, S., Cliffe, J. and Lawrence, J. (eds), *Learning to Teach Physical Education in the Secondary School: A Companion to School Experience*. Abingdon: Routledge.

Bolton, G. and Delderfield, R. (2018) *Reflective Practice: Writing and Professional Development*. London: Sage.

Bozeman, B. and Feeney, M. (2007) 'Toward a useful theory of mentoring; A conceptual analysis and critique', *Administration and Society*, *39* (6), pp. 1-32.

Bradley-Levine, J., Lee, J.S. and Mosier, G. (2016) 'Teacher mentoring as a community effort', *School Science and Mathematics 116* (2), pp. 71-82.

References 311

Bransford, J.D., Brown, A.L. and Cocking, R.R. (2000) *How People Learn: Brain, Mind, Experience and School*. Washington, DC: National Academy Press.

Brickhouse, N.W. (2007) 'Scientific Literates: What do they do? Who are they?', in: *Proceedings of the Linnaeus Tercentenary Symposium Promoting Scientific Literacy: Science Education Research in Transaction*, Uppsala University, Uppsala, Sweden, May 28-29, 2007, pp. 90-94, viewed 10 December 2019, from: https://eprints.qut.edu.au/12883/1/Linnaeus_Tercentenary_Symposium.pdf#page=88

Broadfoot, P. and Black, P. (2004) 'Redefining assessment? The first ten years of assessment in education', *Assessment in Education: Principles, Policy & Practice*, 11 (1), pp. 7-26.

Broadfoot, P., Daugherty, R., Gardner, J., Gipps, C., Harlen, W., James, M. and Stobart, G. (1999) *Assessment for Learning: Beyond the Black Box*. England: Nuffield Foundation and University of Cambridge.

Brookfield, S.D. (1995) *Becoming a Critically Reflective Teacher*. San Francisco, CA: Jossey Bass.

Brookfield, S.D. (2017) *Becoming a Critically Reflective Teacher*. 2nd edn. San Francisco, CA: Jossey Bass.

Brown, S.W. and Grant, A.M. (2010) 'From GROW to GROUP: Theoretical issues and a practical model for group coaching in organisations', *Coaching: An International Journal of Theory, Research and Practice*, 3 (1), pp. 30-45.

Bruner, J.S. (1960) *The Process of Education*. Cambridge, MA: Harvard University Press.

Bryce, N., Wilmes, S.E.D. and Bellino, M. (2016) 'Inquiry identity and science teacher professional development', *Cultural Studies of Science Education*, 11 (2), pp. 235-251.

Bryson, B. (2004) *A Short History of Nearly Everything*. London: Black Swan.

Bucat, R. (2005) 'Implications of chemistry education research for teaching practice: Pedagogical content knowledge as a way forward', *Chemical Education International*, 6 (1), pp. 1-2.

Bullough, A. and Booth, J. (2013) 'Science for all', *Education in Science*, 251, pp. 12-13.

Bullough, R.V. (2008) *Counternarratives: Studies of Teacher Education and Becoming and Being a Teacher*. New York: State University of New York Press.

Bullough, R.V. and Draper, R.J. (2004) 'Making sense of a failed triad', *Journal of Teacher Education*, 55 (5), pp. 407-420.

Butler, R. (1988) 'Enhancing and undermining intrinsic motivation: The effects of task-involving and ego-involving evaluation on interest and performance', *British Journal of Educational Psychology*, 58 (1), pp. 1-14.

Capel, S., Lawrence, J., Leask, M. and Younie, S. (eds) (2019a) *Surviving and Thriving in the Secondary School: The NQT's Essential Companion*. London: Routledge.

Capel, S., Leask, M., Turner, T. and Heilbronn, R. (eds) (2004) *Starting to Teach in the Secondary School*. London: Routledge, https://doi.org/10.4324/9780203338940

Capel, S., Leask, M. and Turner, T. (2010) *Readings for Learning to Teach in the Secondary School: A Companion to M Level Study*. London: Routledge.

Capel, S., Leask, M. and Younie, S. (eds) (2019b) *Learning to Teach in the Secondary School: A Companion to School Experience*. 8th edn. Abingdon: Routledge.

Carter, A. (2015) *Carter Review of Initial Teacher Training (ITT)*. London: Department for Education (DfE). Viewed 17 January 2020, from: https://assets.publishing.service.gov.uk/government/uploads/system/uploads/attachment_data/file/399957/Carter_Review.pdf

CBI (Confederation of British Industry) (2012) *Learning to Grow: What Employers Need from Education and Skills*. Education and Skills Survey 2012. London: CBI.

CCT (The Chartered College for Teaching) (2012) *The Charted College of Teaching (CCT)*, London: College of Teaching Limited, viewed 19 January 2020, from: https://chartered.college

312 *References*

Cepeda, N.J., Vul, E., Rohrer, D., Wixted, J.T. and Pashler, H. (2008) 'Spacing effects in learning: A temporal ridgeline of optimal retention', *Psychological Science, 19* (11), pp. 1095-1102.

Chandler-Grevatt, A. (2018) *How to Assess Your Students: Making Assessment Work for You.* Oxford: Oxford University Press.

Cheminais, R. (2015) *SEN for Qualified and Trainee Teachers.* 3rd edn. Abingdon, Oxon: Routledge.

Child, A. and Merrill, S. (2005) *Developing the Secondary School Mentor: A Case Study Approach.* Exeter: Learning Matters.

Cho, C.S., Ramanan, R.A. and Feldman, M.D. (2011) 'Defining the ideal qualities of mentorship: A qualitative analysis of the characteristics of outstanding mentors', *The American Journal of Medicine, 124* (5), pp. 453-458.

Chu, Y. (2019) 'Mentor teacher professional identity development in a year-long teacher residency', *Mentoring & Tutoring: Partnership in Learning, 27* (3), pp. 251-271.

CIPD (Chartered Institute of Personnel and Development) (2012) Coaching and mentoring fact sheet, viewed 25 January 2018, from: www.cipd.ae/knowledge/factsheets/coaching-mentoring

Clarke, A., Triggs, V. and Nielsen, W. (2014) 'Cooperating teacher participation in teacher education: A review of the literature', *Review of Educational Research, 84* (2), pp. 163-202.

CLEAPSS (2019) Student safety sheets: Fieldwork including any science work outside the laboratory, CLEAPSS, viewed 16 March 2020, from: http://science.cleapss.org.uk/Resource/SSS075-Fieldwork.pdf

Clutterbuck, D. (2004) *Everyone Needs a Mentor: Fostering Talent in Your Organisation.* 4th edn. London: Chartered Institute of Personnel and Development (CIPD).

Coe, R., Aloisi, C., Higgins, S. and Major, L. (2014) *What Makes Great Teaching? Review of the Underpinning Research.* London: Sutton Trust. Viewed 19 November 2018, from: http://dro.dur.ac.uk/13747/1/13747.pdf?DDD45+DDD29+DDO128+ded4ss+d700tmt

Cordingley, P., Higgins, S., Greany, T., Buckler, N., Coles-Jordan, D., Crisp, B., Saunders, L. and Coe, R. (2015) *Developing Great Teaching: Lessons from the International Reviews into Effective Professional Development.* London: Teacher Development Trust.

Costa, A.L. and Kallick, B. (eds) (2000) *Integrating & Sustaining Habits of Mind. A Developmental Series. Book 4.* Alexandria, VA: Association for Supervision and Curriculum Development.

Crawford, B.A. (2007) 'Learning to teach science as inquiry in the rough and tumble of practice', *Journal of Research in Science Teaching, 44* (4), pp. 613-642.

CUREE (Centre for the Use of Research and Evidence in Education) (2005) National framework for mentoring and coaching, viewed 25 January 2018, from: www.curee.co.uk/files/publication/1219313968/mentoring_and_coaching_national_framework.pdf

Daloz, L.A. (2012) *Mentor: Guiding the Journey of Adult Learners.* New York: Wiley.

Davis, B. and Sumara, D. (2009) 'Complexity as a theory of education', *TCI (Transnational Curriculum Inquiry), 5* (2), pp. 33-44.

Davis, J.S. and Fantozzi, V.B. (2016) 'What do student teachers want in mentor teachers?: Desired, expected, possible, and emerging roles', *Mentoring & Tutoring: Partnership in Learning, 24* (3), pp. 250-266.

Davis, P., Florian, L. and Ainscow, M. (2004) *Teaching Strategies and Approaches for Pupils with Special Educational Needs: A Scoping Study.* Nottingham: DfES Publications.

Denby, D. (2018) Making measurements, Royal Society of Chemistry (RSC), viewed 21 February 2020, from: https://edu.rsc.org/cpd/making-measurements/3009329.article

Department of Education, University of York (2018) Developing diagnostic assessment, Department of Education, University of York, viewed 1 December 2018, from: www.york.ac.uk/education/research/uyseg/projects/developingdiagnosticassessments/

Dewey, J. (1933) *How We Think Buffalo.* New York: Prometheus Books.

Dewey, J. (1934) 'The supreme intellectual obligation', *Science, 79* (2046), pp. 240-243.

Dewey, J. (1938) *Experience and Education*. New York: Free Press.

DfE (Department for Education) (2011) Teachers' Standards Guidance for school leaders, school staff and governing bodies, DfE, viewed 11 December 2019, from: https://assets.publishing.service.gov.uk/government/uploads/system/uploads/attachment_data/file/665520/Teachers__Standards.pdf

DfE (2013) Science programmes of study: Key stage 3 National curriculum in England, DfE, viewed 2 January 2020, from: https://assets.publishing.service.gov.uk/government/uploads/system/uploads/attachment_data/file/335174/SECONDARY_national_curriculum_-_Science_220714.pdf

DfE (2014) Science programmes of study: key stage 4 National curriculum in England, DfE, viewed 20 January 2020, from: https://assets.publishing.service.gov.uk/government/uploads/system/uploads/attachment_data/file/381380/Science_KS4_PoS_7_November_2014.pdf

DfE (2015) National curriculum in England: Science programmes of study, DfE, viewed 19 January 2020, from: https://dera.ioe.ac.uk/22953/1/National%20curriculum%20in%20England%20science%20programmes%20of%20study%20-%20GOV_UK.pdf

DfE (2016a) *A Framework of Core Content for Initial Teacher Training (ITT)*. London: Crown. Viewed 19 April 2020, from: https://assets.publishing.service.gov.uk/government/uploads/system/uploads/attachment_data/file/536890/Framework_Report_11_July_2016_Final.pdf

DfE (2016b) *National Standards for School-Based Initial Teacher Training (ITT) Mentors*. London: DfE. Viewed 19 April 2020, from: https://assets.publishing.service.gov.uk/government/uploads/system/uploads/attachment_data/file/536891/Mentor_standards_report_Final.pdf

DfE (2016c) Specialist and non-specialist' teaching in England: Extent and impact on pupil outcomes, DfE, viewed 19 November 2018, from: https://assets.publishing.service.gov.uk/government/uploads/system/uploads/attachment_data/file/578350/SubjectSpecialism_Report.pdf

DfE (2016d) *Standard for Teachers' Professional Development*. London: Crown. Viewed 19 April 2020, from: https://assets.publishing.service.gov.uk/government/uploads/system/uploads/attachment_data/file/537031/160712_-_PD_Expert_Group_Guidance.pdf

DfE (2018a) Health and safety on educational visits, DfE, viewed 16 March 2020, from: www.gov.uk/government/publications/health-and-safety-on-educational-visits

DfE (2018b) Respectful school communities self-review and signposting tool, DfE, viewed 20 December 2019, from: HL11980_Respectful_School_Communities_publication_attachment.pdf

DfE (Department for Education) and DoH (Department of Health) (2015) Special educational needs and disability code of practice: 0 to 25 years, DfE and DoH, viewed 19 April 2020, from: https://assets.publishing.service.gov.uk/government/uploads/system/uploads/attachment_data/file/398815/SEND_Code_of_Practice_January_2015.pdf

DfENI (Department of Education Northern Ireland) (2015) The career entry profile, DfE-NI, viewed 9 January 2020, from: www.education-ni.gov.uk/publications/career-entry-profile-cep

DfES (Department for Education and Skills) (2004) *Pedagogy and Practice: Teaching and Learning in Secondary School, Unit 7: Questioning*. London: DfES. Viewed 1 December 2018, from: http://dera.ioe.ac.uk/5671/8/cea27fdd968639560cb245efafd9c2ff_Redacted.pdf

diSessa, A.A. (2014) 'A history of conceptual change research: Threads and fault lines', in Sawyer, R. (ed), *The Cambridge Handbook of The Learning Sciences: Cambridge Handbooks in Psychology*. Cambridge: Cambridge University Press, pp. 88-108.

Driscoll, L.G., Parkes, K.A., Tilley-Lubbs, G.A., Brill, J.M. and Pitts Bannister, V.R. (2009) 'Navigating the lonely sea: Peer mentoring and collaboration among aspiring women scholars', *Mentoring & Tutoring: Partnership in Learning*, *17* (1), pp. 5-21.

314 *References*

Driver, R. (1983) *The Pupil as Scientist?*. Milton Keynes: Open University Press.

Driver, R., Squires, A., Rushworth, P. and Wood-Robinson, V. (1994) *Making Sense of Secondary Science: Research into Children's Ideas*. London: Routledge.

Duschl, R.A., Schweingruber, H.A. and Shouse, A.W. (2007) 'Taking science to school: Learning and teaching science in grades K-8', *National Academies Press, 49* (2), pp. 163–166.

Eames, C., Williams, J., Hume, A. and Lockley, J. (2011) *CoRe: A Way to Build Pedagogical Content Knowledge for Beginning Teachers*. Wellington: Teaching and Learning Research Initiative. Viewed 27 September 2019, from: www.tlri.org.nz/sites/default/files/projects/9289_summaryreport.pdf

Eberlein, T., Kampmeier, J., Minderhout, V., Moog, R.S., Platt, T., Varma-Nelson, P. and White, H.B. (2008) 'Pedagogies of engagement in science', *Biochemistry and Molecular Biology Education, 36* (4), pp. 262–273.

Education Endowment Foundation (2018) Improving secondary science: Seven recommendations for improving science in secondary schools, Education Endowment Foundation, viewed 19 April 2020, from: https://educationendowmentfoundation.org.uk/tools/guidance-reports/improving-secondary-science/

Education Endowment Foundation (2020) Special educational needs in mainstream schools, viewed 28 May 2020, from: https://educationendowmentfoundation.org.uk/tools/guidance-reports/special-educational-needs-disabilities/

Education Scotland (2018) Self-evaluation framework for Initial Teacher Education, Education Scotland, viewed 27 December 2019, from: https://education.gov.scot/improvement/Documents/SelfEvalFrameworkforITEDec18.pdf

Education Scotland (2020) The national model of professional learning, Education Scotland, viewed 19 April 2020, from: https://professionallearning.education.gov.scot/explore/the-national-model-of-professional-learning/

Edwards, F. (2017) 'A rubric to track the development of secondary pre-service and novice teachers' summative assessment literacy', *Assessment in Education: Principles, Policy & Practice, 24* (2), pp. 205–227.

Eglington, L.G. and Kang, S.H. (2017) 'Interleaved presentation benefits science category learning', *Journal of Applied Research in Memory and Cognition, 6* (4), pp. 475–485.

Ehrich, L.C., Hansford, B. and Tennent, L. (2004) 'Formal mentoring programs in education and other professions: A review of the literature', *Educational Administration Quarterly, 40* (4), pp. 518–540.

Ethel, R.G. and McMeniman, M.M. (2000) 'Unlocking the knowledge in action of an expert practitioner', *Journal of Teacher Education, 51* (2), pp. 87–101.

Evens, M., Elen, J. and Depaepe, F. (2015) 'Developing pedagogical content knowledge: Lessons learned from intervention studies', *Education Research International, 2015*, pp. 1–23, doi: https://doi.org/10.1155/2015/790417

EWC (Education Workforce Council in Wales) (2018) Professional learning passport enhancements: September 2018, EWC, viewed 10 April 2020, from: www.ewc.wales/site/index.php/en/professional-development/professional-learning-passport.html

Facer, K. and Manchester, H. (2012) *Mapping Learning Lives: Final Report*. Manchester: Education and Social Research Institute, Manchester Metropolitan University.

Farrell, J.J., Moog, R.S. and Spencer, J.N. (1999) 'A guided inquiry general chemistry course', *Journal of Chemical Education, 76* (4), pp. 570–574.

Fautley, M. and Savage, J. (2013) *Lesson Planning for Effective Learning*. Maidenhead: McGraw-Hill Education.

Feez, S. and Quinn, F. (2017) 'Teaching the distinctive language of science: An integrated and scaffolded approach for pre-service teachers', *Teaching and Teacher Education, 65*, pp. 192–204, doi: 10.1016/j.tate.2017.03.019.2016.

References   315

Feynman, R. (1985) *'Surely You're Joking, Mr. Feynman'; Adventures of a Curious Character.* New York: W.W. Norton.

Firth, J. (2017) 'Experts in learning', in Rycroft-Smith, L. and Dutaut, J.L. (eds), *Flip the System UK: A Teachers' Manifesto.* Abingdon, Oxon: Routledge, pp. 20–28.

Firth, J. (2018) *How to Learn: Effective Study and Revision Methods for Any Course.* Glasgow: Arboretum Books.

Fitzgerald, M., Danaia, L. and McKinnon, D.H. (2019) 'Barriers inhibiting inquiry-based science teaching and potential solutions: Perceptions of positively inclined early adopters', *Research in Science Education, 49* (2), pp. 543–566.

French, R.B. (1960) *The Bases of Social Power.* London: Group Dynamics: Research and Theory.

Furlong, J. and Maynard, T. (1995) *Mentoring Student Teachers: The Growth of Professional Knowledge.* London and New York: Routledge.

Gareis, C.R. and Grant, L.W. (2014) 'The efficacy of training cooperating teachers', *Teaching and Teacher Education, 39* (10), pp. 77–88.

Gee, J.P. (2000) 'Identity as an analytic lens for research in education', *Review of Research in Education, 25* (1), pp. 99–125.

Gilchrist, G. (2018) *Practitioner Enquiry: Professional Development with Impact for Teachers, Schools and Systems.* Abingdon, Oxon: Routledge.

Godec, S., King, H. and Archer, L. (2017) *The Science Capital Teaching Approach: Engaging Students with Science, Promoting Social Justice.* London: University College London. Date viewed 15 January 2020, from: https://discovery.ucl.ac.uk/id/eprint/10080166/1/the-science-capital-teaching-approach-pack-for-teachers.pdf

Goldacre, B. (2009) *Bad Science: Quacks, Hacks, and Big Pharma Flacks.* London: Fourth Estate.

Golder, G., Arthur, J., Keyworth, A. and Stevens, J. (2019) 'Supporting beginning physical education teachers to deliver and evaluate their lessons', in Capel, S. and Lawrence, J. (eds) *Mentoring Physical Education Teachers in the Secondary School.* London and New York: Routledge, pp. 221–235.

Goleman, D. (2008) *Working with Emotional Intelligence.* London: Bloomsbury.

Gotwals, A.W. and Birmingham, D. (2016) 'Eliciting, identifying, interpreting, and responding to students' ideas: Teacher candidates' growth in formative assessment practices', *Research in Science Education, 46* (3), pp. 365–388.

Gourlay, H. (2019) 'Supporting the development of preservice science teachers' reflectivity using action learning and the diagnostic teaching cycle: A case study', EdD thesis, University of East Anglia, School of Education and Lifelong Learning, Norwich, viewed 19 April 2020, from: https://ueaeprints.uea.ac.uk/id/eprint/74469/

Gray, M.A. and Smith, L.N. (2000) 'The qualities of an effective mentor from the student nurse's perspective: Findings from a longitudinal qualitative study', *Journal of Advanced Nursing, 32* (6), pp. 1542–1549.

Griffiths, V. (2000) 'The reflective dimension in teacher education', *International Journal of Educational Research, 33* (5), pp. 539–555.

GTCNI (General Teaching Council for Northern Ireland) (2018a) Professional competencies, GTCNI, viewed 27 December 2019, from: https://gtcni.org.uk/professional-space/professional-competence

GTCNI (2018b) Teaching: The reflective profession, GTCNI, viewed 16 March 2020, from: https://gtcni.org.uk/professional-space/professional-competence/teaching-the-reflective-profession

GTCS (General Teaching Council for Scotland) (2012) The Standards for Registration: Mandatory requirements for Registration with the General Teaching Council for Scotland,

316 *References*

GTCS, viewed 11 December 2019, from: www.gtcs.org.uk/web/FILES/the-standards/standards-for-registration-1212.pdf

Hacking, I. (1983) *Representing and Intervening: Introductory Topics in the Philosophy of Natural Science*. Cambridge: Cambridge University Press.

Haggard, D.L., Dougherty, T.W., Turban, D.B. and Wilbanks, J.E. (2011) 'Who is a mentor? A review of evolving definitions and implications for research', *Journal of Management*, *37* (1), pp. 280-304.

Hagger, H., McIntyre, D., & Wilkin, M. (Eds) (2013) *Mentoring: Perspectives on School-based Teacher Education*. London: Routledge.

Hall, K., Murphy, P. and Soler, J. (2008) *Pedagogy and Practice: Culture and Identities*. London: SAGE Publications Ltd.

Hand, B. and Keys, C. (1999) 'Inquiry investigation', *Science Teacher*, 66 (4), pp. 27-29.

Hanover Research (2014) *Encouraging Students to Embrace STEM Programs*. Washington, DC: Hanover Research.

Hanson, S.G. (2010) 'What mentors learn about teaching', *Educational Leadership*, *67* (8), pp. 76-80.

Hanson, S.G. (2017) 'What mentors learn about teaching?' *Educational Leadership*, 67 (8), 76-80

Harri-Augustein, S. and Thomas, L. (1991) *Learning Conversations*. London: Routledge.

Harrison, C. (2013) 'Testing and exams', Seminar given as part of Science PGCE Programme, King's College London, London, 1 December.

Harrison, C. (undated) Oranges: Will they sink or float? What's happening?, Strategies for Assessment of Inquiry Learning in Science, viewed 23 November 2019, from: www.sails-project.eu/units/floating-orange.html

Harrison, J., Dymoke, S. and Pell, T. (2006) 'Mentoring beginning teachers in secondary schools: An analysis of practice', *Teaching and Teacher Education*, *22* (8), pp. 1055-1067.

Hattie, J. (2011) *Visible Learning for Teachers*. London: Routledge.

Helmenstine, A.M. (2019) How to read a meniscus in chemistry, ThoughtCo, viewed 20 December 2019, from: www.thoughtco.com/how-to-read-a-meniscus-606055

Henderson, B. (1970) *The Product Portfolio*. Boston, MA: Boston Consulting Group Publisher.

Hennissen, P., Crasborn, F., Brouwer, N., Korthagen, F. and Bergen, T. (2008) 'Mapping mentor teachers' roles in mentoring dialogues', *Educational Research Review*, *3* (2), pp. 168-186.

Hennissen, P., Crasborn, F., Brouwer, N., Korthagen, F. and Bergen, T. (2011) 'Clarifying pre-service teacher perceptions of mentor teachers' developing use of mentoring skills', *Teaching and Teacher Education*, *27* (6), pp. 1049-1058.

Higgins, M.C. and Thomas, D.A. (2001) 'Constellations and careers: Toward understanding the effects of multiple developmental relationships', *Journal of Organizational Behavior*, *22* (3), pp. 223-247.

Hobson, A.J. (2016) 'Judgementoring and how to avert it: Introducing ONSIDE Mentoring for beginning teachers', *International Journal of Mentoring and Coaching in Education*, *5* (2), pp. 87-110.

Hobson, A.J., Ashby, P., Malderez, A. and Tomlinson, P.D. (2009) 'Mentoring beginning teachers: What we know and what we don't', *Teacher and Teacher Education*, *25* (1), pp. 207-216.

Hodson, D. (2009) *Towards Scientific Literacy: A Teachers' Guide to the History, Philosophy and Sociology of Science*. Rotterdam, the Netherlands: Sense Publishers.

Horvath, J., Lodge, J. and Hattie, J. (2016) *From the Laboratory to the Classroom: Translating Science of Learning for Teachers*. Abingdon, Oxon: Routledge.

House of Lords (2012) *Higher Education in Science, Technology, Engineering and Mathematics (STEM) Subjects*. London: The Stationery Office Limited.

HSE (The Health and Safety Executive) (2011) School trips and outdoor learning activities: Tackling the health and safety myths, HSE, viewed 16 March 2020, from: www.hse.gov.uk/services/education/school-trips.pdf

Hudson, P. (2016a) 'Forming the mentor-mentee relationship', *Mentoring & Tutoring: Partnership in Learning*, 24 (1), pp. 30-43.

Hudson, P. (2016b) 'Identifying mentors' observations for providing feedback', *Teachers and Teaching*, 22 (2), pp. 219-234.

Hudson, P. (2004) 'Specific mentoring: A theory and model for developing primary science teacher practices', *European Journal of Teacher Education*, 27 (2), pp. 139-146.

Hudson, P. (2005) 'Identifying mentoring practices for developing effective primary science teaching', *International Journal of Science Education*, 27 (14), pp. 1723-1739.

Huxley, T.H. (1882) 'Science and culture', in T. H. Huxley, *Science and Culture, and Other Essays*. US: D Appleton & Company, pp. 7-30, doi: https://doi.org/10.1037/12819-001

Ingersoll, R.M. (2003) 'Turnover and shortages among science and mathematics teachers in the United States', in Rhoton, J. and Bowers, P. (eds), *Science Teacher Retention: Mentoring and Renewal*. Arlington, VA: NSTA Press, pp. 1-12.

IoE (Institute of Education) (2020) ASPIRES 2: Longitudinal research project studying young people's science and career aspirations, IoE, viewed 2 April 2020, from: www.ucl.ac.uk/ioe/departments-and-centres/departments/education-practice-and-society/aspires-2

Izadinia, M. (2016) 'Student teachers' and mentor teachers' perceptions and expectations of a mentoring relationship: Do they match or clash?', *Professional Development in Education*, 42 (3), pp. 387-402.

Jian Wang, J., Odell, S.J. and Schwille, S.A. (2008) 'Effects of teacher induction on beginning teachers' teaching', *Journal of Teacher Education*, 59 (2), pp. 132-152.

Johnson, W.B. and Ridley, C.R. (2018) *The Elements of Mentoring: 75 Practices of Master Mentors*. 3rd edn. New York: Macmillan USA.

Kang, D.Y. and Martin, S.N. (2018) 'Improving learning opportunities for special education needs (SEN) students by engaging pre-service science teachers in an informal experiential learning course', *Asia Pacific Journal of Education*, 38 (3), pp. 319-347.

Katz, L.G. (1995) *Talks with Teachers of Young Children: A Collection*. Norwood, NJ: Ablex Publishing.

Kell, E. (2018) *How to Survive in Teaching: Without Imploding, Exploding or Walking Away*. London: Bloomsbury Publishing PLC.

Kind, V. (2009) 'Pedagogical Content Knowledge in science education: Potential and perspectives for progress', *Studies in Science Education*, 45 (2), pp. 169-204.

Kind, V. and Taber, K. (2005) *Teaching School Subjects 11-19: Science*. Abingdon: Routledge.

Knight, O. and Benson, D. (2014) *Creating Outstanding Classrooms: A Whole School Approach*. London and New York: Routledge.

Kochan, F.K. and Trimble, S.B. (2000) 'From mentoring to co-mentoring: Establishing collaborative relationships', *Theory into Practice*, 39 (1), pp. 20-28.

Kolb, D. (1984) *Experiential Learning: Experience as the Source of Learning and Development*. Englewood Cliffs, NJ: Prentice Hall.

Kornell, N. and Bjork, R.A. (2008) 'Learning concepts and categories: Is spacing the "enemy of induction"?', *Psychological Science*, 19 (6), pp. 585-592.

Korthagen, F.A.J. (2004) 'In search of the essence of a good teacher: Towards a more holistic approach in teacher education', *Teaching and Teacher Education*, 20 (1), pp. 77-97, doi: 10.1016/j.tate.2003.10.002.

Kroll, J. (2016) 'What is meant by the term group mentoring?', *Mentoring & Tutoring: Partnership in Learning*, 24 (1), pp. 44-58.

Kumpulainen, K. and Wray, D. (eds) (2002) *Classroom Interaction and Social Learning: From Theory to Practice*. London and New York: Psychology Press.

Kyriacou, C. (2018) *Essential Teaching Skills*. 5th edn. Oxford: Oxford University.

Laminack, L. (2017) 'Mentors and mentor texts: What, why, and how?', *The Reading Teacher*, 70 (6), pp. 753-755.

318 *References*

Langdon, F.J. (2014) 'Evidence of mentor learning and development: An analysis of New Zealand mentor/mentee professional conversations', *Professional Development in Education, 40* (1), pp. 36–55.

Laudan, L. (1981) *Science and Hypothesis*. Dordrecht and Holland: Reidel.

Lave, J. (1991) 'Situating learning in communities of practice', in Resnick, L.B., Levine, J.M. and Teasley, S.D. (eds), *Perspectives on Socially Shared Cognition*. Washington, DC: American Psychological Association, pp. 63–82.

Lave, J. and Wenger, E. (1991) *Situated Learning: Legitimate Peripheral Participation*. Cambridge: Cambridge University Press.

Lawson, H., Norwich, B. and Nash, T. (2013) 'What trainees in England learn about teaching pupils with special educational needs/disabilities in their school-based work: The contribution of planned activities in one-year initial training courses', *European Journal of Special Needs Education, 28* (2), pp. 136–155.

Le Cornu, R. (2010) 'Changing roles, relationships and responsibilities in changing times', *Asia-Pacific Journal of Teacher Education, 38* (3), pp. 195–206.

Leahy, S., Lyon, C., Thompson, M. and Wiliam, D. (2005) 'Classroom assessment: Minute by minute, day by day', *Assessment to Promote Learning, 63* (3), pp. 19–24.

Light, D. (2017) Stretch and challenge in your classroom, SecEd, viewed 9 June 2019, from: www.sec-ed.co.uk/best-practice/stretch-and-challenge-in-your-classroom/

Lock, R., Salt, D. and Soares, A. (2011) Acquisition of science subject knowledge and pedagogy in initial teacher training, welcome trust, viewed 19 December 2018, from: https://wellcome.ac.uk/sites/default/files/wtvm053187_0.pdf

Lofthouse, R., Leat, D. and Towler, C. (2010) *Coaching for Teaching and Learning: A Practical Guide for Schools: Guidance Report*. Reading and Berkshire: CfBT Education Trust. Viewed 15 July 2019, from: www.nationalcollege.org.uk/coaching.

Loughran, J., Berry, M. and Mulhall, P. (2012) *Understanding and Developing Science Teachers' Pedagogical Content Knowledge*. 2nd edn. Rotterdam and Boston: Sense Publishers.

Luehmann, A.L. (2007) 'Identity development as a lens to science teacher preparation', *Science Education, 91* (5), pp. 822–839.

Luft, J.A. (2009) 'Beginning secondary science teachers in different induction programmes: The first year of teaching', *International Journal of Science Education, 31* (17), pp. 2355–2384.

Lyon, E.G. (2013) 'Learning to assess science in linguistically diverse classrooms: Tracking growth in secondary science preservice teachers' assessment expertise', *Science Education, 97* (3), pp. 442–467.

Malthouse, R. (2012) *Reflecting Blues. Perceptions of Policing Students in Relation to Reflective Practice and Associated Skills*. Saarbrucken: Lambert Academic Publishing.

Malthouse, R. and Roffey-Barentsen, J. (2014) 'Are science teachers immune to reflective practice?', in Watts, M. (ed), *Debates in Science Education*. Abingdon: Routledge, pp. 179–194.

Malthouse, R., Roffey-Barentsen, J. and Watts, M. (2014) 'Reflectivity, reflexivity and situated reflective practice', *Professional Development in Education, 40* (4), pp. 597–609.

Malthouse, R., Roffey-Barentsen, J. and Watts, M. (2015) 'Reflective questions, self-questioning and managing professionally situated practice', *Research in Education, 94* (1), pp. 71–87.

Mascolo, M.F. (2009) 'Beyond student-centered and teacher-centered pedagogy: Teaching and learning as guided participation', *Pedagogy and the Human Sciences, 1* (1), pp. 3–27.

Maynard, T. and Furlong, J. (1995) 'Learning to teach and models of mentoring', in Kerry, T. and Shelton-Mayes, A. (eds), *Issues in Mentoring*. London: Routledge, pp. 10–14.

McClune, B. and Jarman, R. (2012) 'Encouraging and equipping students to engage critically with science in the news: What can we learn from the literature?', *Studies in Science Education, 48* (1), pp. 1–49, doi: 10.1080/03057267.2012.655036

References 319

McDonald, L.Y.N. and Flint, A. (2011) 'Effective educative mentoring skills: A collaborative effort', *New Zealand Journal of Teachers' Work*, 8 (1), pp. 33-46.

McGinnis, J.R. (2002) 'Preparing prospective teachers to teach students with developmental delays in science: A moral perspective', in *Annual Meeting of the National Association for Research in Science Teaching*, New Orleans, LA, 6-10 April. Maryland Univ., College Park, Dept. of Curriculum and Instruction: ERIC (ED463969).

McIntosh, P. (2010) *Action Research and Reflective Practice, Creative and Visual Methods to Facilitate Reflection and Learning*. Abingdon: Routledge.

McIntyre, D. and Hagger, H. (1993) 'Teachers' expertise and models of mentoring', in McIntyre, D., Hagger, H. and Wilkin, M. (eds), *Mentoring: Perspectives on School-Based Teacher Education*. London: Kogan Page, pp. 86-102.

McIntyre, J. and Hobson, A.J. (2016) 'Supporting beginner teacher identity development: External mentors and the third space', *Research Papers in Education*, 31(2), pp. 133-158, doi: 10.1080/02671522.2015.1015438.

McNally, J.C. (2016) 'Learning from one's own teaching: New science teachers analyzing their practice through classroom observation cycles', *Journal of Research in Science Teaching*, 53 (3), pp. 473-501.

Melville, W. and Bartley, A. (2010) 'Mentoring and community: Inquiry as stance and science as inquiry', *International Journal of Science Education*, 32 (6), pp. 807-828.

Merrill, M.D. (2002) 'First principles of instructional design', *Educational Technology Research and Development*, 50 (3), pp. 43-59.

Millar, R. (2004) 'The role of practical work in the teaching and learning of science'. *High school science laboratories: Role and vision*. The University of York Department of Education, October 2004. Washington, DC: National Academy of Sciences.

Millar, R. and Abrahams, I. (2009) 'Practical work: Making it more effective', *School Science Review*, 91 (334), pp. 59-64.

Ministry of Education and Research (2010) *Differentaited Primary and Lower Secondary Teacher Education Programme for Years 1-7 and 5-10*. Oslo: Ministry of Education and Research.

Monk, M. and Dillon, J. (eds) (1995) *Learning to Teach Science: Activities for Student Teachers and Mentors*. London and Washington, DC: Routledge Falmer.

Montgomery, B.L. (2017, April-June) 'Mapping a mentoring roadmap and developing a supportive network for strategic career advancement', *SAGE Open*, 7 (2), pp. 1-3.

Moog, R.S. (2014) 'Process oriented guided inquiry learning', in McDaniel, M.A., Frey, R.F., Fitzpatrick, S.M. and Roediger, H.L. (eds), *Integrating Cognitive Science with Innovative Teaching in STEM Disciplines*. St. Louis, MO: Washington University Libraries, pp. 147-166.

Moog, R.S. and Spencer, J.N. (2008) *Process-Oriented Guided Inquiry Learning (POGIL)*. Washington, DC: American Chemical Society.

Morehead, K., Rhodes, M.G. and DeLozier, S. (2016) 'Instructor and student knowledge of study strategies', *Memory*, 24 (2), pp. 257-271.

Mosston, M. and Ashworth, S. (2002) *Teaching Physical Education*. 5th edn. San Francisco, CA: Pearson.

Moules, J., Horlock, J., Naylor, S. and Keogh, B. (2018) *Science Concept Cartoons Set 2*. England and Wales: Millgate House Education Ltd. Viewed 17 January 2020, from: www.millgatehouse.co.uk/product/science-concept-cartoons-set-2/

Muijs, D. and Reynolds, D. (2018) *Effective Teaching: Evidence and Practice*. 5th edn. London: SAGE.

National Academies of Sciences, Engineering, and Medicine (2019) *The Science of Effective Mentorship in STEMM*. Washington, DC: The National Academies Press. Viewed 20 January 2020, from: https://doi.org/10.17226/25568.

National Research Council (1996) *National Science Education Standards*. Washington, DC: National Academy Press.

320 *References*

NCTL (National College for Teaching and Leadership) (2012) Ofsted criteria for outstanding teaching. England: NCTL, viewed 25 November 2018, from: www.nationalcollege.org.uk/cm-mc-lds-resource-ofsted-criteria.pdf

NERIS Analytics Limited (2020) 16 personalities: Personality test, viewed 2 January 2020 from: www.16personalities.com

New Teacher Centre (2011) *NTC continuum of mentoring practice*. Santa Cruz: New Teacher Centre.

Newton, D.P. (2000) *Teaching for Understanding: What It Is and How to Do It*. London: Routledge.

Newton, D.P. (2008) *A Practical Guide to Teaching Science in the Secondary School*. Abingdon, Oxon and New York: Routledge.

Nuffield Foundation (undated) Practical work for learning, Nuffield Foundation, viewed 7 June 2019, from: www.nuffieldfoundation.org/practical-work-learning

O'Leary, M. (2016) *Reclaiming Lesson Observation*. Abingdon, Oxon: Routledge.

OECD (2012) CX3.1 special educational needs (SEN), OECD, viewed 19 April 2020, from: www.oecd.org/social/family/50325299.pdf

Ofqual (The Office for Qualifications and Examinations Regulation) (2015) GCSE subject level conditions and requirements for combined science, Ofqual, viewed 19 April 2020, from: https://assets.publishing.service.gov.uk/government/uploads/system/uploads/attachment_data/file/819655/gcse-subject-level-conditions-and-requirements-for-combined-science.pdf

Ofsted (2015) *The Common Inspection Framework: Education, Skills and Early Years*. London: Crown Copyright.

Ofsted (2019) *The Education Inspection Framework*. UK: Ofsted.

Ohio Department for Education (2015) Ohio standards for professional development. Ohio: Department for Education, viewed 25 January 2018, from: http://education.ohio.gov/Topics/Teaching/Professional-Development/Organizing-for-High-Quality-Professional-Development

Pajares, M.F. (1992). 'Teachers' beliefs and educational research: Cleaning up a messy construct', *Review of Educational Research*, *62* (3), pp. 307–332.

PCAST (U.S. President's Council of Advisors on Science and Technology) (2014) Report on education technology – Skills & jobs, PCAST, viewed 19 April 20, from: https://obamawhitehouse.archives.gov/sites/default/files/microsites/ostp/PCAST/PCAST_worforce_edIT_Oct-2014.pdf

Pedersen, J., Isozaki, T. and Hirano, T. (eds) (2017) *Model Science Teacher Preparation Programs: An International Comparison of What Works*. Charlotte, NC: Information Age Publishing.

Pedrosa de Jesus, M.H., Leite, S. and Watts, D.M. (2016) 'Question moments': A rolling programme of question-opportunities in classroom science', *Research in Science Education*, *46* (3), pp. 329–334.

Piaget, J. (1952) *The Origins of Intelligence in Children*. 2nd edn. New York: International Universities Press.

Piaget, J. (1971) *Biology and Knowledge*. Chicago, IL: Chicago University Press.

Piaget, J. (1973) *To Understand Is to Invent: The Future of Education*. New York: Grossman.

Piggott, A. (2002) 'Putting differentiation into practice in secondary science lessons', *School Science Review*, *83*, pp. 65–72.

POGIL (Process-Oriented Guided Inquiry Learning) (2019) The POGIL project, POGIL, viewed 20 January 2020, from: https://pogil.org/about-the-pogil-project

POGIL (undated) POGIL: High school implementation guide, POGIL, viewed 20 January 2020, from: https://pogil.org/uploads/attachments/cj5mtm1x501moekx4n3zhh6zu-pogil-high-school-imp-guide-for-web.pdf

Pollard, A. (2004) *Reflective Teaching in Schools*. 4th edn. London: Bloomsbury Publishing.

Price, B. (2004) 'Mentoring: Becoming a good mentor', *Nursing Standard, 19* (13), pp. 56–56

PSQM (Primary Science Quality Mark) (2016) Activity 5 Knowing about science in your school. University of Hertfordshire, PSQM, viewed 28 March 2019, from: www.psqm.org.uk/__data/assets/pdf_file/0011/85088/Activity-5-Knowing-about-science-in-your-school-Mar-16.pdf

QCAA (Queensland Curriculum & Assessment Authority) (2014) Why do the seasons change? Australian Curriculum Year 7 Science sample assessment, QCAA, viewed 28 March 2019, from: www.qcaa.qld.edu.au/downloads/p_10/ac_sa_sci_yr7_why_do_seasons_change.pdf

QCAA (2017) Year 10 standard elaborations – Australian curriculum: Science. England: QCDA, viewed 1 December 2018, from: www.qcaa.qld.edu.au/p-10/aciq/standards-elaborations/p-10-science

QCDA (Qualifications and Curriculum Development Authority) (2009) Assessing Pupils' Progress: Science assessment criteria. England: QCDA, viewed 1 December 2018, from: https://webarchive.nationalarchives.gov.uk/20110810020820/http://nsonline.org.uk/node/263985

Quigley, A., Muijs, D. and Stringer, E. (2018) *Metacognition and Self-Regulated Learning: Guidance Report*. London: Education Endowment Foundation, viewed 8 December 2018, from: https://dera.ioe.ac.uk//31617/1/EEF_Metacognition_and_self-regulated_learning.pdf

Qureshi, S., Bradley, K., Vishnumolakala, V.R., Treagust, D., Southam, D., Mocerino, M. and Ojeil, J. (2016) 'Educational reforms and implementation of student-centered active learning in science at secondary and university levels in Qatar', *Science Education International, 27* (3), pp. 437–456.

Ragins, B. (2016) 'From the ordinary to extraordinary: *High quality mentoring relationships at work*', *Organisational Dynamics, 45*, pp. 228–244.

Rawson, K.A. and Dunlosky, J. (2011) 'Optimizing schedules of retrieval practice for durable and efficient learning: How much is enough?', *Journal of Experimental Psychology: General, 140* (3), pp. 283–302.

Rennie, L., Stocklmayer, S. and Gilbert, J. (2019) *Supporting Self-Directed Learning in Science and Technology beyond the School Years*. New York: Routledge.

Rhodes, M.G. and Castel, A.D. (2008) 'Memory predictions are influenced by perceptual information: Evidence for metacognitive illusions', *Journal of Experimental Psychology: General, 137* (4), pp. 615–625.

Rizzo, K.L. and Taylor, J.C. (2016) 'Effects of inquiry-based instruction on science achievement for students with disabilities: An analysis of the literature', *Journal of Science Education for Students with Disabilities, 19* (1), p. 2.

Roediger III, H.L. and Karpicke, J.D. (2006) 'Test-enhanced learning: Taking memory tests improves long-term retention', *Psychological Science, 17* (3), pp. 249–255.

Roffey-Barentsen, J. and Malthouse, R. (2013) *Reflective Practice in Education and Training*. 2nd edn. London: Sage.

Rogoff, B. (1995) 'Observing sociocultural activity on three planes: Participatory appropriation, guided participation, and apprenticeship', in Wertsch, J.V., del Río, P. and Alvarez, A. (eds), *Learning in Doing: Social, Cognitive, and Computational Aspects*. Sociocultural Studies of Mind. Cambridge: Cambridge University Press, pp. 139–164.

Rohrer, D. (2015) 'Student instruction should be distributed over long time periods', *Educational Psychology Review, 27* (4), pp. 635–643.

Rohrer, D. and Pashler, H. (2010) 'Recent research on human learning challenges conventional instructional strategies', *Educational Researcher, 39* (5), pp. 406–412.

Rohrer, D. and Taylor, K. (2006) 'The effects of overlearning and distributed practice on the retention of mathematics knowledge', *Applied Cognitive Psychology, 20* (9), pp. 1209–1224.

322 *References*

Rowe, M.B. (1986) 'Wait time: Slowing down may be a way of speeding up!', *Journal of Teacher Education*, 37 (1), pp. 43–50.

Rowland, T., Huckstep, P. and Thwaites, A. (2005) 'Elementary teachers' mathematics subject knowledge: The knowledge quartet and the case of Naomi' *Journal of Mathematics Teacher Education*, 8 (3), pp. 255–281.

Rowland, T. Thwaites, A. and Jared, L. (2015) 'Triggers of contingency in mathematics teaching', *Research in Mathematics Education*, 17 (2), pp. 74–91.

Sachs, J. (2005) 'Teacher education and the development of professional identity: Learning to be a teacher', in Denicolo, P.M. and Kompf, M (eds), *Connecting Policy and Practice: Challenges for Teaching and Learning in Schools and Universities*. London: Routledge, pp. 5–21.

Sachs, J. (2016) 'Teacher professionalism: Why are we still talking about it?', *Teachers and Teaching*, 22 (4), pp. 413–425.

Salehjee, S. and Watts, D.M. (2019) 'Nudges into science: A study of science education interventions', British Educational Research Association (BERA), Manchester University, 10–12 September 2019. London: BERA.

Salehjee, S. and Watts, M. (2020) *Becoming Scientific*. Cambridge: Cambridge Scholars Publishing.

Savage, J. (2015) *Lesson Planning*. Abingdon: Routledge.

Schneider, R.M. and Plasman, K. (2011) 'Science teacher learning progressions: A review of science teachers' pedagogical content knowledge development', *Review of Educational Research*, 81 (4), pp. 530–565.

Schön, D.A. (1983) *The Reflective Practitioner: How Professionals Think in Action*. New York: Basic Books.

Schön, D. (1987) *Educating the Reflective Practitioner*. San Francisco, CA: Jossey-Bass.

Schwille, S.A. (2008) 'The professional practice of mentoring', *American Journal of Education*, 115 (1), pp. 139–167.

Sears, J. (2018) 'Collaborative working: The heart of good mentoring', in Wright, T. (ed), *How to Be a Great Mentor: Developing Outstanding Teachers*. 2nd edn. Abingdon: Oxon Routledge.

SERP (2020) The challenges of science text. Washington, DC: SERP, viewed 7 January 2020 from: www.serpinstitute.org/reading-science/challenges-of-science-text

Shabatura, J. (2013) Using Bloom's taxonomy to write effective learning objectives, TIPS, viewed 15 April 2020, from: https://tips.uark.edu/using-blooms-taxonomy/

Shaw, M. (2019) 'Active learning', in Capel, S., Leask, M. and Turner, T. (eds), *Learning to Teach in the Secondary School: A Companion to School Experience*. 8th edn. London and New York: Routledge, pp. 316–317.

Shea, K. and Greenwood, A. (2007) 'Mentoring new science teachers', *The Science Teacher*, 74 (5), pp. 30–35.

Sheffield Hallam University/Sheffield Institute for Education (undated) Science for all, Sheffield Hallam University/Sheffield Institute for Education, viewed 7 June 2019, from: https://scienceforall.shu.ac.uk/about.html

Shrager, J. and Carver, S. (eds) (2012) *The Journey from Child to Scientist: Integrating Cognitive Development and the Education Sciences*. Washington, DC: American Psychological Association, pp. 227–244.

Shulman, L.S. (1987) 'Knowledge and teaching: Foundations of the new reform', *Harvard Educational Review*, 57 (1), pp. 1–22.

Simons, D.J. and Chabris, C.F. (2011) 'What people believe about how memory works: A representative survey of the US population', *PloS ONE*, 6 (8), p.e22757, doi: https://doi.org/10.1371/journal.pone.0022757

Smith, M. and Firth, J. (2018) *Psychology in the Classroom: A Teacher's Guide to What Works*. Abingdon, Oxon: Routledge.

References 323

Snow, C.P. (1959) 'Two cultures', *Science*, *130* (3373), pp. 419–419.

Soderstrom, N.C. and Bjork, R.A. (2015) 'Learning versus performance: An integrative review', *Perspectives on Psychological Science*, *10* (2), pp. 176–199.

Spence, G.B. and Grant, A.M. (2007) 'Professional and peer life coaching and the enhancement of goal striving and well-being: An exploratory study', *The Journal of Positive Psychology*, *2* (3), pp. 185–194.

Stanulis, R.N. and Brondyk, S.K. (2013) 'Complexities involved in mentoring towards a high-leverage practice in the induction years', *Teachers College Record*, *115* (10), pp. 1–34.

Starling, A., Lo, Y.Y. and Rivera, C.J. (2015) 'Improving science scores of middle school students with learning disabilities through engineering problem solving activities', *Journal of the American Academy of Special Education Professionals*, *98*, p. 13.

STEM Learning (2020) Enrichment, STEM Learning, viewed 19 March 2020, from: www.stem.org.uk/enrichment

Straus, S.E., Johnson, M.O., Marquez, C. and Feldman, M.D. (2013) 'Characteristics of successful and failed mentoring relationships: A qualitative study across two academic health centers', *Academic Medicine: Journal of the Association of American Medical Colleges*, *88* (1), pp. 82–89.

Swanson, L.H. and Bianchini, J.A. (2015) 'Co-planning among science and special education teachers: How do different conceptual lenses help to make sense of the process?', *Cultural Studies of Science Education*, *10* (4), pp. 1123–1153.

Sweller, J. (2005) 'Implications of cognitive load theory for multimedia learning', *The Cambridge Handbook of Multimedia Learning*, *3* (2), pp. 19–30.

Szyjka, S.P. and Mumba, F. (2009) 'Preparing science teachers for inclusive classrooms: Components of a suggested model for science teacher training', *Southeastern Teacher Education Journal*, *2* (4), pp. 5–16.

Taber, K. (2002a) *Chemical Misconceptions: Prevention, Diagnosis and Cure* (Vol. *1*). London: Royal Society of Chemistry.

Taber, K. (2002b) *Chemical Misconceptions: Prevention, Diagnosis and Cure* (Vol. *2*). London: Royal Society of Chemistry.

Teacher Tapp Website (undated) Ask. Answer. Learn, Education Intelligence Ltd Venture, viewed 7 April 2020, from: http://teachertapp.co.uk/

Teachers TV (2010) Teachers TV: Secondary formative assessment, TES, viewed 1 December 2018, from: www.tes.com/teaching-resource/teachers-tv-secondary-formative-assessment-6039026

TES (Times Educational Supplement) (2017) TES community: Science, TES, viewed 20 January 2020, from: https://community.tes.com/forums/science.42/

The State Education Department/The University of The State of New York (2011) *The New York State Mentoring Standards*. Albany, NY: The State Education Department/The University of The State of New York, viewed 25 January 2018, from: http://usny.nysed.gov/rttt/docs/MentoringStandards.pdf

Tonna, M.A., Bjerkholt, E. and Holland, E. (2017) 'Teacher mentoring and the reflective practitioner approach', *International Journal of Mentoring and Coaching in Education*, *6* (3), pp. 210–227.

Toth, E.E. and Graham, M.S. (2016) 'Preparing scientifically literate citizens: Pre-service teacher candidates' use of normative and logical thinking for critically examining news-media', *Electronic Journal of Science Education*, *20* (1), pp. 1–17.

Trevethan, H. (2017) 'Educative mentors? The role of classroom teachers in initial teacher education. A New Zealand study', *Journal of Education for Teaching*, *43* (2), pp. 219–231.

Trubowitz, S. (2004) 'The why, how, and what of mentoring', *Phi Delta Kappan*, *86* (1), pp. 59–62.

Tyson, N.D. (2017) *Astrophysics for People in a Hurry*. New York: W.W. Norton and Company.

324 *References*

United Nations (1989) Convention on the Rights of the Child, The United Nations, viewed 19 April 2020, from: https://downloads.unicef.org.uk/wp-content/uploads/2010/05/UNCRC_united_nations_convention_on_the_rights_of_the_child.pdf

United Nations (2008) Convention on the Rights of Persons with Disabilities, The United Nations, viewed 19 April 2020, from: www.ohchr.org/Documents/Publications/AdvocacyTool_en.pdf

van Merrinboer, J.J.G. (2007) 'Alternate models of instructional design: Holistic design approaches and complex learning', in Reiser, R.A. and Dempsey, J. (eds), *Trends and Issues in Instructional Design and Technology*. 2nd edn. Upper Saddle River, NJ: Merrill/Prentice Hall, pp. 72–81.

Villanueva, M.G. and Hand, B. (2011) 'Science for all: Engaging students with special needs in and about science', *Learning Disabilities Research & Practice*, 26 (4), pp. 233–240.

Vygotsky, L. (1978) *Mind in Society*. Cambridge, MA: Harvard University Press.

Wallace, J. and Gravells, S. (2005) *Mentoring in Further Education: Meeting the National Occupational Standards*. 1st edn. London: Learning Matters.

Watson, S.B. (2006) 'Novice science teachers: Expectations and experiences', *Journal of Science Teacher Education*, 17 (3), pp. 279–290.

Weiland, I.S., Hudson, R.A. and Amador, J.M. (2014) 'Preservice formative assessment interviews: The development of competent questioning', *International Journal of Science and Mathematics Education*, 12 (2), pp. 329–352.

Welsh Government (2017) The Career entry profile, Welsh Government, viewed 9 January 2020, from: https://gov.wales/career-entry-profile-cep

Welsh Government (2018) Professional Standards for teaching and leadership, Welsh Government, viewed 27 December 2019, from: https://hwb.gov.wales/storage/19bc948b-8a3f-41e0-944a-7bf2cadf7d18/professional-standards-for-teaching-and-leadership-interactive-pdf-for-pc.pdf

Welsh Government (2019) Professional Standards, Welsh Government, viewed 3 April 2020, from: https://hwb.gov.wales/professional-development/professional-standards

Wenger, E., McDermott, R. and Snyder, W. (2002) *Cultivating Communities of Practice*. Boston, MA: Harvard Business School Press.

White, H.B. (2008) 'Pedagogies of engagement in science', *Biochemistry and Molecular Biology Education*, 36 (4), pp. 262–273.

Whitmore, J. (2002) *Coaching for Performance: Growing People, Performance and Purpose*. London: Nicholas Brealey.

Wiliam, D. (2008) 'Improving learning in science with formative assessment', in *National Science Teachers Association (NSTA)* (ed), *Assessing Science Learning: Perspectives from Research and Practice*. Arlington, VA: NSTA, pp. 3–20.

Wolf-Watz, M. (2000) 'Student teachers' beliefs about science', *Journal of In-Service Education*, 26 (2), pp. 403–413.

Wright, T. (2012) Guide to mentoring advice for the mentor and mentee, Association of Teachers and Lecturers, viewed 10 June 2018, from: www. atl.org.uk/Images/ATL%20Guide%20to%20mentoring%20(Nov%2012).pdf

Wright, T. (ed) (2017) *How to Be a Brilliant Teacher Mentor: Developing Outstanding Trainees*. Abingdon: Routledge.

Yan, V.X., Bjork, E.L. and Bjork, R.A. (2016) 'On the difficulty of mending metacognitive illusions: A priori theories, fluency effects, and misattributions of the interleaving benefit', *Journal of Experimental Psychology: General*, 145 (7), pp. 918–933.

Yusko, B. and Feiman-Nemser, S. (2008) 'Embracing contraries: Combining assistance and assessment in new teacher induction', *Teachers College Record*, 110 (5), pp. 923–953.

AUTHOR INDEX

A

Ainscow, M. 295
Allen, Michael 155
Amador, J.M. 192
Anderson, L. 34
Archer, L. 282
Ashworth, S. 106

B

Bates, Gareth 73, 265
Bergen, T. 118
Berry, M. 163
Biesta, G.J.J. 181
Bjork, R.A. 205, 209
Bjork, E.L. 205
Black, Alison 291
Bozeman, B. 171
Brickhouse, N.W. 228, 229, 231–233
Brookfield, S.D. 55–58
Brouwer, N. 118
Brown, S.W. 146
Bruner, J.S. 119
Bullough, R.V. 27

C

Chabris, C.F. 204
Chandler-Grevatt, A. 185
Child, A. 20
Cho, C.S. 20
CIPD 13
Clarke, A. 1
Clutterbuck, D. 265, 284, 287
Crasborn, F. 118

D

Daloz, L.A. 17, 265
Danaia, L. 247
Davis, J.S. 60, 295
Day, Stephen P. 32
DeLozier, S. 205
Dewey, J. 53
Dillon, J. 196
Driver, R. 160
Dunlosky, J. 206

E

Edwards, F. 184
Eglington, L.G. 207
Essex, Jane 278

F

Fantozzi, V.B. 60
Feeney, M. 171
Feldman, M.D. 20
Feynman, R. 180
Findlay, Morag 73, 93, 116
Firth, Jonathan 201
Fitzgerald, M. 247
Florian, L. 295
Furlong, J. 16, 20, 93–94, 96, 100, 286

G

Godec, S. 282
Golder, Gill 11
Gourlay, Helen 183
Graham, M.S. 228–229, 234, **235**, 239

326 Author index

Grant, A.M. 146
Gravells, S. 180
Griffiths, V. 54

H

Hand, B. 296–297
Harri-Augustein, S. 180
Harrison, C. 193, 195
Hattie, J. 178
Hennissen, P. *118*
Higgins, M.C. 13
Hobson, A.J. 48
Hudson, P. 32, 36, 119, 121, **122**, 127, *131*
Hudson, R.A. 192

J

Jared, L. 173

K

Kang, S.H. 207
Kang, D.Y. 295–296
Katz, L.G. 18–19, 76, 183, 265, 278, 284, 288
Key C. 297
Keyworth, Alison 11, 150
King, H. 282
Kolb, D. 55–56, 58, 73–74
Kornell, N. 205
Korthagen, F. **118**

L

Larson, Adam H. 244
Lee, C. 193
Littler, Ralph 73, 265
Lo, Y.Y. 299
Loughran, J. 163
Lyon, E.G. 185

M

Malthouse, Richard 47
Martin, S.N. 295–296
Maynard, T. 16–17, 20, 93–94, 95, 96, 100, 284, 286
McDermott, R. 265, 270, 272
McGinnis, J.R. 293

McIntosh, P. 50
McKinnon, D.H. 247
Merrill, S. 20
Monk, M. 196
Montgomery, B.L. 12–13
Moog, R.S. 254
Moore, Darren 291
Morehead, K. 205
Mosston, M. 106, 113
Mulhall, P. 163
Mumba, F. 299

N

Newton, D.P. 4, 21, 179
Nielsen, W. 1

P

Parry, Simon 155
Piaget, J. 179

Q

Qureshi, Shelia S. 244

R

Ragins, B. 20
Ramanan, R.A. 20
Rawson, K.A. 206
Rhodes, M.G. 205
Rivera, C.J. 299
Rizzo, K.L. 298–299
Roffey-Barentsen, Jodi 47
Rowland, T. 171, 173, 176
Rushworth, P. 160

S

Sachs, J. 25
Salehjee, Saima 73, 93, 228, 305
Schön, D. 53–54
Shabatura, J. 281
Shaw, Clare 11
Shulman, L.S. 156
Simons, D.J. 204
Snyder, W. 265, 270, 272

Spence, G.B. 146
Squires, A. 160
Starling, A. 299
Szyjka, S.P. 299

T

Taylor, J.C. 298–299
Thomas, D.A. 13
Thomas, L. 180
Thwaites, A. 173, 176
Toth, E.E. 228–229
Trevethan, H. 28
Triggs, V. 1

V

Villanueva, M.G. 296
Vishnumolakala, Venkat Rao 244
Vygotsky, L. 67

W

Wallace, J. 180
Watts, Mike 171, 228
Wenger, E. 265, 270, 272
Wolf-Watz, M. 30
Wood-Robinson, V. 160
Wormald, Michelle 59

SUBJECT INDEX

Bolded locators indicate tables. *Italicized* locators indicate figures.

A

abstract conceptualisation (AC) 55, 74

action plan 48, 69, **146**, 159-160, 164, 196-198, 200, 301

active experimentation (AE) 55, 74

active observer 239, 241

active reflector 239, 241

active/reactive *see* mentor/ing, style

action plan(ing) 48, 69, **146**, 157-158, 164, 196-195, 200, 301

action steps 147

AE 55, 74

AfL 190-191

analogy 175

apprenticeship plane (Rogoff) 76, 78, 265, 273-274; *see also* three planes of development (Rogoff)

assess 3, **14**, 20, 34, 38, 81, **82, 83**, 85, 123, **146**, 148, **184**, 185, 189-190, 218, 230, 234, 256-257, 268, 281, 300-301; *see also* AfL

assessment for learning *see* AfL

assessment: formative 123, 125, **142**, 183-184, 190-191, 196-198; laboratory 220; peer-assessment 107, 183, 194-195, 199, 255; pupil **142**, 150; risk 220, 223; self-assessment 107, **146**, 183, 194-195, 255; summative 123, 183, 184, 188, 190, 196-197, 239; three-dimensions 183, **184, 185**

astrophysics 161, 228

atomic structure/number **167**, 234

atomic mass 125

atmosphere 63, 96

attitude 17, 34, **146**, 218, 296, 302, 308; *see also* scientific attitude

autonomous teacher 60, 76, 91, 265-269, 270, 272, 275-276, 307; *see also* autonomy

autonomy: increasing 268-269; of a teacher 266, **273**, 274-276, 305; *see also* autonomous teacher

B

beginning teacher, development of: areas for development 101, 129, **130**, 145; development 28, 38, 76, 90, 93-94, 97, 100-101, 106, 113, 117, 123, 147, 155, 159, 226, 265, 267, 286, 305-306; developmental journey of planning 76; learning journey 52, 140; memory and learning 201, 203-205

beginning teacher, knowledge: PCK 155, 157-158, 164-165; subject knowledge 120, 155-156, 158-160, 164; scientific knowledge 156; supporting 76

beginning teacher, mentor/ing: mentoring 33-35, 51-52, 62, 131, 148, 158, 162, 211, 229, 309; mentoring checklist 131-132; mentoring, traditional model 28; mentor-mentee relationship, building 60-61; weekly mentoring meeting 137-139, **140**

beginning teacher, self: autonomy 266; beliefs and values, impact on 26-27; confidence 60, 67, 98-99, 113, 275; constructivist perspective 36; emotions 68, 70, 129; expectations 32-35, 37, 41-42, **43**, 44-45; levels of resilience 61; perception **51**, 64, 284; perspective 32-36, 37, 45, 149; queries **39, 40**, 41; real-life experiences 306; responsibilities **44**, 307; retrieval practice, views on **209**;

Subject index 329

self-reflection 246; SEND, reflection on 293; unreflective beginning teachers 55-58
beginning teacher, teaching: activities **40**; assessment of 183-199; basic teaching skills 93-95, 100-103, 105-106, 109-111, 113, 115, 119, 123-124, 249; effectiveness **15**, 305; evaluation of 110-112, 137, 239-240; induction programme **15**, 32, 39, 45, 149, 271; lesson planning 73-92; prior teaching 5, 37-38, 42; progression profile 42, **43**; questioning practices 192-193; school community, involvement with 271-273; self-evaluation 110-111
beliefs and values 22, 24-67, 29-30
biology 6, 106, 160, 163, **166**, 176, 179, 228, 268-269
Bloom's taxonomy 193, 198, 281
book scrutiny 186
Brookfield's lenses 56-57

C

calmness 96
care 98
case studies: autonomy 267; beginning teacher, support of 103; enrichment 283; Hudson's mentoring factors 36-37; learning and memory 209; learning outcomes 280; mentoring beliefs and values 26-27; mentoring meeting 202-203; mentoring support 268; mentoring, non-directive approach 118; mentor–mentee discussion 232; mentor–mentee relationship 66; PCK 120; post-lesson discussions 128; scientific literacy 232
challenge: high 17, 76, 78, 273; low 17; *see also* Daloz, L.A.
chemistry 6, 47, **167**, 250, 260, 267-268, 280
citizens, scientifically literate 1, 228, 231; *see also* scientific literacy
civic dimension (Brickhouse) 231, 235
clarity 97
classroom management 45, **65**, 66, 104, 140, 178, 278, 280
classroom-teacher 1-2, 307-311
climate change 229, 238
coaching 12-13, **15**, 19, 66, 145, 209; solutions-focused coaching 288
collaboration **43**, 67, 295
collaborative learning 244, **248**, 259; *see also* collaboration

community of practice 3, 5, 49, 210, 265, 268, 270, 272, 275, 277
complex learning theory (CLT) 176, 176
concept map 112, 180, **297**
concrete experience (CE) 55, 74
Confederation of British Industry (CBI) 1
confidence 98-99; beginning teacher 60, 67, 113, 275; building 81, 179, 192; lack of 98, 236, 267, 269, 295, 303
consistency 97
consolidation stage (Katz) 18, 76; *see also* models
Content Representation *see* CoRe
Context: learning 2, 296; mentoring 7, 13-16; school 41, 206, 236, 244, 274; teaching 197, 252
contingent question 3, 172, 175, 177-178, 180
continuing professional development *see* CPD
co-planning 42, 67, 75, 78, 89, 162-163, 233, 279
CoRe 163, **169-170**
co-teaching 42, 67, 295
counselling 19, 172, 284
CPD 163, **188**, 275, 291, 307
critical dimension (Brickhouse) 231-232, 235
cultural dimension (Brickhouse) 231-232, 235
curiosity 171-173, 176, 179
current **79**, **82**, 84-85, **88**, 234
curriculum, science 34, 78, 80, 106, 108, **142**, 156, 158-159, 160, **166**, 172, 214, 217-218, 229, 231-232, 241, 247-248, 256, 282-283, 306-307; English National Curriculum 7; Northern Ireland Curriculum 7; Queensland Curriculum & Assessment Authority 189-191; Scottish Curriculum for Excellence 7; Welsh School Curriculum 7

D

Department for Education (DfE) 6, **16**, 24, 32, 139-140, 155, 172, 217, 228, 257, 279, 292
developmental mentoring 19; *see also* models
developmental plane: apprenticeship plane 76-78, 265, 273-274; guided participation plane 78-85, 274-275; participatory appropriation plane 85-91, 265-266, 275-276; differentiation 91, 279-280, 291, 293, 300; differentiated questions 86-87; differentiated tasks 87-90; planning for 86; *see also* developmental mentoring
discussion: class 82, **192**, 208; mentor–mentee 38, 111, 113, 115, 232, 306; post-lesson 116, 119-120,

330 *Subject index*

123-124, 127-130, 132-133, **135**, 137, 139, 162-163, 225, 257, 259, 268, 300-301; pre-lesson 86, 116, 119-123, **126**, 129, **131**, 132, 257-258, 300
disequilibrium 179
dyslexia 292, 296, 303-304

E

Education Workforce Council in Wales (EWC) 141
effective: basic teaching skills 109; lessons 74, 76-77; mentor-mentee relationship 48, 59-60, 64; mentor/ing, characteristics of 33, **34**, **35**; mentoring 32, 140, 160, 215, 275, 305; mentoring, constructivist approach of 36-37; mentoring, models of 16-21; planning 77-78; science learners 3; science teachers 1-2; *see also* effective teaching
effective teaching 14, 36, 93-96, **101**, **102**, 119, 121, 139, 156, 158, 231, 246; linking subject knowledge with PCK 161-164; PCK mediated 160-161; successful learning 202-203; *see also* effective
electricity 79, 81, **82**, 84-85, 87, **88**, **168**, 222
emotional intelligence 60, 68-70
emotions 23, 49-50, 64, 68-70, 129, 180, 272, 306; *see also* emotional intelligence
English National Curriculum 7
enrichment 282-283; activities 61, 81, 278, 284, 286-289, 296; practices 278, 289; pupils' learning, framework 284-289
environment: classroom 96, **101**; learning **35**, 97, 172, 238, 280; physical 39, 84; school 33, 39, 44, 139
enzyme 160, 163, **169**, **170**
erosion, coastal 229-230
evaluation: beginning teacher, progress of 110-112; lesson evaluation template **240**; mentor-mentee 239-240; self-evaluation **42**
evidence 86, 123, 156; assessment evidence 144; evidence-based practice 2, **35**, 202; lessons 139; meetings 144-145, 147; mentor-mentee discussion 38
expectations: beginning teacher 32-58, 271; managing 64; pupils' learning 80; reinforcing **101**, 103; unreasonable expectations 33, 43, **44**
experiential learning 73-75, 91, 245, 292, 296-297, 301; *see also* POGIL
explanation: beginning teacher 98; mentor 161; question 172-173; scientific 174-179, 193, 208-209, 217

extension: activities 255, 278-279, 282; implementation of 278-290
extension questions, planning for 85; *see also* extension
external forces 30-31; bodies 43, 223, 287; communities 275; drivers **14**, 140-141; examination 186, **188**; expertise support 278, 283-284, 286-287; organisation 24, 286-287; *see also* communities of practice

F

facilitator 17, 34, 145, 238, 245, 253
feedback: constructive 37, 67, 116, 127, 129; focused dimensions 121-123; improving 193-192; lesson 66, 128; lesson observation 121, 126, 134, 142, 161; providing 123, 194; pupil 81, 93, 111-113, 307; WRAP feedback 126, 129, **130**, **131**
field trip 61, **222**, 282-285, 296
formative assessment 123, 125, **142**, 183-184, 190-191, 196-198; *see also* AfL; assessment

G

General Certificate of Secondary Education (GCSE) 6, 160
General Teaching Council for Northern Ireland (GTCNI) 32, 141
General Teaching Council for Scotland (GTCS) Standards for Registration 32, 43, 140
group work 30, 84, 104, 192, 236, 238, 240, 245, 257, 258, 304; beginning teacher, support **233**; incorporating 107-108; inquiry-based learning practices 299; responsibilities 253-254; roles 253-254
GROW model 138, 145, **146**, 146; *see also* model
growth 16-18, 20, 48, 76, 147-150, 194, 276, 278, 307-308
guided participation plane (Rogoff) 78-85, 274
guiding 19, **82**

H

health and safety 34, **40**, 61, 103-104, 124-125, 214-215, 219, 225-226, 285; beginning teacher, incorporation into 220-224
higher order thinking skills *see* HOTS
high-quality teaching 295, 298; *see also* effective teaching
HOTS 281

Subject index   331

I

ice crystals 175
induction: beginning teacher 187; laboratory 222–223; programme **15**, 32, 39, 45, 271
initial teacher education *see* ITE
initial teacher training *see* ITT
inquiry: classroom 211; implementation of 249; inquiry-based learning 139, 247, 298–301; inquiry-based pedagogical approaches 244–249, 259; inquiry-based teaching 215, 245; levels 244, 247, **248**; mentored 211; planned 258–259; scientific inquiry skills 189; science as inquiry 247–245; *see also* inquiry-based learning; POGIL
ITE 23–25, 28, 32, 36, 47, 53, 60, 94, 110, 137, 139, 141, 144, 157, 159, 163, 188, 191, 205, 223, 266–268, 272, 278, 286, 305
ITT 13, **14**, **15**, 20

J

judgement 62, 93, **132**, 176, 238, 307
judgementoring 48

K

key question *see* KQ
knowledge quartet 171, 173
knowledge, scientific 1, 6, 30, 156, 174, 215–216, 228, 231, 237–238, 267; *see also* subject knowledge
KQ **80**, **82**, **83**, **88**, **89**

L

laboratory: assistant 5, 270, 274; induction 222–223; technician 35, **40**, 187, **188**, 223
Leadership 13, **14**, **15**, 32, **39**, 143, 270, 273, 276, 287–288, 307
learning cycle: experiential 73–75, 91; Kolb 55–56, 58, 73–74; POGIL, 245, 249–254, *251*, 256, **257**, 258–259
learning outcomes: key questions **80**; planned 79, 84, 86, 195; planning 78–81, 107, 234, 279; pupils learning 78, **79**, 80, 250; scientific literacy elements 234, *235*; writing **235**, 250
learning progression, approach 78, 91, 112, 121, 155, 157–159, 161, 164; *see also* learning outcomes

learning, science 2, 176, 185, 187, 280, 291, 301, 306
lesson debrief 93, 113, 116, 119, 137–139, 208, 306; purpose **140**; self-evaluation 110–111; *see also* post-lesson discussion
lesson discussions: post-lesson 116, 119–120, 123–124, 127–130, **132**, 133, 137, 139, 162–163, 225, 257, 259, 268, 300–301; meeting 105; pre-lesson; discussions 75, 86, 116, 119, 120–123, 126, 129, **131**, 132, 257–258, 300; meeting 123; *see also* lesson debrief
lesson evaluation 85, 127, 144, 239, **240**; *see also* evaluation
lesson observation 123–127
lesson observation cycle 116–117, 119–120, 123, 131–132; *see also* lesson observation
lesson plan 74, 78, **82**, **83**, 87, 98, 104, 120, 127, 162, 192, 215; POGIL 245, 256, **257**; pre-lesson planning 75; pro forma 215, 219, 223, **224**; three-part 81, 84–85
lesson planning 56, 73, 80, 85, 208, 226, 229; assisting beginning teachers 233–239; developmental journey, supporting 76; four dimensions, incorporation of 233; reflective process 74–75
lesson: individual lesson plans 90–91, 234; series of lessons 73–77, 81, 85, 89–90, 94, 96, 98–99, 100, 107, 109–111, 113, 133, **140**, 192, 232, 234, 256–259
lifelong learning 5, 308
LO **79**, **80**, **82**, **88**, **89**; *see also* learning outcomes
long-term curriculum plan 73

M

maturation stage (Katz) 76; *see also* models
maturity stage (Katz) 18; *see also* models
memory trace 203
mentor/ing: actions **35**; approaches 48, 59, 62, 74, 78, 94, 109, 113, 118, 120, 128–129, 132–133, 183, 215, 272, 305; dictator 34; effective mentoring factors 36; guidance documents 12–14, 215, 266; mentoring standard 140; models 11, 16–17, 28, 42; policy documents 12–14, 215, 266; readiness 23; reflective mentoring 48; skills 22, 117, 148, 233; strategies 42, 52, 55, 60, 67, 69, 76, 89, 91, 93–95, 99, 110, 113, 118, 156–157, 183, 198, 205, 210, 214–215, 218, 233,

332 Subject index

241, 266-268, 272, 275-276, 278, 280, 283, 288, 305-306; style 22, 27, 30, 48-49, 54, 116-118, 129, 131, 133, 301; top-down 12-13; understanding 11-12, 215; *see also* mentor-mentee, relationship; weekly mentoring meetings

mentoring relationship 19, 118, 144, 266; *see also* mentor/ing; weekly mentoring meetings

mentor-mentee, relationship 20, 41, 48, 51, 62-64, 119, 148-149, 210, 272, 306; approaches to 62-66; beginning teacher, developing confidence of 66-67; need for building 60-61; *see also* emotional intelligence; mentor/ing

menisci/meniscus, 103

mercury 103

MERID model 116-117, **118**, 128

micro-planning 73, 77-78, 307

micro-teaching 98, 100, 102-104, 110, 307

mind map 64, 108

mini-plenaries 77, 85

mini-section 84, 100

misconception: pupil 84, 160; science 160; teacher 163

models: apprenticeship 16; competence 16-17; Daloz mentoring model 17; developmental mentoring (Clutterbuck) 19; GROW model 145, **146**, 147; guided participation 73, 76, 78, 81, 265-266, 273-274; Henderson *23*; Hudson 121, *122*; learning partnership 28-29; lenses (Brookfield) 56-57; MEIRD 116-117, **118**, 128; mentoring 11, 16-17, 20, 28, 42-43, 73; participatory appropriation 73, 76, 78, 85-90, 265-266, 273-276; reflective 16-17, 21, 42, 47-48, 75, 215, 288; scientific literacy *235*; situated reflective practice (Malthouse and Roffey-Barentsten) 57-58; traditional model 28-29; *see also* learning cycle; stages of development; three planes of development (Rogoff)

motivation-readiness matrix 23

multi-modal learning 176

multiple-choice questions 103

N

National Model of Professional Learning 141

nature of science: beginning teacher's, understanding of 215-217; *see also* NoS

networking 13, 19, 287

New Teacher Centre **15**

newly qualified teacher *see* NQT

next steps 57, 65, 101, **102**, 104, 129, **131**, **146**, 163, 185, 195-197, 219, 226, 233, 237, 240, 246, **257**, 269, 275, 302

Northern Ireland Curriculum 7

NoS 214-216, 223-226

NQT 6, 42, 110, 141

O

Observation: beginning teacher 7, 18, 67, 124; experienced teacher **40**, 42, 98, 101; observation cycle 116-117, 119-120, 123, 131-132

Ohm's law **82**, 84-85, **88**, 234

ONSIDE 48, 62

P

participatory appropriation plane (Rogoff) 78, 85-91

PCK 61, 94, 107, 116, 120-122, **132**, **134**, 155-157; development of 169; learning progression approach *156*, 160-161; linking subject knowledge 161-162

PDW 162-161, 214, 224-226

pedagogical content knowledge *see* PCK

Pedagogy 34, **35**, 91, 156, 215, 244, 269, 293, 298

periodic table **167**, 234

personal dimension (Brickhouse) 231-232, 235

Personal Record of Progress *see* PRoP

philosophy 63, 245-247

physics 6, 163, **168**, 268-269

POGIL 245-248; activities 249, 253, 255-257, 259; learning cycle 249-250, *251*, 252, 256, **257**, 258-259; lesson plans 256-259; POGIL plan 245, 249-250, **251**

population, coastal 230

Post Graduate Certificate in Education (PGCE) 6, 188, 194

post-box 175, 178

post-lesson: discussions 116, 119-120, 123-124, 127-130, **132**, 133, 137, 139, 162-163, 225, 257, 259, 268, 300-301; meeting 105; *see also* lesson debrief

practical activity/work 29-30, 61, 67, 87, 121, 128, 161, 163, 187, **188**, 214-215, 218-220, 223, **224**, 225-226, 237, 247, **297**, 299-300

Subject index 333

practical guidance 2

practical lesson 61-62, 116, 215, 219-221, **224**, 300; observation 223; planning 220, 225-226; *see also* practical activity/work

practical skills 21

practical tasks 64, 68, 187, **186**; *see also* practical activity/work

practical technique 34

pre-lesson: discussions 75, 86, 116, 119, 120-123, 126, 129, **131**, 132, 257-258, 300; meeting 123

process skills *see* POGIL

Process-Oriented Guided Inquiry Learning *see* POGIL

professional development walk *see* PDW

professional efficacy 137-138, 145

professional standards: guidance documents 12-14, 21, 215, 266; mentor (mentoring) standards 140

progression profile 42, **43**

PRoP 37-38, 42-43, 46, 64, 271

protein **166**, 175, 231

pupil assessment **142**, 150

pupils: enrichment of 284-289; feedback 81, 93; learning 18, 73-75, 78-81, 90, 93, 107-109, 112, 119, 140, **155**, 156, 161-163, 183, 188, 190, 192, 194, 202, 210-212, 218, 234, 236, 238-239, 246, 256, 268; learning needs 77, 269, 278; progress **40**, 81, 113, **184**, 187, 239, 268; promotion of 93, 105-106, 191; pupil-centred learning 245, 249, 259; pupil-centred teaching style 93-95, 100, 107, 110-111, 113, **115**; self-evaluation of 111-112; support of 78, 90, 123, 197; work 27, **83**, 183, **184**, 186, 190, 194; *see also* pupil assessment

Q

QTS 1, 5-6, **14**, 42, 116, 141, 305, 307

Qualified Teacher's Status *see* QTS

qualities *see* effective mentoring

question/ing: contingent questions 3, 172, 176, 178, 180; differentiated 86-87; inquiry questions 245, 252, 256, 257-259; key questions 69, 78, 80-81, 84-85, **88**, **89**, 91, 120, 125; practices 192-193; reflective question 49-50, 52, 104, 138, 143, 145, **146**, 147, 149; types 87, **88**, 192, 207, 252

R

rates of reaction 250, 252-253, 256, 260-261

reactive/active *see* mentor/ing, style

readiness 3, 22-23, 30; *see also* motivation-readiness matrix

reflection-in-action 53, 58; *see also* self-reflection

reflection-on-action 53-54, 58; *see also* self-reflection

reflective accounts: documentation 53-55; sharing conversations 53

reflective journal 53-55, 255, 307

reflective observation (RO) 55, 74

reflective practice (RP): elements 52-53; model 57-58, 157, 261; *see also* RP

renewal stage (Katz) 18, 76, 284; *see also* models

resistance, current **79**, **82**, 84-85, **88**, 234

resourcefulness *19*, **34**, 37, 229

responsibility 13, 18, 41, 45, 52, 76, 78, 90, 100, 110, 113, 119, 131, 144, 147, 149, 180, 202, 220, 221, 226, 266, 303; beginning teacher 95; mentor 45, 93-94, 156; practitioner 52; teacher 178; *see also* beginning teacher, responsibilities

RP 47-48, 157; beginning teachers, change among 52-55; elements 49-55; models 55-58

rusting 232

S

safe space 48, 116, 144, 149

sample 55-56, 75, 104, 141, **142**, 186, 190, 197, 219, 247, 250, 252-253, 256

school placement 36, 42, 63, 141, **142**, 209, 246-247, 250, 268-269, 273, 280

School-Centred Initial Teacher Training (SCITT) 6, 28

science specialist 2, 34, 228

science teacher: autonomy 266, **273**, 274-276; development, professional 54, 94-95, **142**, 289; early career 1, 6-7, 59-60, 30; effectiveness 1-2, 21, 123, 305, 308; NQT 6, 13, **14**, 42, 110, 141, 305; recruitment, training and retention 1; training **15**, 63

scientific attitude 217, 227; *see also* attitude

scientific inquiry 189; *see also* inquiry

scientific knowledge *see* knowledge, scientific; subject knowledge

334 *Subject index*

scientific literacy 81, 229; development of 228, 236, 239, 298; elements 229, 239; embedment of 228-241; enhancement of **238**; four dimensions 228, 231; implementation 229, 232, **233**, 241; pedagogical practices 230-231; promotion of 297; teaching approaches 231; *see also* knowledge, scientific

scientists, future 1

Scottish Curriculum for Excellence 7

self-audit 159

self-awareness 29, 58

self-direction 204, 210, 228, 271

self-esteem 62, **185**

self-evaluation 42, **101**, 110-111, 113, 239; *see also* evaluation

self-reflection 91, 144, 245; beginning teacher 33, 246; mentor 75, 147, 266-270

self-study 160

SEND 18, 61, 270; beginning teachers, activities for 300-304; meaning of 292-293; research 295-299

show-me-boards 103, 107

single lesson 75, 91, 109, 202-203, 209; *see also* solo-lesson

situated reflective practice 57-58

solo-lesson 96, 100, 303; *see also* single lesson

solo-taught lesson 105; solo-teaching 66, 100, 118, 266

special education needs and disability *see* SEND

spider diagram 230

staff members; *see also* communities of practice

stages of development: Maynard and Furlong 93-95, 96, 100; Katz 18-19, 76, 93-94, 96, 100; *see also* consolidation stage (Katz); maturity stage (Katz); models; renewal stage (Katz); survival stage (Katz)

strength 37-38, 46, 53, 63, 77, 99, **101**, 104, 108, **126**, 127, 130, 132, 135-136, 145, 159, 176, 185, 187, 216, 233, 239-240, 246, 254, 259, 269, 279, 301-302

strengthen 33, 36-38, 67-68, 81, 100, 105, 107-108, 110-111, 113, 161, 216, 223, 250, **251**, 266-267, 268, 272, 290; *see also* strength

subject knowledge: developing 155, 159, 164; linking of 121, 132, 161, 164; teacher 120, 156-160, 164; *see also* knowledge, scientific; subject specialist

subject specialist 47, 176, 178; *see also* subject knowledge

subordinate role 28; *see also* mentor/ing, top-down

success/ful 20, 59-60, 63, 70, 73, 94, **130**, 138, 164-167, 175, 193, 197, 198-199, 211-217, 219, 244, 256, 259, 281-282, 288

summative 123, 183, 184, 188, 190, 196-197, 239; *see also* assess; assessment; assessment for learning; formative assessment

support: beginning teacher 37-39, 42, 61, 73, 75-76, 78-80, 86, 99-100, 103, 112, 123, 138, 149, 156, 164, 171, 174, 180, 188, 190, 192-194, 210-211, 213-214, 229, 236, **237**, 241, 249, 254, 265, 278, 282-283, 286, 304; emotional 41, 59-60, 178, 308; mentoring 100, 145, 180, 283, 285; progression 158; social 63, 171

survival stage (Katz) 18, 59, 76, 94, 96, 98, 101-104, 110, 181; *see also* models

SWOT 108

T

targets 38, 51, 55, 71, 86, **88**, 118, 123, 137, **140, 141, 142**, 143-144, 147, 150, 151, 187, 215, 233, 252, 263-267, 278, 282-285, 288, 295, 301-303, 307

teacher education programmes 1, 14, **35**, 119

teacher educator 187, 190, 307-308

teacher standards 7, **14**, 24, 32-33, 37, 39, 42, **43**, 44, 45, **65**, 116-117, 119-123, **126**, 137, 140-141, **142**, 145, 146, **150**, 157, **184**, 266, 279, 292-293, 306-307; *see also* professional standards

teacher-pupil relationship 98, 291

teaching: effective 14, 36, 121, 139, 156, 158, 160-161, 201-202, 231, 246; skills 93-95, 100, 101-103, 105-106, 109-111, 113, 115, 119, 123-124, 249; strategies 77, 93-95, 100, 105-107, 109-115, 121, 145, 173, 201, 229, 237, 245, 249, 254, 261, 265, 288, 292, 295, 299, 301; style 18, 30, 93-95, 100, 106-107, 110, 111, 113, 115, 241, 267

textbook, science 108

three planes of development (Rogoff): apprenticeship plane 76-78; guided participation plane 78-85; participatory appropriation plane 85-91; *see also* models, stages of development

three states of matter 172-173

three-part lesson plan 81, 84-85

time: extra time 127, 178; given time 192; learning time 206

traffic lights, assessment 112, 193; *see also* assess; assessment; assessment for learning; formative assessment; summative assessment

trust 24, 28, 48, 58-63, **65**, 70, 118, 149, 223, 271

two star and a wish, technique 195

U

units of work 6, 75, 78-80, 90-91, 110, 144, 157-158, **166**, **168**, 218, 234, 256, 307

university: course 27; staff 1; tutor 2, 26, 28, 63, 205

V

video 98, 127, 193, 204, 223, 295

voltage **79**, **82**, 84-85, **88**, 234

W

weekly mentoring meetings 34, 41, 51, 53-54, 64, 68-69, 97, 101, 110; external drivers 140-143; internal drivers 143-144; purposes 138-139, **140**; reflection 147-148; structure, pre-planning of 144-145; *see also* GROW model; mentor/ing

Welsh School Curriculum 7

workload 36-37, 163

WRAP 110, 117, 126-127, 129, **130**, **131**, **132**

writing frames 297-298

Printed in the United States
By Bookmasters